COLONIAL MEXICO

COLONIAL MEXICO

A Traveler's Guide to Distinctive Lodging,
Dining, and Shopping in Historic Districts and
Artisans' Communities Throughout Mexico

FIRST EDITION

CHICKI AND OZ MALLAN

MOON
TRAVEL
HANDBOOKS

COLONIAL MEXICO
FIRST EDITION

Published by
Moon Publications, Inc.
P.O. Box 3040
Chico, California 95927-3040, USA

Printed by
Colorcraft Ltd.

Please send all comments,
corrections, additions,
amendments, and critiques to:

**COLONIAL MEXICO
MOON TRAVEL HANDBOOKS
P.O. BOX 3040
CHICO, CA 95927-3040, USA
e-mail: travel@moon.com
www.moon.com**

Printing History
1st edition—September 1998

ISBN: 1-56691-109-5
ISSN: 1095-8878

Editor: Karen Gaynor Bleske
Production & Design: David Hurst
Cartography: Bob Race, Brian Bardwell, Chris Folks, Mike Morgenfeld
Index: Asha Johnson

Front cover photo: La Pila, Chiapa de Corzo, by Oz Mallan

All photos by Oz Mallan.

Distributed in the United States and Canada by Publishers Group West

Printed in China

To the best:
Barb, Tony, Denise,
Scott, Elizabeth, Guy,
Patti, and Bryant

Contents

Introduction 1~25

THE CONQUEST 2; THE GROWTH OF CITIES 9; ARTS AND ARTISAN COMMUNITIES 15; FIESTAS AND FEASTS 19

SPECIAL TOPICS: HERNÁN CORTÉS AND HIS SOLDIERS 4-5; THE DOG—HISTORY AND RITUAL 6-7; THE WORD *HIDALGO* 12; WHY *ZÓCALO*? 13; SILVER AND THE WORLD 18; THE *CHINA POBLANA* 20; THE BULLFIGHT 21-23; PULQUE, MESCAL, TEQUILA 25

Trail of Cortés 27~99

Veracruz 28

This old city served as gateway and first port into 16th-century Nueva España.

SPECIAL EXCURSIONS: JALAPA 38; SANTIAGO TUXTLA 41; LA ANTIGUA 41
SPECIAL TOPICS: PAPANTLA FLYERS OF EL TAJÍN 28; STAR MOUNTAIN 40

Tlaxcala 42

Spanish firepower and trickery forged an alliance with the Tlaxcaltecans that conferred great power on Cortés in his campaign against Moctezuma.

SPECIAL EXCURSIONS: PARQUE NACIONAL LA MALINCHE 49; JARDÍN BOTANICO TIZATLÁN 49; TIZATLÁN 51; SANTA ANA CHIAUTEMPAN 51; SANCTUARY OF SAINT MICHAEL 52; HUAMANTLA 52; TLAXCO 53

SPECIAL TOPIC: THE NEW CITY OF OUR LADY OF ASSUMPTION 1525 43

Puebla 55

Founded in 1531, with a charter from Isabella, the Queen of Spain, Puebla served as a safe haven for Spaniards traveling between Veracruz and Mexico City.

SPECIAL EXCURSIONS: CENTRO CIVICO CINCO DE MAYO 68; CHOLULA 69
SPECIAL TOPICS: MARKET DAYS IN OUTLYING VILLAGES 66; THE TOWER OF CHOLULA 70

Mexico City 73

Once the center of the Aztec world, then the heart of Spain's New World, today this ancient site is the hub of modern Mexico.

SPECIAL EXCURSIONS: CHAPULTEPEC PARK: ITS CASTLE AND MUSEUMS 87; BASÍLICA DE NUESTRA SEÑORA DE GUADALUPE 92; COYOACÁN 92; SAN ANGEL 94; PARQUE NACIONAL DESIERTO DE LOS LEONES 97; THE CANALS OF XOCHIMILCO 98

SPECIAL TOPIC: DEATH FROM A BROKEN HEART 96

Silver Cities 101~159

Taxco 102
*Pink Santa Prisca Church, built atop Spain's first mine in the New World,
is a baroque masterpiece of colonial art in a fairytale city.*
SPECIAL EXCURSIONS: CACAHUAMILPA CAVES 111; ACAPULCO 111;
 NEAR ACAPULCO 118
SPECIAL TOPICS: *JUMILES* 110; THE *POZOLE* CRAWL 118

Guanajuato 120
*A city improbably hewn from a convoluted landscape reveres the unlikely
conquistador Don Quixote and his companion, Sancho Panza.*
SPECIAL EXCURSIONS: MUSEO DE LAS MOMIAS 133; VALENCIANA MINE 133;
 VALENCIANA CHURCH OF SAN CAYETANO 134

Zacatecas 135
*The narrow streets wind along the Cerro de la Bufa, with its "face of stone
and heart of silver."*
SPECIAL EXCURSION: GUADALUPE 145
SPECIAL TOPIC: THE GHOST OF MINA EL EDÉN 142

San Luis Potosí 146
*This modern city has preserved its classical culture, including the
traditional* callejoneadas, *musical/street tours performed by*
estudiantinas *dressed in satin capes and ribbons.*
SPECIAL EXCURSIONS: VILLA DE REYES 153; MEXQUITIC 154;
 SANTA MARÍA DEL RÍO 154; THE HILL OF SAN PEDRO 154;
 REAL DE CATORCE 155
SPECIAL TOPIC: THE SPENT SHOES OF ST. FRANCIS 159

Royal Cities 161~205

Cuernavaca 162
*In one of his favored spots in Nueva España, the conqueror built a rugged
fortress, the Palacio de Cortés, atop the ruins of an Aztec pyramid.*
SPECIAL EXCURSION: TEPOTZLÁN 169
SPECIAL TOPIC: THE CHURCH MURALS 166-167

Oaxaca 171
*The native cultures survive in Oaxaca, another of Cortes's favorite
spots and now a rich blend of Spanish royal architecture and native art.*
SPECIAL EXCURSIONS: SANTA MARÍA ATZOMPA 186; ARRAZOLA 186;
 SAN BARTOLO COYOTEPEC 187; TEOTITLÁN DEL VALLE 187;
 OCOTLÁN 187; TLACOLULU 187; ZAACHILA 188
SPECIAL TOPIC: GUELAGUETZA—AN ANCIENT CELEBRATION 183

Morelia 189
  The "Aristocrat of Colonial Cities" carries the majestic stamp of the
  crown's representatives in Nueva España.
  SPECIAL EXCURSIONS: BUTTERFLY SANCTUARY 198; PÁTZCUARO 198;
    LAKE PÁTZCUARO 202
  SPECIAL TOPIC: SWEET MORELIA 197

Seeds of Independence 207~257

San Miguel de Allende. 208
  The former frontier town was the birthplace of famous freedom fighters.
  SPECIAL EXCURSIONS: SANTUARIO DE ATOTONILCO 220;
    DOLORES HIDALGO 220

Guadalajara 224
  An important Spanish supply center, Guadalajara is the city of 100 plazas.
  SPECIAL EXCURSIONS: ZAPOPAN 235; TLAQUEPAQUE 236; TONALÁ 238;
    TEQUILA 239
  SPECIAL TOPIC: RODEO WITH A TAPATÍO TWIST 234

Querétaro 241
  Here arose the whispered beginnings of the Mexican War of Independence.
  SPECIAL EXCURSIONS: BERNAL 253; THE SIERRA GORDA MISSIONS 255
  SPECIAL TOPIC: DOÑA JOSEFA'S ARREST STARTS A WAR 246

Maya Country 259~303

Campeche 260
  Stone baluartes protected the city from pirates of the world.

Mérida 267
  Appropriately for a modern city with a colonial heart, Mérida's Banamex
  office is housed in the Casa de Montejo, built in 1542 by conqueror
  Francisco Montejo and occupied by his family into the 1900s.
  SPECIAL EXCURSIONS: IZAMAL 280; VALLADOLID 282
  SPECIAL TOPICS: HOW TO BUY A HAMMOCK 277; IF THE HAT FITS 278

San Cristóbal de las Casas. 284
  Though the Spanish put their architectural stamp on this city, they had less
  success influencing the native cultures, stronger here than anywhere else in
  the Mexican highlands.
  SPECIAL EXCURSIONS: SAN JUAN CHAMULA 297; CHIAPA DE CORZO 300
  SPECIAL TOPICS: CHIAPAS INDIAN GROUPS 285; AMBER 294-295;
    THE LACONDÓN 297

Appendices 305~341

Cities of Colonial Mexico 305

ACAPULCO 305; CAMPECHE 306; CUERNAVACA 307; GUADALAJARA 308;
GUANAJUATO 310; MÉRIDA 311; MEXICO CITY 312; MORELIA 314;
OAXACA 315; PÁTZCUARO 316; PUEBLA 317; QUERÉTARO 318;
SAN CRISTÓBAL DE LAS CASAS 319; SAN MIGUEL DE ALLENDE 320;
SAN LUIS POTOSÍ 321; TAXCO 322; TLAXCALA 323; VERACRUZ 324;
ZACATECAS 325

Hotels of Colonial Mexico............................ 326

Transport Tips..................................... 334

Useful Terms...................................... 335

Phrasebook 338

Booklist 342~343

Index 344~365

Index of Churches and Cathedrals 364

The dates listed here trace the Spaniards' arrival and conquest and the subsequent establishment of Mexico's colonial cities.

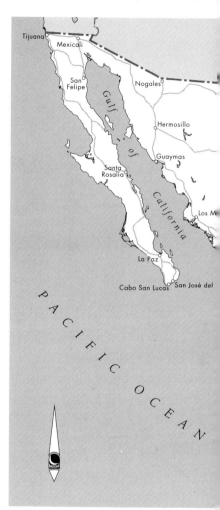

1	Introduction
27	**Trail of Cortés**
	Veracruz 1519
	Tlaxcala 1519
	Puebla 1519
	Mexico City 1519
101	**Silver Cities**
	Taxco 1524
	Guanajuato 1526
	Zacatecas 1546
	San Luis Potosí 1582
161	**Royal Cities**
	Cuernavaca 1521
	Oaxaca 1521
	Morelia 1541
207	**Seeds of Independence**
	San Miguel de Allende 1526
	Guadalajara 1530
	Querétaro 1531
259	**Maya Country**
	Campeche 1517
	Mérida 1527
	San Cristóbal de las Casas 1528

Map Symbols

▬▬▬	Divided Highway	⚓	Archaeological Ruin
———	Main Road	✗	Airport
———	Other Road	•	Accommodation
- - - - -	Unpaved Road	▪	Point of Interest
— · — · —	Track / Trail	○	City
═══	Bridge	○	Town / Village
⬭	Federal Highway	▲	Mountain
⬭	State Highway	⛪	Cathedral / Church

Trail of Cortés	27
Silver Cities	101
Royal Cities	161
Seeds of Independence	207
Maya Country	259

Veracruz 29; Downtown Veracruz 32; **Tlaxcala 44**; State of Tlaxcala 50; **Puebla 57**;
Mexico City 74-75; Historic Downtown Mexico City 78; Chapultepec Park 88;
Coyoacán 93; San Angel 95

Taxco 104; Acapulco's Historic District 114; **Guanajuato 124**; **Zacatecas 136**;
Downtown Zacatecas 138; **San Luis Potosí 148**

Cuernavaca 165; **Oaxaca 172**; Downtown Oaxaca 175; Oaxaca Valley 186;
Morelia 190; Pátzcuaro 199; Around Lake Pátzcuaro 202

San Miguel de Allende 210; **Guadalajara 226**; Downtown Guadalajara 230;
Querétaro 242

Campeche 263; **Mérida 268**; Downtown Mérida 271;
San Cristóbal de las Casas 286; Downtown San Cristóbal de las Casas 289

Acknowledgments

How lucky we have been to explore and learn about Mexico's beautiful cities and friendly people—both from the past and the present. Thank you, Mexico, and we look forward to the discoveries of the future. And especially, thanks to our editor, Karen, who really cares.

We Welcome Your Comments

Even though this book's subject is the Mexico that has lasted hundreds of years, things do change. We want to keep this book as accurate and up to date as possible and would appreciate hearing about any errors or omissions you encounter while using *Colonial Mexico: A Traveler's Guide to Distinctive Lodging, Dining, and Shopping in Historic Districts and Artisans' Communities Throughout Mexico.*

If you have any noteworthy experiences (good or bad) with establishments listed in this book, please pass them along to us. If something is out of place on a map, please tell us. All contributions will be deeply appreciated. Address your letters to:

> *Colonial Mexico*
> c/o Moon Travel Handbooks
> P.O. Box 3040
> Chico, CA 95927 USA
> e-mail: travel@moon.com

The Philosophy of *Colonial Mexico*

This book was designed for the traveler who's interested in investigating the oldest cities of Mexico and who believes that the best way to learn about a city is to explore it on foot. For the most part, our central coverage is contained in the sections titled **Exploring the Streets of** ____. In several cases in which the historical centers have sprawled over a larger territory, such as in Mexico City, we've added a **Special Excursions** section. So if the site is out of the *centro histórico* area, or there are unique areas outside of a city—notable villages, outstanding architectural structures, remarkable hotels—we have included them in that section.

Ratings Key

The accommodations listed in this book use the following price rating categories, based on high-season, double occupancy:

Budget: under US$35   Expensive: US$85-110
Inexpensive: US$35-60   Premium: US$110-150
Moderate: US$60-85   Luxury: over US$150

Introduction

THE FREE-SPIRITED VAGABONDS who crossed the seas after Columbus were an amazing lot. Particularly courageous were the conquistadors, a handful of men led by Hernán Cortés. Cortés was a gutsy man of great vision and immense confidence, with a con artist's tongue—who else, while surrounded by six million hostile natives, would burn his ships to stop grumbling in the ranks, precluding any possible escape from a strange land thousands of miles from home? He had tremendous motivation that most attribute to greed and a compelling desire for power. Against amazing odds, he conquered the unknown land, subjugated its people, and made the first sweeping strokes on a landscape that would become the Americas, then and now the richest piece of the earth.

In his search for new lands and riches, Cortés discovered a civilization that worshipped multiple gods and that had an appetite for human blood. Though the Spaniards were revulsed by the Indians' religious practices, their leaders wore trinkets of gold, which kept the adventurers on their way to the city of Tenochtitlán and to the leader of the Aztecs, Moctezuma.

The society they discovered was in many ways advanced beyond that of Europe. Pope Alexander VI had already given the Spanish explorers carte blanche in any lands they discovered, *as long as they "taught the heathens the word of the Christian God."* That's all the Spaniards needed, another reason, besides gold, to conquer the new land—save the souls of the people.

The Conquest

From Veracruz to Tenochtitlán the Spanish passed through beautiful, well-developed cities in their quest to find the Aztec leader. Tales of the Aztecs' cruelty to their subjects and captives were repeated many times along the way; they did not intimidate Cortés. The Indians on the other hand were terrified and shocked at the loud, powerful explosions that erupted from the conquistadors' "fire sticks." At first they believed that the soldier and the horse were one creature—another frightening vision. And the fighting dogs the Spaniards brought with them (enormous mastiffs and swift greyhounds) were fierce, nothing like the fat little dogs the natives raised for the nobles to eat.

From the beginning, Cortés spread Christian doctrine among the Indians—and extracted promises (under pain of death) that they would give up their beliefs and worship the Christian God. Bernal Díaz de Castillo, other conquistadors, and the letters from Cortés to the King of Spain spelled out clearly the lifestyle of the native people, their rulers, and especially their powerful priests, who encouraged the sacrifice of their captives.

Along the trail to Tenochtitlán, Cortés observed on many occasions that indeed there *was* gold in this vast country. But until the first order of business was completed (making peace with his opponents), finding the source of gold had to wait. As it turned out, the Spanish did find gold, but in much smaller quantities than silver.

It took Cortés and the Spaniards only three years to totally subdue the Aztecs and the Valley of Mexico. Once that was accomplished the rest of the country fell into line. Aztec temples and cities were systematically destroyed. New European-style structures took their places, almost always constructed over the old.

Cortés cannot take all the credit (or blame) for bringing an entire nation to its knees. Much of it was the natives' bad luck, and the most profound event was the smallpox plague brought by a Cuban soldier who came with the Spaniards. It swept across the country, killing as many as 80% of the people—precisely at the moment when the Indians began to realize what had to be done to conquer the Spaniards; fight back! Note: In 1519 the indigenous population was 25.2 million. By 1650 disease and destruction had reduced their number to fewer than one million; however, by 1810 the indigenous had recouped and their numbers were more than tripled to 3.7 million.

Communication between colonial officials and the crown moved slowly. Ships carrying official correspondence sailed only once a year between Spain and Mexico.

That first trek from Veracruz to Tenochtitlán (in 1519) was filled with unexpected discoveries. The Spaniards were impressed with the layout and design of Indian cities, the rich farmlands with unusual fruits and vegetables, the clever infrastructure (plumbing and roads), the use of color, and the amazing woven textiles often incorporating beautiful feathers. But they were particularly wide-eyed at the gold and silver trinkets and religious ornaments they saw.

Cortés learned much about Moctezuma once he and the Tlaxcaltecans became loyal allies. From them he learned how Moctezuma collected tribute from the provincial city-states. Even before the final conquest of Tenochtitlán, he demanded a copy of the tribute rolls of subject cities and studied the books carefully kept by Moctezuma's "bookkeepers." From the rolls, painstakingly recorded in paintings (Indian writing), he learned that 370 villages were under the Tenochtitlán "umbrella," and each paid Moctezuma one-third of its production. These rolls gave him information concerning the geography, industries, and how much each city paid in tribute, but most important, it told him who paid in silver or gold. Cortés—and his men—were more anxious than ever to find the precious metals.

The Spoils

Almost immediately after Cortés' victory, the lands of the country were divided and given to the conquistadors for their valor and bravery, but they did not receive nearly what they expected. All were interested only in finding precious metals.

In the beginning, they found small quantities of gold and silver, and the seeds of a village took hold at each new mine. They were very simple towns at first, but with each new strike, each new vein of metal, the towns grew bigger and better. The first 20% cut of gold and silver went to the king in Spain. However, there was more than enough left in Nueva España to create rich men, magnificent cities, and to found a new culture—thanks mostly to the slave labor of the Indians in a marriage that ultimately became Mexico. Despite the fact that Cortés and his followers destroyed a civilization, raped the land, spread disease and destruction, and looted and pillaged what was left, the resulting marriage of Indian and Spanish culture, Catholicism and native ritual created the rich legacy that Colonial Mexico has bequeathed the world.

Hernán Cortés and His Soldiers

Hernán Cortés was born in 1485 in Medellin, Spain, a descendant of the Lombard kings. As a student, he was sent to Salamanca to be educated in law. It was a short-lived experience; he was not a man of books. Even at an early age he was prone to adventure, though then it was amorous adventure. He dreamed of Columbus's New World and the mystery that it held. At 17 he became a cavalier and eventually sailed to Hispaniola in search of gold and adventure, but he found there instead a life as a country gentleman, owning land and servants but still yearning for his dream. In 1511 Cortés sailed with Diego Velasquez to conquer Cuba. From that voyage it became evident that Cortés had definite talents for risk-taking and leadership. When Velasquez became governor of Cuba, he brought the young explorer along. Again Cortés was awarded land and slaves, and he ended up owning gold mines that paid off handsomely. But his life was still driven by dreams of the swashbuckling antics that frequently landed him in Cuban prisons—luckily for him, he was clever enough to escape each time. Cortés and Velasquez had a precarious relationship, including moments of respect and/or jealousy. They united when Velasquez appointed Cortés the captain general of an expedition from Cuba to find several Spaniards believed held prisoners by the Indians in Mexico. Cortés's explicit orders were to patronize the Indians and to barter with them, to learn about the races of their people and the natural resources of the country, and above all to do nothing to embarrass the crown or offend God.

As Cortés threw himself into preparations for this expedition, with the good-spirited cooperation of many fellow adventurers, Velasquez's seeds of jealousy regarding the possible outcome of the mission began to germinate. After hearing rumors that Velasquez was about to change his mind and appoint a new captain, Cortés made the first of what would turn out to be many gambles. He and his men sailed, ill-prepared and in a hurry. In Cortés's defense, he did spend a considerable amount of his own funds equipping the ships and the stores. More than anything, he could not accept being denied the opportunity to further explore.

Thus, on 10 February 1519, 34-year-old Hernán Cortés sailed from Cuba. With 11 ships, 120 sailors, 550 soldiers, 200 Indians, and 16 horses he set out in search of his dream, with or without the blessings of governor Velasquez. The search for the Spanish prisoners began on the Yucatán's Caribbean coast. But it was on the Gulf of Mexico coast, in what would become the state of Veracruz, that Cortés's destiny was put in motion.

In the days after his arrival the Indians presented Cortés a variety of gifts, including gold trinkets, but one gift in particular would prove to be the most helpful of all—a young woman named Marina (also called Malinche and Malintze). Doña Marina would become his skilled interpreter, adviser, and eventually his lover and the mother of his son. Today most Mexicans consider her a traitor to her homeland because of her assistance in the conquest.

Those of Cortés's soldiers who survived the amazing and often violent subjugation of Moctezuma and the Aztecs were promised a piece of the booty. In 1522, instead of the gold they all had hoped for, each man was rewarded with a piece of land—his own little kingdom.

Unlike today's professional soldiers, many of the explorers who accompanied Cortés not only didn't receive pay, they actually paid a share of the expedition's cost, at least for their own equipment, arms, and horses. Some went into debt to go on this venture. When it became obvious to the men under Cortés that they had no gold to divvy up, their leader agreed to award each of these irate men, who had suffered so much and fought so hard, native villages and villagers.

The idea was that the *encomendero,* the master of these *encomiendas,* would receive the tribute of the natives as well as their (free) labor. They, in turn, would treat the Indians kindly and teach them to be good Christians. In truth, however, the Indians became virtual slaves. In some cases the conquistadors treated them paternally, but in many cases they were treated inhumanely; thousands died as a result. Most of the *encomiendas* were small parcels, not the thousands of acres that later were given to important people. Every conquistador expected to fulfill his dreams of striking it rich by finding gold and silver; in reality few of the soldiers found the precious metal they all longed for.

Cortés was a man of many appetites. One was his love of riches, but perhaps his cravings for adventure, conquest, and fame were even more important to him. His conquest of the Aztec empire and Moctezuma included the annihilation of millions of Indians. After Cortés, in the early 16th century, the door was open for the exploration and colonization of the millions of acres then called New Spain and now called Mexico. With tremendous amounts of silver and gold being returned to Spain and the crown, a flood of Spaniards descended on the new country, and cities grew. Though the conquest and ensuing deluge of riches were obviously a direct result of the courage and cleverness of Cortés, he never received the recognition he desired.

When King Charles V allowed Cortés to choose 22 towns for his personal *encomiendas,* he naturally selected the richest areas in New Spain. By the mid-1530s, thanks to his sugar mills, livestock, mines, and tribute from 23,000 Indian families on his widespread *encomiendas,* Cortés was the richest Spaniard in the world with the exception of King Charles. However, his real desire was for power: to be the governor of the lands that he had conquered, or at the least a duke in the court of Spain. He was awarded neither, although he was given the title of count along with his *encomienda.*

Cortés left Mexico in 1540, never to return alive and never to carry the titles he dreamed of for so long. He died in Spain in 1547. At his request, his remains were returned to Mexico. Today, one seldom hears or sees reminders of Cortés in Mexico, despite his impact on the country. Only a small bust of Cortés lingers over his bones in the **Templo y Hospital de Jesús** in Mexico City. The only other public memorial is a statue in the Cuernavaca Hotel, which occupies the palace he built and the home he most enjoyed in Mexico.

The Church

Cortés laid the Christian groundwork. He preached and prodded the indigenous to give up their "wicked gods," and if that didn't work he used more extreme measures—all the while tearing down idols and temples, replacing them with Catholic images. Even before all Indians were gathered into the fold, more and more priests and nuns came to Mexico. They began by building humble churches, often with thatched roofs. The idea was to get a building up quickly. And since they were there to preach the gospel to people who had never worshipped within a building before, the *open* chapel was generally the first "church" built. Some of these lovely old open chapels still stand. They were a unique concept built on the outside of a wall of the main church. The worshippers looked on from familiar open spaces while the priests stood under cover at an altar with (usually) a wide arched opening toward the people. In many of these open chapels, small

Until 1702, only one ship a year was allowed to sail from Manila to Acapulco filled with goods; after that two a year.

The Dog—History and Ritual

Before the Spaniards reached Mexico, only two creatures were domesticated here; the dog and the turkey. Two breeds of dog have since been regarded typically as Mexican; these are the Chihuahua and the *sholo*. A considerable amount of nonsense has been written about both.

The tiny Chihuahua, the world's smallest dog, is actually uncommon in Mexico. Its origin remains an enigma. For whatever reason, some writers have incorrectly said the Chihuahua was known to the ancient Aztecs (probably because of their little ceramic dancing dogs). But no reliable evidence exists—skeletal, in codices, linguistically, or otherwise—that the animal was known in the regions to which these writers attribute it. It might be a case of mistaken identity with the *sholo*.

Another story suggests that the dog evolved from a wild canine that lived among the rocks in the Chihuahuan Desert. Another says it developed after a

dog mated with a rodent, perhaps a gopher or prairie dog of Chihuahua. Both claims are biologically impossible. Zoologists agree that no wild canine ever lived in America that could have been the progenitor of any domestic dog. Another story mentions a pair of tiny dogs brought from China at the end of the 18th century. This may be closer to the truth.

The other Mexican dog, called the *xolo-itzcuintli* (usually abbreviated to *sholo*), is believed to be the first domestic animal in

escape doors to the main building opened in the wall close behind the altar.

Of course the simple thatched-roof church was not to last very long, and as the cities grew in importance, and silver and gold were discovered, the churches became opulent structures. The Indians had their own churches, and they were seldom allowed in the churches of the Spaniards; according to historians the native churches were dark and dingy by comparison.

The Catholic church was all-powerful in those early days. The Spanish would totally ignore a village until a priest was assigned and a church was built. Then, they took either a paternalistic attitude toward the Indians (most of the priests took this attitude), or they looked down on them and used them as slaves. However, once the Spanish crown learned of some of the treatment given the flock, it tried to correct the difficulty. This didn't stop many priests from bearing down very hard on those

Since the Spaniards found no beasts of burden in use when they first arrived, they hauled all their goods as the Indians hauled them, on someone's back. The Spaniards called these carriers *cargadores,* and they carried everything—enormous pottery jars filled with water, baskets filled with a variety of goods or foodstuffs, even people, in chairs strapped to the backs of the *cargadores.*

North America. The dog is almost totally hairless or "nude." Much of its history is conjecture: perhaps it accompanied early man from Eastern Asia across the Bering Straits; possibly its nearest relative is another form of "naked" dog formerly known in Manchuria; maybe it never was a distinctly wild animal but developed right alongside humans.

At the time of the conquest, the Indians in Mexico held the *sholo* in great esteem; it held important religious significance, they used it medicinally, and they also ate it. The Nahuatl name *xoloitzcuintli* means "he who snatches his food with teeth sharp as obsidian, and who is the representative of the god *Xolotl.*"

The Indians also believed that the dead needed to be ferried across at least one flaming subterranean river before their souls could reach the "promised land," and they thought only black dogs were capable of doing this. These dogs would save their masters from the fiendish crocodiles encountered on the journey. Consequently, the dog of the deceased was killed and buried with him. The *sholo,* normally black or at least dark gray, was the black dog chosen for this ferrying operation. In museums you will notice pottery dogs found in ancient burials.

Today the naked—and consequently flealess—*xoloitzcuintli* finds employment as a living hot water bottle that never cools off. Their bodies emit so much heat that the sick in the Balsas River Valley use the *sholo* to warm themselves, and in the state of Guerrero some still believe that possession of such a dog protects them from colds and other ailments.

Early Spanish historians reported that dog flesh was relished by the Indians. Bernal Díaz del Castillo, for one, mentioned hairless dogs among the innumerable exotic food items the conquerors found for sale in the fabulous marketplace of Tlateloctl. In the 16th century, many Spaniards acquired a taste for dog flesh.

The viceroy was the most powerful man in Mexico. However, he was constrained by the judges of the *audienca*, who were appointed by the king.

Columbus's last visit to the new world he discovered was in 1502.

who had a problem accepting the "new" God of their conquerors. But many Catholic priests will always be remembered for their efforts not only to treat the Indians humanely, but to help them in this new life: men such as Bartolomé de las Casas and Don Vasco de Quiroga.

The church was rich, and the bishops wielded *almost* more power than the viceroys. Perhaps this was a way for the crown to keep its thumb on the progress, the development, and the religious accomplishment of this new world so far from home. The rich and powerful, successful miners especially, sponsored elaborate churches. They used the immense proceeds from their mines and haciendas for personal benefit, except for what they gave to the church. And even the poorest were expected to donate to the church.

These rich temples used fine woods, often inlaid with precious minerals, and especially generous amounts of gold to decorate beautifully carved wall ornamentation. The best artists, sculptors, and architects created these incredibly rich buildings—but only with the labor of the indigenous. Many of these churches took years to construct, and the Indian touch marks many of these carved masterpieces. Despite the pillaging and destruction of many insurrections over the years, many of the churches were somehow protected or rebuilt through the centuries, so that the art lover continues to admire them today, in whatever capacity they serve. Many churches and convents when taken over by the government were put to use in a variety of occupations—libraries, offices, especially government offices, and museums, to mention just a few.

Some of the first monastic orders that arrived, such as the Franciscans, established large, successful haciendas. They operated the haciendas with great efficiency and used the profits or goods to take care of the many hospitals and schools in the cities. Many haciendas operated well-known Indian schools for craftsmen in all fields. It was the church that lent money to mestizos, and it was the church that cared for the indigent and orphans.

All of this changed with the Reform Laws adopted at the end of the Reform War in 1860. During the war many churches and haciendas were burned and destroyed and church valuables stolen. The government took over all church properties and assets. Priests and nuns could not wear clothes that indicated they belonged to a "cult" of any kind. Only limited processions, religious holidays, and bell ringing were allowed. Monastic orders were outlawed. Marriages, births, and cemeteries were now under civil law, and priests could no longer charge for weddings—that practice had often kept poor Indian couples in a state of "singleness" for years, even after they had children. The state had crippled the religious. It was the end of an era, and the rural areas suffered the most.

For the student of history who would like more than a few paragraphs on the fascinating history of Mexico, many books are available. One of the best is *The Course of Mexican History* by Michael C. Meyer and William L Sherman.

The Growth of Cities

Many of the streets of colonial Mexico are lined with antique domed and porticoed structures, boasting ornate stone and tile façades—and they were built to last for centuries. Looking closely at these churches, palaces, and homes, you'll notice the touch of the Native American artisan within these creations—the intrepid fusion that has evolved into the rich Mexican culture. Nowhere is it more apparent than in the colonial cities of Mexico.

Silver in large quantities was found in Zacatecas during the years 1546-1548 and a few years later in San Luis Potosí, Guanajuato, and other sites.

Trail of Cortés

The cities of Colonial Mexico developed in several ways. The original trail of Cortés led from Veracruz through Indian cities: Jalapa, Tlaxcala, and to Tenochtitlán, now Mexico City. Cortés needed Indian allies during his march to Tenochtitlán, and in his way he manipulated the Tlaxcaltecans as friends. Though he didn't know it at his first meeting with this courageous group of Indians, he would lean on them many times before his final success over Tenochtitlán. Cortés didn't forget the help he received from the Tlaxcaltecans, and with his support their Indian settlements eventually developed into major cities.

A few miners became very wealthy and lived in ostentation. Other entrepreneurs made fortunes as suppliers, at first by carrying their goods through the dangerous Chichimeca country. Eventually, they set up supply houses and other services for the miners. The next richest men in the country were the farmers who eventually occupied enormous spreads of land where they raised livestock.

Early Spanish settlers were given home lots within the township and also plots of ground farmed by Indians on the outskirts of the city.

Silver Cities

The Spaniards found gold, but not in the quantities that they found silver. The silver cities are among the oldest, growing from primitive mining camps in the mountains. In most cases the silver cities (Zacatecas, San Luis Potosí, Guanajuato, and Taxco) had little planning. They usually were established at the edge of a rushing river where the silver was processed and gradually spread up the sides of the hills—the more silver, the more growth. The miners were often flooded out and lived under harsh conditions. Once they found the metals in any quantity, the miners established better living conditions and the amenities of real towns.

Only Spanish ships with Spanish crews were allowed to bring in trade goods and they could bring them only to the official port of Veracruz. The custom house collected duties here and at the Spanish end.

detail of the Templo del Carmen façade, San Luis Potosí

The Legacy

Once the silver was extracted from the mines, it was taken to Mexico City to be stored and minted, waiting for the once-a-year shipment to Spain. Some of the most prestigious mines lay in the northern part of the country, forcing the shipments to travel through the dangerous lands of the Chichimeca, some of the most violent Indians. Roads (generally along existing ancient trails) were established and mule trains consisting of many mules and carts and men carried the metals to Mexico City. It was almost inevitable that there would be those who wanted to help themselves to the silver—highwaymen proliferated. Guards were sent along with the trains, but often that wasn't enough. Eventually, presidios were established at the small pueblos along the way; the presidios held a garrison of Spanish troops who would escort the trains through the most dangerous territories. These pueblos grew, providing safe inns for overnight stays, gradually vendors set up shops for travelers' necessities, and more churches and convents were built. Eventually these pueblos grew into large self-sufficient cities, and though the men who became rich did not own mines, they were swept along by the legacy of silver successes. San Miguel Allende and Querétaro originated this way.

Royal Cities

In other cases cities resulted from evangelization. Since the salvation of souls by conversion to Catholicism was a condition of conquering a pagan land, the Spanish crown approved the creation of churches, convents, schools, and hospitals. Logically they were built in the midst of the largest settlements of Indians —usually within the bounds of the Indian ceremonial centers. Cortés made a point of destroying the ancient religious centers, considered evil, and then forced the Indians to use the stones to create the Spanish cities. The largest and richest cities were built early, directly above the remnants of the ceremonial centers with the largest populations. They were then filled with beautiful cathedrals and government buildings, bishops and many teachers, and they became the administrative centers of the Royalist representatives, complete with Casas de Reales, Royal Houses. In many cases, the crown presented the lands to one of the conquistadors or to some other high-ranking official from Spain, who owned them as *encomiendas*. The Indians were essentially relocated. When the Spanish laid out a city, they allowed Indians to build their huts on the outskirts of the city. These neighborhoods were called barrios. Each barrio had its own simple church, school, and priest. Morelia, Pátzcuaro, and Oaxaca cities had their beginnings in this way.

Haciendas

As more and more settlers came to Nueva España, more and more food was needed to provide for them. Many who came were farmers and ranchers. If they were in agriculture *and* had a connection with the crown, they were given immense grants of land. But for the most part these were unusual. It was more common to receive small plots and as the settlers required it, they helped themselves to Indian land or bought other smaller plots from their neighbors. Most of these plots were originally in the wilderness, where the settlers would run cattle and goats, and the crown also gave them a plot in the nearby city (if there was one) for a townhouse. Farmers were given land conveniently close to the towns they supplied. Many people were drawn to the New World by stories of cheap land and cheap labor. In the beginning haciendas either farmed foodstuffs or sugarcane introduced by Cortés from Cuba and the Caribbean. Many of these haciendas were the embryos of villages.

Because of pirates, Spanish ships after the 1560s traveled in convoys for the spring trip to Mexico; armed vessels provided escort.

Though Veracruz was the official port, the trade goods were eventually brought to Jalapa and each year their arrival was cause for a big celebration. Veracruz was ridden with yellow fever and malaria, so Jalapa was a safer depository for the silver that was stored before being transferred to the ships. The same, though on a smaller scale, occurred in Acapulco.

In the 1760s, ports in Campeche and Yucatán were opened for financial reasons; merchants and guilds held monopolies in Veracruz and Acapulco.

In the 55 years after the independence from Spain, a total of 75 presidents, good and bad, tried to organize the country.

Independence

The leaders of the cities were criollos, those of pure Spanish blood but born in Nueva España. These people were in a strange position; in most cases they had status, they were rich, most owned *encomiendas*, but they had no say in conducting government business, nor were they even allowed a (public) opinion on how the country should be run. High-ranking positions, even in the clergy, went only to people directly from Spain. The government began to falter in 1809: among other things, a drought caused a shortage of the corn used to feed the draft animals that supplied much of the muscle in the mining business. Layoffs resulted, mines were shut down, silver production stopped, and there were murmurs of European intervention. The criollos knew this state of affairs could not be allowed to continue. Those in the big cities continued with their leadership positions and social activities. Many were too busy or too close to the problem to worry about it. But in the small provincial cities the momentum grew. Leaders began to evolve in the growing ferment—Spain must be ousted. Querétaro and Guanajuato were in the middle of these events.

Maya Country

The first encounters the Spaniards had with the Maya on the Caribbean coast were violent, and the Indians managed to run the Spanish off each time. It was a number of years before they came back to settle the Yucatán Peninsula. But ultimately they returned and, thanks mostly to the slave labor of the Indians, they built colonial towns and managed to put their stamp on the region. Mérida was settled by the Montejo family; Valladolid was an important city for the religious; and Izamal was considered a bright gem with a convent/church containing one of the largest courtyards in Mexico. Bishop Diego de Landa used Izamal as his hub in his search for "souls." But the cities of Maya Country still retain a much stronger Indian heritage than do other parts of the country.

The Word *Hidalgo*

Hidalgo is a word heard frequently in Mexico, perhaps because of Miguel Hidalgo, who precipitated the War of Independence, ultimately freeing Mexico from Spain. But the word itself has meanings leading much farther back into the history of Spain. It is rooted in the Spanish class system: *Hidalgo* is a contraction of the words *hijo de algo*, which mean "son of something," in other words a hereditary title. It was bestowed upon the lesser nobility, distinct from those with more clout, such as the *ricos hombres* (rich men), and distinct from those nobles who traveled in an even less-honored path, *caballeros villanos* (commoner knights). Actually, the *hidalgos* had a good position, but they were not rich men. They were generally presented land that paid them some rents and bestowed other prestigious privileges. From the 15th century on, they were all Christian (after the long siege of Muslim rule in Spain). For a really good look into the life of an *hidalgo*, read *Don Quixote*, by Miguel de Cervantes, and *Lazarillo de Tormes*, by Hurtado de Mendoza.

City Layout

What a surprise to the Spaniards to discover that the Indian cities were laid out in much the same way as the "newer" European Renaissance plan. The Indian square was laid out according to the cardinal points, north, south, east, west. Only the names were different; the cardinal points were described in colors. The Indians' important buildings, temples, and palaces were situated the same way, around the perimeter of the squares.

The arrival of the Spanish almost paralleled the spread of the art nouveau of Europe's Renaissance era. In a departure from the feudal system, in which houses were built hither and thither around the "castle," the new way of thinking called for planning a city in a particular, logical manner. Construction began with a town center, plaza, park, or garden, and the most important buildings of the city were situated on the perimeter of that center space: the church or cathedral, the priest's home, maybe a royal house or two for the most important people, such as the viceroy or the bishop, government administration buildings, and generally a presidio for the troops. Streets ran perpendicular to the center going east-west and north-south. At the edges of town, Indian villages were built on a smaller version of the center with churches, priest's house, and plaza. If the Indian population were large, there was more than one Indian center; they were called barrios.

Plazas

As the Renaissance and its classical logic took hold in Europe, the plaza became commonplace in Spain. How convenient it was in Mexico for the conquistadors to tear down the "evil" buildings and destroy the "evil" statues and to build directly on top of the Indian structures, using the fine Indian stone now at hand. Often this stone had been brought originally from a great distance. Mexico City was built around the immense plaza of the Aztecs, and the surrounding extraordinary tall temples were torn down. Today the plaza in Mexico City is second in size only to Red Square in Moscow.

Why *Zócalo?*

Those familiar only with its colloquial usage may be surprised to find out that the literal translation of the word *zócalo* is "base of a pedestal." It seems that many years back, the powers that be in Mexico City decided to construct a statue in the square and began by building the pedestal. For whatever reason, that's as far as the project got, so with their usual good humor when observing the confusion of their government, the Mexicans just laughed and began calling the square the Zócalo. The name stuck, and now, no matter what formal names are given to plazas, squares, and central gardens all over Mexico, they are often called *zócalos*. And by the way, the statue was never placed, and eventually the *zócalo* was removed.

The plaza and its surroundings were the most important part of any Mexican city, and the open space has served a variety of functions over the centuries. In the earliest days, the public market was held on the plaza, and villagers got water from a fountain in the plaza designed and built for that purpose. The soldiers' quarters were usually attached to the government buildings facing the plaza, so it was here that they exercised, drilled, and marched (probably the reason so many plazas are called Plaza de Armas). They were conveniently close in case the leaders were attacked. If there was to be an execution, this was the place, especially so during the infamous days of the Inquisition, when heretics were burned at the stake.

This too passed and by the end of the first half of the 1800s, the plaza was used for more gracious occupations. Townspeople spent evenings getting fresh air and strolling with families on the plaza (this was a custom straight from Spain). In the midst of the Porfiriata, well-dressed ladies emerged from elegant carriages and handsome young men pranced on handsome muscled horses.

From the balconies of the *palacios* (government offices) that were always built on the plaza, city leaders delivered important proclamations. And even though the church on the plaza possessed its own *atria* (square), large religious events frequently spilled out onto the public plaza.

Today's plazas have become social gathering places, everyone's outdoor living room. Fountains no longer serve as a utility, but as works of art, throwing fine sprays of water in the warm air and attracting small children to splash and laugh around the water. On many plazas, abundant trees have been planted for shade, and the city provides benches and usually an ornate raised kiosk where city bands play music several evenings during the week. The plaza is the running-place for small children; it's a place for young adults to eye potential sweethearts; and it's the scene of *posadas*.

Every town has at least one plaza, and since so many convents and schools were built, each with one or two plazas of its own, those too are part of the city today. A large, important city will have many plazas. Some cities have additional tiny but locally beloved pocket plazas with one or two benches and a fountain or a statue. The plaza is the center of life in the historical villages, and for the visitor it's quality entertainment and it's free. The Mexican plaza is one form of Mexican art.

Original colonial structures around the plazas were built with thick (some 5-6 feet) and wide *portales,* broad covered walkways, with wide arches. The *portales* were used for a variety of things, sheltering vendors of "everything" to scribes who wrote letters for those who didn't know how to write. The *portales* provided protected walkways from the rain and the sun. The same *portales* today are often outdoor cafés where locals and visitors love to crowd together and chatter, sip or sup, and watch daily life in progress.

Porfirio Díaz: Renovator and Builder

In 1864, with the arrival of Maximilian and Carlota, and then later in 1876, when Porfirio Díaz came into power, Mexican art made a prevalent shift into European styles. Díaz was a dictator and he decided that Mexico would gain more respect from the world if it were more European-like. Most of the buildings constructed during his reign (1876-1911) were beautiful structures decorated and built in the style of France. He also took many decaying structures from the 16th and 17th centuries and remodeled them in the French style, adding still another dimension to the art and architecture of Mexico.

Arts and Artisan Communities

The Spanish found a talented people in the Indians; their use of color and design was brilliant. The Spanish brought with them the talents of their own artists, along with the themes of European Christianity and the Moors. As only could be expected, the architecture of the colonial cities is a New World combination of European/Moorish/Native American.

Most of the arts that had developed over the centuries before the Spanish arrived were connected in some way to ancient religious beliefs and ceremonies. Later, the Spanish influence would become apparent. Neither the Indians nor many of the Spaniards had an understanding of each other's art. Early artists in Europe painted ridiculous scenes portraying ceremonies and events of the Indians; many of them had never seen an Indian. They portrayed the New Fire Ceremony, a very serious Aztec religious event, as a May Day frolic. Most of the paintings and sculptures the Indians saw were religious paintings of the saints and the Virgin.

The early teachers, the priests, devoted much of their time trying to overcome language differences; priests often painted murals on the walls of churches and monasteries to demonstrate their doctrine while instructing the populace. Soon, colonialists from Spain brought artisans who passed on their handicrafts to the indigenous people. Local artists were already great masters of wood and stone carving, gold and silver, masonry, paper art, and painting; they found their color pigments in nature. These existing skills, along with newly introduced European crafts, such as making lace, lacquerwork, and new, more efficient ways to work their already developed skills, blended to create a special flavor. The unique art of Mexico has continued to evolve and flourish throughout the centuries, making Mexican art comparable in quality and originality to that of any country in the world.

All over Mexico you'll see the "tree of life," a pottery rendition of the beginnings of life. Usually an Adam and Eve will grace the very top; there are places for candles, and the tree is a mass of many small figures, which can be angels, flowers, fruits, and animals, all showing the creation of the world according to Catholicism. The tree varies in size from 10 inches (with few ornaments) to eight feet tall (with many ornaments). The trees are vividly painted in bright colors.

Eclectic Mexican Art

Some of the most brilliant art is often the work of Indians from small out-of-the-way villages. After the Spaniards relinquished control of New Spain and Catholicism was thwarted, many of the small villages were isolated. The people of the villages maintained most of their ancient cultures; they continued to weave fabrics on waist looms using ancient designs. They made dyes of tree bark and cochineal insects; they fired pottery in primitive kilns. These valuable traditions have lingered in remarkable works of art—and that's just the beginning. In many areas of the country, these artisan communities are thriving, and they have gained a new way of thinking of their traditions. The indigenous have a new pride for *who* they are. This new consciousness has made them aware of the danger of losing their past. Study groups now get together to learn more about the old ways. Successful villages have tried new crafts and they have a ready market for their product.

The art of Mexico continued to develop for centuries and today offers some of the most flamboyant artistic endeavors in the world, whether in textiles, architecture, mosaic tiles, or pottery. Their intriguing murals tell the history of the country for many people who won't or don't pick up a history book.

Village Specialties

Artisan communities often specialize in one craft, some of collectible quality. The specialties of several cities and villages are listed below.

Veracruz: Palm leaf mats and other woven palm items, Huastecan Indian cactus fiber bags, and coral jewelry.

Puebla: Talavera pottery and ornate tiles of every description, beaded and embroidered clothing, including cross-stitch embroidered blouses called *quechquemetl,* onyx, and *amate* paper artwork.

Tlaxcala: Wool serapes and sweaters.

Guanajuato: Varied styles of pottery and ceramics, including a Talavera type, papier mâché piñatas and masks.

Guerrero (Acapulco): Silver jewelry, traditional ceramics, decorated gourds, and traditional jaguar masks.

Michoacán (Morelia): Inlaid gold lacquerware, special green-glazed pottery, copperware of every description, colorful woven textiles, exceptional carved furniture, guitars, woven fibers, and wooden carvings.

Querétaro: Jewelry with semiprecious stones such as opals, basketry, and other woven items.

Jalisco (Guadalajuara): Ceramics and glass, both traditional and ultramodern, and excellent quality pre-Columbian reproductions.

San Cristóbal de las Casas and its surrounding villages: Textiles and pottery.

The newer artisan communities are cities that have attracted artists from all over the world: Oaxaca, San Miguel de Allende, and Coyoacán and San Ángel in Mexico City are just a few filled with modern artists.

Mexico's Muralists

After Porfirio Díaz was defeated a movement began to regain the Mexican heritage. The Mexican mural became popular; artists such as Diego Rivera began painting huge scenes depicting the history of the people. Artists such as Rufino Tamayo concentrated on Mexican subjects. For the first time, the people of the country were illustrated in their own reality and beauty, along with immense stylized flowers and modern impressions of all nature.

Mexico's muralists have made an enormous impact on the world of art. But more than that, they have interpreted political messages that graphically point out the failings and successes of society since the time of the Aztecs; they have painted the history of the country brilliantly telling the story from the artists' point of view. Some of the most well-known artists are from Mexico's central plateau. A few of the famous muralists to look for are: Diego Rivera, José Clemente Orozco, and David Alfaro Siqueiros. Other great Mexican artists included Pedro Coronel, Rafael Coronel, Miguel Covarrubias, Jean Charlot, Juan O'Gorman, Tamayo, and Pablo O'Higgins.

Everyday Art, the Piñata

For centuries, families have provided swinging piñatas (pottery or papier-mâché covered with brightly colored crepe paper in the shape of a popular animal or perky character and filled with candy and small surprises); children and adults alike enjoy watching the blindfolded swing away with a heavy board or baseball bat while an adult moves and sways the piñata with a rope, making the fun last and giving everyone a chance. Eventually, someone gets lucky, smashes the piñata with a hard blow (it takes strength to break it), and kids skitter around the floor retrieving the loot. Piñatas are common, not only for Christmas and Easter but also for birthdays and other special occasions in the Mexican home. Piñatas are no longer just for Mexicans; they can be found in shops all over the U.S.

For the Shopper

Mexico is a wonderful place to shop; the rich crafts vary from region to region, and the problem isn't *finding* something to take home, but making the choice of *which* of these wonderful gifts to pass by. And speaking of passing by, if you see something you really like and want, and presume that you'll get it later on down the road, you may be making a big, disappointing mistake. You may *never* see it again. The quantity, variety, and quality of all these things create an atmosphere of marvelous shopping, whether it is for the curiosity seeker looking for a souvenir, or the collector, or the interior decorator searching for ideas and goods to replicate the sunny, open style of Mexico. Some shops will ship for you, and in that case it's smart to pay with your credit card.

The Art of Music

The people of Mexico love music. They sing at the drop of a hat, and most little boys learn to play guitar if they can just get their hands on one. Some more affluent communities provide free music instruction to all children. The music most often identified with Mexico is mariachi music.

Silver and the World

When you hear that the amount of silver extracted from the Pachuca mines is one million ounces a year, it becomes hard to imagine that silver (one of the five so-called "precious metals" of the earth) makes up only 0.05 parts per million of the earth's crust. Archaeologists have found silver ornaments in royal tombs around the world dating from 4000 B.C. Historians tell us that silver (and gold) money was in use as long ago as 800 B.C. in countries between India and the Nile. By 1960, the demand for silver for industrial use outweighed its total world production. A few of its practical uses include photography, cloud seeding for rainmaking, antiseptics, cauterizing wounds, and treating diseases of the skin and eyes. But in Mexico you're probably more interested in seeing silver used for jewelry and decorative art, and in that regard you've come to the right place; some of the most modern, beautiful silverwork in the world is done in Mexico. Strictly regulated by the government, certified sterling must contain 92.5% silver and 7.5% of another metal, usually copper. By law, genuine sterling pieces are stamped with "925" somewhere on the item.

Some cities have mariachi plazas where the musicians gather, and they serve as outdoor "hiring-halls" where potential clients come to listen and negotiate deals for parties and weddings. These plazas have evolved into entertainment centers where visitors come to listen, eat, and drink. The musicians *do* expect a tip, especially if you request a song—US$3-5 per is good.

Music has been important from the time the Spanish arrived. Although the Indians made music on simple percussion and wind instruments, it was mostly for religious ceremonies. Historians say that if it wasn't performed properly the musician was killed. Fortunately that's not the case anymore. Prehistoric ceremonies are frequently linked to flutes and drums of many varieties. While around Jalapa, if you have the opportunity, watch the Totonac *voladores* (fliers) pray to the rain god. Five men climb to a rotating platform on the top of a 30-meter pole. Four of the men tie ropes to their ankles and carefully rotate the ropes around the pole. The captain sits in the center and to the beat of his tiny drum and the haunting whistle of his flute, the other four men "dive" off backward and "fly" around and around the pole, getting ever closer to the ground. All the while the captain plays his ancient harmonies as an offering to the gods (and today to the tourists' tips).

As travelers make their way from one colonial city to the next, they will discover many types of music. *La bamba* is a favorite, a beat that combines African, Indian, and Cuban rhythms and is said to have originated in Veracruz. *Tamboras* are loud and happy with bass wind instruments and a great oompah drum, which is said to have been brought along with German immigrants. *Estudiantinas* sing in beautifully trained voices accompanied by strings of many varieties. This tradition began in Spain, where young students made spending money by serenading others' choices for those who were less talented. Their costumes are straight out of Renaissance Europe. And last are the discos, where the majority of young locals like to hang out and listen to the modern beat, and the romantic string trios who play sentimental music and sing love songs in intimate cafés.

Fiestas and Feasts

Special Events and Celebrations

Plazas and fiestas go hand in hand. Having a good time in Mexico is easy, and it doesn't matter whether you're in a big city or a small village—if you plan. One of the simplest but most charming celebrations is Mother's Day. Children, both young and old, serenade mothers (often with a live band) with beautiful music outside their windows on the evening of the holiday. On a recent Mother's Day in Oaxaca, virtually everyone passing by carried a bouquet of flowers. If invited to a fiesta, join in and have fun. Even the most humble family manages to scrape together money for a great party on these occasions.

Beware the "Egg"

In the smaller villages you'll find innocent-looking little old ladies sitting at small tables selling the "dreaded eggshell," filled with confetti, ready to be smashed on an unsuspecting head; usually only the children have the nerve to begin. So be prepared if you're the only gringo around! Your head or any convenient body part will be pummeled with the colorful bombs by anyone tall enough. This is followed by a quick getaway by the bombardiers and lots of giggles from onlookers. The more you respond good-naturedly, the more you will continue to be the target—and what's the difference, whether the headache is from too much tequila or too many eggs doesn't matter. (Besides, it might be time for you to plunk down a few pesos for your own bombs!)

Independence Day

Some celebrations are huge affairs, and the plazas are jammed with people. You can expect thousands of people in a plaza on Independence Day, especially in Mexico City. The president repeats the Grito de Dolores just before midnight, and then a flamboyant show takes to the sky; fireworks and cannons go on for an hour. Everyone waves the Mexican flag and feels very patriotic. If you don't mind crowds it's a moving celebration.

Religious Holidays

Many festivals in Mexico mark religious feast days, which honor Catholic saints. (If someone were so inclined, he or she could travel the length and breadth of Mexico and find a fiesta going on every day of the year.) You'll see a unique combination of Catholic fervor and ancient beliefs mixed with plain old good times.

In the church plaza, dances that have been passed down from family to family since before Cortés continue for hours. Dancers dress in symbolic costumes of bright colors, feathers, and bells, reminding onlookers of their Indian past. Inside the church is a constant stream of the candle-carrying devout, each repaying a promise made to a deity months before in thanks for a personal favor, a healing, a job found, or similar good fortune. Some travel long distances to peregrinate (make a devout journey), sometimes even traveling several kilometers entirely on their knees to a church.

Christmas and Easter are wonderful holidays. The *posada* of Christmas (a procession) begins nine days before the holiday, when families and friends take part in processions that portray Mary and Joseph and their search for lodging before the birth of Christ (*posada* is also the word for inn). The streets are alive with people, bright lights, and colorful nativity scenes.

The *China Poblana*

China poblana is the national feminine folk costume, worn on occasion by city girls and women of all classes. It is the dress of those who dance the Jarabe Tapatío and of the *charras* in the *charreada*. This traditional costume consists of a full red flannel skirt falling to the ankles, heavily trimmed with sequined designs (the top 25 centimeters are green); a white, short-sleeved, embroidered blouse; a rebozo folded over the shoulders and crossed in front; multiple strings of brightly colored beads; a red or green bow atop the head; and high-heeled dancing shoes. While the costume follows a conventional pattern, there are differences in materials and adornments. *Charras* and folk singers top the outfit with a sombrero.

Legend of the *China Poblana*
There are several variations of the story regarding the origin of the *china poblana*. All begin with a Chinese slave girl acquired by Captain Miguel Sosa of Puebla. Differing versions relate that the girl was a Mongol princess named Mina, or a Hindu princess named Mirrha; all agree that she was noble at birth and a servant girl at death. She is said to have married a Chinese slave, but she refused to consummate her marriage with someone of common blood. Some say her piety was so great that she spoke with saints and possessed the power of healing. Her funeral was attended by the nobility of church and state, who carried her coffin on their own shoulders.

All agree that she was a devout Catholic who took the name of Catarina de San Juan and performed good deeds among the poor, inspiring all who met her. The female servants at the time (early 17th century), called *chinas,* were enamored of Catarina and emulated her outfit, which today is called the *china poblana.*

Fiesta Practicalities

Here are a few practical things to remember about fiesta times. Location cities will be crowded. If you know in advance that you'll be in town, make hotel and car reservations as soon as possible. Easter and Christmas at any resort city will be jammed, and you may need to make reservations as far as six months in advance. Some of the best fiestas are in more isolated parts of the country. Respect the privacy of people; the native people have strong feelings and religious beliefs about having their pictures taken—ask first and abide by their wishes.

Foods of Mexico

We could imagine that if it weren't for the ancient Romans, Mexico might be Dutch, Portugese, French, or British, serving boiled potatoes in local pubs on the Paseo Reforma. But no, the Romans were the earliest to realize that the taste of food could be enhanced with herbs and spices. Black pepper was the favorite. By the fall of the Roman Empire in the fifth century, this spice had become so valuable that the cost of a pound of black pepper was a pound of gold. For centuries tales were told of pepper growing in exotic lands. Marco Polo titillated the courts of Europe with grand stories of unlimited quantities of black pepper when he returned from his travels around the Orient. For the next 200 years, all of Europe's sea captains tried to find the shortest route to the so-called "Spice Islands." To be the first was to have control of the sea route to these exotic lands.

The Bullfight

The bullfight is not for everyone. Many people view it as inhumane treatment and torture of a helpless animal, and prefer not to witness the bloodletting and death. If you can't tolerate this sort of thing, you'd probably be happier not attending a bullfight. However, bullfighting is still a big business and a major attraction in Mexico, Spain, Portugal, and South America.

The *corrida de toros* (running of the bulls) is performed by a troupe of (now) well-paid men, each playing an important part in the drama. The country's largest arena (in Mexico City) fills with 50,000 bullfight enthusiasts for each performance on Sunday and holidays. The afternoon starts off promptly at 4 p.m. with music and a colorful parade of solemn pomp with matadors and picadors on horseback, banderilleros, plus drag mules and many ring attendants. The matadors ceremoniously circle the crowded arena to the roar of the crowd. The afternoon has begun! *(continues)*

Excitement of the Bull

This confrontation is the ceremonial test of man and his courage. Traditional customs of the ring have not changed in centuries. The matador is the star of the event. He's in the arena for one purpose, to kill the bull—but bravely, with formal, classic moves. First the preliminary *quites* and then a series of graceful *veronicas* heighten the excitement; he brushes the treacherous horns with each move. The matador wills the animal to come closer with each movement of the *muleta*. He is outstanding if he performs his ballet as close to the bull's horns as possible (oh, how the crowd cheers!). He must elude the huge beast with only a subtle turn of his body (now they love him!). To add to the excitement, he does much of this on his knees. At the moment of truth, the crowd gives its permission for the matador to dedicate the bull to a special person in the crowd. He throws his *montera* (hat) to the honored person and prepares to reveal his ultimate skill.

At just the right moment he slips the *estoque* (sword) into the bull's neck. If he's an artist, he severs the aorta and the huge animal immediately slumps to the ground, killed instantly. If the matador displays extraordinary grace, skill, and bravery, the crowd awards him the ears and the tail along with its respect. If he kills ungracefully and quickly, and performs unsatisfactorily, it loudly lets him know.

Bullfighting has long been one of the most popular events in Mexico. Aficionados of this Spanish art form thrill to the excitement of the crowd, the stirring music, the grace and courage of a noble matador, and the doomed bravery of a good bull. Students of Mexican culture will want to take part in the *corrida*, to learn firsthand about this powerful art. *Art* is the key word. A bullfight is not merely a fight, it is an artistic expression of pageantry and ceremony, handed down from the Middle Ages, and was once celebrated all over Europe.

History of the Bull

The first records of primitive bullfighting come to us from the island of Crete, 2,000 years before the time of Christ. Also at that time, savage wild bulls roamed the Iberian Peninsula. When faced with killing one of these vicious animals, young Iberian men, not to be outdone by the Cretans, would dance as closely as possible to the brute, demonstrating their bravery before finally killing the animal with an ax.

The Romans began importing Spanish wild bulls for Colosseum spectacles, and the Moors in Spain encouraged *tauromachia* (bullfighting). In 1090, El Cid (Rodrigo Díaz de Vivar), the hero of Valencia and subject of romantic legend, is believed to have fought in the first *organized* bull festival. Showing great skill, he lanced and killed a wild bull from the back of his horse. In this era, only noblemen were allowed to use a lance, and the *corrida* soon became the sport of kings. Even Julius Caesar is said to have gotten in the ring with a wild bull. Bullfighting quickly gained popularity, and was regarded as *the* daring event for the rich. Spain used its ancient Roman coliseums. A feast day celebration wasn't complete without a *corrida de toros*. The number of noblemen killed while participating in this wild event began to grow.

To try to stop the *corrida*, Pope Pius V issued a papal ban threatening to posthumously excommunicate anyone killed while bullfighting. This didn't dull the enthusiasm of the Spanish; the ban was withdrawn, and the danger and the fight continued. Queen Isabella and then finally King Philip ordered these encounters halted, and the fight ceased.

Since the lance was forbidden, commoners intrigued by excitement of the event began fighting bulls on foot (they did not own horses), using a cape (*muleta*) to hide the sword (*estoque*) and confuse the bull. This was the beginning of the *corrida* as we know it today.

The *corrida* has changed little in the past 200 years. The beautiful clothes originally designed by the famous artist Goya are still used. Richly embroidered silk capes add a gala touch draped over the railing of the arena. Even in the smallest village *corrida*, the costume design persists. Though made of simple cloth (rather than rich satin and gold-trimmed silk) and delicately embroidered with typical designs, the village *torero's* costume is impressive.

Gone are the wild bulls; the fighting bulls (all of Spanish ancestry) are now bred on large Mexican ranches specifically for the bullring. Only the finest—those showing superior strength, cunning, and bravery—are sent to the ring. *El toro* is trained for one shining day in the arena.

The season begins in December and lasts for three months. The rest of the year you will see only the *novilleros* (neophyte matadors) in the plazas across the country. They must prove themselves in the arena before they are acknowledged as respected (which means highly paid) matadors. Bullfighting is as dangerous now as when the pope tried to have it banned in the 16th century. Almost half of the most renowned matadors in the past 250 years have died in the ring.

Outside of special events, bullfights take place on Sunday afternoon and the best seats are on the shady side of the arena (*la sombra*)—and are more costly. Ask at your hotel or local travel agency for ticket information. But remember, the *corrida* is not for everyone.

A Kinder Gentler *Corrida*

Some villages perform a *corrida* (bullfight) as part of their festivities. Even a small town will have a simple bullring, and the country *corrida* has a special charm. If celebrating a religious holiday, a procession carrying the image of the honored deity might lead off the proceedings. The bull has it good here; there are no bloodletting ceremonies and the animal is allowed to live and carry on his reproductive life in the pasture beyond the *corrida*. Only a very tight rope around its middle provokes sufficient anger for the fight. Young local men perform in the arena with as much heart and grace as professionals in Mexico City. And the crowd shows its admiration with shouts, cheers, and of course, *música!*—even if the band is composed only of a trumpet and a drum. Good fun for everyone, even those who don't understand the art of the *corrida*.

One of them, Columbus, made his way to what he thought was India, called the people Indians, and named *their* fiery spices "pepper." He was wrong on all counts, and though he never actually stepped on land in Mexico, he launched a gastronomic discovery that has benefitted the entire world. Experts (or food-lovers) consider Mexican to be one of the world's top cuisines, along with French, Italian, and Chinese.

Until the Spanish arrived, the Indians did not have cattle, pigs, sheep, chickens, or goats, and they had never seen a horse. As the settlers came to the New World, they brought all of these creatures with them. Before Cortés, the poorest common folk survived on maize, beans, and squash. Only the nobles occasionally ate the flesh of turkey, quail, deer, small fat hairless dogs, and the denizens of the sea.

The Indians grew countless varieties of beans and chiles, along with tomatoes, squash, corn, avocados, cacao beans (chocolate), and many other vegetables never seen by Europeans. The Europeans introduced wheat, rice, onions, garlic, citrus fruits, and sugarcane. This began a marriage of foodstuffs that was automatically influenced by 27 generations of Moorish occupation in Spain. The results continue to get better each day.

The Indians had only honey to sweeten their foods. After the conquest, sugar became very important. The nuns taught their young students the kitchen arts, including the delight of European sweets, candies, pastries, and glazed fruits, to mention just a few. Mexico is a pastry-lover's dream today.

In many of the more moderate restaurants, a fixed-price menu is common, as is its cousin, the *comida corrida.* The only difference is that you usually don't know in advance exactly what is being served as the *comida corrida,* even after you order. As you finish each course you automatically receive the next, sight unseen! The *comida* is generally changed from day to day. This is a great way to eat on a budget.

Every evening if there are people on the plaza you can expect to find a corn salesman with his large bubbling pot of water, shaker of chile powder, and carved limes. A rolling ice-cream cart dispenses frozen bars, and the cotton candy man attracts children's attention with tall plastic-wrapped bundles of bright pink sugar fluff. On holidays you can buy homemade hot tamales; and there's always a place to buy cold drinks. In the days before bottled soda, vendors would set up tables and fill clear glass vats with colored, flavored sugar water, for about a penny a cup. Today soda vendors also sell bottled water, a very "in" thing to carry around in any country, and of course the best water to drink in any country.

In 1686, 326 stalls existed in the public market of Mexico City.

Beer was brewed in Mexico as early as 1544.

The crown allowed the settlers to grow no olive trees or grape vines as it wished to keep the profit from these commodities in Spain.

Initially the new territory imported only expensive fabrics, hats, candle wax, wine, liquors, vinegar, olive oil, paper, steel and iron implements, fruit preserves, and other luxuries that only the rich could afford. The masses had to rely on the public market and the products of the land.

Montejo, Negra Modelo, and Léon Negro are all fine-bodied *cervezas* produced on the Yucatán Peninsula.

The first primitive corn was grown in Mexico in 4500 BC.

Pulque, Mescal, Tequila

The heart of the maguey plant (known as the century plant in the U.S.) is the source of the most popular Mexican alcoholic drinks: pulque, mescal, and tequila. Contrary to what some people believe, there's a great deal of difference among these three drinks.

A Few Facts
Mescals are distilled saps from various maguey plants. They are called "firewater" because the Spaniards in their search for a potent distilled alcoholic beverage came up with this high proof (80 and up), usually clear and colorless intoxicant; it's not unusual to find a worm at the bottom of a mescal bottle. It's not just any worm, but a moth larvae that grows in the maguey plant and is fried crisp before its immersion.

Pulque, on the other hand, is a fermented, milky, slightly foamy, and somewhat viscous beverage, mildly alcoholic (more like beer), and touted to be a good source of vitamins. Pulque was used by the Indians long before the Spaniards arrived, but for the Indians pulque intoxication was a religious event. Indians who drank pulque and got intoxicated for any other reason were sentenced to death. It seems, however, that exceptions were made for people who achieved old age.

Tequila is the star of the three drinks. It's a distilled beverage derived from the juice of the blue maguey plant, which proliferates in only two areas in Mexico, both near the city of Guadalajara. Probably the most well-known area encircles the town of Tequila, and the other area is around the town of Tepatitlán.

Tequila Production
The maguey hearts, weighing 36-80 kilograms, are chopped into several pieces and roasted. The primitive method is to bury the pieces, cover them with maguey leaves, and build a fire on top. Modern distilleries use huge steam ovens. The cooked substance is then shredded and the juice pressed out. Mexican tequila producers are just as concerned about "authentic" tequila as the provincial vintners of France who proclaim that authentic Burgundy wine (for example) is produced only in the region of Burgundy, France.

Tequila must conform to the government regulation requiring that all liquor labeled as "tequila" contain at least 87% distilled blue maguey juice. While production continues to flourish each year as the demand grows, the plant itself imposes limits; its sap will not yield the characteristic tequila flavor except when extracted from maguey grown in Tequila and Tepatitlán.

The university in Guadalajara offers a course and degree in Tequila Engineering.

THE TRAIL OF CORTÉS

I f you like Indiana Jones adventure, then you have to be dazzled by the
exploits of Hernán Cortés, no matter how history may judge him.
What nerve! What audacity! to drop anchor in a strange port, step on
unknown land, and trek through the midst of often violent men. Even
though his troops had doubts, Cortés was up for the job. And though it
took him only a few weeks to reach the fabled city of Tenochtitlán with
its gold accouterments and superstitious leader Moctezuma, it would take him
several years to fully conquer the millions of people who inhabited the rich
territory. In those years, Cortés's quick wit and chicanery won him several
important allies among the Indians. Through their heroic cooperation he eventually captured a country. Along the path of this first trek to Tenochtitlán, the
villages of these Indians became the first cities of Colonial Mexico. In some
cases they were granted broad privileges. Elegant buildings housed schools to
teach the Spanish way and the Christian religion. Young men became priests,
and young women learned the arts of sewing and cooking in the Spanish style.
Their leaders continued to be treated as royalty, but life as they had known it
was changed forever, even after the Spaniards were ousted 300 years later.

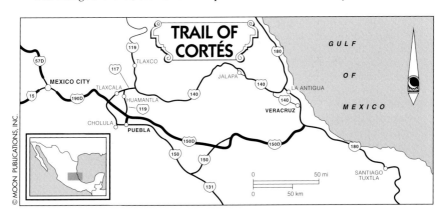

Veracruz

THE SPANISH CONQUEST BEGAN HERE on Good Friday, 1519, with the arrival of Hernán Cortés, his small fleet of 11 vessels, 16 horses, and 550 men. Lives would be forever changed after this moment, in this place and in all the land. The Spaniards quietly slipped into a world both wonderful and frightening.

Cortés was met by the Totonacs, who had ceremonial centers scattered about the coast and inland. By the time the conquistadors had come ashore, selected a strategic location and built a fort, the Aztecs in their Valley of Mexico stronghold had been warned that strange foreigners with "hair on their

Papantla Flyers of El Tajín

One of the highlights of a visit to the El Tajín archaeological zone northwest of Veracruz is watching the *voladores* or flyers (local Totonac Indians) who perform in the front of the visitor's center. No matter how many times you see it, it's still a remarkable feat. The men ascend a 30-meter pole (steel, with protruding rungs to assist their climb to the top) till they reach a small rotating platform. One man (the captain) sits in the middle and plays a flute while tapping a tiny drum hanging from the flute. The other men rotate the platform and carefully wrap their ropes around the pole. While they are doing this, the captain plays his flute, taps his rhythms, and even does a little rain dance on the precarious, half-meter square platform. The men, dressed colorfully in red pants, handsome boots, beaded aprons, and brightly colored hats adorned with mirrors and plumes, perform this dance to beseech the rain gods to send moisture to the earth. While they're at it, the flyers ask all the other gods in nature to go to bat for them, and then they pay tribute to the gods representing the four cardinal points. Thus, the four men fall over backward and fly upside down, around and around, arms outstretched, each attached to a rope by the ankle, making 13 broad circles in the sky (there are 13 months in the Aztec calendar). They look like colorful birds floating on the air currents, descending gradually with each revolution, till at last they gracefully step to the ground without missing a beat. Quite a performance. The flyers circulate through the crowd, asking for donations; US$3-4 is customary. If you wish to take photos, ask—they seem perfectly willing. The flyers generally perform Mon.-Sat. at midmorning, noon, and about 3 p.m.; Sunday noon-4 p.m. Admission to El Tajín is US$3.50, free on Sunday; open daily 8 a.m.-5 p.m.

faces" were looking for Moctezuma. Moctezuma was anxious. Was the stranger Quetzalcoatl, the "white-skinned god" of legend that the Aztecs feared would someday return? Moctezuma soon made his first mistake—he sent rich gifts of gold to Cortés and his men, and with a few words of dismissal hoped the strangers would be satisfied and leave. There it was. Gold! There was no turning back for Cortés; he made the decision for his men as well, whether they wanted to stay or no. With commitment made, Cortés passed through the gateway and the New World was open for business.

Veracruz was the first port in Nueva España. In the 16th century, as the colony developed, ships would arrive yearly from Spain's sailing/trading world, laden with treasures to exchange for New World silver and gold to take to the crown. The arrival of these ships was an exciting event; the *tianguis* (market-place) attracted traders from all over Nueva España. Large tents were put up; food and wine flowed. Wives would come or instruct their husbands to bring home the lovely silks, velvets, jeweled mirrors, decorative combs, exotic scents, and all manner of frivolous wonders from Europe and the Orient that

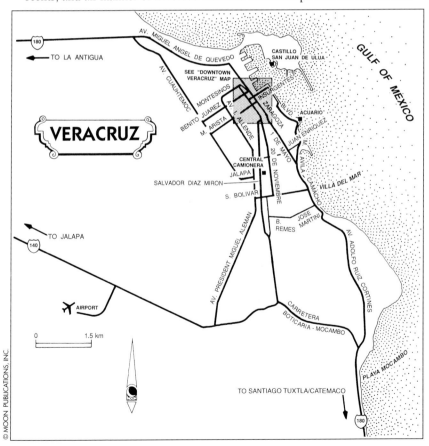

were not always available in the New World. Only the vicious mosquitoes and fear of contracting yellow fever eventually moved the *tianguis* to nearby Jalapa.

During the colonial period, tons of silver and gold were shipped from Veracruz to Spain, tempting pirates from all over the world. Sea rovers frequently raided Veracruz. Sir Francis Drake (the privateer) visited Veracruz at least once and continued to harass Spanish ships and purloin their booty at every opportunity. After years of pirates' constant pillage, the Spanish crown finally saw fit to okay the funds (i.e., to let the people in Mexico keep the money they earned) to build a rugged escarpment and nine forts in Veracruz to protect it from the onslaught. Apparently, the protection was not good enough; Lorencillo and his men ravaged the town and its people in 1683. Pirates sacked the town again in the early 1700s. Eventually, pirate activity slowed down; Spain's power had begun to decline at the end of the 17th century and by the time it was ousted, ships stopped carrying gold and silver across the sea.

Street names are posted on some corner houses, and some signs relate the name that street was called in the past—there can be several numbers visible on each building. If confused, ask—or just wander.

The modern Veracruz seaport and dramatic Spanish Fort doubled as Cartegena in the 1984 movie *Romancing the Stone.*

The port has since been the entry point for *millions* of people and the entry point for every subsequent invasion in Mexico's history. It was the last safe haven of the Spanish after the War of Independence, 1821-24, but only until 1825, when Spain quietly gave up its "jewel" in the New World.

The French took the port in 1837 in the Pastry War, so-called because it involved restitution for a French baker. Not surprisingly, the irascible Santa Anna played his typical comic-opera role, only this time he lost a leg in the fracas. After that, Americans under Gen. Winfield Scott took the town in 1847 during the first war of intervention, which ended with Mexico forfeiting half of its total area to the United States; Santa Anna's name will forever be blackened by that affair. The French returned in 1861 with the English and Spanish to settle payment of past due accounts. But only the French would stay, this time to establish their dominance over the land. And in 1862 they landed in force to depose the president, Benito Juárez, and to install Emperor Maximilian and his wife, Carlota, to the throne; that too was short-lived and Benito Juárez was back in power by 1867. Maximilian was executed in the state of Querétaro that year, and Carlota slowly went insane in Europe.

Veracruz has played a part in many important historic events over the years. In 1914 the U.S. once again took Veracruz, trying to speed the end of General Huerta's regime. Four times, heroic Veracruz played a key role in Mexico's struggle for liberty. But despite its important role, other cities grew larger and more illustrious. Other Mexican cities may attract more attention today, but visitors find Veracruz reminiscent of a Mexico from 35 years past; it has yet to catch up to the glitz of tourism, and for many that's the best reason to visit.

Along the coast of Veracruz, the people are a mix of European, Indian, and African descendants, the most diverse of anywhere in Mexico. Life is lively on the streets of the cities, especially in the sidewalk cafés along the historical plazas, where it's "party time" most of the time. This is *la bamba* country, where it originated, where it continues, and where it takes very little searching to find the music and its dancing aficionados. Coastal vendors sell fish tamales, fish tacos, and fresh grilled shrimp and crab. Veracruz displays a different personality than the Acapulcos and the Cancúns. It's not glitzy—no long white beaches and streamlined high-tech discos. Rather, it's a steamy seaport city presenting still another side of Mexico; it's the city of Carnaval. This celebration vies with that of Rio and all the finest celebrations in the world. Today's Veracruzanos (known locally as Jarochos, the "Rude Ones") are a fun-loving, hardworking lot.

> Popular author Carlos Fuentes is a native of Veracruz.

Exploring the Streets of Veracruz

Veracruz spreads north and south along the sea, and the center of activity clusters around the *zócalo,* officially called the **Plaza de Armas** (either name will get you there). Edging the center, most of the historic colonial buildings, many hotels, cafés, and museums lie within easy walking distance and just one block from the waterfront. The *zócalo* is the beating heart of Veracruz. Musicians are everywhere; marimba bands, guitarists, and mariachis serenade couples on benches near the fountain, diners under the *portales,* and everyone nearby. Natives and visitors alike sit in large hotel restaurants drinking *lechero* (coffee with milk) in the morning, or *cerveza o coctels* (beer or cocktails) in the afternoon, and dining on a wide array of seafoods, day and night. This is also the bubbling center of festivities during Carnaval.

> See the city from a (rubber-wheeled) trolley. They depart from the corner of 16th de Septiembre and the Malecón each hour from 10 a.m. to 10 p.m. They don't run in bad weather.
>
> *La bamba* bands consist of musicians playing many types of stringed instruments (all sizes of guitars, violin, harp, and sometimes a standup bass).

Behind the *zócalo,* across Zaragoza, stroll along the **Plaza de la República,** where you'll see the beautiful pastel yellow buildings of the **post** and **telegraph offices,** with stone lions guarding the columned entrance (designed by Salvador Echagaray); also notice the **Custom House,** with its frets and battlements, and the **train station.** At night spotlight beams bathe them in an eerie glow. The old-fashioned, clustered street lamps hint at what the area might have been like when the buildings were new. Plaza de la República is an island in the swift current of vehicles during the day. Close by, near the train station, look for the sculpture of Benito Juárez, created by Italian artist Francisco Durini and surrounded by metallic plaques bearing the laws of reform. This well-kept park is a cool refuge when the fountains are on. Buses and taxis queue here.

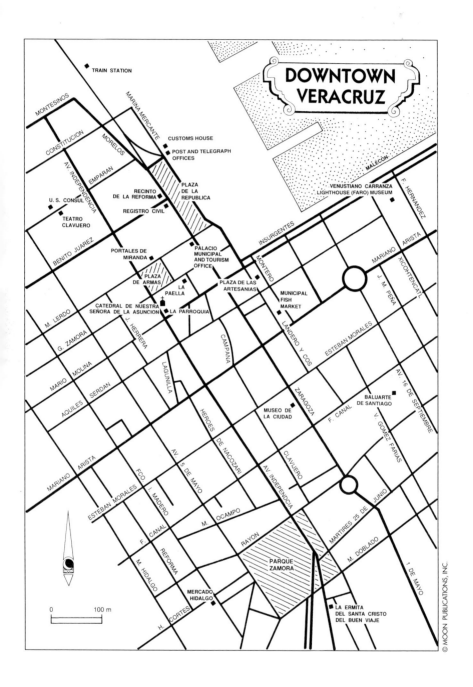

DOWNTOWN VERACRUZ

TRAIN STATION

MONTESINOS

CONSTITUCION

MARINA MERCANTE

MORELOS

AV. INDEPENDENCIA

EMPARAN

CUSTOMS HOUSE

POST AND TELEGRAPH OFFICES

U.S. CONSUL

RECINTO DE LA REFORMA

PLAZA DE LA REPUBLICA

MALECON

VENUSTIANO CARRANZA LIGHTHOUSE (FARO) MUSEUM

F. HERNANDEZ

TEATRO CLAVIJERO

REGISTRO CIVIL

BENITO JUAREZ

PORTALES DE MIRANDA

PALACIO MUNICIPAL AND TOURISM OFFICE

INSURGENTES

MARIANO ARISTA

XICOHTENCATL

PLAZA DE ARMAS

LA PAELLA

PLAZA DE LAS ARTESANIAS

MONTERO

J. M. PEÑA

M. LERDO

CATEDRAL DE NUESTRA SEÑORA DE LA ASUNCION

LA PARROQUIA

MUNICIPAL FISH MARKET

J. HERRERA

G. ZAMORA

CAMPANA

LANDERO Y COS

ESTEBAN MORALES

AV. 16 DE SEPTIEMBRE

MARIO MOLINA

LAGUNILLA

AQUILES SERDAN

ZARAGOZA

MUSEO DE LA CIUDAD

F. CANAL

BALUARTE DE SANTIAGO

V. GOMEZ FARIAS

MARIANO ARISTA

ESTEBAN MORALES

FCO. I. MADERO

HEROES DE NACOZARI

AV. 5 DE MAYO

CLAVIJERO

AV. INDEPENDENCIA

MARTIRES 25 DE JUNIO

M. DOBLADO

1 DE MAYO

F. CANAL

M. OCAMPO

RAYON

REFORMA

M. HIDALGO

PARQUE ZAMORA

MERCADO HIDALGO

LA ERMITA DEL SANTA CRISTO DEL BUEN VIAJE

H. CORTES

0   100 m

© MOON PUBLICATIONS, INC.

On Av. Zaragoza at the ex-church of San Francisco (1715), Benito Juárez pronounced the Laws of Reform in 1859. Today the **Recinto de la Reforma** displays bold bronze statues of the courageous *Heroes of the Reformation*. On the corner of Juárez at **Registro Civil**, the first birth certificate of the city was officially registered, framed, and displayed near the entrance. Don't be surprised that it's the birth record of Jeronima Francisca, the daughter of priest and liberator Benito Juárez. Note the beautiful stained glass window created by Alberto Beltran.

The old **Teatro Clavijero**, on Emparán west of Av. Independencia, was built of wood in 1700, and then destroyed by fire and rebuilt in 1834. For years it was ignored and neglected and ravaged by the elements, but the city took it over and restored it to its present incarnation. The theater is a showcase for good music and theater.

The **Catedral de Nuestra Señora de la Asunción**, (built in 1721 and elevated to cathedral status in 1963), south of the Plaza de Armas on Av. Independencia, is little more than a village church when compared to the massive cathedrals of other cities. If this is your first look inside a Mexican church, note the glass-enclosed statues, and the people who kiss their fingers before touching the glass. Old women sitting behind tables or on the cathedral steps sell religious medals and holy cards (cards depicting holy subjects).

Catedral de Nuestra Señora de la Asunción

The **Palacio Municipal** was built in 1627, greatly inspired by the Moorish architecture of Spain. The Italian-style tower, whose bell would ring to announce each ship arrival, was added a century later. The bandstand nearby holds the military band on Monday and Saturday evenings.

The **Portales de Miranda** (arches), near the cathedral, are named for the merchant who did big business here. Browse through the many shops where once the scribes wrote letters. All around, the colorful façades of balconied houses bring reminders of islands touched by trade winds; shades of blue, green, yellow, and pink abound. Many old houses around the plaza post plaques announcing the residence or birthplace of Mexican leaders and scholars, including native son Miguel Alemán, once president of Mexico.

From the boulevard the *malecón* runs along the harbor and seafront. This is a good lookout to watch freighters and tankers come and go; or from here take a tour on one of the ships tied up close by. Harbor tours are available on one of several launches (7 a.m.-7 p.m.). Prices vary, and they are often negotiable. Guides usually speak only Spanish (ask at your hotel about foreign-language tours).

Castillo San Juan de Ulua, visible across the bay, is the squat, menacing fort built to defend the city in the 16th and 17th centuries. Also known as Rampart of the Shackles, it later was used as a prison; Benito Juárez was a one-time guest (1858-61). Now it's a museum, where it's easy to imagine the massive cannon that stood ready and the soldiers who watched for unfriendly sails on the horizon. After looking through short doorways into airless black cells, all must surely cringe at the thought of occupying this cold, dank dungeon; the prison was notorious for cruelty. From this fort the last royalist force in Mexico was ousted in 1825, and Venustiano Carranza lived here in 1915 when he briefly made Veracruz the seat of government. It's accessible by bus (marked "San Juan de Ulua") or taxi from the *malecón* at Landero y Coss. The museum is open Tues.-Sun. 10 a.m.-4:30 p.m.

Venustiano Carranza Lighthouse stands at the corner of Aquiles Serdan and Xicohtencatl, and a large statue of Venustiano Carranza graces the small park in front of the old *faro* (lighthouse). It's a museum filled with the memorabilia of the famous general and onetime president. Peek into a one-room version of his life as he lived in 1914-15, while he and other leaders of the era composed the Mexican Constitution.

On Canal, between 16 de Septiembre and Gomez Farias, you'll find **Baluarte de Santiago,** the only one of nine forts still standing (from 1635). About a seven-block walk from the *zócalo,* it once marked the outer limits of the city. The cannon on its massive walls created a link to the defenses of the city and menaced attacking vessels. Now it's a museum, open daily 9 a.m.-5 p.m.

At the waterfront, look at the *Marigalante,* a 15th-century-style galleon built in the state of Veracruz 1981-87. This is a true replica of Christopher Columbus's flagship, the *Santa María,* originally named *Marigalante.* This reproduction was built with blueprints obtained from the Marine Museum of Spain. Not only does the fine wooden ship look like the *Santa María,* but it has proven its seaworthiness by duplicating the journeys of the original ship. Built to celebrate the "500 Years of America" project, it set out from Veracruz to Tampico, went on to Brownsville, Texas, and then across the Atlantic Ocean, reaching Spain with a crew consisting of natives of each of the countries of the American continent before returning to the Veracruz. The small ship is a floating museum with typical nautical paraphernalia as well as arts and crafts from each of the countries it has visited. When you're in Veracruz, check with your hotel or tourism office to see if the ship is in port.

Museo de la Ciudad, three blocks from the *zócalo* on Av. Zaragoza, was once an orphanage. The old two-story building is nicely arranged around a central courtyard and houses a small collection of pre-Columbian artifacts. Other displays exhibit local traditions, arts, crafts, and regional costumes.

The **Parque Zamora,** at the corner of Rayon and Av. Independencia, is a lovely green realm in which to retreat from traffic. On Sunday evening, it's a place of stringed instruments, as well as *huapangos* and *danzones* (traditional dances).

A visit to Veracruz would not be complete without a visit to the spirited restaurant called **Café de la Parroquia** (no doubt named for its location near the *parroquia*) just off the Plaza de Armas on Independencia 105. La Parroquia is a restaurant, but it's also a famous landmark; no one visits the city without stopping for a little nosh or a coffee. Here you find the real life of the city. The sounds are a steady mingling of spoons clinking glasses, music, laughter, conversation in a multitude of languages, and a steady stream of vendors passing through trying to sell anything from lottery tickets to live parrots—it's loud and noisy and fun.

Whether you're stopping just for a cup of coffee or a platter of *anything,* it's a pleasant experience. Waiters are quick, the café serves no-frill meals for breakfast, lunch, and dinner, and prices are reasonable. For breakfast try the *huevos* (eggs) cooked in sundry ways: eggs in beans, eggs with enchiladas, eggs in Veracruzano sauce, eggs with asparagus, eggs with chiles, or *al gusto*—which means any way you want them. With coffee it probably won't cost you more than US$3-5.

And it's important to learn the coffee customs at La Parroquia. It's traditional to sit and be seen banging a glass mug with a spoon to summon the bustling waiters. The ritual begins by ordering *lechero* (coffee with milk); your waiter pours black coffee and disappears. Pick up the spoon and clink it, as if a toast were in order; another waiter, with a pot in each hand, will eventually appear. He pours milk or coffee till it's just the right color for you. You will learn quickly—just watch. The day starts early here and goes on till well into the night; it's open 6 a.m-1 a.m. Need a shoeshine? The shine man sets up his chair right in the middle of La Parroquia.

South of Parque Zamora on Independencia stands one of the oldest churches in the Americas, **La Ermita del Santa Cristo del Buen Viaje** (Hermitage of the Holy Christ of Good Journey). Originally, the church was built outside the walls of the city, but the old stones were torn down in 1880 and the church has been gathered into the community. The bells hanging in their niches are reminiscent of those of the California missions.

The house breakfast at Veracruz's famous Café de la Parroquia restaurant is a potato omelet in turkey broth garnished with slices of jalapeño peppers and onion.

When drinking coffee at Café de la Parroquia downtown, take a gander at the lovely old gold-plated bronze Italian coffeemaker that's been doing the job since 1926; it's been polished to a brilliant shine every one of those days.

Modern-day Diversions

Simply called **Acuario** (aquarium), this compound sits in the midst of a modern shopping center, south of downtown on Av. Avila Camacho. The complex is enormous—10,000 square meters of floor space. In the aquarium itself, the main tank holds 1.25 million liters of water and includes a reef. Along with sea turtles, large sharks, barracuda, and other impressive fish glide through the clear water. You look at each other nose to nose through 13 eight-ton acrylic windows that reach from the floor to a height of 4.5 meters. A colorful light and water show entertains visitors as they wait for tickets. The entrance curves through lush greenery, parallel to a winding stream inhabited by small water creatures. Close by, a fine waterfall and hanging green vines cover the wall. Other galleries offer smaller water tanks in modern shapes and settings, all with a huge variety of fish. The Acuario was designed by Hiroshi Kamio, and it's a favorite for all; the touching table includes shark teeth, blowfish, coral, turtle shells, and much more. Another hands-on table features live tidal flats. This is a learning institution, and at any time you will find at least 60 interns helping in all capacities, along with visiting authorities from many parts of the world. The aquarium is open daily 10 a.m.-7 p .m.

This is the city to buy "walking shrimp"—shrimp to go, sometimes on a skewer.

Throughout Mexico, Veracruz has many claims to fame, one of which is its fine cigars. Tobacco is an important crop in the south of the state, and while there have been many factories, for more than 100 years one small factory called **La Prueba Cigar Factory** has been turning out cigars. Follow the aroma of fresh tobacco and you'll find workers "rolling leaf" at Miguel Lerdo 500. The factory is open to the public, and tours are available Mon.-Fri. 9 a.m.-11 a.m. From the *zócalo*, walk one block north on Independencia and turn left on Lerdo; keep going for another few blocks and watch on the left—you can't miss it.

Veracruz Highlights

For the Shopper

In Veracruz, shop for special foodstuffs. Take home a bag or two of locally grown coffee. Jalapeño peppers somehow have more pizzazz in Veracruz. And, if you love pistachio nuts, get a bag or three of those as well (another home-grown item). Crafts include baskets, hats, and other woven palm items.

¡Música!

Trying to trace the beginnings of a type of music or dance is difficult. But when it comes to **la bamba**, various "stories" and "histories" are floating around. No matter which you decide to believe, the dance is still the same—fun!!! Some say that if you tried to pinpoint the exact beginning of the popular *la bamba* dance, it would take you to a West African town called Mbamba, which supplied the slaves who arrived in Mexico with the Spaniards in the 16th century. By the end of that first century in the New World, the dance we know today was born in Veracruz. But it didn't stop there. The melodies are catchy, and the dance spread. Former president (1946-1950) and native-born Veracruzano Miguel Alemán added his contribution to the popularity of the trademark song at every appearance he made anywhere in Mexico; a band would strike up "La Bamba"! As the years went by, the song spread even farther; first across

Mexico, then north of the border until Ritchie Valens recorded it for a rock and roll hit.

Locals say the older generation now performs the *danzon*, a more sedate traditional dance (8-10 p.m. Tuesday, Thursday, and Saturday to the music of the City Band in front of the Palacio Municipal). When it's

> **La Paella,** Zamora 138, offers a taste of Spain on the south side of the *zócalo*. Of course try the paella, a saffron-flavored rice dish made with meat, seafood, and vegetables. Situated in a colonial building, this pleasant little restaurant is decorated with reminders of famous bullfights. It also serves a good *comida corrida*. The generous menu offers many choices (but remember, in Spain a *tortilla* is an omelette). Moderate.

la bamba time, everyone is invited to join in and since the music is so infectious everyone does. Both mariachis and marimba bands play 1-2 p.m. on the Plaza de Armas. Look around and you'll find *la bamba*. The military band plays at the bandstand near the Palacio Municipal on Monday and Saturday evenings.

Special Events

The busiest times of the year are during Carnaval, from the Sunday before till Ash Wednesday; Easter week, from Palm Sunday to Easter; July-Sept.; and mid-November to mid-January.

Pickpockets flourish during Carnaval, working through the crush of people along the parade route. Take precautions.

Carnaval: In Veracruz this is a time of joyous debauchery before the fasting of Lent begins. A parade of extravagant colorful floats is the highlight of **Fat Tuesday,** flamboyant dance groups perform *danzones* down the boulevard, grand balls and masquerade parties are held all over town, and wherever more than two people gather it becomes a party whether in the park, the plaza, the *malecón*, cantinas, restaurants, or a front porch; there's music everywhere. For a list of Carnaval events, check with the tourism office on Plaza de Armas. In the past, men dressed as women would perform and dance at the *bomberos* (firehouse). Ask around town if this is still the custom, and if outsiders are welcome. If you plan to visit Veracruz during this busy time, be sure you make reservations well in advance; hotels are filled to capacity. Don't miss the fun; the Veracruz Carnaval is rated as one of the best in the country.

Regional Food

There's a lot to be said for fresh seafood, and it doesn't get any more varied or delicious anywhere else in Mexico. *Pulpos en su tinta* (squid in its ink), *caldos* (broths) of many kinds of fish, *jaiba* (crab), and the famous *snapper Veracruzano* (made with tomatoes, onions, and peppers) are just a few of the specialties. *Camarones* (shrimp) come any way you can imagine and then some. Another great dish is called by many names, but basically it's *arroz y pescado* (rice and fish), much like paella, but the sauces have taken on the subtle flavors of Veracruz. A bowl of shrimp soup is often used to start the day, and shredded crab tacos are good all day long.

Catemaco south of Veracruz is considered Mexico's premier center of witchcraft; here those who need them can buy love potions, commission the casting of a spell, or have a curse removed. The **Municipal Fish Market**, Landero y Coss, between Arista and Serdan, contains a long line of identical stands (*ostionerias*), where you can sample *coctels* of shrimp, oysters, and octopus—low-priced and good for a snack or a meal with an icy *cerveza* or bubbling *refresca*. Check out the upstairs, and don't neglect the soups: *caldo largo* (a whole fish simmered in stock with onions and tomato), or *chilpachole de jaiba*, a spicy preparation of crab. Entrees include such dishes as *paella, huachinango Veracruzano, ostiones al diablo*, or *camarones en mojo de ajo*.

Special Excursions

Jalapa

Quotations by Bernal Díaz del Castillo and Cortés, later synopsized by Torquemada, paint the following picture:

> When the Spaniards entered Zempoala and saw the splendid city—so new and attractive, with houses made of adobe and others of lime and *cantera* (a local stone)—the streets filled with people who came out to look back at them. The Spaniards corroborated Grijalva's choice name, *Nueva España* . . . Zempoala at that time had a very large population with great buildings, finished with fine wood construction, and each house had its own orchard and irrigation system. Altogether, this garden place seemed like a delightful paradise, not only because it was verdant and cool, but also because it was laden with fruits as well. A market was held every day of all the salable products, to which the many persons present did justice . . . the Spaniards saw that the Zempoalans lived under a well-organized political order and that all held their Lord Ruler in high veneration. Our men admired them because of these things and because unlike other Indians of the islands (the Caribbean), the Zempoalans did not go around nude.

The capital of Veracruz state is the "City of Flowers," and it offers a modern, open attitude, most likely because of its large student population from the University of Veracruz. Most travelers come with the intention of seeing the renowned Museo de Antropologia and the nearby ruins. But once here, they almost always stay longer—the city is a pleasant surprise.

Like Veracruz, Jalapa sits on the historical road used by history's famous: Cortés and his conquistadores, Spanish colonists, American invaders, the French (including Maximilian), and its favorite and/or most notorious native son, Antonio Lopez de Santa Anna. The "often-ex-president" of the country was made president 11 different times between 1833 and 1855. He built and lived in a wonderful hacienda outside Jalapa, now a museum called Ex-Hacienda El Lencero.

The road to the city rises from humid jungle plains to alpine heights and offers a varied and verdant climate. Colorful houses with plenty of wrought iron front winding streets. Jalapa can even brag about its tree-capped volcano. Coffee is grown here as well as varied other crops, including the orchid from which the aromatic vanilla pod grows.

¶¶ La Casona del Beaterio, Calle Zaragoza 20, tel. (281) 8-2129, boasts high ceilings crossed by large open beams hung with plants. Students congregate here, discussing anarchy over *hamburguesas,* and society women sit gossiping over coffee and rich desserts. Casement windows frame a view of the populace on the busy streets and allow a rain-tinged breeze to come inside. It serves excellent *picante* sauce, soups, sandwiches, and *antojitos.*

A variety of good cafés lie along the streets of Jalapa, especially around Parque Juárez and the walking-only street of Callejon del Diamante.

Exploring the Streets of Jalapa

Parque Juárez, across from the cathedral on Zamora, lies in a hilly part of the city. It's a beautiful park with flowers in bloom year-round. Facing the park are the Palacio de Gobierno and the Palacio Municipal. Don't leave the park until you have explored all of its levels. You'll find students poring over texts, lovers looking into each other's eyes, old men playing chess or checkers, children competing in decibels with the birds, and the ever-present vendors of tamales and cold, colorful sugar water.

The **Catedral** was built in 1773 and improved in 1896. Semi-Gothic, with one tower high and imposing, the other squat and square, it has a lopsided appeal. Inside, the three naves are supported by columns forming pointed arches. The chapel contains the tomb of Bishop Rafael Guizar Valencia, who was beatified by the Vatican. A painting by Miguel Cabrera hangs in a place of honor.

Jalapa is built in the hills, and even downtown you encounter hilly climbs. But for the most part walking is somewhat easier around the central area.

Jalapa is known all over Mexico as the jalapeño capital of the world.

Across the way, **Palacio de Gobierno** was built in 1855 on the site of the old Hospital of San Juan de Dios. The murals of José Chavez Morado, depicting the coats of arms given by Charles IV to Jalapa, Cordoba, Orizaba, and Veracruz, grace the walls inside the side entrance.

The **Church of San José** on Calle Cuauhtémoc is the city's oldest, built in 1770 in the colonial style. Sebastian Lerdo de Tejada and Gen. Santa Anna were baptized here.

The impressive **Ex-Hacienda El Lencero** (formerly called Hacienda Manga de Clavo) has been restored to the grandeur it knew when strongman, general, and several-time president Santa Anna was entertaining artists and visiting nobility. It's a look back to a time when a man's hacienda was truly (literally in this case) his castle. Now a fine museum, it is still quite impressive with carefully tended grounds, flowers and shade trees in courtyards, and elegant furniture from around the world filling the rooms that were often the site of high-level diplomatic powwows. The restaurant facing a small lake was once the servants' quarters. El Lencero is 10 kilometers south of Jalapa on the Mexico/Veracruz highway.

The **Museo de Antropología de la Universidad Veracruzana,** built in 1986, was designed by the firm of Edward Durell Stone of New York, and it is a truly imposing museum and folk culture center. A must-see, this museum is ranked the fifth-finest of its kind in the world. The L-shaped structure, built on a 50,000-square-meter plot, covers 9,000 square meters and is surrounded by a lovely botanical garden. Ultramodern, with six spacious exhibition salons, high roofs, patios, and many open spaces, it provides an exotic light that fools you into feeling you're outdoors. Thousands of notable artifacts are on display; probably the most extraordinary are seven colossal Olmec heads carved from stone, including the only smiling head discovered so far. The largest of these monoliths weighs 27 tons.

The three major cultures of Veracruz state are well-represented. **Totonac** art is marked by scrollwork and well-defined curves. Their figurines depict frontal lobe deformation, and some are smiling, which is very unusual in ancient indigenous art. The **Huastecs,** a splinter group of the Maya, occupy the northern part of the state, as well as the bordering states of Tamaulipas and San Luis Potosí. Their sculptural style includes deities with conical headwear, and striking black-on-white pottery. The monolithic **Olmec** heads, which are mounted on pedestals, are thought to represent ballplayers or warriors because of their headgear; there are also smaller, more human figures.

The Olmecs were the first great civilization of Mesoamerica. Their major sites are La Venta, San Lorenzo (from 1150 B.C.), and Tres Zapotes, in the southern part of Veracruz, where their massive basalt sculptures continue to stand guard. Their influence is found in all other cultures, and they are

Star Mountain

The Aztecs' legends were rooted in their observations of nature. Undoubtedly, the smoke, fire, and lava that occasionally erupted from the immense mountains nearby inspired justfiable fear. The peaks surrounding the Valley of Mexico were given sacred names by the Aztecs, and each bears at least one legend. Citlaltepetl means "Star Mountain" in Nahuatl, but it is more commonly known as Pico de Orizaba. Legend tells us that Quetzalcoatl, revered as the Plumed Serpent, was devoured by sacred flames in the heart of this volcano, but then he miraculously took human form and sailed off across the seas, promising to one day return to his people.

Mt. Orizaba, seat of this legend and the highest mountain in Mexico at 5,747 meters (18,675 feet), is the most prominent mountain you'll see while meandering in and around Veracruz state.

credited with inventing the Mesoamerican calendar and "long dates," as well as glyphic writing. Most of what is known about these people is from the trail of sculptures they left behind; the characteristics of these carvings were always the same: thick lips—sometimes snarling—jaguarlike features, and often chubby infant faces. One of the most unusual finds is a bearded figure in the pose of a wrestler. Archaeologists are still unsure exactly where these people were from, though a large number of artifacts were found along the Gulf of Mexico coastal plain, which is today southern Veracruz and neighboring Tabasco. But new finds are now turning up in Guerrero, and it seems there's a connection in Yucatán Maya country as well. In May 1994, the 17th Olmec head was found in San Lorenzo, Veracruz.

For the Shopper

To the right of the cathedral the streets climb to a **public market** on Calle Zaragoza; here, in several alleys, the wares of the merchants are spread on tables. An **indoor bazaar** runs between Zaragoza and Zamora. Look at **Artesanías Piros** on the far side of the Parque Juárez on Ursala Galvan, and check the coffeehouses and the better shops for quality merchandise. The **Agora de la Ciudad** on the south side of the park is frequented by students and contains bookstores and still more assorted *things* to buy.

Santiago Tuxtla

If you're wandering around south of Veracruz and find yourself at all close to the small city of Santiago Tuxtla (151 km south of Veracruz city), stop and wander through the **Regional Anthropology Museum**. The most well-known exhibit is called *Magnetic Black,* a sculpture found during the 1950s at Tres Zapotes, where two of the colossal Olmec heads were found. For many years the odd-shaped sculpture remained in the city's public park. Today many visitors make pilgrimages to touch this statue, convinced that it has special power.

La Antigua

La Antigua is a sleepy town on a sluggish river where songbirds, livestock, and falling fruit are the only afternoon sounds. In this quiet backwater, Cortés first founded Villa Rica de la Vera Cruz, his "rich city of the true cross." It's almost a religious experience to wander the crumbling ruins that were once the home of Cortés, now held together by roots and branches of the dense jungle—aflutter with birds. The only recognizable artifacts are the oven and the cannon in front. The arches and doorways lead out to a tiny plaza where the original, oldest church of all, **Capilla de Santo Cristo del Buen Viaje**, still stands. From here, walk toward the river. Legend holds that along this shore and under the sacred ceiba tree, Cortés tied his vessels and that somewhere nearby is the place where he destroyed them, guaranteeing that his crew would not mutiny and sail away while he slept.

Tlaxcala

CORTÉS AND HIS FELLOW SPANIARDS ARRIVED AT TLAXCALA at the end of August 1519, just months after the first landfall in Veracruz. Archaeologists believe the original site of Cacaxtla was built at the zenith of the Olmec Xicalanca culture around A.D. 700, and that it lasted until A.D. 1200. What Cortés found when he arrived in Tlaxcala was part of a unique civilization that approached a democracy, with voting conducted in a senatorial atmosphere. The Tlaxcaltecans, as they were called, comprised four important dominions: Tepeticpac, Ocotelulco, Tizatlán, and Quiahuixtlán, each with its own chieftain. The Spaniards called these four chiefs the Cuatro Señores.

The Tlaxcaltecans were bitter enemies of Moctezuma and the Aztecs. After learning of the rich gifts Moctezuma and Cortés exchanged, they presumed that Cortés would be their foe. As Cortés and his 300 men approached, the Tlaxcaltecans, 60,000 warriors strong, were ready for him. The Tlaxcaltecan army first offered Cortés the opportunity to turn around and leave. Cortés and his men stood their ground. The Indians charged the Spaniards with slingshots and javelins. The battle raged for 12 days and even though they fought a worthy fight, many of the Indian warriors were killed: they were unable to overcome the Spaniards' firepower, horses, or their fighting dogs. Cortés's army captured many Tlaxcaltecans, including two of their captains, and gave them two options: alliance or death. Though Cortés really sought peace, the Tlaxcaltecans believed his death threat and chose an alliance. This alliance would prove all-important to Cortés; without their help and knowledge, Cortés more than likely would not have conquered millions of Indians. The Tlaxcaltecans' hatred for the Aztecs kept them at Cortés's side, eventually resulting in the downfall of Tenochtitlán.

Because of their early loyalty to the crown, the Tlaxcaltecans were later treated with privilege. They joined Spanish expeditions to South America, the Philippines, and in the colonization of northern Mexico. By order of Charles I, they were given honorific titles, were exempt from taxes, and were allowed to ride horses, which was an honor seldom granted to Indians. But their important position could not help them escape the worst scourge of the conquistadors; smallpox. The diseases brought from Europe devastated the Tlaxcaltecans. Their population was estimated at 4 million at the time of the conquest; less than a quarter of that number remained a century later.

The country's first bishopric was established in 1527; in those years the bishopric meant the difference between development and no development in a town. Tlaxcala was officially founded in 1537 with the construction of chapels of the San Francisco convent. The town was built on land donated by the Indian dominions of Ocotelulco and Tizatlán.

During the period immediately after the conquest, the Tlaxcaltecans were for the most part treated very well. As long as they followed the maxims of Catholicism, Cortés granted the leaders a respect ordinarily paid to heads of state. As time went by, Tlaxcala became the site of many grand pulque and bull-raising haciendas, and later was a leading provider of textiles. After Independence, the state slipped into anonymity, and like many others, into a poverty-level subsistence. Historians comment on the ill treatment given the textile makers during the Porfiriata: long hours and short pay. In some cases the workers were locked into the factories until quitting time. Strikes and violence were rampant.

But the state is historically important. It has preserved its lovely old colonial buildings, and Cacaxtla, the nearby archaeological site (uncovered only in 1975), is proving to be one of the most important discoveries of the era. Its color and design still impresses after hundreds of years.

> ## The New City of Our Lady of Assumption 1525
>
> The city is much larger than Granada and very much stronger, with as good buildings and many more people . . . and very much better supplied with the produce of the land, namely bread and fowl and game and fresh-water fish and vegetables and other things they eat, which are very good. . . . many beautiful valleys and plains, all cultivated and harvested, leaving no place untilled.
>
> —HERNÁN CORTÉS *Letters from Mexico*, describing his first view of Tlaxcala to the Spanish king

Exploring the Streets of Tlaxcala

The streets are laid out around the **Plaza de la Constitución** (the squarish plaza) and **Plaza Xicotencatl** (oblong and erratic shape), in a pretty straightforward grid. However, the names of the streets change frequently, so get your bearings quickly. The neatly planned city was not designed for today's traffic; let's hope the roads around the plaza are turned into pedestrian walkways one day, as they have been in many other Mexican cities. The sidewalk cafés near the plaza cluster around the arched buildings, and they are always crowded. The downtown area is a labyrinth of antiquated buildings and historical sites. The best way to see it all is to walk.

TLAXCALA

TO MEXICO CITY

EMILIO SANCHEZ

GUILLERMO VALLE

PALACIO DE LA CULTURA

ESCALONA

MERCADO EMILIO SANCHEZ PIEDRAS

CARILLO

LIRA Y ORTEGA

ZITLALPOTOCATL

BASILICA Y SANTUARIO DE NUESTRA SEÑORA DE OCOTLAN

SEE DETAIL

ALCOCER

DIEGO MUÑOZ

1 DE MAYO

LARDIZABAL

JUAREZ

XICOTENCATL

MIGUEL HIDALGO

BLVD. M. SANCHEZ

ALLENDE

20 DE NOVIEMBRE

P. DIAZ

PLAZA XICOTENCATL

MORELOS

TO MEXICO CITY

GUERRERO

BUS DEPOT

PLAZA DE TOROS

EX-CONVENTO Y IGLESIA DE SAN FRANCISCO

MUSEO REGIONAL

INDEPENDENCIA

DETAIL

LARDIZABAL

TEATRO XICOTENCATL

SECRETARIA DE TURISMO

PARROQUIA DE SAN JOSE

OFFICINA TURISMO EX-PALACIO JUAREZ

JUAREZ

EX - PALACIO LEGISLATIVO

PALACIO DE JUSTICIA

PALACIO DE GOBIERNO

0   250 m

CORREO (POST OFFICE)

PLAZA DE LA CONSTITUCION

THE ARCHES OF HIDALGO

TO PUEBLA AND CACAXTLA

DIAZ

POSADA SAN FRANCISCO/VILLA ARQUEOLOGICAS

DIEGO MUÑOZ

MORELOS

© MOON PUBLICATIONS, INC.

Plaza de la Constitución in the center of the city lies near the **Parroquia de San José** and the government offices. Colorful flowers surround a 19th-century bandstand; it's next to an octagonal fountain, a gift from Philip IV in 1646, topped by a stone cross engraved with angelic faces. On Monday at 8:30 a.m., the army band plays, and chosen citizens raise the flag amid a fanfare of brass and drums.

The 16th-century **Palacio de Gobierno,** on the north side of the plaza at Plaza de la Constitución 2, is actually three buildings. The Royal Houses, where traveling nobles were billeted when they came to town, are on the right. The lower part of the façade and the interior arches are all that remains of the building, burned during an Indian uprising in 1692 and partially leveled by an earthquake in 1711. Repaired again in 1761, it received its present French rococo-plaster-and-brickwork look in 1928. On the walls above and between the arches on the first floor are the murals of Desiderio Hernandez Xochitiotzin, artist and historian of Tlaxcala. They depict the arrival of man to Tlaxcala, the legend of Quetzalcoatl, the *tianguis* of the four Indian dominions, the alliance with Spain, the departure of 400 families to settle other areas and the seals of the cities that they founded, and of course, Mexican Independence. The work, which began in 1957, was interrupted for years because of philosophical differences between artists and politicians and it is still in progress. The central building, which now houses the state government, was the seat of the elected governor of the four dominions. The original arches, some with carved stone lacework, are intact. An upstairs room, used for state functions, is beautifully appointed, its decorations including a French crystal chandelier. Known as the Red Room, it is not always open for viewing. Ask around if you really want to get inside. The third building was the corn exchange, where the grain was bought and stored. The flower-decorated façade is well-preserved.

The antiquated **Ex-Palacio Legislativo** was completed in 1551 to house visiting dignitaries. Its many incarnations include a slaughterhouse, bakery, and hotel. It was renovated in 1982 to house the state legislature; only the arches remain of the original edifice. It's one block north of the plaza on Juárez.

> **Posada San Francisco/Villa Arqueológicas,** Plaza de la Constitución 17, tel. in the States, (800) 258-2633, in Mexico (246) 2-6022, fax (246) 2-6818, occupies an elderly building renovated to reflect the era ending the 19th century and beginning the 20th century. Often referred to as Casa de las Piedras, it's operated by an arm of Club Med and has a terrific location in the center of the old city. The hotel adjoins the central plaza, and the lovely rooms are situated around a patio or pool. The two-story hotel offers a dining room, coffeeshop, and bar with live entertainment. The dining room, La Trasquila, occupies the second floor and overlooks the charming lobby. Expensive.

Plaza de Toros, Av. Independencia 10, corner of Calle Capilla Abierta, was built early in the 19th century of adobe, *tepetate* stone, and limestone; it is named for Tlaxcala's most famous bullfighter, Jorge "Ranchero" Aguilar. Used only during the state fair in late October and early November, this may be Mexico's oldest surviving bullring. It's open for touring daily 10 a.m.-10 p.m.

The Cuatro Señores helped pay for the Palacio de Justicia, begun in 1528.

Palacio de Justicia, also known as the Royal Chapel, was begun in 1528 by Fray Andres de Córdoba. Dedicated to Spain's Charles I, it was paid for by the four Indian chieftains of Tlaxcala. This chapel was called "Royal," not for the Spanish viceroyalty, but for the Indians of noble birth who were allowed to use it. It was redecorated in the 17th century; stone bas-reliefs represent the coats of arms of Castile and Léon. A fire in 1796, an earthquake in 1800, and almost two centuries of neglect followed until the state took on the task of restoring it in 1984.

Across from Plaza de la Constitución note the **Arches of Hidalgo**, the fine old stone portals that covered what was once the public market. Construction of the arches was begun in 1550 to protect the merchants and their customers from sun and rain. Because they were built in stages, the columns and openings differ in size. The fine carved stone arcade lines two sides of the square. In the early years, shoppers found all of their supplies here as well as fine merchandise from Spain and the Orient. Of course only the affluent could buy the imported goods. Today a series of small stores and the mayor's office are tucked under the broad arches.

🍴 **El Bodegon,** upstairs at Av. Díaz Varela 8-A, serves national and international food. The view of the street market from the wide window gives visitors a feel for the bustle of Tlaxcala.

🍴 The **Teatro Xicoténcatl,** Av. Juárez 21, tel. (246) 2-4073, has been "doing business" since 1873. Historically, it was the site of cockfights, opera, and the city's first movie theater. Inside you'll find an inexpensive place serving breakfast, lunch, or dinner (contemporary live music on Friday night). High ceiling, tall French windows, dark woods, and yards of red curtains and red cloth create an elegant atmosphere.

The art nouveau building at the corner of Juárez was erected at the turn of the century during the era of Porfirio Díaz. Known for years as **Palacio Juárez**, it served as Legislative Palace until 1982. Now it is the home of the state tourism office.

The **Parroquia de San José**, on the Plaza de la Constitución, was built early in the 17th century, with mortar images and the Talavera-tiled façade mandated by then-Bishop of Puebla, Juan de Palafox y Mendoza. The dome was retiled later to cover damage caused by an earthquake in 1864. The lone tower is built in neoclassical style.

The **Ex-Convento de San Francisco** is officially the Convent of Our Lady of the Assumption. Although dates are not certain, historians believe that the main buildings of the immense compound were erected between 1537 and 1540. If these dates are correct, this is one of the first four Franciscan convents built in America. The large open chapel was built to serve this convent, the hub of evangelization. Within the convent grounds the monks operated an Indian school with lodging. Indians used these lodgings until the Reform in 1861. Wander around this graceful old relic to appreciate its art and architectural styles: fluted columns carved with unexpected Elizabethan gothic crosses, stones with representations of St. Francis and St. Dominic, ogee arches (reminiscent of a Moslem arch) characteristic of the 16th century, barely discernible paintings done by the Indians.

Also part of the complex, the **Catedral de Nuestra Señora de La Asunción** exhibits one of the best coffered ceilings (a series of recessed panels) in Mexico from the 16th century. Unusual architectural features and artifacts of interest to note: the heavy cedar crossbeams that glitter with stars, and a Mudejar look, the wrought-iron gate of the Virgin's Chapel, a 19th-century organ, the first pulpit, and in the Chapel of the Third Order, the stone baptismal font in which the four Tlaxcaltecan leaders were converted to Catholicism in 1520, the first step in forging the strong alliance with Cortés. The painting behind the main altar depicts the event. Like so many churches and convents after the Reform, the complex was used as a barracks and a jail. Today the large compound houses the Regional Museum of Tlaxcala. The north entrance from the Plaza Xicohtencatl passes between fluted columns that support the arches connecting the cloister and bell tower.

> (¶) Noted for serving the city's finest food, **Las Casuelas** is a moderately priced restaurant offering indoor and outdoor dining. Everardo Reyes Mendoza, the genial host/owner, caters to your every need. His wife presides over the open kitchen, filling the dining room with mouth-watering aromas. Perfect pictures of Tlaxcaltecan landmarks and prints of Cacaxtla adorn the walls; large windows overlook the patio. Gourmet adventurers should taste a few of the specialties: *queso asado con nopales* (melted cheese with tender cactus leaves), *chorizo santanero* (grilled sausage), or *chiles rellenos con queso o pollo mole poblano*. Figure about US$15 per person for dinner and drink; steaks US$10-12; desserts US$2-3. Open 1-10 p.m., it's at the 20 Km mark of the San Martín-Tlaxcala Highway, one km from the plaza, tel. (246) 2-7467.

The **Museo Regional de Tlaxcala**, in the old cloisters of the ex-convent, was inaugurated in 1978 and contains exhibits from pre-Hispanic to modern times. Pieces of importance include a *chac mool* (sculpture of the ancient Maya god) and the original State Constitution; take a look at the sun clock. A bookstore and library are on the premises.

The **Basílica y Santuario de Nuestra Señora de Ocotlán**, begun in 1670, is the lovely church perched on a hill above the city. Called the high point of Tlaxcaltecan baroque, the church presents an exterior described as a "wedding cake with all of the guests represented, along with the bride and groom." Plaster columns frame the four doctors of theology, the 12 apostles, the seven archangels, and saints Joseph and Francis of Assisi. The star-shaped stained-glass window above the choir depicts the Immaculate Conception. The antevestry, vestry, and the Virgin's dressing room, behind the main altar, are not open to the public. The dressing room, called the "Virgin's Well," was envisioned by Father Manuel de Loayzaga. An Indian artist, Francisco Miguel Tlayoltehuanitzin, spent 25 years completing it. Their masterpiece can only be seen in photos. Traditional processions carry the Virgin through the city on the first and third Mondays in May. The church is on Calz. de los Misterios, at the corner of Independencia. Close by is the **Chapel of the Little Well**, built around a spring that, according to legend, contains curative miracle water produced by the Virgin Mary. Murals by Desiderio Hernandez Xochitiotzin grace the octagonal chapel. In the atrium traditional red clay ducks are sold to transport the water.

The façade of the **Teatro Xicotencatl**, Av. Juárez 21, in operation since the Cinco de Mayo celebration in 1873, was covered with cut stone from Xaltocan in 1923 and again in 1940. The decor is neoclassic; embedded columns topped with Corinthian capitals and bearing a distinct French look frame the 12 windows. In the front of the upper story a coffeeshop still attracts comers. The theater passed into the hands of the government in 1906.

Palacio de la Cultura, Av. Juárez 62, corner of Miguel Lira, was built as the Institute of Advanced Studies in 1939. Neoclassic in design, it was built in a special brickwork with gray stone ornamentation. The building was restored in 1991 and now houses an art gallery and exhibition rooms. The programs change monthly and a newsletter lists all cultural events in the state. Lots of things go on here: art and music workshops, musical events, open air shows, and art shows in the gallery. Everyone is welcome; ask at the tourist office for the bimonthly publication listing events.

The **Aqueducto de Atempa** is on Blvd. Revolución on the way to Santa Ana Chiautempan. The 19th-century viaduct was built to run a hydroelectric plant, which operated early in the 20th century. The viaduct shows skilled stonework. The graceful arches and greenery present a picturesque sight designed by Desiderio Hernandez Xochitiotzin.

Tlaxcala Highlights

Arts and Artisans

The traditional crafts of Tlaxcala state are made for everyday use. Textiles from Santa Ana and Contla, polished clay, huipiles and seed paintings from Atlapa, and silver from Tlaxco are famous for their quality. However, production quantities are small, making them difficult to find at times, ask and look.

Taller Escuela de Platería (Silversmith School), Domingo Arenas 26, tel. (246) 6-0307, is not a common visitor's stop. Strolling from the plaza along Calle Domingo Arenas will bring you to the silver school, operated by Señora Eva Martinez. She takes children ages 13 or 14 and teaches them the art of Mixtec and Aztec jewelry making. The students stay for six years to learn, at their own pace, the 17-step process called *cire perdu* (lost wax). Wax molds are placed inside a larger mold of metal or clay and heated; the wax melts and is replaced by molten silver. Each wax design must be perfect or the piece will be flawed. The students learn by their mistakes.The finished products are symbolic as well as beautiful: birds represent purity, hands—friendship, grapes—religion. The items made are for sale; earrings are in great demand but everything is made in very small quantities. A very friendly, talented woman, Señora Martinez speaks only Spanish; call first to see if she's willing to receive visitors.

For the Shopper
Bazar del Claustro at Plaza Xicoténcatl 8 makes for great browsing, with local art, history books, jewelry, and candies. The **Museo de Culturas** sells the work of its artisans and the quality is very good, but also check out the town of **Santa Ana Chiautempan**, renowned for its woolen products. **Mercado Emilio Sanchez Piedras** is on the corner of Lira y Ortega, a *típico* marketplace with the usual adventure of goods.

Regional Foods
When wandering through the markets of Tlaxcala and if you're early enough, you'll see bright orange squash blossoms for sale. Harvested mostly in the rainy season, these are used for many things, including crepes, fritters, stuffing, and special soups. They have a delicate flavor, and for years only the farmer or those who raised their own squash had the luxury of the blossom. If you see it on the menu, don't hesitate; *flor de calabasa* is a delightful change of pace.

Special Excursions

Parque Nacional la Malinche
One of the most well-known hiking areas in Tlaxcala is La Malinche Mountain Camp in Parque Nacional la Malinche. This national park, 3,000 meters high, sits on the flanks of **Malinche Volcano**, the sixth highest mountain in Mexico at 4,462 meters. From the campground the summit of the volcano is a fairly easy three-hour hike. The gates open at 9 a.m.; daytime visitors can stay until 5 p.m. The park has simple camping facilities available as well as spartan but adequate cabins with kitchens for six to nine people, and firepits, volleyball and basketball courts. For more information talk to the Tlaxcala Tourist Office or call (246) 2-3822 or 2-3900.

Jardín Botánico Tizatlán
This lovely botanical garden on the road to Tizatlán was inaugurated in 1989 for conservation of endangered species, education, research, and spreading the

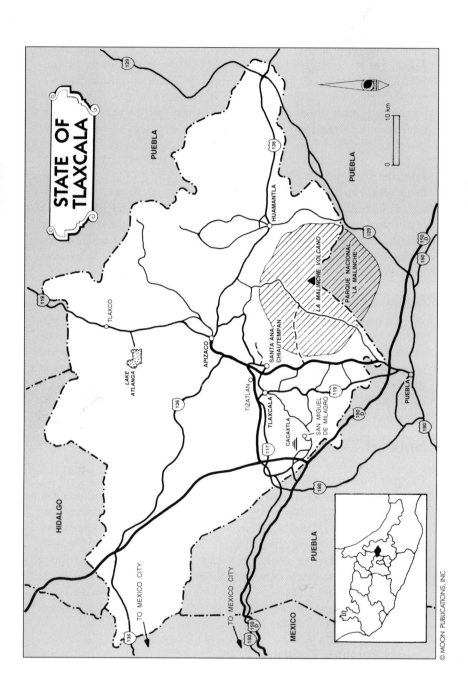

STATE OF
TLAXCALA

PUEBLA

PUEBLA

HUAMANTLA

136

129

150 D

150 D

119

TLAXCO

LA MALINCHE VOLCANO

PARQUE NACIONAL
"LA MALINCHE"

LAKE
ATLANGA

APIZACO

SANTA ANA
CHIAUTEMPAN

136

TIZATLAN

TLAXCALA

SAN MIGUEL
DE MILAGRO

119

190

PUEBLA

190

CACAXTLA

117

190

HIDALGO

PUEBLA

TO MEXICO CITY

TO MEXICO CITY

136

150
150 D

MEXICO

10 km

0

© MOON PUBLICATIONS, INC.

word about ecology and use of resources. The area covers eight hectares, and the dominating vegetation is subaquatic; you'll also see lots of alder, willow, cypress, and juniper pines. A nursery on the grounds grows seedlings that are later used in the state's reforestation program. Two rivers, the Zahuapan and the De Los Negros, run through the property, and a deviation of the Zahuapan has formed a lake where aquatic plants are nurtured and studied. In other sections of the garden you'll find medicinal herbs (sage, dill, aloe, and arnica). Fruit-bearers include apple, pear, peach, and orange trees, as well as grape-vines. A high-tech greenhouse imitates the humidity and shady conditions of tropical areas with a waterfall and an artificial lake, encouraging the growth of typical tropical plants such as ferns, orchids, and palms. The exhibit includes an on-site auditorium, herbarium, and lecture hall, and parking is ample. This is a favorite place for students or laymen to learn about Mexico's ecosystems. These gardens were also popular in pre-Columbian Mexico. During the Aztec era, the people collected plant specimens from various parts of the country to study ancient medicines and cures. The garden is three kilometers out of the city on the road to San Esteban Tizatlán, at Blvd. Revolución and Antigua Camino Real.

Tizatlán

This was one of the four feudal states that together kept the Aztecs at bay. It's about five kilometers northeast of Tlaxcala on the road going to Apizaco; visitors will find a few remnants of what was once a major stronghold of Xicohtencatl. Even though Cortés needed and befriended the people, he never faltered in his demand that they give up their "false images" and become Catholics. In the conquistadores' usual manner, they built an open chapel on the site of Xicohtencatl the Elder's palace (probably after Xicohtencatl the Younger was hanged by his own people, who were under the influence of Cortés and his men). One of the other four chiefs, Maxixcatzin, with Hernán Cortés placed a cross here on the site. Remnants of old artwork linger at this archaeological zone where, it is said, the Cuatro Señores allied themselves with Cortés. Mixtec-style columns and altars are decorated with frescoes depicting legendary figures such as the god of the underworld, god of war, god of the morningstar, and Xochiquetzal, goddess of Tlaxcala. This spot is believed to have been the birthplace of Xicohtencatl the Elder, as well as a training site for the fierce warriors called the Telpochcalli.

Santa Ana Chiautempan

Don't miss Santa Ana's two colonial churches. Most of the sights and markets lie fairly close to the central area. The **Church and Ex-Convent of Our Lady of Santa Ana Chiautempan,** on Agustín de Iturbide 6, was built in 1588 on what was then the town center. The **Parish of Saint Ann,** on Parque Hidalgo 18, was finished at the end of the 17th century. Visitors will enjoy yet another look at the neoclassical and baroque styles. A visit to the markets and shops for a round of bargaining is a must. But that's not all—this is the place to check out hand-woven woolens. The town is known for good quality, and since so many of the townsfolk are employed at the same industry, you might find some good deals. Some quality is really first rate, but other products are mass-produced, so browse and hunt first, compare prices, and then be ready to bargain. Santa Ana is six kilometers east of Tlaxcala and easy to reach by taxi or *colectivo*.

The fields of Tlaxcala are fertile, producing many vegetables, including corn and maguey, from which Tlaxcalans make pulque. Many haciendas grew large and rich producing the alcoholic beverage. Since the breakup of the large properties, many smaller farmers have scattered across the countryside, raising any number of food crops and farm animals. The region is known for *barbacoa en mixiote*, a barbecue of meat or chicken heavily sprinkled with chile, wrapped in the tough skin of the maguey plant, and cooked in pits lined with maguey leaves. Pulque and *mixiote* go hand in hand.

Sanctuary of Saint Michael

This 17th-century sanctuary in San Miguel de Milagro was built under the sponsorship of the Bishop of Puebla, Juan de Palafox y Mendoza. The small corner chapel was built in 1712 to replace the original built in 1631. The legend that has persisted for hundreds of years says that Archangel Michael appeared to a local Indian boy, Diego Lazaro, telling him to spread the news of a curative spring. When he didn't comply, Diego was stricken by illness. The water of St. Michael cured him. When the priests were told of the miracle they weren't receptive; they needed proof. Once again Diego was laid low; this time (it is written) he was cured by drinking from the fountain as they watched. Inside the sanctuary is a statue of an angel sculpted from Mexican alabaster (*tecali*), bearing the date 1708. Eight paintings by Ysauro Cervantes, dated 1899, adorn the walls. Seventeenth-century works that tell the story of the miracle are also quite beautiful. Behind the altar is the burial place of Diego Lazaro and an 18th-century baroque carving of St. Michael. The sanctuary is on the main square; visitors are welcome daily.

Huamantla

This small city is one of the ancient boundaries of the Tlaxcaltecan republic, inhabited then and now by the Otomi people. The city was founded in 1534, but Huamantla is most famous for the annual fair that starts on 1 August and concludes on 15 August with a solemn procession through the streets to the church; it's the **Feast of the Assumption of the Virgin Mary.** Highlights include the running of the fighting bulls through the village streets. On the night of 14 August *la noche en que nadie duerme* (the night when no one sleeps), the two-kilometer-long procession route is decorated by local artists who create a flower and sawdust "carpet," which usually takes from sundown to sunup to craft. This is a fun-filled religious event and it's as much fun to watch the "colorful carpet" come to life through the night as it is to follow along with the procession on the short-lived masterpiece.

Typically Huamantla's most intriguing sights lie close around the town center. **Parque Juárez**, the *zócalo*, is surrounded by most of the important buildings. The cloister of **The Church and Convent of San Luis Obispo**, a 16th-century construction of the Franciscans, is still occupied. The main courtyard floor is covered with marble and obsidian, forming graceful geometric designs.

The church foundation was laid in the 16th century, but it wasn't finished until much later, in the early 18th century. Architecturally, the building exhibits elements of baroque (the entrance), Romanesque (the floor plan), and Churrigueresque (the altarpiece) features. To the side is the chapel containing the image of *The Lord of the Convent*, which is carried in the procession for the Feast of the Assumption.

Huamantla's two museums of special interest are dedicated to what some call the two national "love affairs"—*toreadors* and marionettes. **Museo Taurino** (Bullfight Museum), next to the bullring of the same name on Calle Allende 203, offers four rooms of bullfighting paraphernalia and memorabilia for the aficionado and novice alike. Huamantla has a large appetite for the sport; two native sons have made a name for themselves in the ring: Antonio "El Marinero" Ortega and Fernando "El Callao" de los Reyes Pichardo. On display you'll find posters, photos of famous matadors, costumes, capes, swords, and models of modern bullrings in Mexico. A bright mural decorates one wall. The museum is open Mon.-Fri. 9 a.m.-2 p.m.

Modern-Day Diversions

The National Puppet Museum, Parque Juárez 15, is a tribute to Mexico's other national love interest. Housed in the 19th-century residence of, and donated by, the Barrientos-Carvajal family, the museum was opened in 1991. In Huamantla, the tradition of puppet-making and shows was started in 1850 by Julian Aranda and his brothers. A later collaboration with Antonio Rosete was a success and the Rosete-Aranda troupe gained widespread fame in Mexico and abroad. A pleasant change of pace from the usual museum, it is nonetheless an important facet of Mexican culture. The puppets, only a fraction of Aranda's work, are complemented by puppet creations from around the world; even the U.S.A. is represented. Creative displays include a wall map that pinpoints, with lights, the countries of origin, as well as a line of puppets that moves at the touch of a button. Tours in English are available by appointment.

Tlaxco

The word Tlaxco is from the Nahuatl word *tlachtli*, meaning place of the ball court. This is a quiet town of (predominantly) Indians, who speak only their native language. If you happen to be passing through, stop and take a look. In itself it's not usually a destination, but it's a silver center the site of a silver crafts school. Several colonial structures illustrate once again the great artistic care taken while building.

An 18th-century edifice, **Parroquia de San Agustín** on the main plaza is notable because the builder, Vincenzo Barroso de la Escaloya, was responsible for the cathedral of Morelia. The pink stone is marked by empty niches and the depiction of St. Augustine atop a two-headed eagle. Recently renovated, the main altar, built in 1760, the octagonal dome, and the lovely stained-glass window inside the outer doors are of particular interest. Antique lovers, check out the 19th-century organ in the choir loft.

Lake Atlanga, on the Atlangapec-Tlaxco highway, is the largest lake in the state and has areas for barbecue picnics, as well as boat and horse rentals and a restaurant that serves fresh trout and *mojarra*. The **Atlanga Cattle Ranch** nearby was once a large hacienda, and it continues breeding outstanding bulls. Some of the old hacienda buildings are still standing, including the chapel.

wander the ruins of this colonial convent

Puebla

CORTÉS ARRIVED IN PUEBLA TO FIND A PEOPLE READY TO HELP HIM in his war against Moctezuma and the Aztecs. Historically, Puebla was a buffer zone between the kingdoms of Cholula, Tlaxcala, Cuautinchan, Totimehuacan, and Tepeaca as well as a stopover for pre-Hispanic traders on their way to the major *tianguis* (market) in Tlaxcoco. These small city-states were in a perpetual state of war, and though Puebla had maintained its independence for centuries, eventually it fell to the mercy of Moctezuma and the Aztecs. With their increased power and daring, the Aztecs from Tenochtitlán were becoming more frenzied in their raids. They regularly kidnapped or demanded the wives and children from the people of Puebla, using them for sacrifices to their gods and in the "flowery" battles. In the terrible famine of the 1450s, sacrificial victims had been dying on their own, cutting short the Aztec supply. The Aztecs believed they had to satisfy their bloodthirsty gods *immediately* to end the drought. Since they had no time to venture to distant provinces and kidnap or wage war to get their sacrificial victims (which often took as long as a year) they had made an agreement with Puebla's neighbor Tlaxcala, which needed sacrifical victims for the same reason and for the same gods. The Aztecs and the Tlaxcalans signed a pact that they would wage limited war with each other and take live captives for sacrifice. The grim logic was that they would not waste young lives that ordinarily would die on the battlefield, and at the same time, young soldiers got a lesson in war games. It's no wonder then that with neighbors such as these, the indigenous people of Puebla didn't hesitate to join Cortés against the Aztecs. After Cortés finally defeated the Aztecs, Puebla grew as a commercial center; because of the cooperation and friendliness of the people of Puebla (Poblanos), it became a "safehouse" for Spaniards on the road between Mexico City and Veracruz, the main port of entry for ships to and from Spain.

The region is heavily populated (4.5 million people). State industries run on well-developed hydroelectric power. A few of the most vigorous industries are connected to automaking; the Volkswagen Beetle is manufactured here —and the factory can't keep up with the local demand.

Before the Spaniards arrived the city-site was called Cuetlaxcoapan, "The Place where the Snakes Change Their Skin." The Spaniards first called it "City of the Angels," Puebla de los Angeles. The name was destined to change. On 5 May 1862, after the battle of Cinco de Mayo in Puebla territory, the Juaristas defeated Maximilian and the French; Benito Juárez decreed the name of the city change to Puebla de Zaragoza in honor of the Mexican general Ignacio Zaragoza Seguin, who led his men in the Cinco de Mayo victory. In 1987, UNESCO gave Puebla the honorific title "Cultural Patrimony of Humanity." Often you will hear tour guides or those who promote the city call it "City of Monuments" or "City of Tiles." Most, however, know it as plain old Puebla.

For Mexicans, 5 May 1862 was a day of great triumph. On a dark note, it was a good excuse for Napoleon's government in Europe to oppose the French people and to send more troops to Maximilian in his ongoing struggle in Mexico. Napoleon sent an additional force of 30,000 troops when he heard the outcome of the battle. It took almost a year after the first Mexican victory, but this time the French outnumbered and overpowered the Mexican army. Though the Mexican victory was short-lived, Cinco de Mayo remains one of the most enthusiastically celebrated holidays in Puebla today.

Exploring the Streets of Puebla

The city was founded in 1531, with a charter from the Queen of Spain, Isabella of Portugal, and designed by Hernando de Saavedra. He laid Puebla out in the typical pattern, which includes a central plaza surrounded by a grand church and government buildings. As in most colonial cities of Mexico, the historical central section is a lively conglomeration of striking buildings with more than 400 years of experience serving as a backdrop for bustling commerce, thick traffic, dozens of cafés, bars, shops, shoppers, museums, students, and scores of tourists savoring the design of a past era. The architecture here is almost too overwhelming, and after just a few minutes of walking around you'll suffer sensory overload. The baroque design is dressed with rich carved woods, ornate stucco abstractions, curlicues, flowers, and cherubs, which are applied in combination with colorful tiles—it creates a very distinct look. Those with an eye for "antique" enjoy the baroque churches, the Churrigueresque façades, and the magnificent carved stonework that appears on most of the colonial structures. Many of these old buildings now house hotels, trendy shops, and outstanding restaurants.

> **Mesón Sacristia de la Compañía,** on 6 Sur 304, Callejon de los Sapos, tel. (22) 32-4513, fax (22) 42-1554, is a charming bed and breakfast with an unusual approach to life. It's an "antique shop" rather than a "museum." Marvelous antiques are on display in a 200-year-old building. All of the large rooms are on the second floor on the street-side balconies (the inside rooms are windowless). Live music goes on till quite late below in the courtyard, which is also the dining room. This is a small intimate hotel (nine rooms) with a very special charm. Premium.

It's around the **Plaza de Armas** in the city center and surrounded by colonial buildings of church and state that visitors experience the real flavor of Puebla. The *zócalo* (plaza), in front of the cathedral, is bordered on three sides by the original broad stone arcaded buildings called *portales* (arches). The buildings display typical styles including

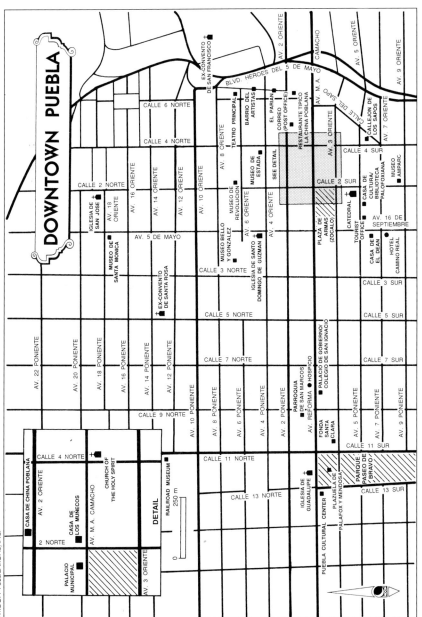

DOWNTOWN PUEBLA

EX-CONVENTO DE SAN FRANCISCO

CALLE 6 NORTE

CALLE 4 NORTE

BLVD. HEROES DEL 5 DE MAYO

AV. 2 ORIENTE

AV. 5 ORIENTE

AV. 9 ORIENTE

AV. 7 ORIENTE

CAMACHO

CALLEJON DE LOS SAPOS

CALLE DEL SAPO

M. A.

TEATRO PRINCIPAL

BARRIO DEL ARTISTAS

EL PARIAN

CORREO (POST OFFICE)

RESTAURANTE TIPICO LA CHINA POBLANA

AV. 3 ORIENTE

CALLE 4 SUR

MUSEO AMPARO

CASA DE CULTURA/ BIBLIOTECA PALOFOXIANA

CALLE 2 SUR

SEE DETAIL

AV. 8 ORIENTE

MUSEO DE ESTADA

MUSEO DE REVOLUCION

AV. 16 ORIENTE

AV. 14 ORIENTE

AV. 12 ORIENTE

AV. 10 ORIENTE

AV. 6 ORIENTE

AV. 4 ORIENTE

AV. 18 ORIENTE

CALLE 2 NORTE

IGLESIA DE SAN JOSE

MUSEO DE SANTA MONICA

AV. 5 DE MAYO

MUSEO BELLO GONZALEZ

IGLESIA DE SANTO DOMINGO DE GUZMAN

PLAZA DE ARMAS (ZOCALO)

CATEDRAL

TOURIST OFFICE

AV. 16 DE SEPTIEMBRE

CASA DE EL DEAN

HOTEL CAMINO REAL

EX-CONVENTO DE SANTA ROSA

CALLE 3 NORTE

CALLE 3 SUR

CALLE 5 NORTE

CALLE 5 SUR

AV. 22 PONIENTE

AV. 20 PONIENTE

AV. 18 PONIENTE

AV. 16 PONIENTE

AV. 14 PONIENTE

AV. 12 PONIENTE

CALLE 7 NORTE

CALLE 7 SUR

PARROQUIA DE SAN MARCOS

HOSPICIO

AV. REFORMA

PALACIO DE GOBIERNO/ COLEGIO DE SAN IGNACIO

CALLE 9 NORTE

AV. 10 PONIENTE

AV. 8 PONIENTE

AV. 6 PONIENTE

AV. 4 PONIENTE

AV. 2 PONIENTE

FONDA SANTA CLARA

AV. 5 PONIENTE

AV. 7 PONIENTE

AV. 9 PONIENTE

CALLE 11 SUR

CALLE 11 NORTE

RAILROAD MUSEUM

250 m

CALLE 13 NORTE

IGLESIA DE GUADALUPE

PUEBLA CULTURAL CENTER

PLAZUELA DE PALAFOX Y MENDOSA

PARQUE PASEO DE BRAVO

CALLE 13 SUR

DETAIL

CASA DE CHINA POBLANA

CALLE 4 NORTE

AV. 2 ORIENTE

CASA DE LOS MUÑECOS

CHURCH OF THE HOLY SPIRIT

AV. M. A. CAMACHO

2 NORTE

PALACIO MUNICIPAL

AV. 3 ORIENTE

0

© MOON PUBLICATIONS, INC.

baroque, Churrigueresque, neoclassic, Herreresque, and Renaissance. Sidewalk cafés and shops under the arches sell shoes, clothes, jewelry, and tacos. Almost anything you need you'll find under the 16th-century arches, including Spanish and English newspapers (*The Mexico City News* in English). The spacious *zócalo* is an island of tranquility with abundant shade trees, benches, and a bandstand within the crowded noisy ocean of cars, honking horns, and scurrying people. On Sunday locals and families from outlying villages escape their routine to enjoy the fresh air together. Before 1854's renovation, however, the center of town was more popular for public hangings, the *tianguis*, bullfights, fiestas, and as a forum for *politicos*. For a flavor of the city today, get there early on a Sunday when families in their best clothes (little girls in white dresses, with their hair in big red bows, or little boys dressed as clones of their papas) meander around the plaza after mass. Faded umbrellas shade the shoe-shiners and their customers, a huge fountain sends out sprays of water, and vendors carrying clusters of bright balloons, pink cotton candy, and a variety of food specialties crowd the walkways.

On the south side of the *zócalo* stands the **Catedral de Puebla**, considered by many visitors, art specialists, and Catholic-church buffs as the most beautiful church in all of Mexico. That's a huge compliment considering how many lovely churches still thrive in the country (a country that on more than one occasion tried to destroy all Catholic churches). The cathedral was begun in 1575 by Francisco

Catedral de Puebla

Becerra and completed in 1648. Twin-towered and tile-domed, this cathedral shows three distinct architectural/historical influences: medieval, Renaissance, and neoclassical. It truly rivals any in the country. Manuel Tolsá designed the altar, which is carved from marble and onyx. The carved wooden doors are

beautifully executed, and in the choir loft you'll find a 12-meter-high pipe organ. The 14 gilded chapels contain religious paintings by well-known artists of the 17th century (Balthazar Echeverioja, Diego de Borgraf, Cristóbal de Villalpando, Miguel Jeronimo de Zendejas), as well as relics and sculptures of several centuries. During its period of construction, it outlived several Spanish sovereigns: Charles I (who ordered the construction to begin), Phillip II, III, and IV; check the high reliefs on the north façade, which commemorate those kings.

The cathedral towers are 74 meters high.

The towers rise gracefully above the city, 74 meters high. The second tower is devoid of bells because it was feared that the weight would cause the cathedral to sink into the ground. See the bells on the tower tour, offered every day at 11 a.m.; English speaking guides can usually be found at the church then. Make your feet comfy, the tower contains more than 200 steps.

A façade of bricks and tiles adorns the structure that was formerly the archbishop's palace; today it houses the **Casa de Cultura** across from the cathedral at Av. 5 Oriente 5, next door to the tourist office. This long building, built in 1597 by Juan Larios, housed the Colleges of San Pablo, San Pedro, and San Juan in the 17th and 18th centuries. In 1891 it became the Palacio Gobierno, and it was rebuilt in 1973 because of its historical significance. Inside you'll find a movie room, exhibition space, workshops, a cafeteria, a coffeeshop, and restrooms. Up a flight of marble stairs to the second floor is the **Biblioteca Palafoxiana**, believed to be the oldest library in the Americas. In 1646, Bishop Juan Palafox y Mendoza donated the first 5,000 volumes, including works of philosophy, theology, and history. The books contain the work of a wide variety of scholars —many were written in Greek and Latin, others in Hebrew and Sanskrit; some were printed as long ago as the 15th century. In 1773 Bishop Francisco Fabian y Fuero built the library, a parallelogram 43 meters long and 12 meters wide, covered by five domes on six Doric arches. Stands of white cedar, divided into 2,472 sections, hold 50,000 volumes. Note the water flasks hung on the ends of the shelves in case of fire. Tables inlaid with onyx stand on a red tiled floor. Faded maps of the ancient world adorn the hand-hewn walls and in one corner is a chapel dedicated to the Virgin Mary. The room is artistically delightful.

Legend has it that the bell in the Cathedral of the Immaculate Conception was put in place by angels. It's just another whimsical tale about the church—but then it might be true considering the size of the bell—8.5 tons.

The bell in the cathedral tower is named *Doña María Palafox*. Its companion bell is the *Flotista*.

Hotel el Mesón del Ángel, Av. Hermanos Serdán 807, tel. 48-2100, fax 48-7935, is a pleasant stopover for "down time" in a tropical green garden with two pools and a health center. Expensive.

Fonda Santa Clara is a popular and sometimes noisy restaurant serving traditional regional food. Try the *mixiotes* (*al vapor*—steamed), the *tingas,* or poblano *mole*. The *antojitos* (snacks) are tasty. Paper decorations hang from the ceiling, and rave reviews are scrawled on the walls. The menu is in English and the bow-tied waiters are efficient and polite. You'll find it at Av. 3 Poniente 307, tel. 42-2659; there's another at Av. 3 Poniente 920, tel. 46-1952.

fountain on the main plaza

Across the plaza from the cathedral stands the **Palacio Municipal**, rebuilt by English architect Charles Hall in 1901 in Italian Renaissance style. The small, elegant, interior patio displays a marvelous staircase of carrera marble and lovely stained-glass windows. The city's ancient Royal Decree, signed by Isabella of Portugal, is kept in the main council room.

Three blocks north of the plaza, look for the **Iglesia de Santo Domingo de Guzmán**, the Dominican monastery consecrated in 1690. Its **Capilla del Rosario** (Chapel of the Rosary), Cinco de Mayo and 6 Poniente, is golden. Inside, walls are ensconced with ornate carvings, tiles, and cherubs, all gilded, and the Virgin is adorned with jewels. This baroque gem of Pueblan colonial art is not to be missed. Behind the church is the **Ex-Mercado Victoria** with three neoclassic façades and formerly the garden of the Santo Domingo Convent. The façade of the *iglesia* is 17th-century baroque, and the inside is similar to that of the Capilla del Rosario, though the elaborate relief figures aren't gilded. The style is somewhat neoclassical; the sculptures are very well done.

Puebla has about 58 churches, one of the largest concentrations in the country. At the **Iglesia de San José**, nine blocks north of the plaza at Av. 18 Oriente and Calle 2 Norte, the columns, tile, and brickwork of the façade give the appearance of a small cathedral. The tile-domed **Chapel to Jesús** adjoins it. **Church of the Holy Spirit**, Av. Camacho and Calle 4 Sur, was consecrated in 1746 and designed by José Miguel de Santa María. This is where the China Poblana Mirrha, baptized as Catarina de San Juan, is said to be buried. The bases of the stone columns are beautifully ornamented and form domes at their tops.

The **Iglesia del Carmen**, at Ave.16 de Septiembre and Av. 17 Oriente, was built at the start of the 17th century by the "Barefoot Carmelites." According to noted architects, the "lines and the contrasting brick-covered spaces are harmonic and artistically attractive."

The **Ex-Convento de San Francisco**, Av. 14 Oriente 1009 and Blvd. Héroes del Cinco de Mayo, was begun in 1535 and completed in 1667 with the

According to legend, Don Leonardo Ruiz de la Pena found himself facing death by drowning in a terrible storm. He prayed to Our Lady of the Immaculate Conception and promised that if his life were spared he would build a convent in her honor. And so her lovely Ex-Convent was built in 1593. Today the convent has been renovated to its original beauty as the **Hotel Camino Real Puebla,** Av. 7 Poniente 105, Centro, tel. (800) 996-7325, fax (212) 223-6499. If staying in Puebla, don't pass it up. The hotel offers all the amenities and luxury the Camino Real is famous for against the backdrop of ancient architecture: Talavera tile is shown off to its best advantage here and there, beautiful antiquated frescos appear on many of the walls, lovely rooms have the high ceilings of another era, plus modern king beds with comfy bed clothes, TV, telephone, computer hookups, private bathrooms, and each offers its own touch of antiquated art. The hotel displays a lovely courtyard, wide arches, dining room, and bar in a convenient downtown location facing the Casa el Dean. Luxury.

Bodegas del Molino sits on the edge of town at San José del Puente, tel. 49-0399 or 49-0651, on the highway to Mexico City. This old hacienda was once a flour mill that turned the land white, giving it the name of Lady of the Snows. Beautifully restored and lovingly decorated, this is one of the best restaurants in town. It's a favorite choice for Poblanos for special occasions, and prices reflect just how special.

addition of the tower and the Churrigueresque façade of stone, brick, and tile. Inside lie the remains of the beatified Sebastian Aparicio under beautifully ornamented domes. The principal one is shaped as an eight-sided star; all are worth a look. *La Conquistadora*, the statue of the Virgin that legend tells us went into battle with Cortés, is also here. One of the oldest gardens in the city, the **Paseo Viejo**, is close by; it holds a monument to the city fathers and a lovely fountain of blue glazed ceramic tiles.

Iglesia de Santa Cruz, in an old neighborhood at Calle 14 Norte and Av. 14 Oriente, is the site of the first mass in Puebla, celebrated in 1530. This is supposedly the land envisioned in a dream by a newly arrived bishop and the reason Puebla was built in this part of the (then empty) countryside.

Templo de la Santísima Trinidad, at Reforma and 3 Norte, is a 17th-century church with a glazed tile depiction of the founding of the city. Farther up at 3 Norte at 4 Poniente, **Santa Catalina** church looms with its Talavera-tiled tower and cupola sparkling in the sunshine.

Museo de Santa Monica, 18 Poniente 103, is a religious museum that preserves a story of the city during the anticlerical era. Some Poblanos dispute these stories, but take a look and decide for yourself. After Catholic nuns and priests were banned from the country in 1857, many went "underground"—literally. This convent was discovered in 1935 after surviving in secret (along with two other convents) since 1857. After the discovery, the convent was left untouched and turned into a museum. The convent was founded in 1610—originally, as one story goes, to harbor the (pregnant) daughters of prestigious citizens. After that era it is said to have been a hiding place for prostitutes (the other option was jail). Some years later it became a cloister for young novitiates. It's characterized by dim narrow halls, winding stairways that step down into the bowels of the earth (where supposedly a crypt holds the bones of babies), a secret window that looks into the church next door (where the nuns could observe mass and other ceremonies), and hidden passageways. Not everyone will be thrilled to tour this former scene of self-flagellation and total silence, for almost a hundred years a secret hiding place for many women. It is also said that many influential families of Puebla helped in the religious conspiracy and saw to it that the women

Puebla is noted for its wonderful cuisine, often copied but seldom matched. Bakeries are prevalent and always great for a quick breakfast. For simple fare local delis offer sandwich meats and cheeses, and *pollo* shops are easy to find, with chubby chickens slowly rotating in front of electric coils and sending out delicious aromas. A fresh whole rotisseried chicken with a loaf of good fresh *bolillos* make great picnic material.

The entrance to **Restaurante Típico la China Poblana's,** one block south of El Parian at Calle 6 Norte 1, is a small storefront room with three tables next to the kitchen and a larger dining room in the rear. It's decorated with local plates, masks, clothing, and a life-sized China Poblana. The food is good here, but there's no written menu and everything is a la carte. If you don't speak Spanish, ask twice to be certain you know what you're getting and at what price.

At one time the art nouveau structure that now houses the VIPS Restaurant on the corner of 2 Oriente and 2 Norte was the home of the wealthy American William O. Jenkins. It was built at the beginning of this century.

had food and medicine. Adding to the mystique, entrance to the convent was through the home of sympathizers through a cupboard in the dining room. Today entrance to Museo de Santa Monica is still through a private home. Apparently, this was just one of three hidden nunneries, and at Santa Monica artifacts are shown from all three. Small admission fee. Next door, the **Church of Santa Monica** contains the glass-enclosed sculpture of *El Señor de las Maravillas* (Jesus of Wonders), admired by both Poblanos and visitors.

The **Museo Amparo** at Calle 2 Sur 708, opened in 1991, is the newest and brightest museum in Puebla. Three blocks from the *zócalo* (follow the signs), this beautifully restored colonial mansion heralds a new policy in museumdom. Manuel Espinoza Yglesias, a banker and philanthropist, has showcased his extensive collection of pre-Columbian and colonial art here. The displays are labeled in Spanish and English; push-button recordings are in every room. Rent headphones at the door, plug them into the audiovisual unit, and choose your language (Spanish, English, French, or Japanese). Follow instructions and learn the history and interesting details about each piece. The high-tech system has a few glitches now and then, but overall it is a fine system.

Museo Amparo

Guided tours are given in Spanish (English guides are available by appointment) through the **Museo Bello y Gonzalez**, Calle 3 Poniente 302. This seemingly endless collection of elegant furnishings from throughout the country, and from Europe and Asia, includes fine art, gold, silver, ivory, jade porcelain, glass, Talavera, wrought iron, pianos, organs, original sheet music by Beethoven, religious vestments, clothing, locks, and countless other curiosities. All of this was collected by José Luis Bello, a businessman who amassed a fortune during his life and, alas, was only an armchair traveler. He vicariously acquired elegant treasures for his home through the efforts of *real* travelers.

The biggest attraction in the rather boxlike **Ex-Convento de Santa Rosa/House of Handicrafts**, Calle 5 Norte 1201, originally built in 1740 as a convent for Dominican nuns, is the Talavera-tiled kitchen (if you have time to see only one Talavera-tiled kitchen, this is the one to see) with huge caldrons and other earthenware utensils. If we are to believe the legends, this is where much of the regional cuisine was created by the now-famous Dominican nun, Sor Andrea de la Asunción. Everyone has heard the story: "Look who's coming to dinner, Sor Andrea—uh oh, it's the bishop." In a flash she cleaned out her kitchen tubs and crocks and created the first *mole poblano,* made of more than 25 ingredients, including a large variety of chiles, spices, chocolate, and turkey. It has been famous ever since, and just one of the dishes that Puebla is known for. After the Reform and the nuns were gone, the building was used as an "asylum" for the demented, and then an apartment house. It was totally remodeled before use as the House of Handicrafts. It displays Mexican art on two floors, and a gift shop offers a selection of local handicrafts.

The word *alfenique* means sugar paste, and while there is a touch of the intricate on the baroque façade of the **Museo de Estada /Casa de Alfenique**, Av. 4 Oriente 416, it doesn't compare to many other more "lacy buildings." Still another explanation/myth is that it was decorated with a sugar paste mixed with an almond oil called *alfenique*. Built in 1790 by Ignacio Morales, it is now the state museum. The first floor houses carriages, armor, weapons, paintings, and old manuscripts, the second floor will delight the history buff, and on the third floor you'll find a display of a typical dining room and drawing room from the 18th-19th centuries. The original *china poblana* dress is here along with other clothing of the colonial era.

Museo de Estada/ Casa de Alfenique

The 18th-century **Museo de Revolución**, Av. 6 Oriente 206, also called the Regional War Museum, was formerly the home of Aquiles and Maximo Serdán Alatriste, who were members of the revolutionary "Light and Progress Club." Opposed to the re-election of Porfirio Díaz, this party would eventually help topple his dictatorship in the revolution that began 18 November 1910. Aquiles was unable to take part in the revolution thanks to an informer who tipped off Díaz. Díaz sent his men, and a barrage of bullets killed almost everyone in the building. Aquiles, who was shot, died shortly afterward. Maximo survived the attack, but along with anyone else who survived he was ultimately captured and killed—look at the hiding place under the floor that *almost* kept him from being discovered. The bullet holes are displayed on the building as a badge of courage. On exhibit are weaponry and photos.

Casa de el Dean, 16 de Septiembre and 7 Poniente, is a Renaissance-style house built in 1580. The historic old *casa* houses a fine display of antique frescoes. Visiting hours are sporadic; ask at the tourist office.

The top floor of the **Casa de los Muñecos**, 2 Norte and Avila Camacho, is decorated with caricatures (some quite gruesome) of the town fathers who refused to let the owner, Don Agustín de Ovando y Villavincencio, add the third floor. Their complaint was that it would be taller than the old City Hall. Don Agustín went to Mexico City where, with proper politicking, he got his way. With this nose-thumbing gesture he immortalized his foes in stone parody. Today it houses the University Museum.

For bullfights, go to Plaza de Toros el Relicario, and remember, you want a seat in the *sombra* (shade).

Lienzo Charro, a *charreada* (Mexican rodeo) stadium holding 4,000 people, is on the Carretera Tehuacan Poniente 1032, tel. 35-2288. *Charreada* is held most weekends and on big holidays.

Puebla is renowned for its pottery.

Though unimaginatively named, **Teatro Principal**, Av. 6 Oriente and Calle 6 Norte, is a lovely old theater begun in 1726 and finally opened in 1760. A fire all but destroyed it in 1902, but the Mary Street Jenkins Foundation lovingly rebuilt it. The intricate stone façade may be all you get to see unless you visit on Sunday or attend a performance. On the ceilings in the lobby and on the second floor are portrait galleries honoring the Patrones of the Comedy Corral. These patrons of the theater proved their commitment by providing their own homes to stage shows before the theater was built.

Across the alley from the theater at Calle 6 Norte and Av. 6 Oriente, check out the **Barrio del Artistas**, once called the *parian de tornos*, where spinning wheels turned out thread vital to the Poblano clothing industry. Formally named the José Luís Rodríguez Alconado Exhibition Hall, it is now occupied by artists. This hall provides small spaces for painters to work portraits and still lifes in pastels, watercolors, and oil. The artists love to capture the roving tourist on canvas given the opportunity; make sure you clarify price before you pose. It's open daily all day.

A little farther, on 6 Norte and Calle Segundo Central, is the only raised park in the city—a quiet green space with flowers, especially bougainvillea, and the ever-present courting couples. The neighborhood is well-kept and the houses reflect an interesting mix of architectural styles. Notice the **Casa de la China Poblana**, on the corner of Av. 2 Oriente and Calle 2 Norte, where the legendary woman lived and died. This is not open to the public.

West on Reforma between 7 and 9 Norte loom two 17th-century buildings of interest. On the left side of the street is the **Palacio de Gobierno/Colegio de San Ignacio**, and on the right side is the **Hospicio**, once a house for the poor that was rebuilt in 1832 and that served as a barracks in the revolution. On the corner of Reforma and Calle 9 Norte is the **Parroquia de San Marcos**, built in 1578 with typical brick and tile façade. At the north end of the Paseo de Bravo on Reforma and 11 Norte is **Iglesia de Guadalupe**, a 17th-century baroque church with a scene of the Apparition of the Virgin captured in another tiled masterpiece. Walk through the **Parque Paseo de Bravo** with its tall swaying trees and spewing fountains dedicated to the brave men and women of Mexico. Sprays of flowers and water beckon. A tiled monument depicts the planting of the cross by Cortés's expedition upon landfall.

Across from the park on Reforma and Calle 13 Sur, look for the **Puebla Cultural Center**. This ex-penitentiary was built in the 1840s, a replica of those that stood in Philadelphia and Cincinnati. The high brick walls, towers, and turrets once held those deemed unfit to remain at large, socially or politically. Today it is a fine library and cultural center.

The **Railroad Museum**, Calle 11 Norte between Av. 2 and Av. 6 Poniente, is a collection of spiffed-up trains that have been put out to pasture. The antique steam engines and rail cars are open for kids (and adults) to touch, examine, and explore. In some of the cars visitors find pictures and displays illustrating the history of Mexican trains since 1837—designing the routes, laying the track, even references to the *bandidos*. The bandits chased after the trains on their horses; once on board the train they confiscated everything of value. The stationlike building also displays pictures. Sunday is family day; lots of picnics are held in the grassy area close by.

Modern-Day Diversions

Agua Azul tel. 43-1330, is a *balneario* (water park), where for a small fee whole families splash and play. Weekdays are less crowded; buses run regularly.

Africam is a safari ride through 6,075 hectares inhabited by an immense variety of wild animals. Buses for Africam leave the Central Camionera (CAPU) three times every day. It's about eight km (15 minutes) from town.

Puebla Highlights

Arts and Artisans

Talavera tile

Today's Puebla, an ornate colonial center, is often referred to as "Talavera-tile country." Taking a stroll through the city is overwhelming; you can't help but notice the patterned tiles on ledges and domes, churches and hotels, ceilings, bathrooms, kitchens, and fountains. A constant reminder of an era dedicated to color and artistic grace, Puebla is a city of culture and colonial splendor as well as a popular visitor's center. Although gold leaf appears everywhere, Puebla's distinct signature is Talavera tile, some centuries old, some brand new.

Long before the Spanish arrival, this area was already an Indian pottery-making center, so the natives readily took to the changing designs and methods brought by the padres. A visit to a family-run Talavera tile workshop illustrates the methods of handmade tiles and pottery. Go from room to room to see the procedure; with a heap of wet clay carefully wrapped, the men (always men) work the wheel turning out saucers, plates, cups, vases, and bowls, as many as 30 plates an hour. Rows of worktables are filled with young women and men using fine-pointed brushes to paint intricate designs. And from the outside of the kiln, one small hole shows an orange glow inside. You'll find dozens and dozens of small pottery workshops; in most cases you can buy from them, and some will even ship your goods home.

For the Shopper

Puebla is an outstanding shopping city. Local arts and crafts are exceptional, and every shop sells Talavera tile and pottery, from top quality to not-so. Excellent onyx from Mexico state is sent to Puebla and its upscale carvers. In the fine shops along the streets, you can browse, bargain, and find souvenir-type gifts. From the surrounding villages the indigenous people bring folk crafts to Sunday market.

Almost every traditional craft that visitors admire began as something utilitarian, often with a religious meaning for a special village. In the ceramic shops of the **Barrio de la Luz** in downtown Puebla, ask to see the vessels made expressly for holding *mole* or those made expressly for tamales. Mexican-style coffee is also made in a pottery pot of a particular shape. In nearby villages the artists create myriad crafts: in **Izucar de Matamoros** the artists create the "tree of life," which can be small or immense with fine intricate figures representing a family, a village, or the story of Adam and Eve. Some of these are 10 feet tall, but that's unusual; traveling shoppers can find them 8-24 inches tall. Most shops will carefully pack these for you. Onyx and marble carvings created in **Tehuacán** and **Puebla** are especially admired. As for textiles: **Cholula, San Martín Texmelucan,** and **Tepeaca** are particularly respected for the quality of wool and cotton they produce. *Amate* paper with unusual designs has long been an important part of religious events in the village of **Pahuatlan.** Today these paper scrolls are sold for souvenirs and framing. All of these are brought to the Sunday market in Puebla.

Mercados

Originally built for clothing merchants at the end of the 18th century, **El Parian** (then known as San Roque, later called Cuauhtémoc) on Calle 8 Norte between Av. 2 and Av. 6 Oriente is a shoppers' getaway. Rows of

---

Market Days in Outlying Villages

Puebla is a small state to scurry around, especially if you have a car. If not, bus transport is simple to these outlying areas, or travel agencies can arrange tours. Market days at a few of the surrounding cities can be an expedition of discovery:

San Martín Texmelucan—Tuesday and Friday

Huejotzingo—Saturday

Cholula—Wednesday and Sunday

Zaragoza—Sunday

Tepeaca—Friday

Tehuacán—Saturday

Puebla—Sunday

brick shops sell clothing, wood, leather, ceramics, silver, and onyx—practice your bargaining techniques here. Check out **Centro de Talavera la Colonial,** Av. 6 Oriente 11, tel. (22) 42-2340, a nifty retail outlet for the tile factory. These craftsmen are renowned makers and merchants of Talavera Poblano.

During the week the **Callejón de los Sapos** (Frog Alley), Av. 7 Oriente and Calle 4 Sur (three blocks south and one block east of the *zócalo*), is a quiet place to meander and discover quality antique shops. On Sunday the alley comes to life with bric-a-brac-laden tables and blankets, and with a flea market where the common man dusts off and displays relics of inheritance and indifference.

The craft of glazed ceramics (majolica) was introduced to Puebla by artisans from Talavera de la Reiva, Spain.

The *mercado publico,* 11 Norte between Av. 2 and Av. 6 Poniente, is chockablock with all the ingredients necessary to make the mouth-watering cuisine of Puebla: meats, fruits, spices, vegetables, innumerable varieties of chiles, tortillas, and breads (cooked and uncooked). Stands also sell flowers, household goods, pots, pans, candles, clothing, and crafts. But maybe the most fascinating is the opportunity to witness the everyday, no-nonsense life of the ordinary Poblano.

¡Música!

Anyone interested in hearing the **mariachis** should go to the **Plaza de los Trabajos,** Calle 11 Norte and Av. 10 Poniente across from the Railroad Museum. Mariachis play every evening; this is loud, sad/sweet happy music. They also play at **Plaza de Santa Inez,** Calle 3 Sur and Av. 11 Poniente.

A tip for readers: do tip the players. They play to earn a living and will circulate, expecting donations—they will let you know if it's not enough.

Special Events

Cinco de Mayo: Each year on May 5 thousands of people come to Puebla to celebrate a famous event in Mexican history. Here, on that fateful day in May 1862, 6,000 French soldiers under Gen. Lorencez attacked the forts of Loreto and Guadalupe, which were defended by about 2,000 Mexican troops under Gen. Ignacio Zaragoza. The defeat of the French earned Puebla the honorific title *heroica.* The defeat certainly didn't add to the popularity of Maximilian in Europe; he was already considered an "enemy" by most of the common folks in Mexico. Today on the battlesite a museum exhibits dioramas of the battle, photos, drawings, and paintings. One work shows Maximilian in Querétaro (moments before his execution) comforting the priest who had come to ease the ex-emperor's last moments. Shortly thereafter he died in front of a firing squad, but not before his final words rang out: "Viva Mexico!" Cinco de Mayo is celebrated each year here with a re-enactment of this battle and a major fiesta.

Regional Food

Many food critics say that Puebla is the birthplace of Mexican gourmet cooking. Its cooks have been creative and clever, with easy access to many rich food products. Not only is the city known for the first *mole*, but a number of other tasty foods are attributed to the cooks of Puebla (mainly the nuns of the old city). The word *mole* comes from the Nahuatl and means concoction. That's certainly apropos since *mole Poblano* is the sauce that contains as many as 10 varieties of peppers, both fresh and dried, along with many other spices and chocolate. When Sor Asunción of the Convento de Santa Rosa put this sauce and her simmering turkey together, she created a gastronomic bombshell in Mexico. Today there are as many varieties of *mole* as there are cooks. Since the 16th century it has been a favorite at home and now in restaurants.

One of nature's dazzling attractions, Popocatéptl volcano is only 45 minutes from Puebla Centro.

Another Puebla creation is one of the most flavorful and colorful: *Chiles en Nogada,* made by stuffing *chiles poblanos* with a zesty mixture of chopped meat, fruit, and nuts. This is smothered with a white cream sauce and crowned with a sprinkle of vivid red pomegranate seeds. This dish is very popular around the independence holiday, as it exhibits the bright colors of the flag. Whatever the holiday, these chiles are delicious, and not too spicy.

Special Excursions

Centro Civico Cinco de Mayo

Take a taxi or a city bus (from Av. 6 Oriente and Calle 2 Sur) marked "Maravillas" or "Fuerte" to a complex less than two miles northeast of the *zócalo* at Blvd. Héroes del Cinco de Mayo. Here, parks, forts, and museums commemorate the scene of Mexico's great (successful) battle with the French. It's worth the bus or cab ride to wander around and imagine the tall-hatted and overly confident French soldiers, so sure they would win. The French didn't count on the motivation and determination of the barefoot peasants who came to fight. These campesinos battled with everything they had—sticks, clubs, and machetes, but mostly their hearts. After the smoke cleared and the shouting and commotion relented, the French soldiers were gone and the outnumbered Mexicans were victorious. The stone horseman (monument) you see is **Gen. Zaragoza**, who led the troops—and received most of the glory.

Many disappointed "monarchists" and Catholic clergy aided the limping French army. New President Juárez issued a presidential decree threatening to fine and imprison "priests of any cult" who further aided the French enemy. And he made it illegal for priests of "any cult" to wear "vestments or any distinguishing garment" outside of the churches. But a year later, the French returned with thousands more troops and finished what they started on that fateful Cinco de Mayo in 1862.

Acuayematepec (Frogs in the Water of the Hill) is the native name of the site of the **Fort of Our Lady of Loreto**, which Ciriaco del Llano ordered built in 1821. Within the fort the church of **Our Lady of Loreto** was built to the exact measurements of the "Saint House" in Loreto, Italy.

Other more modern attractions in the area are the **Planetarium** and **Natural History Museum**, where a 360-degree screen depicts the night sky. The entrance of the natural history museum displays the murals of Poblano artists Salvador Ortega and Fernando Ramirez Osorio. At the **Anthropology Museum** nearby, three rooms of exhibits display pre-Hispanic, colonial, and revolutionary artifacts.

Cholula

When traveling to Cholula, visitors hear tales of the churches; Cortés vowed to tear down every indigenous temple and build a Christian church instead. In pre-Hispanic times, Cholula was one of the most

> **Villa Arqueológicas,** Av. 2 Poniente 601, tel. in the U.S. (800) 258-2633, is part of the Club Med-owned chain of hotels built near various archaeological zones in Mexico, and it offers a/c, tennis courts, swimming, a well-stocked library, and a reasonably good French restaurant. Moderate.

powerful provinces in the country. It had, and still has, the largest ancient structure in the Americas, the Great Pyramid of Tepanampa. It covers 18 hectares, stands 60 meters (195 feet) high, and has a volume of three million cubic meters. But if it weren't for the towers of the Spanish church sitting on the hill marking the spot, you might never know what a valuable piece of historical real estate was hidden underground and around the now-overgrown pyramid.

Great Pyramid of Tepanampa

A visit to the great pyramid is a must. As you approach Cholula from Puebla, about 10 km to the east, you will see the church as you get closer; it's quite a spectacular view. What you *won't* see is evidence of Indian occupation. For that you must go underground.

The Great Pyramid of Tepanampa has had many names: Quetzalcoatl Hill, Tlachihualteptl (Artificial Hill), Tlalolochihuac (Made with Balls of Earth), and Machihualtepec (Hill Made by Hand).

Older than Teotihuacán, it was inhabited before the birth of Christ. It's still larger than anything yet discovered on the North American continent. As was the custom in the ancient Mesoamerican civilizations, the pyramid's builders superimposed seven structures on the original pyramid over an 800-year period. And according to historians the pyramid was in constant use until 1200.

The Tower of Cholula

Traveler Baron Alexander von Humboldt heard an old Indian legend that explained why the great pyramid was truncated. The gods were unhappy with the seven giants inhabiting the land of Tlahuizcalpentecutli. They sent a fierce storm with thunder and lightning, and the torrential downpour destroyed all but one of the seven giants of the primordial world. The last one of the giants built the pyramid in his desperate attempt to reach heaven, but the gods didn't approve of him either, so they destroyed the tall pyramid-tower with fire and confused the language of the builders, eliminating the possibility of ever getting to heaven.

When Cortés arrived in 1519 on his way to attack Tenochtitlán and Moctezuma, Cholula was still an important ceremonial center, with a population of more than 100,000 people. The Cholulans were friends of Moctezuma, and secretly planned a way to get rid of this foreigner. In the guise of friendship, the Cholulans devised a trap to capture the Spaniards. But Cortés's Tlaxcalteca allies discovered the ruse and the Spanish turned the tables; the Cholulans paid with their lives. Formerly called Tlahuizcalpentecutli, (Sacred City of the Evening Sta"), Cholula in Nahuatl means "Place to Escape." The tranquil scene today belies the dramatic bloodbath of the indigenous people that took place at this enormous ceremonial center. Six thousand warriors were slaughtered that day.

Cortés was so incensed by the Cholulans and Moctezuma's almost successful ploy that he vowed to build a Catholic church in Cholula for each day in the year. He didn't quite make it, but there are at least 39.

Three centuries later, in 1804, the explorer Baron Alexander von Humboldt visited Cholula and described the immense pyramid as truncated, with three terraces. He nicknamed it "a mountain of unbaked bricks."

Baron von Humboldt entered through a small opening on the east side of the structure and found a labyrinth of tunnels with walls decorated in yellow and black frescoes with butterflies and insects. In his day only people of importance were allowed into the inner sanctum of the pyramid. Today, anyone (with a paid admission) can wander through the myriad underground tunnels. Hiring a guide (who will undoubtedly find you as soon as you get to the entrance on the north side) is a good idea. You'll see more and have a better explanation of what you see than if you go it alone in this subterranean, though lighted, maze; it doesn't hurt to bring a flashlight. These guides have no posted fees, but they do expect a tip (which is their only pay). After passing through the hill at the entrance, you will find yourself among the ongoing excavations, begun in 1931. Archaeologists have tunneled through about eight km of this amazing den.

On the south side of the pyramid lies the **Great Plaza**, also called Patio de los Altares, which was the primary entrance to the pyramid. Large carved stone slabs rest on the east, north, and west sides. You'll see platforms and diagonal stairways. Human bones were discovered in a pit at the south end, the scene of human sacrifices. A large

> The **Café y Artes** offers an art show and a four-course *comida corrida* at the same time, all pleasantly served under the arches at the north end of the plaza.

> **La Casona,** 3 Oriente 9 one block off the main street, is a lovely restaurant painted a cool white and with plenty of trees and flowers. The outdoor patio tables are usually filled with Mexican families (especially on Sunday), and the two indoor dining rooms open onto the patio. A typical meal can begin with *consomé de pollo,* thick with pieces of chicken, and *sopa de arroz* (rice), followed by an entree of *pipian verde con pollo* (green pumpkin seed sauce with chicken), all with fresh bread; ice-cold Negra Modelo *cerveza* (beer) is available.

building, not generally open to the public, sits west of the plaza. Check it out in case it's open, or ask an attendant; you might be able to get in with a tip. Within, a 50-meter-long mural depicts a pulque-drinking debacle from the third century. Follow the signs to beyond the railroad tracks, where a small museum displays pieces of pre-Hispanic art, obsidian, and ceramics. Entrance to the museum is included in the admission charge to the pyramid; show your ticket to get in.

Finally, to get to the church atop the pyramid, turn back the way you came and follow the steep, winding path to the top of the hill—expect to sweat a little here. Built in 1666, the **Capilla de la Virgen de los Remedios** is so beautifully gilded it will take away any breath you may have remaining after the climb.

Exploring the Streets of Cholula

Downtown, on the east side of the *zócalo,* you can't miss the fortresslike **San Gabriel Monastery** with its Moorish look and 49 domes. The **Ex-Convent and Church of San Gabriel,** started in 1549 by Toribio de Alcarez, was consecrated by the third bishop of Puebla, Martín Sarmiento de Hojacastro. The Franciscan ex-convent is one of the original 12 built after the conquest. Construction began in 1529 and was completed in 1571; it has recently undergone a massive renovation.

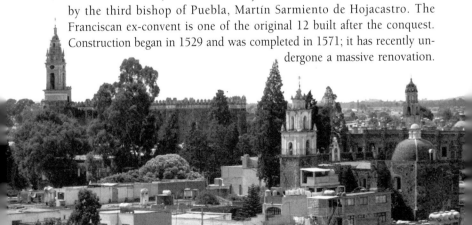

Tour the kitchen, dining rooms, and cloisters and peer into the sleeping quarters upstairs. Period furnishings, religious paintings on canvas, and the black-and-white frescoes of Fray Antonio de Rola adorn the walls. Wander the paths around the compound, noting the small chapels capped with triangular roofs in each corner. The entrance door has 122 Roman nails, each a different design. The **Parroquia de San Pedro** is on the north side of the *zócalo*. This old church dates from 1641.

Near Cholula

The **Santuario San Francisco Acatepec** sits on the old highway to Atlixco, five km south of Cholula. This Indian baroque church's façade is a masterpiece. The builders combined Christian and indigenous ideals in tile and wood carvings. **Santa María Tonanzintla** is a town famous for its pottery, four km south of Cholula, between Acatepec and Cholula. It's the site of another important Indian-style church of the 18th century. When the missionaries introduced the hierarchy of angels and saints to the New World, the natives incorporated many of their old beliefs into the new religion. They used stucco, tiles, and quetzal feathers to adorn the walls and statues—all very impressive, but visitors always remember the gold work.

Special Events

Carnaval: The enormous *zócalo* is the site of the annual Carnaval celebration. Festivals always include fabulous fireworks displays, and at some you'll see flamboyant indigenous dancers.

Festival de Virgen de los Remedios: During the first week of September, *indígenas* perform traditional dances at the Great Pyramid.

Mexico City

WHEN CORTÉS FIRST SAW TENOCHTITLÁN IN LAKE TEXCOCO, its islands were covered with splendid palaces that reflected the sun under clear blue skies. Houses were built on interconnecting canals, the main transport was by canoe, and efficient drawbridges kept out enemies—until the arrival of Cortés. Marketplaces bustled with crowds of people dressed in brilliant fabrics adorned with flamboyant feathers and gold threads. Sellers and buyers bartered generous varieties of fruits, vegetables, fowl, spices, and fresh fish. Rich traders from other parts of the country conducted *big* business with bird-quills filled with gold dust. It was a city of rare beauty, efficient organization, and economic success; however, it was a city that practiced a religion of blood-letting and human sacrifice to placate a pantheon of demanding gods. When the Spanish arrived all of that was to change. The next hundred years brought the destruction of Tenochtitlán, the building of a new city, the ascendancy of viceroys and bishops, the Inquisition, and plagues that would kill 70% of the native people.

The battle for Tenochtitlán was ferocious, and it took many months and many deaths, but the Spaniards finally captured the city with the help of their new allies the Tlaxcaltecans. To conquer the entire country took three years.

For more than 2,000 years the central plateau has been the center of government. As a nucleus, the grounds of Tenochtitlán barely skipped a beat when the Spaniards transformed it into the nerve center of what one day would be called Mexico. Surrounded by some of the most important colonial structures of its time, this ancient center remains the hub of today's Mexico.

Today's Mexico City is a city of high fashion, big money, big business, international trade, modern high-rise structures, the best in *haute cuisine,* and still—some of the most breathtaking structures are the centuries-old colonial buildings and plazas.

The palaces of old vary from the sometimes-stark stone of the 1500s to the baroque façades and tiled domes of the 1700-1800s. Add sleek steel and glass towers of the 20th century and together the landscape provides one of the unique skylines of world capitals.

The city is built on the porous, spongy soil of an ancient lake bed and lacks an underlying bedrock foundation. As the supporting mass of water in the subterranean aquifers has been pumped out, parts of the city have sunk as much as nine meters. Straightening and reinforcing the sinking buildings helps some, but many have sustained stress-related structural damage. Newer buildings ride on floating foundations, and subway tunnels float in the soil, but everything else is sinking.

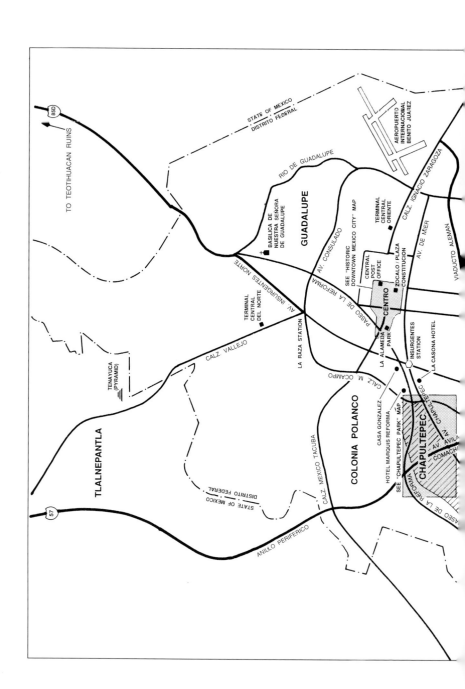

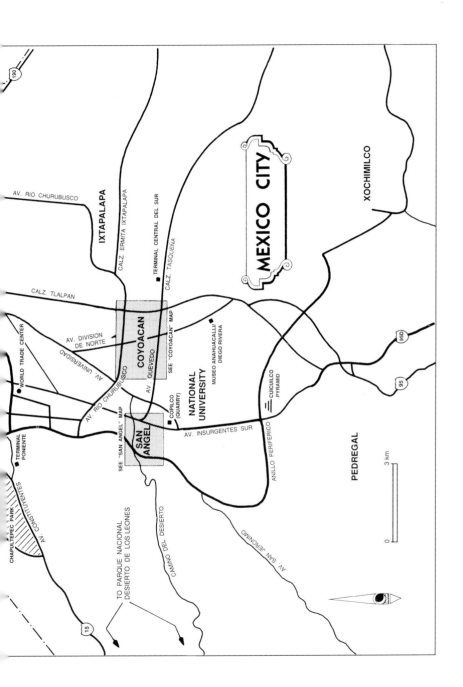

Yes, all roads *do* lead to Mexico City, and they have for more than 2,000 years. That's how long the central plateau has been the center of government, and of population. In 1930 the population of Mexico City was one million people, in 1970 eight million, and by 1980 it had doubled again to 16 million. Today it is estimated that more than 20 million people call Mexico City home—20% of the country's population lives on one percent of the land.

Though life on the avenues is bustling and often hectic, ambling the streets brings a new surprise at every corner. In the center of this monumental concrete city, parks and plazas provide trees and flowers and bubbling fountains—small havens of tranquility. The sounds of dozens of native dialects come from people with chiseled profiles resembling those portrayed in ancient art. Mexico the country is a collection of diverse peoples with a multitude of origins. Mexico City is its nirvana, the paradise that the poorest from distant villages strive to reach. They dream of jobs and education —and not surprisingly, they often accept much less than their expectations. They stay, though, and see the possibilities of modern life all around them. Statistics prove that some of them eventually will enjoy a "piece of the pie" in this ancient, bustling metropolis.

Mexico City is a city crammed with sights to see and sites to explore; archaeology and anthropology, architecture, great art, and a rich history—don't come intellectually unprepared.

Exploring the Streets of Mexico City's Historic Downtown

In and Around the Zócalo

The most famous plaza in Mexico City is called the **Zócalo** or Plaza de la Constitución. A public square from the time of Moctezuma, it was surrounded by Aztec palaces and temples. Today it is surrounded by rich palaces and churches of Mexico's colonial era, and vigorously involved with life in the present. On particular holidays, when the plaza is crammed with locals and tourists, vendors and merchants turn out in large numbers hawking their wares. Women in black rebozos ask for alms at the doors of the cathedral next to itinerant workers sitting by their signs advertising "work for food." The Zócalo is the second largest public plaza in the world, second only to Red Square in Moscow.

Mexico City's transit systems expertly move literally millions of people around the city daily. There are many ways to get where you're going: buses, minibuses, *colectivos*, taxis, or the Metro. (But avoid the Metro during peak business hours!) Buses run frequently, and taxis are reasonable. Once at your general destination plan on walking a lot.

The **Catedral Metropolito** was begun in 1573, consecrated in 1667, and completed in 1813; it was the archbishop's cathedral. Architectural style includes examples of the Gothic, baroque and Churrigueresque. The cathedral was conceived and reconceived by the finest architects: Claudio Arciniega, Damian Ortíz de

The Zócalo has been a public square since the age of the Aztecs.

Castro, and Manuel Tolsá. The main altarpiece is a stunning array of niches filled with statuary covered with gold leaf. Five naves, 14 chapels, three side altars and the sacristy are filled with colonial and European religious canvases representing the past 450 years. The choir balcony is intricately carved and contains still more artwork and an impressive pipe organ. This cathedral is enormous and takes up one entire side of the Zócalo.

The **Sagrario Municipal** to the right of and adjacent to the cathedral is actually a separate church, for the largest parish in the city. The richly worked façade is a monument to José Churriguera, the creator of this architectural form (Churrigueresque) of expression. Inside is a small museum full of plans, drawings, paintings, and other images of the men responsible for and the builders of the cathedral.

The **Palacio Nacional**, with its *tezontle* stone façade, stands on the site of Moctezuma's castle on the east end of the Zócalo. The bell above the entrance is said to be the very one that Fray Miguel Hidalgo y Costilla rang as he proclaimed his Grito to call the people to arms for the War of Independence.The tradition continues each year and the ringing bell starts the Independence Day

It took 240 years to finish the Catedral Metropolito.

festivities, while the overflow crowd in the Zócalo is a scene reminiscent of New York City's Times Square on New Year's Eve. Murals depicting Diego Rivera's visions of the Great City of Tenochtitlán, the Legend of Quetzalcoatl, and the American Intervention grace the main staircase and mezzanine. The **Museo de Benito Juárez** is also here.

If you like flea markets do stroll through **Nacional**

HISTORIC DOWNTOWN MEXICO CITY

© MOON PUBLICATIONS, INC.

Monte de Piedad (National Pawnshop), 7 Calle Monte de Piedad. Opened in 1777, it served the dual purpose of offering no-interest loans and helping the needy (literally translated the name means "Mountain of Mercy"). What a place to browse! All kinds of trinkets and "things" are for sale here, modern and antique, from jewelry to musical instruments. It still does a booming business.

The **Palacio del Ayuntamiento** (City Hall) occupies two buildings, which were once just one, now separated by Av. 20 de Noviembre and sitting directly across the Zócalo from the cathedral. Porfirio Díaz replaced the façade and added a floor. The original building was torched during a riot in 1692 and rebuilt in 1724. Because of the growth of bureaucracy another floor was deemed necessary and was completed in 1948.

The **Museo de las Culturas**, Calle Moneda 13, was formerly the 16th-century mint, where millions of dollars of silver was stored while awaiting the yearly ships to take it to the treasury of Spain. The former mint now houses objects from around the world. The building is undergoing renovation, but it's still open for business.

In 1978, a utility crew stumbled upon the once-holiest shrine in Aztec Tenochtitlán, the **Templo Mayor, the Great Temple of Tenochtitlán**. It was a magnificent discovery. After the conquest, Cortés had torn down the Great Temple

> **Reminder:** Mexico City is about 2,240 meters (7,350 feet) above sea level (higher than Denver), which gives some visitors difficulties at first. If you land at the airport and find yourself huffing and puffing on the *long* walk to the baggage area, it's probably just the altitude. Climbing steps and running will produce the same reaction. If you're bothered (some folks aren't), go easy on *really* strenuous activity for the first couple of days. Sometimes headaches and mild stomach upset accompany the breathlessness; doctors suggest eating lighty and staying away from alcoholic drinks for those first days.

The Hemiciclo de Benito Juárez was built in Alameda Park to celebrate 100 years of independence.

to build the Metropolitan Cathedral. Rediscovery has yielded countless remnants from the earlier era. The Great Temple must have been an awe-inspiring sight; by the time the Spanish arrived it had been rebuilt at least six times and described as a "truncated pyramid crowned by twin temples." A walkway through the site allows visitors to view the twin altars—one to the war god, Huitzilopochtli, the other to the rain god, Tlaloc —and the faded murals that surround them. Because of its location in the heart of Mexico City, the Tenochtitlán site was never investigated, at least not until the temple was uncovered

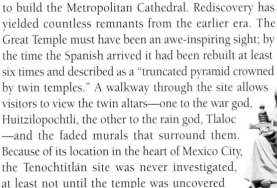

A charming Victorian inn frozen in a past era, **Casa González**, Río Sena 69, in Col. Cuauhtémoc, tel. (5) 566-9688, has 22 rooms, a parlor, and a dining room, all served by a great third-generation family/staff. Yes, the furniture's a little worn, but in a comfortable loving way. This little *casa* hosts some very interesting travelers. It's at a great location near the Zona Rosa, and it's a good starting point for visiting many of the museums and galleries in the city. Tasty meals go for US$10 each. Budget to Inexpensive.

Next door to the Nikko hotel, the **Intercontinental Presidente Hotel**, Av. Campos Elyseos 218, tel. in the U.S. and Canada (800) 462-2427, in Mexico (5) 327-7700, fax 250-9130, is one of the oldest of the Chapultepec Park hotels. The hotel lobby is a multistory pyramid shape with a play of light from the immense skylight at the top. This is a big hotel (660 rooms), with restaurants, bars, and a popular disco. The lively lobby bar is always full and Maxim's serves excellent food. Luxury.

during the 1978 subway excavations. Although many historical documents relate the history of that culture, nothing tells more about a society than walking in its footsteps. In this case, most of those footsteps are buried under a bustling city. The Mexican government was supportive when the temple was discovered; it stopped all construction on the municipal project for as long as it took to plan how to make the modern construction work *with* the temple.

Museo de Templo Mayor alongside the temple relates the story of the discovery and displays many of the artifacts. A large, round stone carving shows the dismembered body of the goddess Coyolxauhqui. It reveals the history of the Aztecs and contains a model of Tenochtitlán. Life-sized statues of eagle warriors stand menacingly over the skulls of their victims. The museum is next to the cathedral; access is through the site at Calle Seminario 8, on the corner of Seminario and Guatemala. Tours in English are available Tues.-Saturday.

A large exhibit of the works of contemporary artist Luis Cuevas are on display at the **Museo de José Luis Cuevas**, Calle Academia 13, two blocks northeast of the National Palace and across from the San Carlos Arts Academy. The *enfant terrible* of Mexican plastic arts now has his own center for the pictorial work of Latin American artists. The museum is arranged in a beautifully renovated 16th-century stone building, the former Santa Ines Convent. Cuevas donated about 1,000 paintings, drawings, and small sculptures to open the museum; many are his own work. You'll find a large collection (32 pieces) by Picasso and many works by Latin American artists of Cuevas's generation. One of the highlights of the museum is a striking eight-meter-high bronze sculpture of a female figure that Cuevas designed especially for the center patio.

Along Avenida Francisco Madero from the Zócalo to La Alameda Park

One of the most beautiful buildings in the city is **Palacio de Iturbide**, Av. Francisco Madero 17. This 18th-century mansion (restored by Banamex in 1972) oozes opulence. It was built in the 1700s by the Marquis del Jaral de Berrio and later passed into the possession of the Marquis de Moncada. And later it seemed a fitting residence for Agustín de Iturbide, who was briefly the self-proclaimed Emperor of Mexico (1822-1823). On the ground floor are the bank offices as well as an area set aside for art exhibits. The courtyard is lively, with three levels of balconies; sculptures and art are beautifully displayed. The chapel on the second floor has also been renovated. Much of this area was residential in colonial times, and the homes all appear to be palacelike.

The **Casa de Azulejos** (House of Tiles), Av. Francisco Madero 4, was built in 1596 by a son to disprove his father's low opinion of him. The father prophesied that the son, who was either shiftless or lacking in business acumen, would "never build a house of tiles." Either way the son proved him wrong. Today the house of tiles is Sanborn's, where you can stop for a drink, a meal, a book, or buy a gift. Across the street is the **Iglesia de San Francisco**, which was built by Cortés in 1524, using masonry stripped from Aztec temples. The painted ceiling has been restored. It was originally part of the Franciscan monastery, which was destroyed in the 19th century.

All around the **Plaza de Santo Domingo**, which is five blocks north of the Zócalo, are buildings rife with history. The **Old School of Medicine** on the northeast corner was the center of the Court Inquisition, where trials were held and sentence passed. The **Portales de los Evangelistas**, where letters were written for the uneducated people, now contains antique printing presses turning out handbills.The interior of the **Ministry of Education** building, República de Argentina 28, is incomparable in splendor; the walls are covered with murals by Diego Rivera and his students Jean Charlot and Amado de la Cueva. The baroque **Templo de Santo Domingo**, with neoclassical features, boasts an altarpiece executed by Manuel Tolsá and occupies the site of the first Dominican church in Mexico. It's on Calle Gonzalez Obregón, between República de Argentina and República de Brasil.

On **Alameda Park** pushcarts and food stands, lovers arm-in-arm on benches, shoeshine stands, and the ever-present balloon sellers create a moving kaleidoscope of people. The **Hemiciclo de Benito Juárez**, a white marble monument built to celebrate 100 years of independence, stands on the south side of the park on Av. Juárez. The **Museo de la Alameda** (also known as Museo Mural Diego Rivera) houses the Diego Rivera mural called *Dream of a Sunday Afternoon in Alameda Park*. This work once graced the lobby of the former Del Prado Hotel, a victim of old age and the 1985 earthquake. The mural portrays many of the sights of this lovely park, as well as the likenesses of Hernán Cortés, Porfirio Díaz, and Francisco Madero. In the forefront of the picture, strolling with La Santísima Muerte (Most Sacred Death) on his arm, is a middle-aged José Guadalupe Posada, the artist who originated the unusual artistic style featuring the dead. La Santísima Muerte is a softer, less frightening descendant of the goddess Coatlicue, sort of a Mexican grim reaper often symbolized by the confectionary skulls and skeleton candies that abound on the Day of the Dead. When death comes for the men of Mexico, it is said to come as a woman. "Most sacred death, beloved of my heart" is a well-used phrase. Study this mural and find the artist as a young boy. Heretics were

(YI) **La Fonda del Recuerdo,** Bahía de las Palmas #37, Colonia Verónica Anzures, serves authentic Veracruzano cuisine in a four-story restaurant with the appropriate Jarocho musicians wandering around. Here seafood dishes from the famous port are faithfully reproduced. Try the paella-
like oysters au gratin or the garlic-cooked octopus.
This place hops, and it seats 750 people. The atmosphere is as authentic Veracruzano as is its food.

(YI) Still an all-time classical favorite, **Fonda del
Refugio,** Liverpool 166, Zona Rosa, tel. (5) 528-
5823, serves traditional dishes in a charming old traditional house. If you can't read the Spanish menu
ask for the English version. It's open Mon.-Sat. 1
p.m.-midnight.

(YI) On the third floor of the Hotel Camino Real,
Mariano Escobedo 700, Colonia Verónica Anzures,
tel. 5-203-2121, across from Chapultepec Park, **Fou-
quet's** is open Mon.-Sat. 7:30-10 a.m., 2-4:30 p.m.
and 8 p.m.-11:30 p.m. It serves excellent French
cuisine, worth donning the required jacket and tie;
about US$60 for two.

burned here during the Inquisition (alive if they refused to repent; renouncing their heresy brought mercy from the executioners, who would strangle them before immolation). In the 1800s, the memories of these dastardly acts were erased: the park was redressed with lovely fountains, a kiosk for the band, and sculptures—indeed a place for romantics, a place to see and be seen. Elegantly dressed dandies would arrive in their fancy coaches and promenade around the park. In the 19th century, La Alameda was the social "event" of the week. Beginning in 1989, the west end of the park was full of squatter shelters, a protest scene for everyone who had a grievance against the government, and there were many. Now they have been moved to the Plaza de la Solidaridad close by.

Just a block farther you can't miss the **Palacio de Bellas Artes** (Palace of Fine Arts) on Av. Angela Peralta. This is the showplace of Mexican culture, bordered by La Alameda, the largest park in downtown Mexico City. Construction began in 1900, during the reign of Porfirio Díaz, but was interrupted by the *revolución* and subsequent turmoil. Completed in 1934, this beautiful vision, rendered in Italian marble with neoclassic, art deco, and art nouveau motifs, was something of a white elephant from an economic point of view (total cost in Depression-era dollars was US$15 million). It is so heavy that it has already settled more than 4.5 meters into the old lakebed underlying the city. The lobby is open to the public, and there's a restaurant off to the side. Several ticket windows open for advance sales to the Ballet Folklorico—showtimes Wednesday at 9:30 p.m. and Sunday 9:30 a.m. and 9 p.m.—and the Orquestra Sinfónica Nacional (National Philharmonic Orchestra)—showtimes Sunday 12:30 p.m. and Friday 8:30 p.m. Murals by Rivera, Siqueiros, and Orozco cover the mezzanine walls. The only opportunity to see the Tiffany glass curtain depicting the volcanoes *Popo y Ixti* is before showtime.

Along Avenidas Juárez and Hidalgo

These two streets border La Alameda Park, and still more historical buildings abound. German-born Franz Mayer collected a vast assortment of art during his lifetime. It is now well-represented at the **Museo Franz Mayer,** Av. Hidalgo 45. This lovely 16th-century, ex-hospital building, sandwiched between colonial churches (and rebuilt after the earthquake) is the ideal setting for such a collection. It contains a few canvases by European Renaissance artists as well as *objetos de arte*, crafted in precious metals, ceramics, jade, ivory, and fabric, but mostly the exhibits are the applied arts, Mexican colonial ceramics, antique rebozos, furniture, weaving, silver pieces, and clocks. The small central courtyard offers a beautiful touch of green and old stone.

Museo de la Estampa (Engraving Museum), Av. Hidalgo 39 just east of Museo Franz Meyer, is another reconstructed 16th-century mansion; this one displays a large collection of printing plates in wood and metal. What was so important in the past to illustrate books and periodicals is now a dead art because of photography, but there is much of interest to see here. The etchings of José Guadalupe Posada, whose works all feature variations of the skeleton figure La Santísima Muerte (Most Sacred Death), are here. He is credited with inspiring the social consciousness of the great muralists, especially Rivera and Orozco, who hung around his studio as neophytes.

Near the Paseo de la Reforma on Av. Hidalgo is the archaic and charming **Hotel de Cortés**, where generations of sightseers have stopped in the cool courtyard for *bebidas y antojitos* (drinks and snacks) and music. This lovely old stone building has a long history (including use as a sanitarium) and is worth a look. Today it's also a nice central place to stay when in town.

> If you crave something sweet look into the **Dulcería Celaya,** Av. Cinco de Mayo 39; it sells a wonderful selection of candies and confections.
>
> If you're in the mood for some off-the-wall entertainment and don't mind being shocked a little, stop in at **El Habito.** Entertainment depicts *anything* or *anyone*, politicians most certainly included (people who understand Spanish will really enjoy this). If you've always wanted to see and hear singing waiters, this is the place; Saturday night is cabaret night. For reservations call (5) 524-2481.

More to See along the Avenidas

North of the Bellas Artes, between Av. Cinco de Mayo and Calle Tacuba on Eje Central Lázaro Cárdenas, are the turn of the century **Bank of Mexico** and **Central Post Office** buildings (ex-palaces!). South, at the corner of Madero and Eje Central Lázaro Cárdenas, stands the **Torre Latino Americana** (Latin American Tower), once the tallest modern building in Mexico. The observation deck on the 44th floor offers the best view of the city and environs (when there's no smog of course). Built to survive the quakes that

> **La Casona Hotel,** Durango 280, Colonia Roma, Mexico D.F. 06700, fax (5) 211-0871; in the States, tel. (800) 223-5652, is one of a kind. In a completely renovated mansion built in 1922, this cozy, luxurious time capsule provides a welcome change from the bustle of sightseeing. The intimate hotel offers just 30 rooms; breakfast is included with the rate. Each room has its own personality, with different decor and different appeal. Burnished hardwood floors, floor-to ceiling shuttered doors, striking antiques, oriental rugs, a charming little dining room, and a fine collection of musical instruments for an unusual ambience all fit together to make this a not-to-miss stay. Service is impeccable, the concierge helpful, and the favorite gathering place with friends is the wine cellar/bar. The hosts/owners, Swiss-trained Rudolfo and Ines, go out of their way to make this an excellent experience. Expensive.

occasionally rattle Mexico City and its spongy foundation, the structure has withstood a couple of good shakes.

Aside from other complex political machinations, the Reform Movement abolished nunneries, closed half of Mexico City's 83 churches, forbade priests to wear their identifying vestments on the street, prohibited religious processions, and allowed the ringing of church bells only during mass.

If you visit Plaza Garibaldi, not only will you find great mariachi bands, but also good representation of the Jarochos from Veracruz playing *la bamba* music.

Around the corner since 1982 is the **Museo Nacional de Arte** (National Art Museum), Calle Tacuba 8. It's a lovely building, with art from all eras represented: pre-Columbian, colonial, and modern. The building, once the home of the Ministry of Communication during Díaz's regime, was later used to store the National Archives. The sculpture of the mounted rider (Spain's Charles IV) in front of the museum is Manuel Tolsá's well-loved and oft-travelled *El Caballito* (only the horse is remembered fondly here in Mexico). This piece has stood in the Zócalo, on the Reforma, and several other places since creation in the 18th century.

The **School of Mining**, across the street at Tacuba 5, is another striking building, also designed by Tolsá. Several meteorites are on display in the lobby.

a grand entrance

Mexico City Highlights

Arts and Artisans

The city is a showcase of the talents of ancient and modern artists. It supports dozens of fine museums, and every little plaza on Sunday offers umbrella-artists illustrating city culture; stop and look—this artist may be the next Orozco or Kahlo. The murals of the city are the most dynamic exposition of the country's history. No subject is sacred. Lovers of Rivera, Siquieros, Orozco, Kahlo, and many other fine artists should go to **San Ángel** and **Coyoacán** to visit the homes/museums where some of these people lived and created, feel their surroundings, walk their steps, see unfinished work.

For the Shopper

Mexico City's public markets, like all *mercados publico,* provide the lifeblood of the ordinary people. Because the city is so spread out, they are everywhere.

> For a historical "experience," check out **Hotel de Cortés,** Av. Hidalgo 85, a fine old establishment with a grand history. The building, originally a convent, dates from the 16th century. The 27 rooms are somewhat archaic, but they're clean and the ambience is very pleasant and very Mexican. The candlelit courtyard is a lovely place to have supper, and on Saturday evening two grand, folkloric supper shows are presented. Twenty-foot-high bushes fill the courtyard, providing a haven for hundreds of singing birds. In the U.S. and Canada, call (800) 528-1234, in Mexico (5) 518-2181, fax 518-3466. Expensive.

If a person had a limitless pocketbook, and limitless time, it still wouldn't be enough to cover Mexico City's shopping scene. Even the most practiced shopper would not have enough time to properly peruse each shop, *mercado,* museum-store, antique shop, stall, mall, flea market, pawn shop, blanket-on-the-ground, table-shoved-along-the-side-of-the-road, art gallery, and junk shop. And you can't miss even one, because you never know where some little treasure will pop up. One place not to miss: the two-story plaza of **Bazar Sábado** in San Ángel, where talented artisans sell wonderful handcrafted items such as jewelry, pottery, leather, and clothing. Some of the finest artists have regular shops here; this is one of the "must-dos" while in Mexico City and it can really get crowded. In the plaza outside, artists under umbrellas display their work, often working at their easels as they sell. Bargaining is taboo *inside* and can cause an ugly response. With the artisans *outside,* haggle all you wish. The selection of quality crafts is unbelievable, and very trendy. The central patio is now a dining room and serves lunch and snacks. This is a great way to spend a Saturday.

Special Events

Independence Day: Just before midnight each 15 September, Mexico City dwellers and people from distant parts of the country gather in the Zócalo to hear the bells ring and see and hear the president of Mexico stand on the balcony of the Palacio Nacional and shout the Grito de Dolores. The famous *grito* shouted

⌂ Next to the Zócalo, **Hotel Majestic,** Madero 73, tel. (5) 521-8600, (800) 528-1234, fax 518-3466, is a 16th-century building with a dab of character. On the first floor you're surrounded with stone archways and fountains; on the second floor the mix includes a glass-brick floor. The small rooms are nothing to write home about, but the wonderful location overlooking the Zócalo makes it all worthwhile. The views across the Zócalo on a (rare) clear day are quite impressive. You can reserve a room with that view, or if staying in another hotel, come here for breakfast on one of the seventh-floor balconies overlooking the Zócalo. It's a lovely way to start the day. If it's early enough (6 a.m.) you'll see the daily flag-raising ceremony, complete with uniformed guards and drums. Or, if you miss that, you may see a practically deserted plaza with only the orange-clad workers sweeping the center of this immense plaza. If you're not a morning person, get a table at 6 p.m. and watch the presidential guards take the flag down. Anyone planning a trip to Mexico around 16 September (Independence Day) and interested in the big celebration, which actually begins at midnight the night before, should plan to stay here. Remember: for these dates you must make reservations a year in advance. Ask for a room facing the Zócalo and keep your fingers crossed. The square comes alive on that night! The president gives the Grito, and then he and his family watch the fireworks along with thousands of Mexicans waving flags. Expensive.

🍴 If you'd like a little history thrown in with lunch or dinner, or just a cold *cerveza,* stop in at the **La Opera Bar,** Av. Cinco de Mayo 10, a long-time favorite. It's almost always crowded and you'll probably have an interminable wait for service. But it's worth it—the walls all but shout classic history. Women weren't allowed in this male domain until the 1970s. This dark, baroque cavern of a place was built with plenty of wood and huge, mirrored booths big enough to hold large parties of revelers or to conceal couples deep in the recesses. It's said that Pancho Villa brought his horse here for lunch and fired his *pistolas* into the ceiling (unhappy with the service perhaps?). That's just one of many stories told about La Opera. It's open Mon.-Sat. noon-midnight.

in 1810 by Miguel Hidalgo in the small village of Dolores Hidalgo became the most famous in Mexican history: "Long live our Lady of Guadalupe! Down with bad government! Death to all Spaniards!" This call to arms and the ensuing War of Independence is Mexico's shining hour, and thousands gather here each year to remember that moment; even the bell is the real thing. This is still a stirring, patriotic moment for all Mexicans, and actually for all who experience it.

Regional Food

Even before this was Mexico City, when the Aztecs ruled Tenochtitlán, food was the centerpiece—at least of the palace. According to chronicler Bernal Díaz del Castillo, the court chefs would cook a selection of dishes for the emperor to choose from. Even fresh fish was brought from Veracruz—and those were the days before FedEx. Runners would wrap the fish in various leaves and pass the important package at running stations to the next powerful runner so that Moctezuma could have his delicacy that night—or not. The rest probably went to the help—they ate well!

It's difficult to name one or two food specialties in Mexico City. During the colonial era some of the country's finest cuisine was found here. It was the center of government, and the viceroys and prelates entertained lavishly—all had their cooks, and all tried to outdo themselves. Later, when Carlota and Maximilian arrived, they brought their French cooks and their French cuisine. Perhaps thanks to the Hapsburgs, the wonderful *bolillo* (small hard rolls, most nearly like French rolls) became the bread of preference. And it is safe to say that with the arrival of the French came the delicate pastries so favored by the Europeans. The nuns passed these fine recipes along, and many young indigenous women contin-ued the trend, each bringing just a smidgin of change using local fruits and ideas.

Today's cuisine in Mexico City is the country's most varied. Visitors have a choice of many ethnicities, and several of the finest restaurants serve *típico* Mexican food from every region. For the curious, several restaurants even serve specialties that date from the era of the Aztecs, including wild game and nutritional insects loaded with protein. The Mexican marketplace is a good place to find fine *masa* creations (tiny tortillas in a multitude of styles stuffed with chicken, cheeses, chiles, and much more).

Special Excursions

Chapultepec Park: Its Castle and Museums

About five km from Centro, Chapultepec Park is the centerpiece of the city. The park is filled with some of the finest museums, a castle, green grass and trees, small lakes, plenty of history, and families, especially on Sunday. Long before the Spanish set foot in the New World, Chapultepec Park was impor-tant to the inhabitants of the Valle de México. Even then it was called Cerro de Chapultepec (Grasshopper Hill). The drinking water for all the people in the valley came from the underground springs in the Chapultepec foothills. Histo-rians tell us that Aztec kings kept summer homes in these woods, and here they would have gentlemen's hunts. Eventually, Spanish viceroy Matias de Gálvez imitated the Aztec leaders, and he too kept a summer home in the park, which ultimately became Mexico's Military Academy.

Castillo de Chapultepec is the castle of the ill-fated couple, Emperor Maxi-milian of Hapsburg and Empress Carlota of Saxe-Coburg, who sought to bring European pomp, ceremony, culture, and court to Mexico. Maximilian com-mented that the views of the valley and the mountains from Chapultepec, which overlooks the city from a 60-meter-high bluff, reminded him of those from his Miramar Palace in Trieste. Carlota stood in her formal rooftop garden and could watch Maximilian in his carriage all the way along the Reforma to the palace. No doubt the air was totally free of smog and remarkably clear then.

Chapultepec was desirable real estate from the time the Aztec kings kept a zoo and botanical garden for medicinal herbs. The Spaniards built a chapel in 1554 and in the 1780s built a summer palace for the Spanish viceroys. But not until Maximilian and Carlota took over did the palace attain the regal flavor of an emperor's residence. Apparently, Maximilian devoted much of his time to creat-ing his own bit of Europe, with flowered terraces, a formal rooftop garden, and grand salons; he was criticized by his contemporaries for the time and money spent to beautify his palace and the city. After Maximilian and Carlota were

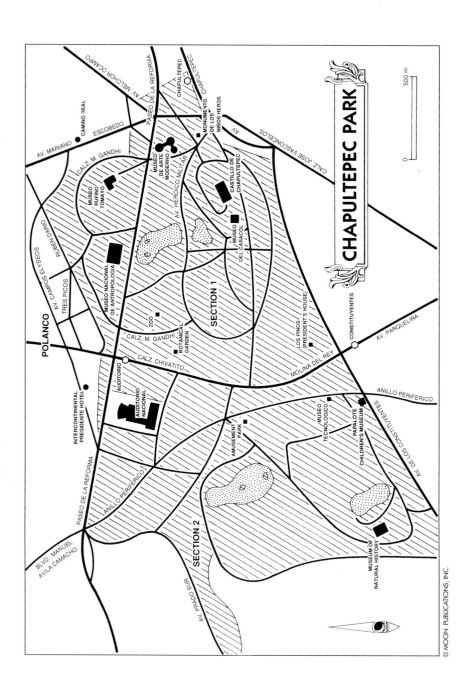

CHAPULTEPEC PARK

500 m

overthrown by Benito Juárez, the castle was never the same. It was used as the presidential residence until the 1930s, and in 1940 it became a museum while the surrounding area became a park. As a museum the castle has been restored to an approximation of its grandeur. Murals by Diego Rivera, José Clemente Orozco, Juan O'Gorman, and David Alfaro Siqueiros have been added since Maximilian's occupancy. Visitors will find a gallery of the viceroys, also known as the "Accountants of the Empire." No one should miss a visit to the castle, with its arrow-straight, statuelike guards dressed in tall crowned hats. They look as though they're straight from a Grimm's fairy tale. Tours are available in English.

Without a doubt, the **Museo Nacional de Antropología** is the most important museum in Mexico. The treasures of all the civilizations that made the country great are displayed in this beautiful, understated, showcase building designed and built in 1964 by Pedro Ramírez Vázquez. As you pass the entrance into the central patio, a sheer curtain of water drops from the top of a huge concrete column. The column is covered with reliefs that portray events in the development of the country, and it's topped with a concrete overhang referred to as an "umbrella." The effect is lovely, tranquil, and cooling—liquid art. The patio is surrounded by exhibit salons. Within the rooms visitors will see precious jade carvings, stylish gold jewelry, funerary pottery, polychrome pieces, animated whistles, obsidian carvings, reproduced murals from excavated sites deep in southern jungles, immense Olmec carvings, and maybe the most exciting of all, the Aztec Calendar Stone in the Aztec Salon.

(¶❶) You might find some intellectual stimulation over a cappuccino at the **Café el Parnaso** (and bookstore), off the plaza at Felipe Carrillo Puerto 2, (5) 554-2225. This is the gathering place for people who aren't afraid of expressing or listening to new ideas, whether they're left or right of the political line. You'll find lots of books here, mostly in Spanish, but covering all subjects. It's open daily 9 a.m.-9 p.m.

(¶❶) **El Hijo del Cuervo**, on the Parque Centenario, is another cantina where women are welcome. Come here to eat *botanas* (snacks), drink Cuervo, and see a show in the little theater in the back. It's open Tues.-Sun. 7-11:30 p.m., performances Thurs.-Sun. 7 p.m.

The museum is arranged on two floors and around several courtyards. Each salon on the first floor exhibits a geographic area or culture; the second floor addresses the ethnography or characteristics of the people in today's Mexico. Each of these salons is well-marked.

A real museum buff would spend a *minimum* of an entire day touring, beginning with the museum's 20-minute orientation film *Man in Mesoamerica*, study its exhibits, browse through its great Spanish and English bookstore (with a lot more than books for sale), walk its four kilometers of walkways and salons. Catch your breath under an umbrella while enjoying an alfresco lunch or snack at the lower-level café, and save a little time to observe a slice of everyday Mexican life; lots of schoolkids come to the museum on field trips.

If you wish to take pictures, you have to get special permission and pay a fee when you buy your entrance ticket. If you have a video camera, it's even less welcome, and the fee is US$10 (for your personal use only; for professional use it's much more). No flash photography is allowed. If you don't want to pay the fee, you can check your cameras and anything else not needed. The museum is free on Sunday (when it's always jam-packed!), but closed on Monday.

Nearby, **Monumento de los Niños Héroes** commemorates the six young cadets who lost their lives when Chapultepec Castle was stormed by U.S. troops during the American Intervention of 1847. On 13 September 1847, the six young men defended their academy with all the strength they could muster. Finally, when their position seemed hopeless, they wrapped themselves in their flags and jumped from the castle to their deaths. A somber memorial relives their deaths on the anniversary of the event. Roll call is taken and as each boy's name is called out to the silent crowd, it answers as one, "He died for his country."

One of the newest and most beautiful lodgings, **Hotel Marquis Reforma,** Paseo de la Reforma 465, tel. (5) 211-3600, fax 211-5561, has already established a great reputation. The exterior is a marvelous mingling of *cantera rosa,* a marblelike pinkish stone, and glass in an art-deco style. Subdued elegance characterizes the lovely lobby, tastefully done in marble and burnished inlaid woods. Rooms are beautifully furnished and carpeted. The hotel pampers each guest with amenities, and provides every convenience that a businessman or -woman might need. The hotel reserves one floor's use exclusively for women. Try Joya, the stylish Italian restaurant, as well as two bars, a gym, a sauna, and jacuzzis, and note the lovely indoor fountain of four Aztec figures. Luxury.

Museo del Caracol is also called Museo Galería de la Lucha del Pueblo Mexicano por su Libertad. Though the museum is quite close to the castle, the entrance is a little difficult to find, so keep looking. This snail-shaped building is named for the struggle of the people on the road to liberty. It contains exhibits that include dioramas, photographs, and displays explaining Mexico's fight for independence, freedom, and reform. Weapons and uniforms are also on display. At the end of the winding corridor the impressive, stark, red-stone display of the Mexican flag depicts a carved eagle standing guard above a replica of Mexico's 1917 Constitution. Look for this building partway down Chapultepec Hill on the south side of the castle.

Modern-day Diversions

The **Museo de Arte Moderno** was designed by Pedro Ramírez Vázquez (of Museo Antropología fame); this modern museum shines with glass and marble everywhere you look. The galleries are in four main salons, and you can't miss the impressive stairway in the main lobby. Three galleries have changing exhibits, and a permanent collection of 20th-century Mexican art is well-represented by the important names of Rivera, Siqueiros, Orozco, and Tamayo. Cross the moat and you'll find other salons and displays. Good stuff here!

Museo Rufino Tamayo honors one of Mexico's most loved artists. Rufino Tamayo, who died in 1991 at the age of 91, was first a Mexican (a Zapotec Indian from Oaxaca), and secondly an artist. The man deeply loved his people and used his talents to bring them beauty and art. On canvas he brought to life what he felt *was* Mexico. He used magnificent deep earth colors, and his imagination would fly like the wind; his works are universal and timeless. In 1981, he and his wife, Olga, gave the people of Mexico this airy museum along with a fabulous collection of modern art, consisting partly of his works and partly of the work of others. A modernistic red sculpture sits in front and fine gardens surround the building. World-class traveling exhibits change frequently. Check the local newspapers or the tourist office for a current list of exhibits.

The museum is east of the Anthropology Museum, very close to Paseo de la Reforma.

A wonderful thing has happened in Chapultepec Park—a brand-new children's museum, the **Papalote Children's Museum.** And it's attracting children from 1 to 100, it's that fantastic. One of the most impressive displays is the musical staircase. Remember the

> A new lodging, the **Hotel Colonial Plaza,** was going up facing Mexico City's Zócalo, at Av. Cinco de Mayo #61. Its very old building, veneered with blood-red volcanic marble, looks charming. The interior renovations planned for the structure are quite spectacular, with the lobby exhibiting a tall waterfall of stone, and the restaurant on the roof providing a spectacular view of the city and the mountains. The project uses the newest high-tech materials, such as double sound-proof glass. Take a look. The location is ideal for anyone interested in Centro Mexico City. Luxury.

giant piano keyboard Tom Hanks "played" in the movie *Big*? This was designed by the same man. Come and "climb" your favorite tune. That's just one of the great presentations that kids young and old will enjoy. Check out the five-story maze, the motion machine that runs for 600 feet, the immense mobile that is either a kite or a butterfly (depending on the viewer's perception), and the wonderful rainforest tree, plus 250 more exhibits that give kids a hands-on, foot-stomping experience they won't soon forget. Probably the most spectacular is the fantasy maze and light show within a green tile sphere that's five stories tall.

It's the newest museum in the park. You can't miss it; it's a beautiful building covered in bright blue tile (the first tile building constructed in Mexico in 100 years.) It's in Chapultepec Park, on Constituyentes s/n, in the second section, and open daily except Monday 9 a.m.-6 p.m., admission US$5, tel. (5) 286-0505 or 286-0510.

Chapultepec is very much a people's park; no signs here say Stay Off The Grass! In fact, on Sunday the grass is littered with people of all ages. Families come to have picnics and relax in the quiet strip of green in the middle of this busy city of concrete. The park offers flowers and trees, sculptures and monuments, lakes with swans and boat rides, and wide paths filled with people bicycling and jogging. The large crowds and the park's size (850 hectares) make the park a logistical nightmare to keep up, and keep clean, but for the most part it's accomplished. It is usually quite inviting, especially after the summer rainy season when the grass is lush and green. The president's official home, **Los Pinos,** is also in the park. If you plan to cover the entire park thoroughly (eight square kilometers), it will take you several days to do it properly. And as with the Louvre in Paris, that's really the way to do it. Study the maps and the various installations, and allot a day or a time for each museum or site that you wish to visit. Otherwise, much of your time will be spent getting from point A to point B.

You'll find many vendors and several cafés at the park; the cafés around the lakes are for the most part expensive and quite nice. Vendor food is available, and of course, this is a favorite spot to bring a picnic.

Basílica de Nuestra Señora de Guadalupe

The shrine of the patroness of Mexico is the most visited in the country. The village around the new basílica (1976) contains the old basílica (1709), the **Capuchin Church and ex-convent** (1787), and the **Capilla Pocito** (1791). The religious art museum displays oils and sculptures of the vice-regency. Every year, 12 May brings a million people from all over the country to worship at the shrine. This is where you see the emotional impact of the holiday of the Virgin Guadalupe. The Basílica de Guadalupe is eight kilometers north of the city center and can be reached by bus or Metro.

Coyoacán

About eight km south of Centro, Coyoacán is still another outlying village that the city has all but swallowed up. Today, Coyoacán, still bearing the historical fingerprint of Cortés, is an affluent suburb boasting some fine museums, and plazas surrounded by outdoor cafés, all side by side with local artists and musicians who add bohemian color with their street displays and impromptu concerts. Coyoacán is a place favored by artists and academics alike. Coyoacán means "The Place of Coyotes"; the only coyotes evident today are in the central fountain of **Parque Centenario**. Coyoacán is a marvelous combination of beautifully sculptured shrubs, rainbow beds of flowers, narrow streets, and alleyways that are barely wide enough for cars. You'll discover good cafés under brightly colored awnings, and organ grinders playing beneath towering trees. Sample the varied menus or just have a banana split at El Fogoncillo. If you're into the "I Love Frida" craze, you'll find a museum filled with artifacts and art that describe the life of Frida Kahlo. If you're just here for the day, wear your good walking shoes and enjoy exploring the city.

Another bit of Cortés's past lies just off **Plaza de la Conchita**; it's the house of his Indian lover/interpreter, Malinche. **Casa de la Malinche** is filled with history, myths, suppositions, and maybe even a ghost. Today's Mexicans revile Malintzin (her Indian name) for her part in conquering Mexico. She was more than just an interpreter; she taught Cortés how the people thought and acted, enabling him to conquer the land.

Built in 1589, the church **Iglesia de San Juan Bautista** graces nearby **Plaza Hidalgo**, and one of Cortés's *casas* lies behind it. The surrounding streets are chockablock with beautifully renovated colonial homes.

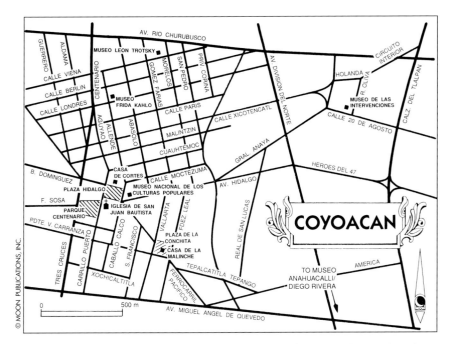

Customs and crafts from all over Mexico are performed and created at the **Museo Nacional de los Culturas Populares**, on Calle Hidalgo 289. Exhibitions are changed frequently, are very informative, and are always fun to watch. On the grounds of the Churubusco ex-Convento, where General Anaya surrendered his sword to the United States, the convent has been turned into the **Museo de las Intervenciones**, Calle 20 de Agosto at Gral. Anaya. *Intervenciones* is a polite Mexican term for "invasions." Here you'll find dioramas of gigantic proportions depicting various battles against French and U.S. forces. Of particular interest to history buffs is that all sides are treated fairly and without animosity. Note a plaque that commemorates a group of Irish-American soldiers who fought on the side of the Mexicans. Members of the St. Patrick Battalion who survived the battle were executed in 1847.

Modern-day Diversions

Coyoacán is lined with signs pointing to the **Museo Frida Kahlo**, Calle Londres 247. It's worth the walk if it's open (sometimes it's not). Acclaimed by critics and collectors worldwide, this artist's works are still selling. Madonna is one of her biggest fans and hopes to portray her in a movie. Frida Kahlo suffered a crippling injury in her early years; according to historians, her life was one of pain and self-loathing. She was married to artist Diego Rivera for many years (actually she married him twice). She was born in this startlingly blue house; later she returned "home" and lived with (and without) Rivera for 25

> **Hacienda de los Morales,** Calle Vázquez de Mella 525, Col. Polanco, tel. 540-3225, dates from the 1500s and is renowned for its Mexican specialties, high-powered service, and beautiful gardens, all in marvelous colonial surroundings. It's open daily 1 p.m.-midnight.

years until her death in 1954. Kahlo collected an eclectic assortment of art. The collections in the museum contain excellent pre-Columbian artifacts and Mexican folk art, as well as representations of some well-known artists including José Clemente Orozco, Paul Klee, and of course Rivera. Probably the most fascinating are the Kahlo's works depicting her lifelong search for serenity, which included a love affair with the Communist ideology. Stalin appears in her work as a champion. Kahlo had a close relationship with Leon Trotsky (his museum is nearby). The garden here is a nice stopping spot for reflection on the artist's life.

Leon Trotsky's house **Museo Leon Trotsky**, on Calle Viena 45, really does look like a fortress; it was built this way intentionally to protect him. Today his retreat is preserved as a historical museum. His furniture and possessions are of less interest than the house itself, except for his study. Once great friends with Rivera, he moved here after an affair with Frida Kahlo. There are photographs of Trotsky, his wife, Natalia, Rivera, and Kahlo. He came to Mexico in 1937 to seek asylum at the invitation of Rivera and Kahlo; because of them, then-president Lázaro Cárdenas allowed him to stay. Convinced that Joseph Stalin was trying to kill him, Trotsky hired mercenaries as protection and seldom ventured out of the house. In 1940 his worst fear became reality. A Spaniard, Ramón Mercader, first convinced Trotsky of his friendly motives, and then murdered him inside the house while he worked at his desk. Visitors to the museum see the room exactly as it was left the day of his death; every paper and book remains the same.

The **Museo Anahuacalli/Diego Rivera**, Calle de Museo 150, was designed and built by Diego Rivera. It contains his massive collection of pre-Columbian treasures, more than 60,000 artifacts from the Zapotec, Toltec, Teotihuacán, Veracruz, Mixtec, and Aztec cultures. The upstairs studio has opened Rivera's life to inquisitive eyes, revealing his day-to-day objects and his sketches, some incomplete as though awaiting his return.

San Ángel

Roughly nine km south of downtown and once a tranquil little village separated from the bustle of the big city by open fields, San Ángel is now an important suburb. Life still proceeds at an even pace, with cobblestone streets and old haciendas converted to restaurants and other businesses, but with a distinct feeling of another era. Like the entire Valle de México, San Ángel has a historic past filled with pre-Columbian events. Its Indian name was Tenanitla (At the Foot of the Stone Wall), referring to El Pedregal, the lava field just south. Another historic footnote: the U.S. Army in a decisive battle here defeated General Anaya, who had disobeyed Santa Anna's order to withdraw his troops during the American Intervention. Anaya chose to fight, a fatal mistake for many Mexican soldiers. And this charming little city was where in 1928 a religious monomaniac assassinated former president General Alvaro Obregón. Fanatics in the world aside, strolling through the cobblestone streets is a pleasant occupation.

The two-story **Museo Estudio Diego Rivera**, on Av. Altavista and Cda. Las Palmas, was designed by well-known artist Juan O'Gorman in 1928; Rivera lived and worked here with wife Frida Kahlo for a time. Mostly this building served them as a studio, and it has been decorated as it might have looked when the artists were in residence. Rivera's life and his work, including a few self-portraits, are depicted on two floors here.

Simply called **Museo Carrillo Gil Arte Contemporano**, Av. Revolución 1608, this museum's other (more complete) name is Museo de Arte Alvar y Carmen T. Carrillo Gil. This slick four-tiered building is publicly owned. Exhibits include an excellent collection of works by the more talented Mexican artists such as Rivera, Siqueiros, and Orozco, along with lesser known, avant-garde artists and well-known foreign masters. But it welcomes the offbeat; one exhibit lampooned the "love affair" with Frida Kahlo. This is one of Mexico's finest art museums.

Walk up the hill (on Calle Madero) to the lovely colonial **Plaza San Jacinto**. A pleasant small plaza surrounded by charming reclaimed colonial buildings, it's always a brilliant splash of color on Saturday. Still another plaque bears testimony that in 1847, U.S. soldiers who chose to fight for Mexico were executed on the plaza by order of Gen. Zachary Taylor. The young soldiers were Irish Catholic immigrants; Mexican Catholic priests persuaded them that the church had been wronged and that they should fight for Mexico. The 16th-

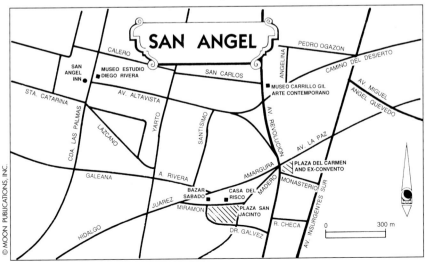

century church of San Jacinto is on the west side of the plaza. The church was at one time part of the Dominican monastery.

While on the north side of the Plaza San Jacinto, look at **Casa del Risco** at number 15. This 18th-century house encloses two museums and two court-yards. The Museo Colonial Casa del Risco exhibits artifacts indicative of the European lifestyle as it was exported to Mexico in the colonial era. Also in the building is the colonial library, Centro Cultural y Biblioteca Isidro Fabela.

Northeast of Plaza San Jacinto, at the 17th-century Carmelite ex-convent, **Plaza del Carmen** you'll find a diverse collection of colonial art. Even more amazing is the basement crypt containing mummified remains of priests and

Death from a Broken Heart

Bazar Sábado is one of the finest in Mexico for quality crafts. A large, 17th-century house on the Plaza San Jacinto's north side, it's the plaza's centerpiece. Both the U.S. (in 1847) and the French (in 1863) used this old building as headquarters during their attacks on Mexico. Built in the Spanish era, it was a lavish home to several important families over the years and features a love story in its past. As love stories often do, this one began with a beautiful young girl. She admired a handsome young man who would ride past her house every day on his beautiful stallion. Eventually, through the corner balcony window, they became acquainted and fell in love. He decided to leave for the gold fields of Peru; he would return rich and marry his sweetheart. Every day the young woman waited at the window and watched for her lover. Many months became years, and finally she died of a broken heart. One day very soon after, the young man jubilantly rode into the plaza with bags of gold tied onto his saddle. He went directly to the balcony window and at first didn't see her, but then he felt a warm embrace, a ghostly embrace. With only a hushed whisper, he quietly joined her in death. Today's caretakers walk through the buildings with their dogs and tell of hearing footsteps and hushed whispers in the hall each midnight. Even the dogs hear something: they stop, look around, and then as though they've met an old friend they wag-along on their nightly rounds.

In 1963, the present owner, Señor Romero, was walking along the desolate plaza past the abandoned building. He became curious because above the stone walls he could see a lovely jacaranda tree in full bloom poking through the caved-in roof. He thought that someone must be inside, and after poking around he found a very elderly gentleman (100 years old) whose family had worked in the old house years before. The old man had continued to water the tree and a few plants that had survived. Señor Romero believed the house had "called" him. With the help of architect Manuel Parra, he took over the task of rebuilding the old mansion to its original style. Romero, an artist, decided to reincarnate the old Indian custom of market day and opened a bazaar on just one day of the week, Saturday. Hence the name, Bazar Sábado, one of the must-do markets in Mexico City.

nuns, discovered during a building project. The plaza itself is small and crowded but filled with working artists protected from the sun by colorful umbrellas.

San Ángel Inn, Las Palmas 50, was formerly a hacienda built in the 17th century. Home for counts and marquéses, San Ángel later served as a temporary home to the likes of Fanny Calderón de la Barca, wife of the first envoy from Spain to independent Mexico in the mid-1840s. Señora Calderón was a talented writer who chronicled Mexico's struggle with the growing pains of independence. Other temporary guests of San Ángel Inn were Santa Anna and his troops, and then many years later the foot soldiers of Emiliano Zapata and Pancho Villa. Today, only tourists visit. Ponderously heavy beams, casement windows, and stone fireplaces dominate indoors; outside, lush, green gardens are a perfect refreshment for the body and the mind.

Near San Ángel, take a look at **Polyforum Cultural Siqueiros**, Av. Insurgentes Sur at Filadelfia. It was designed by muralist David Alfaro Siqueiros, whose work covers immense expanses of this building. Its claim to fame (aside from its multishaped building) is the mural on the uppermost tier inside, Siqueiros's *The March of Humanity*, a three-dimensional sculpture/mural covering thousands of square meters. The multifaceted building covers an art gallery, theaters, a concert hall, a cafeteria, and a bookstore. A plethora of arts and crafts is for sale at fixed prices.

Parque Nacional Desierto de los Leones

Although its title says desert, that's a misnomer since it's really in a lovely forest of mostly pines, *encinas*, and *oyameles* covering almost 2,000 hectares. High in the mountains at about 2,970 meters, it is a lovely national park. Picnickers and those seeking solace from the busy city stroll along paths through the trees. Occasional Sunday concerts are presented in the center of the park at the Carmelite ex-convent within its still-lovely gardens. It was proclaimed a national park in 1917, the first official national park in Mexico.

The history of the Carmelites (and the park) is rich with tales of the crusades and hermits. *Desiertos* were distinctive Carmelite monasteries first built in Spain in picturesque cool forests far from the noise and bustle of everyday life in a city. Monks could live lives of silent isolation and prayer patterned after the lives of the hermits on the Sacred Mount of Carmel in Israel during the crusades of the 11th century. Small cottages/hermitages were hidden in the trees on the hilltop outside the monastery walls for the friars who desired even deeper solitude. Once a day each lone inhabitant rang a bell to signal all was well.

It is believed the *"desierto"* part of the name stems from Christ's 40 days in the desert. The first *desierto* was built in Spain in 1592, by crusaders and pilgrims ready to trade in their nomadic lifestyles as well as their pilgrims' crooks and crusaders' swords for monks' robes. Built in 1606, Desierto de los Leones was the fourth such monastery built, the first in the New World. For almost

200 years, the friars carried on their lives of contemplation. However, as Mexico City grew, requests for spiritual getaways (by influential city dwellers of such importance that the friars could not refuse) became so frequent that eventually "there wasn't a week without guests around." That, coupled with aging and damaged structures from an earthquake in the early 1700s, motivated the Carmelites to move in 1801 to a more isolated region.

The abandoned deteriorating monastery of Leones sat vacant for many years, though anyone who knew about the lovely forest location came to find a special tranquility and harmony with nature. In 1917 Desiertos de los Leones was officially proclaimed a national park.

Today a small war is going on between corporate groups eyeing the desirable property for development and environmentalists who fear the destruction of one of the few forests remaining in the Valle de México. Add to that the claims that reforestation money has not been "planted" as was designated, and further, that the land is really *ejido* land and not available to outside buyers, and it all makes a grand rhubarb, Mexican style. Let's hope the environmentalists win this battle. But in the meantime, don't wait too long for a peaceful afternoon among the trees and a bit of ancient history to boot.

Today's *Desierto*

Today the national park's monastery is a museum. Neat walkways meander under tall shade trees and along well-kept flower beds. One path leads some distance to the chapel of secrets (where it is said that the monks made their confessions). Though many of the buildings are just shells, the main building is still in good condition with a lovely chapel. The domes and arches emphasize the architecture of the 17th century. Thick walls and long corridors define rooms marked with their former uses, such as the monk's barbershop. One large room has been converted into a restaurant, open for breakfast and lunch. On Sunday it is always crowded. The public is invited to camp out in certain areas. Wandering the grounds on the many paths that lead away from the main building, you'll run into the remaining eight hermitages (of the original 10). At the edge of the former commune, in the park's recreational areas, El Retiro and Peteretes programs are operated to breed deer and maintain a trout hatchery. Locals will tell you that armadillos, raccoons, squirrels, rabbits, badgers, and opossums still inhabit the forest.

The museum is closed on Monday. The road into the park from San Ángel, Camino del Desierto, is closed daily 6 p.m.-7 a.m.

The Canals of Xochimilco

In some ways, this centuries-old neighborhood is a living museum. People still live along the canals—as the Aztecs did before the Spaniards arrived. *Chinampas* (artificial islands) were an imaginative solution that could be compared to "bringing the mountains to Mohammed." The low-lying lake water surrounding the islands of the Valle de México could not be directed to the higher land of the islands, making farming almost impossible for the Aztecs on their small island of Tenochtitlán. So the soil was dug from the shallow areas of the lakes and with clever construction using reeds, tree limbs, and soil, they created floating islands on which they planted crops. As these multiplied, canals were formed. The soil was extremely fertile, yielding two or three harvests a year. This method of raising crops saved the Aztecs in the earliest years of Tenochtitlán.

The older more established societies that looked down their noses at the Aztecs took them more seriously when this clever manner of farming proved successful. The method was soon a common practice on other islands. The Aztecs created more canals in and around Tenochtitlán, ultimately building 80 kilometers of canals. When the Aztecs constructed an aqueduct to bring more water, their economy flourished and the centers of commerce subtly moved from the mainland foothills (with their underground springs) to the islands in the lakes. Transporting goods and supplies no longer required live porters; boats became the mode of travel and transport.

Homes lined the canals, bridges connected the islands to the mainland, and the Aztecs were becoming a powerful force. But their time in the sun was short; when the Spaniards arrived, they tore down bridges, houses, temples, and civic buildings, and filled in the lakes with the debris.

Xochimilco was spared since it was the "breadbasket" of the city. Vegetables and flowers continued to grow. Today, you can get an idea of what life was like by visiting Xochimilco. Try to ignore the crowds of tourists, musicians, and vendors that also float around by boat trying to sell you things, from hot corn to tacos to trinkets. On the weekends, hundreds of boats move along the water. The government has set a standard hourly fare that the boatmen charge. Still, agree on a price before you board and give the boat a look; some are nicer than others. Most are decorated with imitation flowers in bright colors. This is popular Sunday fun for Mexican families, and it can be a lively good time, but if you're looking for peace and quiet, go on a weekday.

Xochimilco Park

This, the country's largest urban ecological park, has become the flower garden of Mexico once again. At a cost of $230 million and an investment of four years, one million trees were planted along 200 km of connected waterways that will irrigate the entire canal system. A colossal variety of flowers were planted, and planners hope that the flowers will not only provide a beauty that harkens back to the time of the Aztecs, but that they will also become a thriving industry to provide the nation with flowers—and have enough left over to export. Already the improvement shows.

THE SILVER CITIES

I magine tall mountains set against blue sky for miles beyond miles; as far as the eye can report lie rugged drops, craggy peaks, and rivers carving their way through mineral-rich soil. Horses and mules carried determined men up and down this landscape. All were pushed beyond the extremes of their endurance, but their riders hungered for one thing—gold. Nature played a game: it protected its precious metals and coveted stones for centuries in the bosom of solid rock, often miles underground, but showed a rare hint on the surface occasionally to whet the appetite. The land witnessed a perseverance that was superhuman. Oh yes, gold was found—and celebrated. But the treasure of Mexico turned out to be its silver, in unbelievable volume. Men scratched the earth until they forced it to give up its wealth. Every strike brought people with hopes and rich dreams. With the discovery of each shiny rock, they built new houses, along with a new rich church, a royal residence, a palace, an aqueduct, all around a flat space of trees and fountains. These cities were built to last; it's been almost 500 years, and today the skylines have changed only a little. In high valleys, along gorges wedged between high peaks, or climbing the sides of the mountains, aged spires and shiny domes dot the view, modern skytrams sail across the cities, and those old flat spaces provide a "center" where the old and the new still mix.

Taxco

IN 1524 CORTÉS WAS SEARCHING FOR TIN TO MAKE BRONZE CANNONS. He noted in the Aztec tax rolls that the Tlahuica Indians paid tribute with, among other things, blocks of gold and silver. This excited Cortés, and he put aside his search for tin and headed for the Tlachco mountains to search for gold. The Spaniards did indeed find gold and silver at their first mine in the New World, Socavon del Rey. The Santa Prisca Church now covers the spot. Over the years the Spanish built haciendas, smelters to process the metal, and an aqueduct to bring water into town. You can still see a section of the old aqueduct at the north end of town; the highway passes under it, but little else remains of that first building spree.

The early 16th-century discovery was the first cycle of gold mining in Taxco. Though silver seemed played out to these 16th-century miners, plenty of metal in the earth was still waiting to be found. The hardiest never gave up hope and continued their search for more gold; legend says it was a horse that this time "discovered" the silver. The beast apparently reared, stumbled, and scraped the earth with its hoof, uncovering something shiny. Voila! A rich vein of silver. So, in the early 1700s, news spread all over the country once again: another silver strike in Taxco. The new discovery sparked another building boom, this one creating the beginnings of a fairy tale city of spires and domes, balconies and belfries, crowned by a pink baroque church called Santa Prisca. Artisans from Europe were imported to build still-more beautiful estates. Very active in all of this building was José de la Borda.

The three names most closely associated with Taxco are José de la Borda, William Spratling, and *silver.* In 1708 the de la Borda brothers arrived from France and began working the mines. The eldest, Francisco, died early on; his brother, José, discovered the San Ignacio vein and became a very rich man. Soon hundreds of fortune hunters journeyed to this remote mountain town. Indian workers brought the silver out of the earth; *patrones* gave the king his fifth and then spent the rest on ostentatious homes lining the streets of the hilly village and on their Catholicism, the other important thing in their lives.

From 1751 to 1759 the wealthy Borda supplied the funds to build Santa Prisca, supposedly the richest church in Mexico. Next door he built a lavish home, part of which he shared with the local priests. His son, Manuel, had meanwhile taken the vows, and served as Taxco parish priest for 18 years.

Borda also began acquiring land not just in Taxco but elsewhere in Mexico. At least one of his holiday homes still stands in Cuernavaca.

Then, because his mines played out, or because of his lifestyle, Borda was reduced in 1775 to begging the archbishop of Taxco to return some of the treasure he'd given the church in wealthier times. He was eventually permitted to "borrow" several rich pieces smothered in precious stones and several gold chalices. He died two years later. After the mines closed, all those lured to Taxco for treasure packed up and left for richer pastures. Taxco slipped into poverty and anonymity once again: a silver ghost town. The ornate city languished until 1929.

Enter American professor William Spratling from Tulane University in New Orleans. Spratling originally traveled to Mexico to write a book, but before it was completed his publisher went out of business. The U.S. ambassador to Mexico, Dwight Morrow, then encouraged Spratling to start a silver workshop. Though his early training was as an architect, Spratling possessed a very real artistic flair. While exploring Mexico on horseback, he'd accumulated a large collection of pre-Hispanic artifacts; now, with just a few craftsmen and clever designs and molds patterned after the unique Indian designs in his collection, Spratling began turning out high-quality, unusual jewelry using only the finest silver. His business grew, and soon his pieces were in demand in the elite jewelry stores of the United States.

Today's Taxco silversmiths continue to improve their craft, shifting their designs to accommodate the latest trends. Whatever is in style at the moment, they're on top of it—perhaps they even created it. Several contemporary Taxco silver shops are owned by one-time Spratling apprentices; there are literally hundreds of quality silver shops (300) in Taxco today.

In 1940, the Mexican government imposed controls on the silver industry. It decreed that all silver sales must be contracted through the Bank of Mexico; even silversmiths must buy their silver bars from the bank. Goods made from silver must bear the sterling seal, indicating a content of .925 pure silver. If you see that mark, you can be assured the piece is sterling. Of course there are those who illegally apply the .925 seal. If you acquire proof of a swindle, notify the government of all details of the purchase, including receipts and the name and address of the violators. The government diligently works to eliminate the crooks from the industry, primarily these who substitute the cheap imitation *alpaca* for silver.

Exploring the Streets of Taxco

Silver is just one of the reasons to visit Taxco. The city itself is a Spanish gingerbread lane of cobblestone streets that climb up, down, and about, twisting in and out of the hilly landscape, occasionally opening up to reveal intimate plazas and cooling fountains. The Mexican government has designated the city a "Colonial Monument," which encourages construction in the colonial style and guarantees that the original old buildings will remain in good colonial-era condition.

Folks with physical disabilities may experience problems with the steep, narrow streets. It's not unusual for pedestrians to have to jump out of the way for an oncoming car; there's barely room on some of these streets for a VW bug to get by.

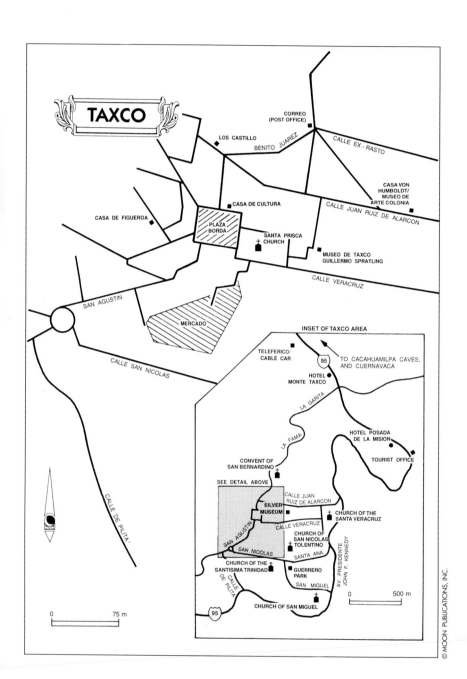

TAXCO

CORREO (POST OFFICE)

LOS CASTILLO

BENITO JUAREZ

CALLE EX - RASTO

CASA VON HUMBOLDT/ MUSEO DE ARTE COLONIA

CASA DE CULTURA

CALLE JUAN RUIZ DE ALARCON

CASA DE FIGUEROA

PLAZA BORDA

SANTA PRISCA CHURCH

MUSEO DE TAXCO GUILLERMO SPRATLING

CALLE VERACRUZ

SAN AGUSTIN

MERCADO

CALLE SAN NICOLAS

INSET OF TAXCO AREA

TELEFERICO/ CABLE CAR

95

TO CACAHUAMILPA CAVES, AND CUERNAVACA

HOTEL MONTE TAXCO

LA GARITA

HOTEL POSADA DE LA MISION

LA FAMA

CONVENT OF SAN BERNARDINO

TOURIST OFFICE

SEE DETAIL ABOVE

CALLE JUAN RUIZ DE ALARCON

SILVER MUSEUM

CHURCH OF THE SANTA VERACRUZ

CALLE VERACRUZ

SAN AGUSTIN

CHURCH OF SAN NICOLAS TOLENTINO

SAN NICOLAS

SANTA ANA

AV. PRESIDENTE JOHN F. KENNEDY

CHURCH OF THE SANTISIMA TRINIDAD

GUERRERO PARK

CALLE DE PILITA

SAN MIGUEL

95

CHURCH OF SAN MIGUEL

500 m

CALLE DE PILITA'

0   75 m

© MOON PUBLICATIONS, INC.

Shops, hotels, and restaurants are all clustered here, some up and down steps and twisting lanes, but locals are happy to direct you if you become befuddled. The main street is Hwy. 95 as you come into town from the north. It then becomes Av. Presidente John F. Kennedy, winding around town to the south end, before heading toward Acapulco and becoming Hwy. 95 again. Any of the many streets and alleys along Kennedy twist back up to the center of town at Santa Prisca Church. Actually it's pretty hard to get too lost here, since wherever you are, just look up: you can see the church from anywhere in the city, and it's the landmark to head for.

Take time to study **Santa Prisca Church**, facing the Plaza Borda. Santa Prisca is truly one of the masterpieces of the colonial era. The energetic façade of this pink church is an eclectic collection of hewn angels, saints, and shells. The baroque style, when interpreted by the Mexican artist, became the enchanting Churrigueresque style of architecture so commonly found throughout the colonial cities. Here, two ornamented steeples lead the eye to a tiled dome. This is the result of a marriage between expert architecture and outstanding artists, actually an *ultrabaroque* creation that works stunningly. On the inside, the walls are hung with magnificent paintings by Miguel Cabrera, a Zapotec Indian and probably the most prominent of the colonial-era artists. Gold leaf is everywhere, and so many gold nooks and crannies, angels, curlicues, designs, patterns, and arrangements—it takes some time to absorb it all. Note: Santa

Hotel Posada de la Misión just off Av. John F. Kennedy on Cerro de la Misión 32, tel. (762) 2-0063 or 2-0533, fax 2-2198, is a big hotel with the colonial feel. Today it features 150 rooms with private baths, suites with fireplaces, two bars, a coffeeshop, a dining room, gardens and views, a swimming pool, tennis, golf, and parking. Expensive.

One of the nicest hotels in town, **Hotel Monte Taxco** perches on top of a bluff on the north end of town near Hwy. 95. If you want a little fun getting there, take the *teleférico*. The view is spectacular. The hotel offers guests (and nonguests) a golf course, tennis courts, restaurants, and other interesting ways to spend your time. If nonguests want to spend the day by the pool or playing golf they're welcome, for a fee. The hotel is old Mexico style, comfortable with both standard rooms and suites. If you're so inclined you have access to horses, a steam bath, and a fitness center. The restaurant serves good food, and a favorite attraction for visitors (wherever they're staying) is **Windows,** an "on fire" disco. You can reach the hotel by taxi. Expensive.

Prisca is supposed to have a small painting of the pregnant Virgin Mary, said to be the only painting of Mary pregnant. Amazingly it took only eight years to complete the church, paid for by rich miner José de la Borda. Santa Prisca is open daily.

Plaza Borda, the flat center of town, is small but shady and comfortable, a serene spot under ancient Indian laurel trees. Along one side of the plaza sits the Santa Prisca Church. Also bordering the square are lovely old buildings containing gift shops that offer fine pottery, Guerrero masks, colorful textiles, but mostly silver.

On the top floors of **Museo de Taxco Guillermo Spratling** on Calle Veracruz, look for the unique pre-Hispanic collection of William Spratling. Gathered during his many years in Mexico, this is a fine collection of ancient art from the immediate area of Guerrero and the central plateau. The bottom floor houses changing exhibits. From the Santa Prisca Church, go left, then make another left at the corner.

For getting around town, the *burritos* (white minibuses) run from 7 a.m. to about 9 p.m.

The **Silver Museum**, next to Santa Prisca (look for a small sign), is a small museum that tells the story of silver in Mexico, with a special emphasis on Taxco. Operated by a silversmith, it includes a pleasant display of award-winning pieces. If you speak Spanish, this is a good place to acquire information about silver.

During Taxco's "first" silver cycle, one of the first haciendas built was the **Hacienda del Chorrillo**, in use today as a language school. The Spaniards first called the town Taxco, a corruption of the Nahuatl word Tlachco.

At the **Convent of San Bernardino** Agustín de Iturbide in 1821 drafted the Plan de Iguala, a major plan to implement what all hoped would bring stability to a Spanish-run nation. Instead, it was a forerunner to independence from Spain.

The **Church of San Bernardino de Siena** is a group of buildings started in the 16th century by Franciscan monks. Like so many other great churches it changed over the centuries; the present façade was put in place in the 19th century. The neoclassical stonework shows architect Manuel Tolsá's influence, even though the two towers were never finished. West of the church is the chapel of **Santo Entierro** (Holy Burial), where, during Holy Week processions, the image of Christ mounted on a donkey is brought from the village of Tehuilotepec. What was once the monastery is today a primary school.

The **Casa de Figueroa**, at Guadalupe 2, was built in 1767 for the Count de la Cadena family. This home has one of the wildest histories of any building in town. Built by Tlahuica prisoners—men who could not pay their tributes and labored with shackles on their legs—it quite justifiably earned the nickname Casa de las Lagrimas, or "House of Tears." Years later a Cadena descendant living here murdered his daughter to keep her from marrying a man he disapproved of. He was taken off to jail, and the house remained empty for decades. Eventually it was used as a barracks for independence soldiers, a jail, a whorehouse, a mint, a residence for priests, and a reformatory. Ultimately another arm of the Cadena family took up residence here. After some years (the story goes on) only one member of the family remained, an elderly woman who, trusting no one, secreted her money in the walls of the house. Somehow, somebody found out about the money, and burglars arrived one night and robbed and killed her. The doomed edifice lay empty until 1943, when the Figueroa family bought it. Stories persist that the house contains a series of tunnels leading to the church. Others say several notable Americans have walked within its walls, including late President Richard Nixon. The Figeroa house is on the square of Los Gallos, where the weekly traditional cockfights were held as depicted in a mosaic embedded in the pavement. The house has a two-story façade delicately built with a colorful tile design. It now houses a folk art museum.

The **Casa von Humboldt/Museo de Arte Colonia** sits on Calle Juan Ruiz de Alarcon 6, just a block and a half from Plaza Borda. The traveling baron barely put his thumbprint on the building. As it turns out, Humboldt spent one night in the building in 1803. The house is a good example of the one-story Moorish design popular during the mining era. The geometric mortar design is colorful, and stone carvings surround two windows, their balconies bordered by wrought iron. A similar stone carving edges the entry door. Originally built in the late 1700s by the Villanueva family, the house served for many years as a guesthouse. Some of the most intriguing collections are in the Borda Salon. The clothing that José de la Borda wore is on exhibit along with a painting of him in his colonial apparel. Ask for a guide to really get all the savory stories about the city, such as "Were many of the exhibits in this museum *really* found in a secret room in Santa Prisca Church?" Tales are still told of secret tunnels in and around the church.

Next to the church on the square, Casa Borda was built for the Borda family in 1759. Today it serves as the **Casa de Cultura**, a good place to see exhibits by local artists. This 18th-century building is Santa Prisca's contemporary. It was the stately home of the famous mine owner Don José de la Borda, later on the parish priest's residence, and then the town hall. In spite of the modifications it has undergone this is one of the few houses in Taxco that maintains the characteristics of its period. The sedate and elegant stone façade reminds one of past grandeur, and it encloses two large interior gardens with breezeways and stairs. The building has two floors facing the smaller Bernal square. The Borda coat of arms is still beside one of the entrances. It's open daily 9 a.m.-5 p.m.

At the end of the 16th century, the **Church of the Santa Veracruz** was built in the neighborhood of Real de Tetelcingo by the *Cofradia de los Disciplinados* (brotherhood of the disciplined). It was actually dedicated as a church in the 19th century. Situated in front of an atrium, the large wall conceals a public washing place built in the 18th century. A clock and two symmetrical towers top the neoclassical façade. The image of Christ on the altar came from Spain; revered in Taxco, the image is carried at the head of a solemn procession during the Holy Week celebrations.

The Church of San Miguel is in the Tlachotecpan neighborhood and (as expected) is dedicated to San Miguel Arcángel. Many locals believe in a link between him and the Indians because of his religious "warrior" attitude and the pre-Hispanic deities with the same attitude. The Franciscans began building the church in the 16th century and it was probably used for some time before the change to the popular baroque style of the 18th century. Two niches flank the door of the façade; above the door is a choir window and above that another niche with a stone statue of the archangel. To the side of the door rises the three-sectioned tower. The inside has changed substantially over the years, but it still contains an image of San Miguel.

The **Church of the Santísima Trinidad** (Holy Trinity) was begun in the 16th century and we know little about the original construction; it was reconstructed in the 18th century. This church possesses unusual features, among them an atrium of slightly elevated black stone slabs. A half-circle stone stairway leads to the main entrance, a simple doorway surrounded by stone. Above the center of the façade a lantern floods the interior with light by day. The tower, on the west, diminishes in size from the bottom to the top. The nave has a split sloped roof. Inside the church is the *Cristo de los Plateros* (Christ of the Silversmiths). The church really is a lovely building with its unusual little touches. It now serves as the oratory chapel for the Concepcionist nuns.

The tiny 19th-century chapel called **Church of San Nicolas Tolentino** is well-known for its *Cristo Negro* (black Christ), also called the *Cristo del Veneno* (Christ of Poison). The original structure dates from the 17th century. The neoclassical façade is done in mortar and is unusual with a squat unfinished tower. The single nave has a tiled roof with two slopes. Inside the church, two 18th-century images (according to the guide) were "carved wooden, baked, and polychromed"—one of Santa Ana (Saint Ann) and one of the Inmaculada Concepción (Immaculate Conception). Several processions begin here during the Holy Week celebrations. The day before the patron saint's celebration, children come with wildflowers and ears of corn to exchange for bread. Then celebrants hold a fair with contests, food and drink, and a fireworks show.

On the steep side of Señor de las Aguas mountain, the **Capilla del Señor Ojeda** was begun in the 16th century and rebuilt in the 19th century. Legend tells that a stranger, a man called Señor Ojeda, arrived in the area with six mules loaded with coal. He requested food and lodgings. His request was graciously granted, and then the man was gone. Soon after, an image of Christ appeared in the chapel, replacing the old one; most believe that it was Señor Ojeda's doing. The church and tower are quite simple.

The *teleférico* (cable car) runs at the north end of town, near the highway from Mexico City. The ride on this Swiss-built cable car (240 meters to the top of a bluff) is a nice experience if you like spectacular views of the city. The cable car runs daily 7:30 a.m.-7 p.m.

Taxco Highlights

Arts and Artisans

The artists of Taxco are famous for intricate, modern, silver craftsmanship. The special work devised and begun by William Spratling many years ago has been reintroduced to Taxco at the **Spratling Ranch Workshop**. While all are invited to look, there are a few things they should know before they visit. The workshop is more than five miles south of town, there's no phone, crafts are not for sale, and there are no showrooms in Taxco. This is much like the industry that was developed in the era when Spratling was in charge; these unique pieces are sold in trendy, expensive shops in Mexico City and in other countries, mostly the U.S. But, for the true artist, this is an ideal opportunity to watch the apprentices work. Visitors are welcome Mon.-Sat. 9 a.m.-5 p.m.

For the Shopper

Bring money if you're planning to buy silver. That's not to say you can't find silver cheapies around town, but they will be ordinary things that you can buy anywhere. Taxco offers some of the finest creations in Mexico. Bargains are almost unheard of on high-quality goods; and in the city's many silver shops, you can expect high-quality merchandise. This is where you come for the originals, the best. Besides silver you can buy items with unusual mixtures of silver and ceramics, or silver, brass, copper, and ceramics and turquoise.

One of the finest shops is owned and operated by the Castillo family. Tony Castillo began as a Spratling apprentice and has gone on to create top-quality designs of his own. His work is sold all over Mexico. Castillo's family now plays an active role in the Taxco business. **Los Castillo,** just off Plaza Borda, is open daily. Walk down the hill next to City Hall until you see the sign. You can watch the silversmiths at work here. If you want to take a gander at the larger operation, visit the Castillo workshop about eight kilometers south of town on the highway to Acapulco. It's open Mon.-Fri. 9 a.m.-5 p.m.

For more traditional gifts, stop by **Arnoldo's** at Plazuela de los Gallos 7. Here there's a fine assortment of masks used in various Indian ceremonies and dances. Wander around; it's impossible not to bumble into some of the town's finest.

Beside the Santa Prisca Church and behind Berta's, visitors enjoy a stop (down) at the *mercado.* The market contains innumerable stalls and *fondas,* featuring stacks of fruits and vegetables, medicinal herbs, and such domestic necessities as serapes, blankets, pots, pans, sombreros, and pottery, plus lots of palm-woven items. On weekends (Sunday is the official market day in the plaza) the *mercado* is crowded with Indians from small villages in the hills around Taxco. These are the best days to look for decorative local crafts.

Special Events

Semana Santa: Easter Week always seems to be a more magnificent celebration in the colonial cities of Mexico, and Taxco boasts one of the finest in the country. The traditions somehow seem closer to home, and the revelry more colorful, more godly. As in the entire country, the Holy Week fiesta begins on the week before Easter. On Palm Sunday, an image of Jesus is placed on the back of a donkey in the village of Tehuilotepec, and the first of many processions begins with the donkey and a journey to Taxco. Nightly it's common to see candlelit processions of *penitentes,* their heads covered with black bags, on their peregrination to the church of Santa Prisca. Many of these *penitentes* make the last part of the journey on their knees. On Holy Thursday, in front of Santa Prisca, locals perform the Last Supper, and on Saturday, the Resurrection is staged about 9 a.m. The last procession takes place on Easter Sunday. Semana Santa is one of the most festive weeks in Taxco.

Jornadas Alarconians: On the last three weekends of May people come from all around for a cultural festival to honor native-born Taxcan Juan Ruiz de Alarcon, a writer of the same era as Miguel de Cervantes. Alarcon's playlets, art exhibits, and band concerts are presented everywhere you go—plazas, alleys, and parks.

Feria Nacional de la Plata: The national Silver Fair is held each year in the first week of December. Artists present their crafts to a prestigious panel of judges, who choose the best silver work in all of Mexico. Anyone intrigued with the newest designs of the precious metal will get an eyeful during this fair.

Regional Food

Although *pozole* is a rich maize stew that's favored all over Mexico, it sometimes appears that the state of Guerrero loves it most! Legend says the dish was first made in Guerrero in the 18th century when an important bishop and his entourage were due to arrive from Puebla, the city of excellent cuisine. The cooks prepared huge quantities of *nixtamal* (softened kernels of dried corn) to make tortillas, but there wasn't enough help in the kitchen to grind it into *masa* for tortillas. So the cook thought fast and used the kernels "straight" in a pot of chopped chicken, spices, herbs, and soup stock. Ever since, Thursday afternoon is "the holy day of *pozole*," and from small hole-in-the-wall cafés to upbeat modern restaurants, *pozole* is always prepared on Thursday. And it seems that lots of folks, including business people, take the entire afternoon off. Call it the "*pozole* crawl." From the original *pozole* many types have developed, some green with *pipian* seeds (pumpkin seeds) or red with chiles, and on and on with anything else the

Jumiles

Jumiles are small beetlelike insects prized as food since the pre-Hispanic era. The locals found these bugs to be a nutritious, protein-filled addition to their diets, as well as a curative for many ailments. These days, on the Monday after the Day of the Dead, families journey north of Taxco for a mass at the cross of the Cerro del Huisteco. Most families arrive the day of the fiesta, with all the fixings to prepare *jumiles*—including griddle, *metate*, and ingredients. Cerro del Huisteco is alive with *jumiles* and the whole family often helps to collect them. They are eaten mixed in a chile sauce, grilled with lemon and onion, or consumed live wrapped in a tortilla. The season runs Oct.-Dec.; you can buy them live in local markets and it's not unusual for vendors to wander the *zócalo* in Taxco with baskets filled with the live delicacy.

cook can think of. Then individual diners add to the *pozole* from small bowls filled with chopped green onions, avocados, lettuce, radishes, tomatoes, chiles, slices of lime, as you please; a glass of mescal (with or without the worm) traditionally accompanies the dish. This is a great hearty stew that with a stack of tortillas or a *bolillo* is a satisfying dinner.

Special Excursions

Cacahuamilpa Caves

Wander through caverns two kilometers long, featuring 20 impressive "rooms" and a wondrous variety of stalactites, stalagmites, and stone formations. The caves are lit with electric lights, which is a good thing, because it's *very* black when they're switched off. Guided tours leave every hour 10 a.m.-5 p.m. Not all guides speak English. Often it's very crowded, with flea-market-style *fondas* at the entrance. Buses leave daily to the caves from Taxco; it's about a 30-kilometer drive. Inquire at the tourist office for the bus schedule and prices.

Acapulco

The word Acapulco is from an old Indian name, Acatil Pulco, and several meanings have been suggested: "place where the reeds were destroyed," "place where the reeds bend," "bending palms." As with the name, we know little about the earliest inhabitants of this broad Pacific bay.

The Spanish first discovered Acapulco in the early 1500s. But not until 1530, when Cortés established a commercial center, did Acapulco enter its first period of fame and respect. The Spanish navy built and repaired ships here, and later Acapulco became the most important port of Mexico's west coast. For 200 years, Spanish galleons traveled between the Philippines and Acapulco, establishing an important trade route.

Merchants and rich buyers came from miles around to buy at a yearly *tianguis* (market) on the golden beach, buying exotic delights from the Orient—ivory, jade, silk, incense, and titillating perfumes. It didn't take long before the pirates of the world crossed oceans to plunder this yearly caravan of ships. After many episodes of pillaging and ransacking, the Spanish king finally gave his permission to build Fuerte San Diego. It was established on a hilltop above the bay, manned by soldiers with cannons keeping an eye to the sea, ready to attack the furtive pirates lying in wait on the horizon. The pirate ships pounced on these floating treasure chests

For excitement, everyone who visits Acapulco generally makes it to the cliffs of Quebrada. This is where man pits himself against the whimsy of the sea. Only a special brotherhood of men (the diver co-op) is "allowed" to take part in this ceremony of nerves. It begins with a barefoot climb to the top of a 38-meter cliff. Here the divers study the movement of the sea as it rushes into a small cove. They say a quick prayer at a convenient shrine on the hill, study the sea until it's just right, and then they fling themselves out over the rocks in a graceful dive at just the right moment—when the small cove is filled with the rushing sea.

headed for Spain. Great bloody battles took place on the sea. Many ships (both Spanish and pirate) never made it to their home ports—(dreamers say) great treasures still lie undiscovered at the bottom of the ocean.

After the War of Independence, Spain's viceroyalty lost its hold on the New World. One of the casualties was the fine port of Acapulco. In the confusion of finding itself, the infant country didn't need Acapulco, and the port slipped into anonymity. The ships of Spain no longer sailed to Acapulco, though it remained a port of call for the occasional vessel from distant ports to take a rest or repairs.

A little after sunrise, we anchored in the harbor of Acapulco, Mexico. This ancient city and her forts face the entrance of the harbor. Nearby stands the old Spanish church almost ready to tumble down. The church was built several hundred years ago of adobe, as most all buildings are in this country. A few other buildings in the countryside, native huts, a mission or two, almost complete the city. It is not a place that a pleasure seeker would fall in love with at first sight. The harbor is land locked; a person unacquainted with navigation might pass by and never know that there was a city behind the rugged hills.

—Written on 29 November 1898 by U.S. Marine Mansfield Moore Hutchison (1869-1958) on sea duty.

Perhaps the above description gives all of us an idea of what Acapulco lapsed into after the Spanish closed up their port and went home. It was home only to fishermen, locked from the rest of the country by mountains and sea. Few travelers made their way through the treacherous mountains that surrounded the lovely bay. But things began to change in 1927, when the first road between Acapulco and Mexico City was built. It was still a trip only the most hardy would attempt— a weeklong adventure. But enough travelers trickled through to prompt the building of the first hotel in Acapulco. Acapulco remained a slow-moving tranquil harbor until the 1950s, when

Acapulco was once the most important port on Mexico's west coast.

more modern engineers under the direction of President Miguel Alemán Valdes created a road that cut traveling time from one week to six hours. That was the beginning.

Acapulco was "discovered" by the rich and famous. The first high-rise hotels began to circle the bay and in 1964 direct international air service put the frosting on the tourism cake. It became the playground of *la gente bonita* (the beautiful people) of

Fuerte San Diego was first built in 1616, destroyed in an earthquake, and rebuilt.

the world. Those were the halcyon days. And contrary to what U.S. Marine Mansfield Moore Hutchison said in 1898, the avant-garde yachting and fishing crowd with big money *did* "fall in love with Acapulco at first sight."

Exploring the Streets of Acapulco

El Centro is the old downtown area where visitors will find the *zócalo*, La Quebrada, Fuerte San Diego, Playa Hornos, and the docks—the historical heart of the city and a very small part of the city. The coast-hugging boulevard, officially called Costera Miguel Alemán, connects the old and new parts of Acapulco for about 11 kilometers. This modern divided waterfront boulevard rambles around the harbor from the north at Playa Manzanillo to the south, where it ends at Escenica Las Brisas (familiarly called the Las Brisas Hill), which heads past the navy base up the hill on the way to the airport.

A visit to the *zócalo* is reminiscent of "old" Acapulco. The feeling is unmistakable. Nothing modern here—the ceiba trees that line the plaza are said to be hundreds of years old. If one were so inclined, one could dig into the past of each of the buildings surrounding the *zócalo* and discover a romantic history. The one exception to this "old" look is the **Catedral Nuestra Señora de la Soledad** with its rather eclectic blue and yellow domed rooftop. Locals really live in their plazas: benches lie in deep shadows and are usually crowded with friends and neighbors enjoying a cool moment near bubbling fountains. Children run along shady paths and climb onto strong limbs and branches of the ancient trees. Men sit in the shade and read while getting their shoes shined. Businessmen gather at outdoor cafés and philosophize over cups of *manzanillo te*. This place is light years away from the hustle and bustle of the tourist world just a few blocks down the road.

Fuerte San Diego is the star-shaped San Diego Fort Museum, situated on a hill (next to the army barracks) in old Acapulco. It is the one remaining shred of stone history from Acapulco's beginnings. Soldiers patrolled the ramparts

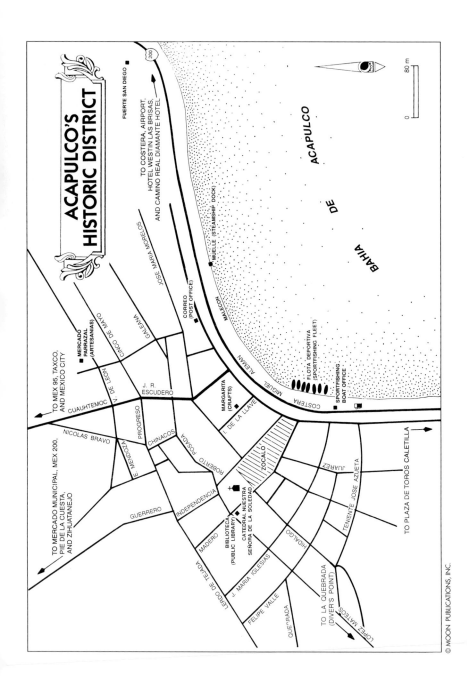

ACAPULCO'S HISTORIC DISTRICT

watching for distant pirate ships. Those were brutal days. The roar of cannons brought terror to the small village; pirates killed and pillaged searching for the treasures waiting to be shipped to the Spanish king. The history of the fort reflects the history of the city. The original fort was built in 1616, and then destroyed in the 1776 earthquake; it was rebuilt before the turn of the century and since then the city has grown up around it. Mexico City's Museum of Anthroplogy directs the old fort-turned-fine museum, which has been restored to illustrate Acapulco's past. Small (air-conditioned) rooms offer exhibits depicting life in another era, including a delightful reproduction of a tile kitchen with stove, utensils, and cooking methods. A bookstore at the entrance offers a few books in

From the airport road at the top of the hill, wind down a steep, curvy road past lovely built and almost-built modern homes till you find the **Camino Real Hotel Diamante,** tucked along the hillside on different levels overlooking the water. The beautifully understated rooms glow with subdued shades of beige, lavender, and moss green. The designers cleverly left many of the craggy rocks in place and built the rooms and dining areas around them, giving the feeling of the outdoors even when you're inside. The rooms are comfortable and the bathrooms dreamy, with everything you could possibly need right down to the shaving mirrors and satellite TV. No, you don't have to hike up and down to the pool and your room; eight elevators make it easy. Located at Baja Catita, tel. (74) 81-2010, in the U.S. tel. (800) 722-6466. Free airport shuttle available. Luxury.

Lunch in the *mercado publico* can be an adventure, especially if you try a terrific quesadilla made at **Sylvia Fonda #1354.** Take a seat on a tall stool at her *fonda* in front of her grill and watch her make it, beginning with raw *masa* dough. You can choose the fillings you prefer: mushrooms, onions, peppers (hot or not so hot), cheese, chicken, and many more choices. As large as a pancake, folded it becomes a filling meal. At the next stall you can watch the vendor squeeze orange juice, or behind, you can get a soda pop.

English, but most publications are in Spanish. Follow the Costera Miguel Alemán north a few blocks to the fort atop the hill (at Morelos).

Modern-Day Diversions

For years Acapulco existed because it was a fishing and boating village. It still is, in a way. The big commercial fishing boats bring in their catch of the day here. Cruise ships dock along here as well. Deep-sea fishing trips can be arranged a little farther west (across from the *zócalo,* off the Costera) where charter fishing boats anchor near the sightseeing boats. Hotels will make arrangements for their guests, or you can meander around the boats and find a captain to take you fishing.

The Costera is lined with beaches, many hidden behind highrise hotels, and the city has made an all out effort to clean the bay. All manner of sea-fun is available: parasailing, sailboarding, water skiing, snorkeling, and scuba diving along with bay cruises and excellent deep-sea fishing. Land sports include golf on a choice of courses, tennis, and biking.

Arts and Artisans

Pal Kapenye's studio is in his home on a mountaintop overlooking the bay. His sleek carved figures are also sold in upscale shops. He lives in Acapulco year-round.

For the Shopper

For a good look into "Old Acapulco" of the 21st century, take an hour or two and wander through the **Mercado Municipal.** This is a great place to practice your Spanish and bargaining techniques. Locals shop for the daily necessities of life; there's no glitz for tourists here, just everyday goods. You'll find a labyrinth of stalls divvied into areas: a section where just raw meat is sold, others for fruit, vegetables, plastic utensils, leather goods, hand-carved wooden items, baskets in all sizes and shapes, gewgaws for tourists with shells glued to "everything," a huge flower market with blossoms and buds in every color of the rainbow and aromas that make life sublime, baskets filled with roots and herbs. If you know the right stall (ask), you can buy a magic potion for just about any purpose. Don't miss the pottery stands. This is not the best place to buy silver. Even though the jewelry may be hallmarked, the safer bet would be a reputable uptown jewelry store. If you should decide to buy silver at the market, never under any circumstances pay anywhere near the asking price. (Acapulco has many jewelers who sell fine Taxco silver; they may not bargain, but they are fairly reliable.) The best time to arrive at the *mercado* is early in the morning when most of the activity is going on.

¡Música!

The visitor can choose among Mexican trios, mariachis, or folkloric ballet. The music of today's Acapulco is legendary. As one of Mexico's premier coastal resorts, and the oldest, the city is busting at the seams with musical entertainment. Probably the most flam-

---

Las Brisas Hotel, the pink and white hotel on the hill, is one hotel that "doesn't get older, it just gets better." Well over 30 years old, and with a lot of new competition, the hotel is still one of the most beautiful hotels in Acapulco. Every white stucco unit is pristine, accented with bright pink trim. Winding roads are filled with the bright pink and white jeeps that carry guests, bellmen, maids, and room service. Las Brisas is built into the mountain, covering 45 hectares over the edge of a hill bathed in the pinks of fuchsia and hibiscus, contrasting with tall green leafy trees. Romance is a key word here, and whether on the first honeymoon or the 50th, lovers come here each year to luxuriate in the privacy of a small *casita* with a private pool afloat with pink flowers, a roomy terrace, a/c, and continental breakfast served to your "magic box" in the wall each morning. Most bungalows have a private pool (300 *casitas,* 250 pools); some share with another *casita.* Las Brisas is pricey and designed for those who want the best. Guests are indulged and they come back year after year for more. The streets of the small "village" called Las Brisas Hotel are steep, and the hardy folk who walk up and down get a good workout; you can telephone for a ride, and quickly a pink and white jeep arrives at the steps of your bungalow ready to take you anywhere on the grounds, including La Concha (the private seaside beach club), restaurants, a deli, an art gallery, boutiques, one of the sport centers, or, at the very top of the Brisas hill, the Chapel of Peace. Jeeps are available for rent from the hotel. The Belle Vista restaurant floats on the edge of the cliff; European chefs prepare remarkable food. The hotel is off Carretera Escenica on Clemente Mejia, tel. (800) 228-3000 in the U.S.; fax (74) 85-2748, 84-1650. Luxury.

boyant are the modern discos (locals say there are 120 of them!). Many feature flashing lights, floor fog, and high-tech sound systems. Most of Acapulco's discos enforce a strict dress code of casual elegance—no jeans, T-shirts, or cutoffs. Enjoy.

Special Events
Aficionados gather Sunday at 5:30 p.m. at the **Plaza de Toros Caletilla** bullring to watch the bull and the matador square off. Yes, this can be bloody. Make reservations through local travel agents; request the shady (*sombra*) side.

Regional Food
The fruits of Mexico are outstanding, and Acapulco on the southwest Pacific Coast is the perfect spot to try them all. The state of Guerrero grows about seven varieties of **mango,** and when they're in season (late spring and early summer), you can just escape into mango heaven. Try mango crepes, mango sorbet, mango on a stick, mango sliced into easy-to-get-to "petals" sprinkled with lime juice and chile powder (or skip the chile if you prefer). Mango sauces will appear on all manner of entrees and deserts. If you order a fresh fruit plate you *won't* find mango; it's difficult to slice for the large quantities necessary for a hotel kitchen, but in a small café at breakfast, ask and you might receive.

bananas for sale at the Acapulco market

You can eat a mango many ways besides all of the above. If you just want to pick up a mango out of the fruit bowl, do it. Be forewarned; you must wrestle with the large seed in the middle that doesn't easily let go of the lovely orange flesh. If you're in a real hurry and at home, after peeling just lean over the sink and let it drip: it's only good if it's dripping *a lot* of that sweet juice. Or, if you're serving mango to guests, make two slices lengthwise, just missing the seed on each long side. Then you have two small halves in the skin. They can be served with a liberal squeeze of lime juice and eaten out of their own "skin-cups" with a spoon. Mango is always best with lime juice.

Driving through a mango orchard (and you'll spot the trees all over the place) is a beautiful sight: tall, full, bushy, the tree has dark green leaves with dollops of color clustered on every branch. The variety of mangoes hanging from the trees

The *Pozole* Crawl

Pozole-crawling is not a creeping critter; it's like pub-crawling in England. *Pozole* is a thick maize-based stew with veggies and anything else the chef wishes to add—meat, chicken, or just a big variety of veggies. It can be very spicy—or not. Ask your waiter if it's *picante;* although the color (white, red, or green) usually gives it away, it's safest to ask. Thursday is *pozole* day in Acapulco (and all of Guerrero), and lots of restaurants cook it fresh in immense stockpots for the locals. However, more tourists are learning the secrets of *pozole* and enjoying the fun that is found at many of these Thursday afternoon sessions, which generally start between 1-2 p.m. and serve until . . . ? The small cafés around the *zócalo* may not advertise, but will have this on Thursday; ask around. Here are a couple of cafés that serve good *pozole,* all the same—but different. **Señor Frog's**, Carretera Escenica, Las Brisas Hill (at La Vista shopping center). The first course is a variety of appetizers; then comes the thick stew with chunks of chicken and vegetables, and platters of goodies (chopped peppers, onion, avocado, lime slices, tomatoes, cheese, chiles, and lots of other things) to drop in the *pozole* bowl, and of course tortillas. Don't forget the tequila or mescal. **Las Cazadores**, Calle 6 at Av. Mexico, is another *pozole* house. This is a zany place for fun at night; you might see transvestite dancers. Do Mexican businesspeople just take the rest of Thursday off? **El Zorrito**, on the Costera at Anton de Alaminos, is still another *pozole* hangout, open daily.

is amazing; some are greenish/orange and the size of a large avocado; others are much larger and the ripened fruit as it hangs on the tree is red; the most colorful are a large bulbous fruit that's a violet/pink/salmon. All that beauty and it tastes heavenly besides.

Cattle too love mango. If they wander through unfenced orchards, they strip the lower branches bare and then lie satisfied under the trees waiting to digest into *another* stomach before starting in again.

Near Acapulco

About 10 kilometers northwest of Acapulco, **Playa Pie de la Cuesta** displays some of the most forceful surf around Acapulco. Here you can maintain a healthy respect for the power of the sea without swimming in it. Walking the beach and watching the rolling breakers is a pleasant way to spend a few hours; usually there are few other people around. The small village near the lagoon is a perfect spot to watch the sunset over a cold *cerveza*. The rough surf deposits flotsam and jetsam, including great seashells, on the beach. Daring locals practice their surfing techniques when the sea rises. Everyone else has good sense!

Next to Pie de la Cuesta, **Coyuca Lagoon** is a tranquil spot, edged by trees and brush. It meanders from Pie de la Cuesta to the Barra de Coyuca and passes through a canal into the Coyuca River, which ultimately empties into the Pacific Ocean. In the pre-Cortesian era the lagoon was home to the Tarascans, some of the most powerful indigenous rulers—until the Aztecs drove them away. Now cranes stand statuelike watching the water until fish come close enough to spear with their beaks. Youngsters paddle around in their *lanchas*, pulling in fish for dinner. Several "Tortilla Flats" places offer simple meals on tin tables under *palapa* roofs. The lagoon is popular for water-skiing and other water activities. You can reach the lagoon's four small islands, La Montosa, La Pelona, Los Pajaros, and El Presidio, by hiring locals to transport you in their brightly colored boats.

South of Acapulco, 32 km south of the Hotel Marqués intersection, veer right toward the beach. Watch for signs and you ultimately end up at **Barra Vieja**, a windswept beach and a collection of *palapa* cafés, all specializing in seafood. On Sunday the beach is alive with families enjoying fresh barbecued fish. From here watch the pelicans "crash" the waves when the sea is rich with bait. Some folks camp along this beach, which is usually no problem. Ask the nearest café or other businesses on the beach. This is really *old Mexico*.

Guanajuato

THE FIRST SPANIARDS ARRIVED IN GUANAJUATO IN 1526, when the territory was granted to Don Rodrigo Vázquez. He, like everyone in that era, came looking for gold and silver. Years passed before anyone found sizable veins of the precious metals. But they found another, homelier treasure early on: fertile plains capable of producing bumper crops of fruits and vegetables. When ships filled with colonists embarked for the New World, Cortés convinced the Spanish crown to reserve space for seeds and saplings from home. Oranges, figs, pears, and peaches thus arrived from Spain. Farmers soon began growing native pumpkins, squash, cacao beans, and corn, this last the most important new crop among the exotic vegetables and fruits in the New World. An eager market waited for these products in nearby settlements—especially Mexico City. Guanajuato state is still known as the "breadbasket" of Mexico.

In 1548, the search for silver paid off. Guanajuato's struggling mining camps finally found it at the San Bernabé mine; two years later the San Juan Rayas mine opened. The discovery of precious metals in the rugged Sierra Madre attracted hordes of hardy miners. Clusters of primitive shelters became the mining camps of Marfil, Tepetapa, Santa Ana, and Cerro del Cuarto. In 1554 these camps merged and became Guanajuato. It was a strange little city, spread along a gorge-bottom and set very close to the river at the foot of tall mountains. The town was frequently wiped out by floods, but people kept coming. Sixteenth-century colonists labored hard to create cities that closely reflected what they left behind in Spain. By the 17th century, Guanajuato towns featured cloistered buildings and labyrinthine rooms, flower-filled courtyards, private chapels, and opulent works of art. Universities were built, musicians and artists encouraged. Newcomers worked hard to achieve a touch of elegance from bare rock and total isolation. And they were successful.

Bring warm clothes to sleep in, especially in the winter, since most hotels lack heaters.

Folks with disabilities should consider the topography of Guanajuato city before choosing to come. It's not an easy place to roll a wheelchair or manipulate crutches.

In 1741, the city had more than 12,000 inhabitants and earned from Philip IV the official designation of "city." The really *big* discovery at Valenciana came in 1760. A thick vein of silver was found that would change many lives, making many men rich while bringing untold hardships to the Indians who labored deep within the earth. Mine shafts were hacked out of the mineral-laden

a bird's-eye view of central Guanajuato

soil, with thousands of primitive steps leading to the rich yields of minerals hidden below. Ore cars were filled using shovel and bucket and then pushed long distances to the surface. Indian laborers working under the jurisdiction of hard and cruel *encomienderos* dug the caverns and brought out the silver, slaving beyond the limits of human endurance. Treated by money-hungry entrepreneurs as expendable commodities, many lost their lives in the tunnels. German naturalist Alexander von Humboldt was shocked at the conditions he witnessed at Valenciana in 1810: men carrying as much as 160 kilograms of ore on their backs for six straight hours, ascending thousands of steps at a 45-degree angle; even boys under 12 and men over 60 were forced to work the mines. In the beginning the ore was pulverized by hand with five-kilogram sledgehammers. Later, donkeys were used to crush the stones with their hooves. (Not until the 1970s did mine operators begin to use pneumatic shovels and electrically driven cars.)

Decades after the discovery of silver, Mexico's War of Independence would change everything. The war began under an unlikely general, Father Miguel Hidalgo, a radical parish priest from the town of Dolores. This reckless band quickly won a few minor skirmishes; Hidalgo then hit the road to Guanajuato city with his ragtag collection of "soldiers." Fearful of attack, city leaders brought Spanish residents and their families, as well as the town treasury, to Alhóndigas de Granaditas, a stout stone building. Folk legend tells us that the inexperienced rebels won their first victory through the bravery of dissident Juan José de los Reyes Martínez, known as Pípila, who flushed the city's royalist defenders from the Alhóndiga.

When the insurgents entered the city they released all the prisoners in the local jail, and then proceeded to fill it with apprehended *gachupines*. Three months later, when it was clear they were about to lose Guanajuato, Hidalgo's people brutally killed all their prisoners. However, within a year Father Hidalgo was captured in Chihuahua, charged with treason and heresy, and executed. His head was carried to Guanajuato, where it was placed in a cage and hung outside the granary building. Three of Hidalgo's comrades—Juan Aldama, Ignacio Allende, and Mariano Jiménez—were executed as well, their heads also placed in cages and hung on hooks in the corners of the Alhóndiga de Granaditas. Historians claim the heads hung in place for nine years and seven months.

Exploring the Streets of Guanajuato

As anyone who stays even a few days soon learns, Guanajuato is alive with music. El Jardín de la Unión is the pulsing center of town, with a silvery kiosk where bands play regularly year-round. Groups of handsome young men called *estudiantinas* walk the streets at night strumming their stringed instruments and singing sentimental ballads of love.

The annual Festival Internacional Cervantino honors Spanish author Miguel Cervantes and his unforgettable characters Don Quixote and Sancho Panza. During the festival, the intimate Teatro Juárez is a lively center for a variety of music, with artists from all over the world. Dancers take to the streets and every small plaza is alive with the excitement of bards, playlets, music, and dance.

This small, romantic city is best explored on foot. Museums are hidden in unlikely corners, housed in lovely old structures. Tiny plazas, old fountains, and pastel houses with wrought-iron balconies enlivened by a host of colored flowers fill the narrow, hilly streets. Leafy vines climb old stone walls, and white lace curtains drape the windows.

Guanajuato is built on narrow, hilly streets.

The architecture is striking—you needn't know a Doric column from a Moorish proscenium to enjoy the grace of the antiquated domes or carved Churrigueresque façades. Intense artistic effort went into so many of these structures. And fortunately for the rest of the world these buildings should be forever preserved; in 1989, the entire city was designated a "World Heritage Zone," preventing modernization of these old structures. The stone statue of Pípila stands guard on a high hill, visible from almost any spot in the city. Wear good walking shoes, as these streets are steep—in some areas they become staircases.

The **Pípila** monument stands as a reminder of the beginning of the war of independence. The monolith, about 10 meters tall, recalls the bravery of Pípila, who during the siege of the city strapped a slab of stone to his back to deflect the gunfire coming his way; then, with a pile of straw, he set fire to the entrance of the Alhóndigas, enabling the insurgents to storm the fortresslike granary. In stone he continues to hold high the torch, standing above a plaque promising "there are still other Alhóndigas to burn." Visitors are welcome to climb an inside stairway of the statue into the torch for a marvelous view of the city. Pípila is open 24 hours a day, and there's always a crowd of vendors selling snacks and souvenirs. For the hardy it's a good hike; the rest should take the bus marked "Pípila." Once there it's easy to spot several paths that return to town.

Locals really appreciate **El Jardín de la Unión**. In Guanajuato there are very few broad areas of flat land conducive to the construction of the typical, broad, square Mexican plaza. So here the favored center/gathering place bears a rather unusual shape; El Jardín is a small flat area in the midst of zigzagging up-and-down streets. This shady, smallish garden is almost entirely covered by a thick canopy of aged Indian laurel trees. A kiosk in the

The **Casa de Espiritus Alegres** (House of Cheerful Spirits) is up in the hills in the suburb of Marfil. This bed and breakfast occupies an ex-hacienda built in the mid-1700s. At one time many haciendas lined the river here, about three kilometers from the heart of Guanajuato. Gold and silver ores were brought here on mules for processing. In 1906, the river raged, flooding out this hacienda—along with many others—and creating a ghost town.

In the 1950s Italian sculptor Georgio Belloli took an interest in the area, restoring the old stone ghosts into charming homes. American artists Joan and Carol Summers took over Casa de Espiritus Alegre in 1979. First they improved the building with plumbing and wiring, and then they built a separate studio. Finally, employing playful sophistication, earthy art, and bright color, they worked their way through the entire house, restoring rooms and building terraces. The building now consists of six bedrooms, four with fireplaces, and the decor includes marvelous folk art from all over Mexico. Guests enjoy a glass-covered, tree-shaded central courtyard with tropical plants and a stone fountain. The traditional kitchen is decorated with bright colors in a style *típico* of Mexico, and it includes hand-painted ceramic tiles, folk art, and a dining table set in front of a large open fireplace. Each bedroom is unique: one features a collection of dolls, another the rich atmosphere of the tiger dance ritual, and a third enhances romance with plenty of lace and flowers. All are quite charming. For more information and brochures write or call Joan Summers, 2817 Smith Grade, Santa Cruz, California 95060, U.S.A.; tel. (408) 423-0181. In Mexico, write to La Casa de Espiritus Alegres La Ex-Hacienda La Trinidad, 1, Marfil, Guanajuato, 36250, Gto., Mexico; tel./fax 3-1013. Expensive.

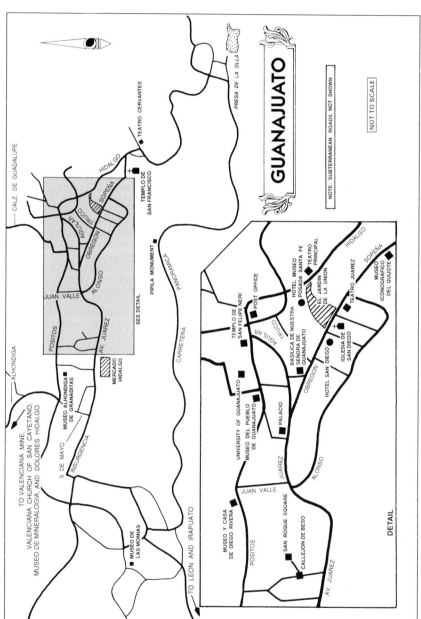

© MOON PUBLICATIONS, INC.

center is the site of music on Tuesday, Thursday, and Sunday each week. This is a pleasant place to spend an hour or two on a shady bench reviewing the social habits of Guanajuatenses. Water spouts vigorously from the silver-colored fountain. Small children dance up and down the steps of the silver kiosk, and students and businesspeople enjoy tranquil breaks. *Mamacitas* and small girls, dressed in white veils like miniature brides, rush to place nosegays of flowers on the altar of the Virgin at the basílica. Elderly aristocratic women take the fresh air strolling on the arms of middle-aged sons. At this great people-watching locus the parade is nonstop.

If staying in downtown Guanajuato, the best way to get around is on foot. Wear good walking shoes with thick soles for protection from the cobblestones. Be prepared for walking up and down steep hills; some streets narrow down to stairways. Walking Guanajuato is a daily exercise in physical fitness.

(🍴) Just across from the *jardín*, the **Hotel San Diego** offers a nice little dining room with small open balconies where diners can enjoy breakfast, lunch, or dinner. Bright red plaid linens cover the simple wooden tables; you'll eat good old-fashioned Mexican food at modern prices.

In the evening teenage girls huddle in bunches, giggling at young boys huddled in bunches watching the girls. Vendors sell supper-in-a-cup, *vasitas de elote*—a corncob pulled from a boiling pot, the kernels scraped off, placed in a cup, sprinkled with chile powder and served with a plastic fork. The music in the park mixes swing, rock, salsa, and samba: something for everybody. Many dining spots lie around the *jardín,* including sidewalk cafés Café de Hotel Museo Santa Fé and Café El Pollo Pitagorico. Favorite hotels stand on the *jardín* and across the street.

Across the street from El Jardín the **Teatro Juárez** stands in lovely elegance. Although theater construction began in 1873, it wasn't until 1903, when Guanajuato was enjoying a period of intense wealth, that the building was finally inaugurated. The opening performance was Verdi's *Aida;* among the many notable celebrities in attendance were Don Porfirio Díaz, then president of the Mexican Republic, and the composer of *Aida,* Verdi himself. The top of the *teatro* is graced with life-sized statues of the nine Muses—Melpomene, Thalia, Polyhymnia, Erato, Terpsichore, Euterpe, Clio, Calliope, Urania. The portico displays Doric-Roman columns, and the walls are stone in layers of light green and blue. Although several architects worked on the project over the years, the last to revise and complete the building was Antonio Rivas Mercado.

The nine Muses decorate the top of the Teatro Juárez.

Established in 1862, **Hotel Museo Posada Santa Fé** is probably the oldest hotel in Guanajuato. During the reign of Maximilian the consulate of Prussia lodged here when on royal business to the city. On the walls, paintings by chronicler Don Manuel Leal depict life in the early days of Guanajuato. All 50 rooms exude a feeling of the 1800s despite the addition of carpets, TV, private baths, self-serve bars, and king-size beds (suites only; in the other rooms the double beds seem quite small). Don't expect 20th-century utility, just old luxury. The gracious historical landmark is filled with antiques and antiquated art. Finely finished wood railings and spindles accentuate the curved stairways. A lobby bar, inside dining room, immense fireplaces, friendly, attentive staff, and a sidewalk café on the edge of El Jardín make this a favorite stopover. Reservations suggested. Write to Hotel Museo Posada Santa Fé, Guanajuato, 36000, Gto., Mexico, tel. (473) 2-0084. Expensive.

The theater is as handsome as ever with the same broad staircase, red wrought-iron fence, and ornate multiglobed streetlamps. The interior is smaller than expected. But in its day it must have been nothing less than opulent, with a European-Moorish flavor. The drop curtain was painted in France by the renowned scenographer Labasta of Paris; his subject is a panorama of the Golden Horn of Constantinople. Rich burnished woods, unique carved designs, French sculptures, foyer furniture covered with elegant damasks, and a grand chandelier from Paris all reflect the wealth of the city at the turn of the century. An announcement poster out front describes the offerings, times, and dates. The theater is open for viewing Tues.-Sun. 9 a.m.-1:45 p.m. and 5-8 p.m. Any opportunity to attend a production in the small theater offers a grand experience.

The **Teatro Principal** and **Teatro Cervantes**, usually open Sunday, Monday, and Tuesday evenings, show international films. All three edifices are fairly close together, near the *jardín*.

Scene of the first bloody battle of the fight for independence, **Museo Alhóndigas de Granaditas** is today one of seven fine Guanajuato museums. This one-time city granary is filled with historical artifacts that relate the story of the city and boasts a pleasing art exhibit. From 1864 to 1964 the Alhóndigas served as a prison. In 1967 the city revamped the old building and displays today include stairway murals depicting the history of Guanajuato painted by popular artist José Chavez Morado. On the corners of the building, still in place, are the hooks from which the heroes' heads were hung. Guanajuato is justifiably proud of its historical part in the fight for independence. And though it's been hundreds of years since these events, the city still exudes an aura of liberty, free thinking, and patriotism.

Established in 1724 by Jesuit priests from Spain, the University of Guanajuato did and still contributes a great deal to the "arts and letters" ambience of the city. The university itself is huge, standing out in the town like a child taller than the rest of the class. The architecture is unusual, and the university draws students from all over. Three **University of Guanajuato museums** present changing art exhibits. Two occupy the ground floor, and one is in the Templo de la Compañia de Jesús next door. They're open Mon.-Fri. 9 a.m.-2 p.m. and 5-8 p.m. Not just naturalists enjoy the **Museo de Historia Natural**

Alfredo Duges on the fourth floor, where exhibits of stuffed specimens of a large variety of animals, some rather unusual, are on display. It's open weekdays only, 10 a.m.-6 p.m.

The Museo del Pueblo de Guanajuato is in the former home of the Marqueses de San Juan Rayas, owners of the rich Rayas silver mine. This graceful old mansion is now an art museum. Built in 1696 with its own chapel, the building exhibits a selection of art ranging from the early colonial period to the modern era. In the chapel in the courtyard a fine mural by José Chavez Morado is on display.

An interesting history surrounds the Fountain of the Baratillo. Originally commissioned by

A few blocks from the center of town sits **Parador San Javier Hotel,** Dolores Hidalgo Hwy. on the Plaza San Javier, tel. (473) 2-0626 or 2-0944, fax 2-3114. This charming old structure features colonial rooms from the old days, with shiny wood floors, fireplaces, and colorful tile. Other rooms are straight out of the 20th century. All are quite lovely—the suites are really comfortable and lie just a few steps from well-manicured gardens with exquisite lawns and brilliantly colored bougainvillea tumbling over old stone walls. You'll spot some fine antiques in the public rooms. Just wandering the grounds is a pleasant experience. A coffeeshop and a lovely old dining room feature high ceilings, a fireplace, and colonial art, linen, and crystal as well as very efficient waiters. Have a drink in the El Pozo piano bar or experience the disco at La Galería. Meals at the hotel restaurant are a fixed price. Remember, a Mexican lunch is the main meal of the day—generally a four-course meal. Expensive.

El Gallo Pitagorico Restaurant and Bar on the *jardín* (6-C) serves good international food. During happy hours (noon-2 p.m., 6-7 p.m.) drinks are two for one and the *botanas* are free. A good-sized combination Mexican platter runs about US$8.50.

Emperor Maximilian in 1864, the fountain was constructed in Florence, Italy. Distinctly Italian in design, it was a gift to Guanajuato and placed opposite the Basílica de Nuestra Señora de Guanajuato in the Plaza de la Paz. But when Maximilian fell from power and was executed, the fountain was moved to a more inconspicuous spot about a block from the *jardín*. Today it's the centerpiece of a small plaza featuring a couple of tiny cafés and a pleasant laid-back ambience.

San Roque Square by day looks like just another small antiquated stone plaza with unusually shaped iron lanterns set in front of an old church. But during the Cervantes festival the square becomes a lavish stage straight out of old Europe, with actors dressed in the velvets and satins of the medieval period. Crowds sit on wooden bleachers to listen to the wit and wisdom of the bard. These evening playlets from Cervantes's masterful pen are productions that rival Hollywood's, and the price is better. The moon, stars, and church architecture present a perfect backdrop for well-performed theater. Visitors who follow the *estudiantinas* up and down the narrow streets will also end up at this square, where a bard tells a sad or happy story.

If you're looking for The Street Lacking Doors and Windows, quit looking. The name refers to the subterranean labyrinth of streets in tunnels that run under and through the city. It looks as though a masterful engineer designed the throughway for the growing vehicular traffic—Mother Nature was the engineer. For centuries homes, churches, and businesses were flooded by the

Río Guanajuato, where in the early days of the city silver was processed. Perfect roadbeds were left when the lusty river was diverted; highways were constructed, and doors of adjacent homes were blocked off.

The Basílica de Nuestra Señora de Guanajuato houses an ancient statue of the Virgin.

Guanajuato is a showcase of charming churches. The **Basílica de Nuestra Señora de Guanajuato** is a marvelous old church well worth a visit. The interior is an opulent dedication to a small wooden statue of the Virgin sent to the New World by King Philip II in 1557. It had been worshiped in Spain since 714, hidden in a cave from the Moors, and is presumed to be the oldest representation of Christian art in Mexico. It stands on a silver base and is adorned with tunics of precious inlaid stones. Each year three days are set aside to celebrate holidays dedicated to the city's protector, the Virgin of Guanajuato.

The Templo de la Compañia de Jesús was originally built as part of the Jesuit University in 1747-1765. When the Jesuits were expelled from Mexico, the order of St. Felipe Neri took over and adopted its present name, **Templo de San Felipe Neri**. The original dome and main altar collapsed in 1808, but were replaced with different designs of neoclassic architecture.

The **Iglesia de San Diego** at El Jardín was built by the Franciscans in 1633. It has survived flood and financial difficulties and was completely reconstructed in 1786 under the patronage of the Count de Valenciana (of gold mining fame). The **Templo de San Francisco** is on Sopeña, close to the *jardín*. The city supports still more churches; keep looking. Not all are flamboyant but each church has its own personality and usually an intriguing history.

On the edge of town, the paths at the **Ex-Hacienda San Gabriel de Berrera** lead to beautiful grounds

The unusual **Hotel Castillo de Santa Cecilia** looks like a medieval castle sitting on a protective bluff overlooking the city. Once inside you'll find a charming, well-decorated hotel with 88 rooms, excellent service, luxurious amenities, and a dining room serving excellent food. Amenities include a swimming pool, cable TV, a handicraft workshop, and parking. Dancing at the La Cava nightclub Fri.-Sat., a great *estudiantina* show, and live music provide entertainment. For reservations write to Camino a la Valenciana Km 1, C.P. 36000, Guanajuato, Gto., Mexico; tel. 2-0485, fax 2-0153. Moderate to Expensive.

and myriad gardens with gracious names: the Orange Garden, Arabian Garden, Pergola Garden, Rose Garden, Italian Garden, St. Francis Garden, and Queen's Garden. Lovely trees, beautiful statuary, sculpture, fountains, and reflecting pools are scattered about. This museum illustrates what life was like for the wealthy and the servants who slaved for them.

> Once a 17th-century convent, **Hotel San Diego,** Apdo. Postal 8, Guanajuato, 36000, tel. 2-1300, fax 2-5626, on the *jardín,* has historical ambience but lacks the pizzazz of some of the other historic hotels in the city. But the location is great, and, for some travelers, it's still one of the all-time favorite accommodations in the city. The rooms meet modern standards, with private bathrooms, hot water, and shower/tubs. Some of the rooms have antique balconies. Ask about the pay-garage one block away. The dining room is open 7 a.m.-11 p.m. for dining, cocktails, and entertainment. Moderate.

Guanajuato Highlights

Arts and Artisans

A visit to **Museo y Casa de Diego Rivera**, Calle Pocitos 47, tells the story of the artist's early life. Born in 1886 in the two-story house on a narrow Guanajuato street, Diego Rivera lived in Guanajuato until he was eight years old. Then the family moved to Mexico City, where he began painting at the age of 10. The first floor of this museum offers a pleasant display of life in the Rivera family, including furniture and antiques. The two upper floors contain about a hundred Rivera paintings and sketches. Rivera attended art schools in Europe and became enamored of the political activists of his era. Returning to Mexico, the flamboyant artist frequently became a center of controversy because of his connections and associations with communism; because of Rivera's influence, Leon Trotsky made his home in Mexico City until an assassin sank an ice ax in his skull.

Another artist revered in Guanajuato is author Miguel Cervantes. Don't miss a visit to **Museo Iconográfico del Quijote**, also known as the Cervantes Museum, at Manuel Doblado 1. The museum is in front of the Templo de San Francisco.

the elaborate façade of the Templo de San Felipe Neri

Anyone who has laughed or cried at the antics of the cross-eyed conquistador and his pal Sancho Panza will enjoy a lighthearted visit through this amazing collection of Quixote art. Cervantes-lover Eulalio Ferrer left Spain for Mexico at the end of the Spanish Civil War, donating his immense collection of Quixotic figures to the city of Guanajuato. Cervantes creations appear in 600 displays, including giant wall murals, a modern depiction by Pablo Picasso, lithographs by Salvador Dali, Pedro Coronel and Raul Anguiano murals, pottery, statues, eggs, and postage stamps—all portraying the sad-eyed knight of La Mancha. The museum was officially opened by Spanish President Felipe González on 6 November 1987.

The Quixote Museum boasts 600 displays honoring the errant knight created by Miguel Cervantes.

For the Shopper

The **Mercado Hidalgo** east of Juárez is an unusually shaped Eiffel-like structure built in 1905 on land formerly occupied by the Gabiria Bullring. On the Centennial of the Independence, 16 September 1910, General Porfirio Díaz inaugurated it. A slender clocktower crowns the structure. On the two inner levels are thirty large windows and four staircases.

This turn-of-the-century building features an immensely high ceiling, and a wrought-iron stairway leads to the wraparound balcony; one story says the building was originally designed to house a train station. The design of the building has a distinctive French flair, and shoppers will find dozens of small stalls offering tin pans, baskets, embroidered dresses, pottery, rebozos, jewelry, huaraches, vegetables, fruit, and Bimbo bread. If you *are* going to find a bargain it will be on the upper levels, a colorful *tianguis* where you can find just about anything.

¡Música!

A favorite evening pastime all year-round is a *callejoneadas,* following the *estudiantinas* up and down the streets of Guanajuato. These young men are well-trained classical musicians with fabulous voices working out on classical guitars, 12-string mandolins, and huge bass fiddles. Between songs they

The estudiantina *tradition originated among poor students in Spain who would serenade sweethearts for a fee.*

entertain the crowds with hilarious stories; translator required for full appreciation of the punchlines. The *estudiantina* tradition began among students in Spain, who, desperate for money, hired themselves out to stroll the streets and serenade lovely *señoritas* at the behest of their lovers or to pay tribute to mothers on their special days.

The evening promenades these days are probably more for the benefit of tourists than for those being serenaded, but it's fun. As the musicians go up and down the lanes and alleys of the city, a small donkey follows behind, carrying the night's wine supply. Originally carried in skins, the vino today is transported in boxes with spigots. Anyone who wants to join in is welcome, for but a small charge for the wine and the *boron,* a spouted ceramic wine carafe.

Some local travel agents have commercialized the tradition with package tours. All tourees meet in a given spot and then wander the passageways behind the musicians, trailing behind the donkey and always passing through the tiny Callejón del Beso, or "Alley of the Kiss." The legend tells of star-crossed lovers who once pined for each other from separate houses directly across from one another, finally daring to kiss from balconies so close together the kiss proved a remarkably easy task. The sad ending of the story finds an angry father catching them in the act, killing his daughter in an inhuman rage; her lover did himself in.

In the 20th century it's considered good luck to buss your lover beneath the infamous balconies, at the narrowest spot on Callejón del Beso. On tours photographers catch these kisses on color film. You're presented the photo at the end of the walk; if it pleases you, it's available for about US$6. Touristy? Yes. But who wouldn't like a reminder of a kiss in such a romantic spot under a star-filled sky? The trip around town lasts about two hours.

Special Events

Festival Internacional Cervantino: Enrique Ruelas, founder and director of the university theater, introduced in 1953 the one-act street farces of Cervantes known as *entremeses*. The word has a double meaning, meaning both "interlude" and "farce"—very apropos, since the *entremeses* were originally written to entertain during the interlude between acts.

> (♈) Not a disco, and not just a bar, **Rincón del Beso,** Alonso 21-A, is instead a *peña,* an intimate bohemian spot with dim light, tiny open rooms, plain wood tables and chairs, and a colorful miniature stage with a backdrop representing the small winding streets of Guanajuato. If you've ever felt the urge to stand and recite that heartfelt poem you wrote over a glass or five of your favorite sangria, here's your chance: everyone here is welcome to recite, sing, or emote. Between the amateurs, plenty of professionals clamber on stage to sing the music of Mexico, Argentina, and Cuba. Only short walk from the *jardín,* it's a fun place where you can start late and stay till early in the morning; the *peña* remains open as long as there are customers. Wine is the drink of choice; no cover charge.

In 1972, the city broadened the affair, creating the Festival Internacional Cervantino and inviting dance groups and musicians from all over the world. In 1993, a group from Russia appeared; the German opera *Moctezume* made its Mexico debut here. For more than 20 years, the festival has enjoyed nothing but success. The streets are filled with dancers, bards, and playlets. Musicians, including Guanajuato's *estudiantinas*, stroll the streets dressed in the clothes of the Renaissance—satin knee breeches, velvet puffed sleeves, and flat velvet caps with plumes up top. The Cervantino Festival is held for two weeks each year in October. For the dates, call a Mexican Government Tourism Office, ask your travel agent, or write to Desmond O'Shaugnessy at the Guanajuato Tourism Office.

Semana Santa: A popular holiday in Guanajuato is Holy Week—ongoing from Palm Sunday to Easter Sunday. The most moving event is the portrayal of the Passion of Christ. Reverent processions bearing Christ on the cross and the Virgin of Dolores peregrinate to the churches. Flowers and palm crosses abound; most homes and businesses display traditional altars.

Regional Food

From the early days, Guanajuato was a rich farming area in the high valley. Many vegetables and fruits were grown here and delivered to surrounding communities. (Even today it's a broccoli center and the Jolly Green Giant has a huge frozen-food processing plant.) Fresh vegetables were served as side dishes, salads, and in wonderful marinades. Artichokes were a fad in 19th-century Mexico, cooked in a variety of ways including stuffed, fried, and baked; this was really a dish for the affluent in the colonial era. Just outside the marketplace you'll catch the aroma of chicken frying with potatoes and carrots, all then snugged into fresh tortillas—this is called the miner's supper. Vegetables are commonly served pickled in Mexico, probably a leftover from the days when there was no refrigeration, and a great way to preserve the bounty. Roasted onions browned on a *comal* or grill are a typical accompaniment to barbecued meat.

If you have a chance, try the glazed strawberries of Guanajuato, plump and sweet—this is strawberry country. They're excellent when fresh and juicy, but the glazed variety are easily taken along in a purse or pocket.

Special Excursions

Museo de las Momias

People wait in long lines to see the otherworldly exhibits at the Museum of the Mummies. The museum simply stores a collection of dried-up cadavers for viewing in glass cases. The dry mountain air and chemical mix of the soil in the tiny local cemetery combine to prevent decomposition in about two percent of bodies buried. In many Mexican cities, when the deceased is buried, the family has five years to pay for the plot. If at the end of five years no payment has been received, the body is exhumed and cremated to make room for "paying" customers. Long before the museum was built, and before the law permitted cremation, evicted bodies were propped along the fence bordering the cemetery and left there until family members retrieved them. One day a curious visitor walking along the cemetery path was assaulted by a dead body that suddenly tipped over upon her; the visitor nearly had a heart attack. Perhaps that's when it was decided that the mummies must be removed, cremated, or, if not claimed, placed in a glass case for display. The museum is open daily 9 a.m.-6 p.m.

Valenciana Mine

As the Valenciana Mine continued to produce amazing quantities of silver, Guanajuato city developed into one of the major cities of New Spain, growing almost as large as

The Valenciana Mine still produces tremendous quantities of silver.

the opulent interior of the basílica

Mexico City. Guanajuato prospered for two centuries, providing the world with one-half of its total silver supply. The Valenciana Mine alone produced one-third. Only 17 Guanajuato mines remain open today. One is the Valenciana, reopened when silver prices resurged. The mine is open for inspection by the public. Statistics tell us the Valenciana mine shaft is 525 meters deep; 80 tons of silver are brought to the surface each month, together with 396 kilograms of gold. Although Taxco is referred to as the silver center of the country, Valenciana produces more silver.

Valenciana Church of San Cayetano

The wealth of the Valenciana mine was unbelievable, hence the (nearby) Valenciana Church of San Cayetano is just what you'd expect a "gold" church to be—golden. The façade is ornate Churrigueresque baroque. On the inside you'll find four enormous paintings by Luis Momay, golden altars with delicate filigree work, statues, stained glass, an alabaster holy water font, and a spectacular pulpit. The walls are one-and-a-half meters thick. If you study the walls, ceilings, altars, and pulpit you'll discover fine gold work, inlaid precious woods, ivory, and other bone. Four barrel vaults make up the ceiling, with a cupola in the transept. This is really a church that says pesos—lots of them.

One historian claims the church was built by Valenciana Mine owner Don Antonio de Obregón Alcocer in thanks to his maker for the vast wealth gathered from the mine. Another historian says the church was built to assuage his guilty conscience for the wealth accumulated at the cost of innumerable Indian lives. In front of the Church of San Cayetano a tiny gift shop sells interesting odds and ends, including silver and gold figurines and earrings.

Valenciana Church

Zacatecas

A FEW LONE MISSIONARIES AS EARLY AS 1530 MADE THEIR WAY into the difficult mountains of the north to save the souls of the wild Chichimecas, but with little success. And from almost the same time Spaniards were seeking the precious metals of the Indians. Lying on the natural path between the arid country of the north and tropical mesoamerica, Zacatecas was ignored for years. But in 1546, treasure hunter Juan Tolosa's luck changed and he found silver. The miner encountered little resistance from the Zacateco Indians who lived on the flanks of Cerro de la Bufa. This mountain on the edge of Zacatecas has played a vital role in the establishment of Zacatecas from the day the first Spaniards arrived. Historically it has suffered through events such as Benito Juárez's bloody victory over rebels in 1871. In 1914 the city was exposed to the violence of war again when Pancho Villa captured the city and fought until the huge garrison of thousands of soldiers was destroyed. Through it all, Zacatecas's special gift continued to be the silver buried within the surrounding mountains.

The Ex-Hacienda Bernardez, which at one time belonged to the former viceroy, Count Laguna, is a trade school for silversmiths; **Santuario de Plateros de Zacatecas** serves as an important adjunct to the city. It certainly makes sense that the highest silver-producing city in the country should train its youth to become talented artisans with the metal in addition to teaching them the business end. Actually, the young folks at the school also learn to work with gold and other metals. Crafts made here are sold both at the school and in the **Central Commercial** in Zacatecas.

From the beginning, once the word "silver" was out, the city attracted more and more people seeking their fortunes. The city spread and grew along the winding river banks of the Arroyo de la Plata at the foot of La Bufa and began an irregular climb along its "face of stone and heart of silver." Large quantities of silver were found, and not only miners came; farmers, toolmakers, leather craftsmen, and people from all walks of life made their way to the Zacatecas highlands, to still another "silver-spawned" city of Nueva España.

The narrow streets twist and climb in no particular way, some so steep they become steps. Wandering around the city you will discover little streets with fanciful names that always have a romantic history. You'll see small balconies with brass lions, stone symbols, architecture reminiscent of the Moors, nouveau art, and imperious coats of arms from the days of viceroyalty. From the broad religious structures built by the earliest arrivals in the 16th century to the elegant buildings of the era of Porfirio, the art and architecture of the city beg to be investigated.

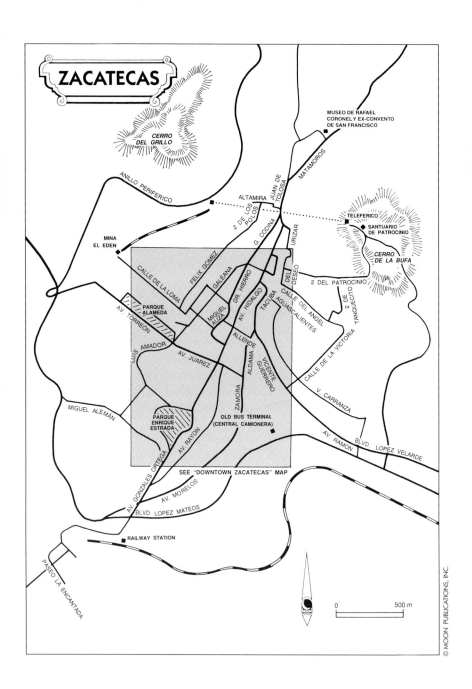

ZACATECAS

CERRO DEL GRILLO

MUSEO DE RAFAEL CORONEL Y EX-CONVENTO DE SAN FRANCISCO

ANILLO PERIFERICO

ALTAMIRA

MINA EL EDEN

TELEFERICO

SANTUARIO DE PATROCINIO

CERRO DE LA BUFA

2 DE LOS POLOS

JUAN DE TOLOSA

MATAMOROS

G. CODINA

URIZAR

2 DEL PATROCINIO

CALLE DE LA LOMA

FELIX GOMEZ

GALEANA

DR. HIERRO

AV. HIDALGO

TACUBA

DEL DESEO

CALLE DEL ANGEL

2 DE TANQUECITO

PARQUE ALAMEDA

AV. TORREON

MIGUEL AUZA

ALLENDE

AGUASCALIENTES

CALLE DE LA VICTORIA

LUIS AMADOR

AV. JUAREZ

ALDAMA

ZAMORA

VICENTE GUERRERO

V. CARRANZA

MIGUEL ALEMAN

PARQUE ENRIQUE ESTRADA

OLD BUS TERMINAL (CENTRAL CAMIONERA)

AV. RAYON

AV. RAMON

BLVD. LOPEZ VELARDE

AV. GONZALES ORTEGA

SEE "DOWNTOWN ZACATECAS" MAP

AV. MORELOS

BLVD. LOPEZ MATEOS

RAILWAY STATION

PASEO LA ENCANTADA

0   500 m

© MOON PUBLICATIONS, INC.

Exploring the Streets of Zacatecas

The city fathers realized the importance of preserving the city long before UNESCO bestowed the title "Patrimony of Humanity" in 1993. It's a badge of honor and to those who wander the streets it becomes apparent the locals are proud of the title. Usually a city's plazas draw visitors together, but here, it's the **Catedral de Zacatecas,** built from 1718 to 1732. This is one of the most flam-

boyant masterpieces of Mexico's baroque creations. Other simple churches had been built on this site since 1537; its ranking as cathedral was bestowed in 1841. But the design, the intricate beauty set it aside. You could study the façade of this structure for days and still find something new among the elaborate carvings. It's a cache of geometric designs, unusual jambs, and a divided three-storied façade. The top story of the façade is a panel, its outer edges curving into a shield. Corinthian capitals top Solomonic and simple columns. This is Churrigueresque at its climax, at its best when the sun lights the pink stone as though under a spotlight. The play of light and shadow in each crevice brings this stone front to life. It's a don't miss, and bring your camera. In total contrast the interior of the cathedral is simple and sedate.

the baroque masterpiece the Catedral de Zacatecas

Palacio de Gobierno, built in the early 1700s, was originally the residence of a wealthy miner, the Count de Santiago de la Laguna. Facing the Plaza de Armas, it is of simple two-story construction with a wrought-iron decor and a stone framed doorway. The lovely central courtyard is lined with arched breezeways on both floors. Other notables have made this their home over the years. Next to the cathedral, it has belonged to the government since 1834, and today it's the city hall of Zacatecas. A mural inside, painted in 1970, graphically shows the history of the city.

The **Palacio de la Mala Noche** is another of the lovely old buildings built in the late 1700s with a story to tell. Its story is a typical "morality play" in which good wins all. A frustrated miner gives his last peso to a starving family and then spends a *mala noche* (bad night) in despair; the next day his mine reveals a silver deposit of indescribable proportions.

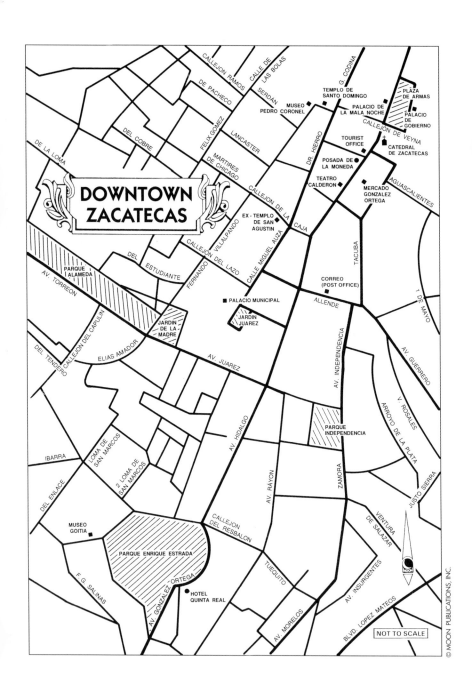

DOWNTOWN ZACATECAS

NOT TO SCALE

© MOON PUBLICATIONS, INC.

Teatro Calderon, built in the 19th century, today plays an important part in the city's culture. At the time of its construction, it was considered one of the most luxurious theaters in Mexico. Since its beginnings it has been used for multiple purposes. The three-story neoclassical building today is used by the University of Zacatecas as a venue for dance, concerts, lectures, theater, and exhibition hall.

The **Templo de Santo Domingo** was built by the Jesuits in the 16th century next to the Real Colegio de San Luis Gonzaga. It was rebuilt in the middle of the 18th century. After the expulsion of the Jesuits, the Dominicans occupied the church and the college. Like most of the structures in the city, it was built of rose stone, and it sits gracefully on its pleasant square. The façade is baroque, and two towers hint at Moorish design. On the inside, the four domes are quite impressive.

Templo de Santo Domingo

Mercado Gonzalez Ortega dates from the Porfirian period. This lovely old building replaced the original, which was destroyed by a fire. It was then used as the city's marketplace, well-situated on the south side of the cathedral and adjacent to Francisco Goitia Square. The building's east façade displays a stylish Mudejar-style archway and wrought-iron balcony giving a very nouveau look, especially when the balcony is filled with chattering people enjoying food, drink, and good company. The wide outside steps are conveniently used as bleachers for events at Goitia Square, especially crowded during the traditional Saturday *callejoneadas* and performances by the *tambora* bands.

Museo Pedro Coronel, formerly the Real Colegio de San Luis Gonzaga, was built in 1616. In 1767 it was taken over by the Dominicans and its name changed to Escuela de la Purísima Concepción. Attached to the building is the Elias Amador Library, where the walls are lined with shelf after shelf in an elegant high-ceilinged room. Here more than 25,000 books dating from the 16th to the 19th century are carefully looked after. This two-story neoclassical structure has passed through various phases over the centuries. It has housed a print shop, a jail, military quarters, a tenement, and finally it houses the rich collection of art donated by Zacatecan artist Pedro Coronel.

the Mudejar-style archway and wrought iron of the Mercado Gonzalez Ortega

The **Posada de la Moneda** (Finance Ministry and Treasury of the State of Zacatecas and former Mint) boasts a long history. During the colonial period, the metal from the mines was taken by animal transport a great distance to Mexico City, where it was coined. However, after independence and for almost a century, the more convenient Zacatecas Mint coined money here. While strolling through the old building with its elegantly proportioned inner courtyard, it's amazing to consider how many millions of dollars passed through this quiet and serene atmosphere. A black and white contemporary mural briefly tells the history of the Posada de la Moneda.

The **Ex-Templo y Bishopric de San Agustín** was built in the 16th century, though the present style has changed along the way to neo-Hispanic 17th-century baroque. Unfortunately, the Presbyterians owned the building at the end of the 19th century and destroyed an extraordinary façade that portrayed Catholic beliefs. On the north side the church has preserved the unique entrance that illustrates the conversion of Saint Augustine. Note the lovely domes and some outstanding altarpieces. The inner courtyard of the two-story convent displays skillful archwork. The chaotic history of both buildings has left its mark; they have been used for more humble occupations during the time of "reform:" a pool hall, gambling house, hotel, tenement house, warehouse, and a stage for cultural events.

As early as 1880, both the United States and England criticized the bullfight as a cruel and barbarous spectacle. Historian William Beezley called it the epitome of a clash of values. He went on to say that while most Mexicans saw "a ballet of cape and animal," foreigners saw "only blood and sand." And though Porfirio Díaz vehemently disagreed with this argument, he placed such value on international respect that he banned (for a while) bullfighting in the Federal District, Zacatecas, and Veracruz, the areas that he thought were most exposed to foreigners at the time.

Some of the most sought-out fighting bulls are raised at the haciendas Malpaso, San Mateo, and Trancoso.

Hotel Quinta Real, Av. Rayon 434, Zacatecas 98000, Zacatecas, tel. from the U.S.A. (800) 445-4565, from Mexico (492) 2-9104, is one of the most unusual hotels in Mexico. Built on the site of the decaying San Pedro Bullring (in 1866), it's spectacular and needless to say sports an unusual backdrop. The public rooms?—charming in the best colonial manner, with lovely arched corridors, vaulted ceilings, small niches holding artistic treasures, and that's before you get to your room. The rooms (all suites) are gracefully superimposed on the old bullring's bleachers, a beautiful formal dining room offers a gourmet menu and overlooks the arena; the decor of the hotel is opulent. It offers lovely armoires, hand-painted dressers, comfy beds with plump bedding, elegant wall decorations, marble bathrooms, pleasing paintings, swimming pool, TV, and all the gracious amenities that make a stay in a fine hotel perfect. Have a drink in the bull "chute;" the only things missing are the bulls. At the entrance of the hotel you can't help but notice the graceful old aqueduct standing next to the Quinta Real Hotel. Luxury.

Hotel Quinta Real incorporates an old bullring. The old aqueduct runs nearby.

The **Museo de Rafael Coronel** (Rafael is brother to Pedro) is housed in the ex-church and ex-monastery of San Francisco northeast of the Plaza de Armas. The church was constructed in the 16th century. And though the vault collapsed in 1924, the ruins just add to the whimsy and beauty of the building wide open to the blue sky. Wandering the grounds of this once-lovely complex is a very pleasant way to spend a couple of hours.

Museo de Rafael Coronel

The masks of the Museo de Rafael Coronel

It's not a surprise that the grounds are often used for weddings. The remaining walls and gardens are warm and inviting, still vibrant with the once-beautiful design of the building. The original carved stone baroque façade is still in place. The presbytery and the chapels are used for art exhibits, and in the monastery, the remaining cells, cloisters, library, and sacristy are the backdrop for a fine collection of memorabilia of prehistoric and colonial artifacts. But mostly this fine old museum is known for Rafael Coronel's magnificent collection of Mexican masks. Included are masks from eras beginning with prehistoric through colonial to modern; they are beautifully displayed. Even without the fine displays of historical memorabilia, San Francisco invites all for a little meditation. If you stand in just the right spot in the garden closest to the fallen vault, you'll see a white chapel that appears to sit on the crest of the curved arch of the museum. But it's just an optical illusion. The lovely white church and tall tower sit on a hilltop on the other side of town.

The **Santuario de Patrocinio** was built in 1548 to commemorate the conquest of the city. The hermitage, which sits on the crest of Cerro de la Bufa, eventually was transformed into the 18th-century church that stands here today. It features a single nave, two simple

The Santuario de Patrocinio overlooks the city from the crest of Cerro de la Bufa.

At one time one-third of the country's production of silver came from Mina el Edén.

façades, and a large atrium surrounded by archways where pilgrims can take shelter from the weather. This hub of the mountain's modern complex includes a meteorological observatory, a mausoleum of famous people, the **Museum of the Capture of Zacatecas**, and a perfect vista overlooking the city. You can reach this spot by cable car from the Eden Mine, by road, or by a cobblestone walkway that begins behind the cathedral.

Mining began in 1586 at the **Mina el Edén**. The tunnels were hand-hewn by the Indians whose lives were cut short for the cause of silver. If one is to believe the stories, a day never went by that at least one person wasn't lost in one of the deep chasms of the mine, and according to some historians it was many more than one. Flooding was common, and if a miner fell a thousand meters down, there was no way to get him back up, dead or alive. The whole job of extracting the silver was precarious, with unhealthy fumes, low light, rickety wooden ladders, and rope bridges that crossed these drops into the depths of the earth. But the job was accomplished; a lot of silver came from Zacatecas. One-third of the country's production of

> ⦿ Spending an evening at the **Eden Mine Disco** is another reason to venture into Cerro de la Bufa after dark. Only this time it's for music and fun. It's open Thurs.-Sat. only, cover charge.

The Ghost of Mina el Edén

Legends rooted in local superstition are rampant in these old cities. The story goes that the miners lived in a constant state of temptation, dreaming of what it would be like to possess just a *little* of the precious metal for themselves. One day a miner found a large piece of gold when no one was close by. He couldn't resist; he made his way to the lowest level of the mine to squirrel away "his" treasure. He finished his day's work in great anticipation and hastened to get the gold—but it was gone. He cowered in fear all night expecting the mine bosses to burst in and grab him. Who could have seen him? Who else—besides God—knew where he hid the gold? It must still be there, he rationalized; tomorrow he would search again. The next day he returned to the mine and again at the end of the day he scurried to the lowest level, but before he had a chance to search, the mineshaft caved in, crushing out his life beneath tons of stone. But that's not the end of the story. For decades, those who have spent much time in the Edén tunnels have reported encountering a ghost who wanders the tunnels—searching, searching, searching. . . .

silver came from here during the busy centuries of mining, more than from any other mining city. Though the Eden Mine no longer operates, the bright red **Eden Mine Tram** takes visitors into the tunnels of the old mine. The tram enters the tunnel on the fourth level, three levels lie below and three more above. The trip imparts a hint of what life must have been like working in this dark, drafty, underground world, day in and day out. Today, small bare light bulbs light some of the rough-hewn stone tunnels, while the really sensational sites—where you look down into deep crevasses or walk across the short suspension bridge to the tiny miner's chapel—are dramatically lit. Along the tram tracks sits a small shop where you can buy trinkets or stones. The tram takes you almost .6 kilometers (2,000 feet) into the mountain. From the top of Bufa, you can approach or depart the tunnel by elevator.

Zacatecas Highlights

For the Shopper

Mercado Gonzales Ortega is just one of the fine gathering places for craftsmen of all genres. By today's terms it's a "mall" filled with trendy shops and charming cafés, all within the building that at one time *was* the public market. The shops sell leather purses and belts, fine beadwork done by the Tarahumara Indians, and many other great souvenirs—trendy clothing, lovely silver jewelry, trays, and candlesticks, and lots more for the looking.

On Tacuba St. going downhill, (behind the Mercado Gonzales Ortega), the real *mercado publico* is just as expected, a place for the locals to buy fruits, vegetables and all the necessities of life. This is always a place to learn about the people and their city.

The first ragtag group of men cum army commanded by Miguel Hidalgo passed through Zacatecas in 1811, looking for funds to continue financing his campaign for independence. Shortly after, he was captured at the battle of Calderon Bridge and executed, bringing an end to the first faltering step on the path to independence.

Gray Line Tours provides good daytrips in and around the city. A couple of worthwhile trips visit Guadalupe and the old viceroyal Ex-Hacienda Bernardez.

An unusual celebration during Holy Week is the bathing of Christ's statue in the center of town and the gathering of the holy water left behind.

¡Música!

April visitors have the opportunity to hear the lovely **Las Mananitas,** played by the Zacatecas city band in the early morning (about 7 a.m.). Music by both young and old begins the day at Parque Alameda. Everyone should stroll through town behind **La Tambora,** a great brass and drum band that leads all to a good time, wandering through narrow streets and parks, stopping for an impromptu dance here and there. It's not unusual for the band to be coaxed into a popular café to play a tune or two. Look for La Tambora at Goitia Square on Friday and Saturday nights. Ask at your hotel for directions, though it's hard to miss because it's *loud,* but fun!

A cable car sails over the city between the two mountains Cerro del Grillo and Cerro de la Bufa every day (except when the wind comes up.) This ride reveals the city landscape from a marvelous perspective. A stop over on Bufa is a must. The small **Capilla del Patrocinio** was built in the 1700s in honor of the Virgin, who frequently gives the locals (present and past) a helping hand with miracles that heal.

Special Events

Moors vs. Christians: During the last two weeks of August, a reenactment of the war between the Moors and Christians is an several-day affair staged near the Bracho hills. The Moors dress in baggy pants, red berets, and carry unusual backpacks full of vegetables and with a baguette poking out. With shotguns in hand they march through the city streets, shooting to make a ruckus. When both the "Christian army" and the "Moorish army" reach the battlefield, the army band plays and the two squads of men go hard at it. On the first day, John of Austria, leading the Christians, is victorious. On the second day, the Great Turk, leader of the Moors, is the conqueror. On the third day, the armies and their leaders reassemble at the battlefield, and the two captains argue violently until the Great Turk turns and flees into the hills. John stalks him, ultimately captures him, and marches him to the Chapel of Bracho. In a great show of gallantry he beheads the infidel, and the war is ended (remember, all pretend). Bullfights and music accompany the historical events.

Feria Nacional de Zacatecas: Held the first two weeks in September, this is one of the finest regional fairs in Mexico. Highlights include eating, drinking, music of all varieties, and of course the bullfight.

Regional Food

This is meat country. If you like a good piece of beef, ask for a good cut, (preferably the filet) *adobado* style. The beef is marinated in a thick sauce made of *chiles anchos, chiles guajillos,* and a lineup of spices, garlic,

Venture outside Zacatecas to the Church and Viceroyalty Museum of Guadalupe.

onions, and tomatoes. After marinating, the beef is grilled, still coated with this tasty sauce. What better accompaniment than tortillas wrapped around each bite? Although flour tortillas are very common in northern Mexico, most Mexicans still think of corn tortillas first. Another favorite is *cabrito* (young goat) prepared the same way, soaked in the great sauce. Often the meat is cooked on top of the stove, simmering in the sauce.

Early in the morning, the *aguamiel* (honey water) man walks his donkey down the street with a couple of large pottery jugs hanging from each side of the animal. Flag him down. He serves (big) paper cups of *aguamiel* to get the morning going. Very sweet, but said to be nourishing.

Special Excursions

Guadalupe

The sprawling **Church and Viceroyalty Museum of Guadalupe** lies 7 km outside Zacatecas. The museum displays many works by artists from the colonial era: La Bufa, Villalpando, Ovalle, Rodriguez Juárez, Juan Correa, Miguel Cabrera, and others. The library is immense, and you'll find a **Transportation Museum** in the section where once the horses were kept and carriages were repaired; also here are a shop and forge. The old convent was the site of the important **Apostolic School of Propaganda Fide**, opened at the end of the 19th century. Wandering through, visitors will see not only its carved baroque façade, but also the lovely choir benches and another outstanding chapel, **Capilla de Nápoles** from the 19th century.

San Luis Potosí

FOR DECADES AFTER CORTÉS CONQUERED TENOCHTITLÁN, the central plains that would one day be San Luis Potosí were still isolated from the rest of the development of Nueva España. This high country was originally occupied by Chichimec Indians, the Guachichiles (which means red-painted, and it is supposed that the people painted their hair red). Missionaries began their evangelization of the Guachachil Indians in 1582 with a small village called Tangamanga. A group of settlers from Tlaxcala was brought in by 1590 to encourage the growth of a peaceful pueblo. (The Tlaxcaltecans had been pacified by Cortés right at the beginning. Over the years until the independence, they were representatives of the Spaniards and were often brought to various parts of Mexico to help acclimate the indigenous people to their new barrios, their new lives.) According to legend, a Guachachil Indian first found silver in the mountains. Although it was a while before the Spaniards discovered a rich vein at Cerro de Pedro (the Hill of Peter), it turned out to be a phenomenally rich silver deposit. It was initially compared to the Potosí mine in Bolivia; hence the name. Because of the lack of water the city was built about 25 km away. The layout was typically Spanish, with the town center the most important area and Indian barrios on the farthest edges. San Luis has seven barrios, and one can only presume that they were laid out in the original plans. Eventually San Pedro was mined out, but by then San Luis Potosí had grown to be an important center in many other successful aspects, including myriad businesses. It was the political center of northern Nueva España, overseeing an area that covered the entire state of today's San Luis Potosí, many outlying mountainous provinces, plus Coahuila, Texas, New Mexico, Nevada, and Louisiana.

When you travel around the old gold and silver mine country, you always hear stories of the tunnels underlying the town centers. They were supposedly built large enough to admit a horseman or a team of mules and a silver train. So it is in San Luis Potosí. Perhaps they were used to escape from robbers, to store precious metals, or even as hiding places for those who did the robbing. Today the tunnels are said to be flooded.

Over the centuries San Luis Potosí has grown in grace and industry—and very protective of its antiquated city center. You get the feeling San Luis likes being a leader, in anything. The city fathers have always encouraged classic culture, and that culture continues to support the development of the fine arts, whether music, dance, sculpture, or concerts and festivals of many genres. A receptive audience of Potosinos will always attend every performance, whether it's in a large theater or a little "off-broadway" bistro.

Exploring the Streets of San Luis Potosí

The **Catedral** stands at the site of the first church and hermitage (1670-1730). When the Potosina Diocese was created in 1854, its naves were enlarged, altars remodeled, and a choir built, though these changes were not finished until 1886. The main façade is baroque, with Solomonic columns and a choir window, flanked by marble sculptures that contrast with the ashlar building material. The structure is framed by two towers, with columns on the upper level. Fine architectural features inside include beautifully crafted vaults and a lovely altar. Also worth a look are the tomb of bishop Ignacio Montes de Oca and beautiful paintings of Juan Patricio Morlete.

the baroque façade of the Catedral

Replacing the old Royal Houses, the **Palacio de Gobierno** was built in the late 18th century by Miguel Constanzo. The neoclassical building occupies an entire block on the west side of Jardín Hidalgo. In 1910 a clock was installed high on the gray stone façade to commemorate the Centennial of the Independence. In 1960, a replica of the Bell of Dolores was installed to celebrate another 50 years. This impressive building is a landmark of Mexican history. President Benito Juárez denied reprieve for Maximilian right here; the Hidalgo Hall exhibits oil portraits of the insurgent leaders. Inside, octagonal domes crown two staircases.

Mid-winter temperatures in San Luis Potosí occasionally drop to a frigid 0 degrees; every 25-30 years it snows.

Construction of the neoclassical **Teatro de la Paz** was begun in 1889, finished in 1894, all under the direction of architect José Noriega. Ten elegant fluted columns, topped by Corinthian capitals, front the façade; it was remodeled in 1949. The theater is an art gallery in itself. Four mural mosaics by Fernando Leal line the walls, and lovely sculptures are placed here and there. The main hall accommodates 1,500 spectators. Of the other two halls, the Flavio F. Carlos Hall is available for concerts and recitals, and the German Gedovius Hall opens for art exhibits. The elegant Greek-style building is lovely inside and out.

Museo de la Máscara (The National Museum of Masks) is housed in another neoclassical mansion, this one built in 1894 as the home of Ramon Marti Pech.

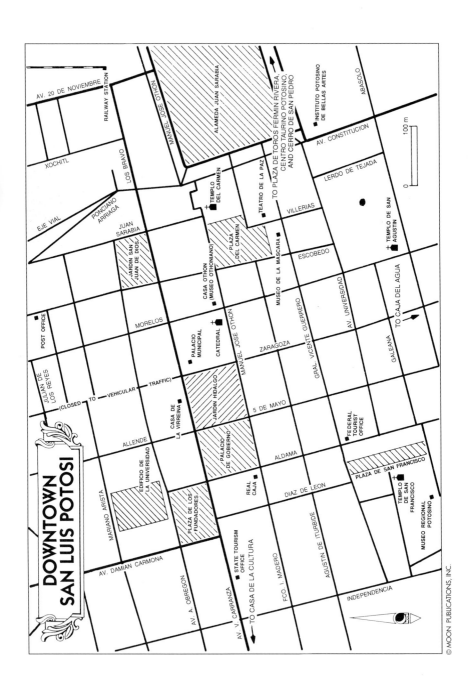

DOWNTOWN SAN LUIS POTOSI

© MOON PUBLICATIONS, INC.

It was used for a while as the Federal Palace. Since 1982 it has been a museum exhibiting a fine collection of more than 2,000 masks, donated by Victor José Moya. The façade that faces **Plaza del Carmen** was built in 1982, when the building was remodeled for its life as a museum. On the inside are a court paved with ashlar slabs, and a lovely staircase and banister. On the aisles note the classical paintings by Italian artists. The artistry of making masks is taught right here, and the history of the various masks is on display.

The **Templo de San Francisco** and the convent were founded in the 16th century. The church displays various styles of the 17th and 18th centuries. In the pink stone façade, graceful columns, reliefs, and sculptures appear;

doorway of the Templo del Carmen

and as one would expect, San Francisco graces the central niche. The church boasts two towers, one topped by a four-arched lantern, and the other crowned by a vault. Inside the designs are mixed and matched in keeping with the trend at the time of each feature's construction. Neoclassical altars have replaced the baroque, but fortunately, the 18th-century woodwork done by imported Italian craftsmen is still on view, along with the old organ and paintings by the colonial artist Antonio de Torres. In the sacristy, note a small metal grate that appears to provide an entrance under the church. Some say this leads to a cemetery; others are convinced it leads to flooded underground tunnels.

An example of colonial civic architecture is the baroque building that at one time housed the Real Caja, the official treasury of the viceroy. Built between 1763 and 1772, its various reincarnations have been as the police station, customs office, an Episcopal palace, a post office, a private home, and now it is part of the university. Bronze gilds its rich façade. Inside more stone carvings appear around doors and windows; the huge carved wooden doors were designed to allow the entrance of the mule trains carrying ore from the mines.

The façade of the Templo de San Francisco is made of pink stone.

A lovely example of Mexican neoclassicism (built in 1827), the **Caja de Agua** (water case), or Conservera, serves as the final depository for water from the Cañada del Lobo Aqueduct. This reservoir and spring, where Potosinos got their water in the 19th century, was declared a national monument in 1953. Since then its unique design has been the city symbol. Made of ashlar, the circular building is decorated by rich carvings. On the upper level sits a garland topped by a beautiful pineapple, or is it a pine cone? No one knows for sure who designed the building, but some attribute it to architect Francisco Eduardo Tresguerras.

The Centro Taurion Potosino houses one of the most complete collections in Mexico of artifacts related to bullfighting.

Today the ex-convent of San Francisco is home to the **Museo Regional Potosino** and the **Capilla de Aranzazu** (Chapel of Aranzazu). Construction of the chapel began in 1749. Art buffs admire the lovely double façade and the mixed arch entrance. Inside are richly decorated dome and vaults, skillful stone and tile work. Note the unusual image of Christ on the exit of the chapel. The lower level, which was part of the convent, is now the Potosino Regional Museum, inaugurated in 1952. On display in one of its halls is a good timeline that shows the development of the Prehispanic cultures—especially the Huasteca—that once occupied the land, along with a fine collection of colonial pieces and handicrafts.

The **Templo del Carmen** was consecrated in 1764; it is considered one of the most ornate examples of baroque art in Mexico. The triple façade displays outstanding craftsmanship in the stonework as well as in the vertical fascia, decorated with flowers and fruits. A small pointed dome supports the double tower. Inside visitors see stone and gilded altarpieces, as well as "the richest and most lavish frontispiece in America." Paintings by Francisco Antonio Vallejo, 18th-century muralist, decorate the walls.

The **Templo de San Agustín** was founded in 1603, and offers a 17th-century façade and an 18th-century nave. Here note some of the more primitive popular sculptures in the façade. The main tower is quite lovely in Mexican baroque style. The interior was remodeled in 1840 and again in 1930.

a Templo de San Agustín tower

The beautiful **Casa de la Cultura** occupies an extraordinary neoclassical building with a fascinating history/legend/myth. Today it sits well back on a lush green lawn, with beautiful sculptures here and there, and displays permanent and temporary shows of archaeological pieces, historical works of art, and arts and crafts.

a Templo del Carmen tower

The history of the lovely building is almost as important as the actual structure. Its story begins in 1400 with a Dutch family named Meiak living in the town of Cork, Ireland. Political intrigue forced the head of the house to change his name to Mead. (A historical footnote recounts that in 1470 one of his descendants fell in love with and wished to marry Ann Boleyn, but —much to her later chagrin—Ann considered Henry VIII a much better catch.) Eventually the family's descendants established themselves in Mexico and became quite wealthy. At this point San Luis Potosí enters the picture, for it was here that one Harold Mead decided to build this lovely home for his young family in the early 1900s. The family's successes continued; they invested in gold mines in Guanajuato (where they built another grand home now converted to the Hotel San Javier), and they founded the Bank of San Luis Potosí, whose original building still stands across the street from the Club la Lonja. The family remained in San Luis Potosí until 1939, when the Hotel Vista Hermosa rented their mansion, remaining until 1961. After 1961 it was only rented out twice—once to Princess Grace Kelly's father.

A school occupied the house until the governor of San Luis bought it with the intention of turning it into an art school; ultimately it was decided to make it the showcase of the present Cultural Museum. Excellent displays of paintings and all manner of life's leftovers tell the story of San Luis Potosí's cultural background. It's said that the Casa, opened in 1967, was the first Cultural Center in Mexico.

> Ⓨ The **Casa de la Verreina** possesses a lovely faux colonial dining room with 18-foot-high ceilings, unusual columns, and a striking five-foot-tall "tree of life" sculpture. The lovely proprietress (for many years) has been Chita Rodriguez Alvarez. If you have a chance, talk to this elegant elderly lady—you'll really feel you've stepped back into another era. The food is delicious, well-prepared, and beautifully served by well-trained waiters. A piano player provides wonderful mood music.

> San Luis Potosí has been called the **City of the Seven Barrios** for its old, traditional neighborhoods.

> The **Casa Othón,** where the poet Manuel José Othón was born and lived, exhibits manuscripts, photographs, period furniture, and other objects owned by the artist.

> Check out the **Centro de Difusion Cultural del Instituto Potosino de Bellas Artes** (Center of Cultural Extension of San Luis Potosí Institute of Fine Arts)—a fine example of contemporary architecture. It contains four exhibition halls, a library, and an auditorium.

San Luis Potosí Highlights

Arts and Artisans

Santa María del Río, 48 km south of San Luis Potosí, is famous for its arts and crafts. Tradition says the silk rebozo originated here, and take a look at the fine inlaid wooden boxes and unique baskets. The rebozo, or shawl, is fine enough to slip through a ring, traditionally a gold wedding ring. At the **Rebozo School and Workshop**, you can watch the shawls being made. These very special shawls, made from fine silk, are sold at the school and at shops as

> Check out the **Centro de Difusion Cultural del Instituto Potosino de Bellas Artes** (Center of Cultural Extension of San Luis Potosí Institute of Fine Arts)—a fine example of contemporary architecture. It contains four exhibition halls, a library, and an auditorium.

well; rebozos here are also made in other, less expensive fabrics. The shawl is a favorite gift, and if the rebozo is not nice enough, buy one of the lovely inlaid boxes of fragrant woods to carry the shawl to its recipient.

¡Música!

Callejoneadas are musical/street tours. Groups of people follow the *estudianti-nas* dressed in 1500s costumes, their satin capes layered with ribbons (apparently pinned on by their special sweethearts—the more ribbons, the more sweeties). These classically trained musicians play both traditional and modern music on fine guitars and strings; often one or two of the musicians breaks into classical traditional dances along the way. Small clay cups hung on red ribbons are placed around your neck to have handy in case the thirst should overtake you, in which case a swish or two of a local pulque drink solves the problem.

Special Events

Semana Santa: This celebration, important in San Luis Potosí, begins the week before Easter on Palm Sunday. On Good Friday, Christ's Passion is presented first in the morning at Barrio de San Juan de Guadalupe. Later in the afternoon the torchlit Procession of Silence passes through the middle of town. Hooded celebrants carry images of saints with hundreds of participants following along, all in a dramatic silence.

Festival de Arte Primavera Potosina: For 10 days in May, usually in the middle of the month, the city comes alive with concerts, folkloric and modern dance, theater productions, and art exhibits. Every plaza and park in the city is filled with music and activity.

Feria Nacional Potosina: At the end of August, the fair kicks off bullfights, *charreadas*, cockfights, and a marathon that attracts people from all over the country.

the Greek-style Teatro de la Paz

Festival de Música y Danza de la Huasteca: October brings still another dance and music fete, held the first two weeks of the month.

Regional Food

Ask any Potosino and he'll recommend the great *enchiladas potosinas*. The difference is in the *masa*. When the tortilla *masa* is mixed the cook adds a special sauce made from red *chiles anchos* and salt. This turns the *masa* pink, and the enchiladas are stuffed with a crumbled *queso fresco*. It's not a super spicy dish, but it's a tasty dish sold on every street corner in the city. Another local favorite is the huge tamal called *zacahuiles*, a Huasteca dish. The *menudo* is a hearty soup, made from the "innards" of beef. This is a favorite of those who have tipped the mescal bottle just a wee bit too much the night before. Mexican soups are a meal by themselves, served with lemon slices and a tall stack of tortillas on the side.

You'll see cactus everywhere when you drive through this mountainous arid landscape. It's no wonder then that it is used in a variety of ways in the cuisine. Probably one of the best ways is in a salad with chopped onions, tomatoes, jicama, oregano, and whatever else sounds good. Of course the prickles are removed from the nopales paddles first. Then the paddles are cut up and lightly steamed (with baking soda); after the cactus cools it's mixed with the rest of the ingredients.

> (¶) For a great Argentine barbecue, ask your hotel to direct you to **La Cabanas Pecos,** a very casual eatery with wood floors and plain wooden tables. The airy, pleasant ambience and great food ensure that the place will always be packed at lunchtime. Steak is brought to the table on a hot grill so you can finish cooking it to your own satisfaction. A featured side dish is (of course) enchiladas Potosí.

> (¶) The **Casa de la Verreina** possesses a lovely faux colonial dining room with 18-foot-high ceilings, unusual columns, and a striking five-foot-tall "tree of life" sculpture. The lovely proprietress (for many years) has been Chita Rodriguez Alvarez. If you have a chance, talk to this elegant elderly lady—you'll really feel you've stepped back into another era. The food is delicious, well-prepared, and beautifully served by well-trained waiters. A piano player provides wonderful mood music.

The Tangamanga Park is an important cultural and recreational center in San Luis Potosí. It covers 822 acres where visitors can enjoy tranquil gardens, sports facilities, playgrounds, two theaters, two lakes, a planetarium, an observatory, and other attractions. Visitors will find the Museo Tangamanga park. At the Hall of Architecture a slide show portrays some of the most important architecture of San Luis Potosí.

The Plaza de Aranzazu sits behind the temple; note the lovely window and the chapel of the same name.

At the end of the Calzada de Guadalupe hulks the State Penitentiary, which once imprisoned the Mexican soldier Francisco I. Madero.

Special Excursions

Villa de Reyes

The several haciendas in Villa de Reyes, south of the city, are pretty well preserved and capture the imagination with their old elegance. According to historians, the **Hacienda de Bledos** belonged to the only known woman viceroy of Nueva España, the Vicereine Doña Francisca de la Gandara, wife of Felix María Calleja del Rey. They say that she ran the hacienda after her husband left to fight the insurgents at the beginning of the War of Independence. The 18th-century church of the hacienda is beautifully preserved in all its baroque glory.

The hacienda **San Pedro Gogorron** was also built at the end of the 16th century. It was built and rebuilt, especially during the Porfiran era, into a palace-like home containing all the touches of Porfirian European luxury, with an elegant church, workplaces for a textile factory, and a hydroelectric plant. At

Nahua Indians inhabited the territory that would become the Villa de Reyes municipality for 2,000 years before they were supplanted by the Chichimecas. The Spanish built a fort in 1570, and in 1872 the town received the official title of Villa de Reyes to honor Don Julian de los Reyes.

Another town worth visiting in the central region is Tierra Nueva, known for water sports and for its traditional Lienzo Charro, where rodeos are staged during holidays.

one time it had 17 wells on the grounds. Today a local attraction nearby appeals to those interested in water recreation or soaking in mineral waters. The warm waters of the **Centro Vacacional Gogorron** bubble from the ground at 42 degrees Celsius for five different pools.

The **Hacienda de la Ventilla**, built in the same period as San Pedro Gogorron, features one of the most beautiful and well-preserved haciendas in the state. The two-story house with its tower and the neoclassic style church are outstanding.

Mexquitic

Twenty-three kilometers from San Luis Potosí, the town of Mexquitic was established before the modern state capital was founded. Franciscan missionaries built its church and convent in the 16th century. The church is dedicated to Archangel Michael and displays a fine wooden likeness of him as well as a baroque altarpiece on the high altar. Nearby, the Alvaro Obregón Dam, where the locals go fishing, is a place to relax and enjoy a little peace and quiet. Just before Mexquitic is the turnoff for the **Desert Sanctuary of Our Lady of Guadalupe**. Built in 1735, it houses a 17th-century painting of the Virgin of Guadalupe. On the 12th of each month, pilgrims come to the isolated sanctuary.

Santa María del Río

Santa María del Río, famous for its arts and crafts and known as the home of the rebozo, sits on the banks of the Santa María River, 48 kilometers south of the capital city. It was founded in 1589 by Franciscans working with Guachichil and Otomi Indians.

The lovely old 18th-century parochial church and the Franciscan monastery, with its antiquated sun clock, are considered Santa María's main architectural attractions. The school-workshop, where rebozos, or shawls, are made, occupies an old house on one side of the square.

In Santa María the biggest celebration of the year is the annual **Feria del Rebozo**, commemorating the feast of the Virgin de la Asunción during the first two weeks of August. On 12 December each year, people from all over Mexico gather for the **Pilgrimage of Birds**. They go to the parochial church of the Virgin de la Asunción with their caged birds and ask the Virgin for her blessing.

The Hill of San Pedro

The original mining company that instigated the settlement of San Luis Potosí dug in here; its gold and silver attracted many treasure hunters, who settled in the valley. But without water a real city could not exist, so the "real" city center for the mine was developed 27 kilometers away. Nowadays, very little of the

"Hill's" splendor is preserved. Early on the wealth of its mine apparently was compared with that of the Peruvian mines called Potosí, hence the name of the city. But the mine, though rich, didn't compare to the Peruvian mines. By 1656, the metals brought up had produced more than 72 million pesos for the Spanish crown. Production at the mine began to slow down in the mid-18th century: it was no longer profitable for the mine owners, it was almost impossible to get supplies, and in 1767 rather violent mutinies erupted. Little is left of the once prosperous mines, but the **Church of San Pedro** and the **Chapel of San Jeronimo** are well worth a look; head northeast from the city and follow the signs.

For sightseers, highlights of the area include the mineshafts of San Pedro, the nearby Hacienda Parroquia, and the 18th-century church of our Lord of San Pedro.

Real de Catorce

It's hard to imagine how many "dry" holes men investigated in the hunt for gold and silver, or the lives they must have led day after day in scorching rocky terrain as they searched these high rugged mountains. In the summer they suffered the arid heat, in the winter icy winds and cold. The lure of gold is mighty powerful.

It's not hard to understand that the master architect of lifestyles for the early inhabitants of Nueva España was precious metal. False starts were many; they split the "haves" and the "have nots"—and the "have nots" often turned into the "haves" with the clink of a pickax. As a result, the finest towns and cities began where mines were successful. However, the "haves" also quickly found themselves on the opposite end of fate's whimsy for a variety of reasons: such was the case with Real de Catorce.

The town was named for *catorce* (14) bandits who continually robbed the *real* (royal) mule trains transporting valuable minerals to the king. A vital, affluent town grew in these isolated mountains where there was nothing, not even the remnants of an Indian society. Life here was as amiable and gracious as any in the country. At its zenith Real de Catorce claimed 30,000 residents living the good life. Today it's an isolated nirvana of craggy peaks, abandoned houses—a real ghost town perched 2,749 meters (9,043 feet) up.

Catorce went through several cycles of success. In 1775 its first silver mines opened. Silver flowed through the streets; life was rich and the town grew. Historians call this period the Epoch of Prosperity. The town's important mines, Descubridora, Purísima, Guadalupe, Dolores, Zavala, Refugio, and San Agustín, all produced healthy quantities of silver during the last 25-30 years of the 18th century.

In the 1800s technical advances brought changes: pumps to drain flooded mines, electricity to light mine shafts (albeit bare light bulbs), and in 1901, miners blasted Tunel de Ogarrio through 2.5 km of stone. The tunnel provided quicker transport for mules pulling silver trains. Not too much later tracks were installed and electric trams ran through the tunnel, making delivery quicker and bringing even greater prosperity. The metal had to be taken to the railroad station in Potrero, and from there to the smelters in Cedral and elsewhere. For residents the tram meant a much improved and quicker trip to the other side of the immense mountain. In 1981-1982, the tunnel was paved and expanded to hold one vehicle. A man on each end (with a walkie talkie) directs traffic. At the tunnel stands the small chapel of Our Lady of "Pain" in honor of those who died in the mines. Today flowers and candles represent prayers for safety and well-being in the small town.

> The **Abundancia Hotel** occupies a charming little mid-19th century building that was once the city mint. Burnished wooden floors and creaky old wooden steps lead to bedrooms. The hotel defines simplicity, but it's clean as can be and filled with historical charm. The hotel serves meals, and the proprietors are a young married couple; she's Mexican and he's Swiss. Inexpensive.

At the peak of Catorce's success, the "beautiful people" created their own little world in the top of these mountains. They lived in well-built homes with extravagant furniture covered in linens, silks, laces, and velvets—where you'd have expected cowboy bunks. The well-dressed men and women gathered at lovely plazas and a theater. It was commonplace for high fashion (by way of catalogs) to be imported from France, Spain, Germany, and Italy. Well-educated men and women, counts and marqueses representing the King of Spain lived here; after all, the king received his cut of the silver even from this remote part of the world and somebody had to look out for his interests. The town built a bull ring and brought in the most famous matadors and the best bulls. A fancy *palenque* (for cockfights) was always filled by popular demand. Bands and choirs entertained at every event.

Three newspapers operated and managed to fill their pages with news and gossip. And in the 1800s several small businesses actually minted coins. This rich society thrived until the beginning of the War of Independence. From the time of Hidalgo's *grito* in 1811, until the Spanish crown was ousted in 1825, the town's economy stumbled and halted. Suddenly the built-in market was gone, and the price of silver dropped to rock bottom. The Spanish overseers and efficient business managers left. Laborers were without jobs; Catorce had become a city of the "have nots."

Life was unsettled for years after independence. The mines and equipment needed repair—which took money. But then the Spanish de la Maza family arrived. With an infusion of big money, the Mazas rejuvenated mining in Catorce. They began the successful Santa Ana mines and continued to find quantities of silver. In 1863 Count Santos de la Maza bought a piece of land and with the blessings of then-president of Mexico, Benito Juárez, built Casa de Moneda (the mint), a three-story structure across from the parish church. Here the metals were brought in and either stored in the basement or melted and formed into silver bars or coins. This was a proud occupation for the small town. But it was short-lived; the newly imported Austrian emperor Maximilian ordered the mint closed.

Despite the closure of the mint, the Santa Ana mines were successful for years. The mines in and around Catorce were the most prosperous mines in San Luis Potosí, and one of the largest silver mining areas in Nueva España. As the mines made improvements that would increase the production of silver, the city grew and spread across the mountaintops. It became known all over Mexico; even President Porfirio Díaz visited. The trip meant traveling by train from Mexico City to Potrero and from there by mule-pulled wagons to Maza's Santa Ana mine and hacienda outside of town. Díaz thrilled the people with a visit to the town by horseback, and they honored him with a huge fiesta.

But another decline began in the early years of the 20th century. The Maza family grew old, smelting methods changed, and more adequate roads were needed. And when "political unrest" became the Mexican Revolution, the exodus of managers, tradesmen—and money—was significant. From a city of thousands, Catorce dwindled; this time it really *was* a ghost town.

About 1918, Real de Catorce experienced a different kind of renaissance. Talk of miracles in the church began to reach the outside world. Religious pilgrims began arriving in the remote town to pay homage to St. Francis of Assisi. Legends of St. Francis were rife. The people came to see and pray to the saint, especially on 4 October, the feast of St. Francis. On weekends the town center was hopping with visitors, many believing the saint could and would perform miracles. People from all over Mexico and abroad continue to come, though this weeklong celebration little affects the decay of 90% of the city. The rest of the year the town is pretty quiet, though the European (mostly Swiss) community is growing; they've taken a keen interest in the mountain ghost town.

Real de Catorce also attracts pilgrims of a different kind. For many years the Huichol Indians have made their annual pilgrimage here from Nayarit, Durango, Zacatecas, and Jalisco on foot to collect the hallucinogenic peyote cactus for their religious rites. On foot it takes more than a month; today they still make the trip and collect peyote, but by car or truck.

Exploring the Streets of Real de Catorce

Real de Catorce is a grand place to explore even though the steep cobblestone roads in some areas are almost vertical. The town possesses the charm of age and an amazing history involving the mystique of precious metal. Several small restaurants have opened in various antiquated structures; the wood floors creak and the rooms are tiny. Remnants of the bullring and cock ring are still in place.

The old **Casa de Moneda**, also remembered as Casa Maza, is now a delightful little hotel, complete with the wrought-iron door built to allow only a hand and a sack to pass back and forth. In winter a fireplace still warms the old three-story building—and its resident ghost. People describe hearing the sounds of currency and silver bars being shuffled and moved; the old don Señor Maza himself is said to be taking care of his mint.

The **Church of the Immaculate Conception**, dating from 1780, was built with the pesos of the miners. A Spanish custom allowed the miners each day to take one piece of "mineral" (gold or silver) as large as they could carry to give to the parish priest. Eventually the miners presented the priest 1.8 million pesos. Notice the wood floor of mesquite. It is said to be from the original construction, not a common find. The church is kept up very nicely when compared with many of the surrounding buildings. Many humble *retablos* line the walls—locks of hair, *milagros*, small hand-made paintings—mostly in thanks for favors received.

Real de Catorce Highlights

Thousands of pilgrims gather in the streets for the celebration of the feast day of St. Francis of Assisi on 4 October every year. The celebration lasts for a week, with music, processions, and Chichimeca Indian dances.

the crooked streets of Real de Catorce

Collectors of all kinds have found Catorce virgin territory. Rock hounds and gem collectors are discovering untouched turf. Shuffling through tailings in the mining areas titillates the imagination of would-be treasure hunters (complete with metal detectors). The city never had a real bank; some visitors have found coins (for sale), and locals whet appetites telling tales of bandits and early residents who would bury their valuables: gold, silver, coins, jewelry, and who knows what else.

It's common to see vendors selling the fine antique wrought-iron locks and keys that were designed for the thick wood doors of the colonial days. These pieces are displayed as works of rugged art. Other vendors sell great and not-so-great silver objects. Several outdoor stands across the narrow

The Spent Shoes of St. Francis

The earliest story tells of St. Francis appearing to a peasant, and after praying, he promised great wealth to the town. The first church of Catorce, the tiny **Chapel of Guadalupe**, is where the entire town paid homage to the image of St. Francis. Legend recounts that when the new church was built, many people forgot the old chapel—and St. Francis, and that he missed the noise and cameraderie of the people—so much so that his shoes were worn thin from sneaking over to the big new church to watch the activities. When the people noticed his shoes, they moved the saint's image to the place of honor in the new Church of the Immaculate Conception.

road from the church sell religious publications and other items. And if the word *antique* makes you salivate, you'll find many intriguing bits of furniture, kitchen utensils, brass, glass, old paintings, saddles, spurs that date back to the Spanish era, and just plain old junk for sale.

Perhaps the most avid "collector" is the artist or the photographer. Every day the panorama changes, a new set of clouds filters the sun, highlighting an odd turn of the arch, half decayed carvings, and unnoticed crevices, the wind rearranges, or the tall cactus on the hill sprouts one single bloom of brilliant color against a beige backdrop.

The Church of the Immaculate Conception in Real de Catorce replaced the old Chapel of Guadalupe dedicated to St. Francis.

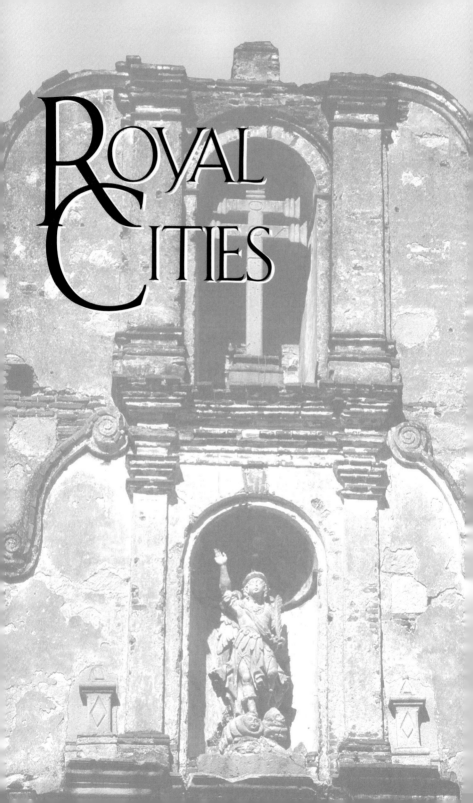

ROYAL CITIES

After five centuries of rule by the Moors, Spain regained control of its lands. Quickly its jurisdiction spread around the world and by the close of the 15th century, Spain had established itself as the colonial power in the Americas. That power was shared by the king and the Catholic church. It followed, then, that the king would send his important subjects to administer the country, to keep the king's thumb on the pulse of the new land, and to ensure the progress of the search for gold and the spread of Christianity. Universities were built to educate the sons of the rich *peninsulares* so far from home. The cities grew under the leadership of the most diligent bishops and viceroyals. Civic and religious construction was the finest, a Spanish legacy enjoyed today. Artistic elegance was important, and the royal cities were beautifully planned following the new modern thinking of the Renaissance. Built to last, most of the public buildings have been renovated to their original gloss and belong to the people. These once-royal cities are sophisticated, successful cities; modern life thrives with high-tech additions, but the "old" is continually polished and maintained and remembered.

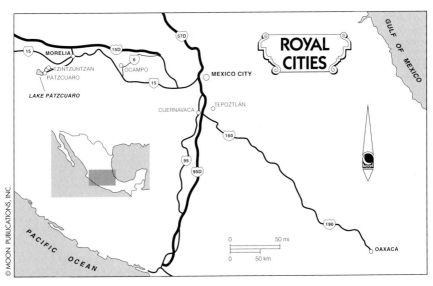

Cuernavaca

CUAUHNAHUAC (PLACE OF GREAT TREES) WAS A LOVELY WOODED AREA that has attracted the "rich and those who have become famous" for centuries. The Tlahuicas and Aztecs established religious sites and hunting grounds for the pleasure of their leaders long before the building of the Augustinian, Franciscan, and Dominican monasteries. Apparently it was the original getaway city, even for the Aztecs, and a favorite of Cortés, even before his final assault on Tenochtitlán. After that success, he torched Cuauhnahuac in 1521 and renamed the ruins Cuernavaca, a collection of letters easier on the Iberian tongue though with a much uglier meaning, horn of the cow.

People who became intrigued with Cuernavaca after reading Malcolm Lowry's *Under the Volcano* should know the city has changed quite a bit since his sad days there.

Emiliano Zapata raised his voice to save the "little" farmers who after the war of independence were losing their land to rich landowners an acre at a time. During the Mexican Revolution of 1910, he incited the farmers to fight for their property. His heartfelt war cry was *"Tierra y Libertad"*—"Land and Liberty." The modern-day Zapatistas in Chiapas continue to pursue their namesake's ideals.

Cuernavaca was a gift to Cortés from Charles V, a fief to do with as he wished. The first thing he did was to build directly over the ruins of an Aztec pyramid; his fortress-home, finished in 1531, was a castle by anyone's description. Cortés, who had learned about sugarcane in Cuba, introduced it in Cuernavaca. His sugar hacienda at the edge of town, now the Hacienda de Cortés, was the site of frequent unrest. The Indians were unfamiliar with sugarcane and unwilling to work with it; as a result, Cortés had to bring in Caribbean slaves.

Many years later, the state of Morelos provided several key insurgents in the War of Independence; after a century more, the region was a seat of revolution, popular with the likes of Emiliano Zapata and his Zapatistas. The ill-fated Emperor Maximilian and his wife, Carlota, both found *romance* and a "royal" aura in this getaway city. Some of the biggest names in government have built luxury villas here throughout the years, using Cuernavaca as a temporary escape from the consequences of their political machinations; today dozens of Mexico's wealthiest families maintain second homes in Cuernavaca.

In the 18th century Cuernavaca was a day away from Mexico City by horse and buggy; today it's an easy one-hour drive on a modern highway. The weather is a happy medium between the cold highlands and the sultry tropics, and the city is forever famous for flowers that seem to bloom year-round. The city streets, however, were not designed for modern autos. When the air is clear (the city gets its share of smog) the great volcano Popocatépetl, 24 km away, dominates the landscape; lately it has been making the *chilangos* (Mexico City visitors) nervous, belching large puffs of steam, rocks, and ash.

Cuernavaca contains at least 20 language schools. Students studying Spanish fill the city; most are from the U.S. Mexican families open their homes to these students, providing an environment where only Spanish is spoken.

Exploring the Streets of Cuernavaca

Plaza de Armas is the larger of the two plazas that make up the center of town. It comes alive in spring with flame-colored blossoms on flowering trees. Continuously abustle with locals and visitors enjoying the outdoors, its benches are always occupied and balloons in bunches float high. The **Jardín Juárez** is the garden next to the Plaza de Armas sporting a charming little kiosk designed by Frenchman Eiffel of Paris Tower fame. Birds chatter in the trees over shady benches. Tables are coveted for a coffee or a snack.

The rugged **Palacio Municipal**, on the south side of Jardín Borda at the corner of Av. Morelos and Callejon Borda, dates from 1883. Discover its central courtyard, and first and second floors; the paintings portray how the Tlahuica Indians made cloth from *maguey* and wove feather mosaics. Also here are rare representations of Aztec goldsmiths. The Palacio is open Mon.-Friday.

The **Jardín Borda**, on Morelos at Hidalgo near the Palacio Municipal, was built in the mid-1700s as the opulent holiday home of José de la Borda, mining entrepreneur of Taxco silver. In 1866 it served as the summer residence of Emperor Maximilian and his wife, Carlota. The "royals" spent the treasury's money to renovate the aged structure, transforming it into a beautiful home and garden, and they took great pleasure in entertaining aristocratic friends. Here Maximilian and his lover, the gardener's wife, conceived a son, the emperor's only known child. After Maximilian's execution the house again began to decay. But in 1987, the gardens, lakes, and kiosks were totally renovated once again, and today it's a popular locale to wander, rent a rowboat,

A wealthy miner built the Jardín Borda in the mid-1700s.

inside the Jardín Borda

attend a lakeside show, feed the ducks, or have a picnic. Paintings reflect the turbulence surrounding Maximilian and his era. Changing art is exhibited in the entrance of the building.

The **Catedral de la Asunción**, at the corner of Hidalgo and Morelos opposite the Jardín Borda and the Palacio, is one of the city's oldest churches; it was begun under Cortés in 1526. One comes away with two startling memories: the skull and crossbones over the main entrance, and the Japanese-style painting depicting the persecution of Christians in Japan. No one seems to know for sure why or who the artist was; it wasn't even discovered until a renovation of the building in the 1960s. The construction typifies the early Franciscan fortress-churches of Mexico; in those early days personal safety was at least as important as universal salvation. And certainly the skull and crossbones gives the aura of something dark and sinister. For something a little different, attend the mariachi mass at the cathedral that begins at 11 am.

Museo Casa de la Torre, Calle Netzahualcoyotl 4, tel. (73) 18-8554, formerly known as the Robert Brady museum, is in the former cloister of the Catedral de Cuernavaca. Brady lived in this wonderful Mexican atmosphere, and today his collection of many years is shown against the eclectic backdrop of a tile kitchen, arched corridors, planted gardens, and old chandeliers. The works of Frida Kahlo and Rufino Tamayo are represented here, along with those of many other well-known artists. Brady collected art from all over the world and displayed it here along with crafts from numerous countries. He lived here until his death in 1986. The museum offers a special service for visitors who speak no Spanish; call to make reservations for a French- or English-speaking guide, included in the price of admission. Spanish guides are available without special notice. The museum is open Thursday, Friday, and Saturday, or make reservations to visit the museum on alternate days.

Dwight Morrow served as the U.S. Ambassador to Mexico 1927-1930. During his term as emissary, besides restoring good relations between the United States and Mexico after the brutal revolution, Morrow promoted the rising interest in Mexican arts and crafts. The gossip columnists in Mexican newspapers made sure everyone knew that his daughter, Anne, was often accompanied by pilot Charles Lindbergh.

The **Museo de Cuauhnahuac/Palacio de Cortés**, on the southeast end of the Plaza de Armas, was built in the rugged fortress-like style of someone interested in protection as much as a comfortable home. Cortés began the structure in 1522 and lived in the palace for several years before returning to Spain in 1540. He never returned. The building was held by the Cortés family for the rest of the century; later it was used as a prison and served as the seat of the Morelos State Legislature. When the

CUERNAVACA

politicians moved to newer quarters, it was converted to a museum. The antiquated building really shows all of its centuries, but it is still a magical place to contemplate the history of the man who built it and walked its chilly corridors. The Diego Rivera mural on the second floor, tracing the history of Cuernavaca from the Spanish onslaught to the 20th century, is a powerful exhibit. Theme: Human barbarism in the name of profit and religion. This mural, one of Rivera's best, was commissioned by U.S. Ambassador Dwight Morrow in the 1920s. Wandering the salons visitors find displays of colonial artifacts, including carriages, furniture, farm implements, and a suit of armor. Artifacts of the Tlahuica are placed about, and if you look around on the ground floor you can see traces of the old walls of the Aztec pyramid Cortés razed. Little stalls sell odds and ends on the bridge to the side of the castle. The most popular is the

The Church Murals, Catedral de la Asunción

In October, 1596, a rich Spanish merchant seaman, sailing from Manila bound for Acapulco, was blown off course by a typhoon and forced to take refuge in a Japanese port. On board was a Mexican Franciscan, Brother Philip of Jesus. Seized by suspicious warlords, he was sent with 25 other local friars on a harrowing winter march to the court of the Emperor Hideyoshi. Interrogated and condemned as spies and heretics, the friars were taken to a hill outside Nagasaki to suffer the agony of crucifixion. Transfixed by a spear, Philip quickly succumbed. He became a celebrated martyr and the first Mexican-born saint, thereafter revered as San Felipe de Jesús.

In the 1950s, as workmen stripped the centuries of accumulated church furnishings from the cathedral to prepare for its renovation, fresco fragments suddenly came to light beneath layers of dirt and whitewash. As the work proceeded, the scale and extent of the murals astounded the excited researchers. The discovery caused a sensation, creating almost overnight a national shrine to San Felipe.

Painted in the early 1600s—perhaps to commemorate the beatification of Philip in 1627—these magnificent murals retell the story of the twenty-six Japanese Martyrs in grisly detail. These narrative frescoes are among the most ambitious, most complete, and most original cycles of murals painted in colonial Mexico. They are also among the last, since by this date, altarpieces were replacing murals as the preferred medium for church embellishment.

Originally covering the entire length of the nave, 75 feet long by 25 feet high, the murals were painted by an unknown artist in vivid blues, greens and warm earth colors—a far richer spectrum than the monochromatic murals in the *convento*.

corn-man, who sells hot corn especially popular with the locals and American language students.

Another name for **Museo de la Herbolaría/La Casa del Olvido**, at Calle Matamoros 200 about 1.5 kilometers southeast of the town center, is Casa Maximiliano. It's also known as the "House of Forgetfulness," for here Maximilian forgot for a time his unhappy marriage to Carlota, consorting with Margarita Lefuisamo Sedano,

If driving to Cuernavaca from Tepoztlán (21 km), stop by the cemetery of **La Transfiguracíon del Señor** church and view the colorfully painted small monuments on the graves. The church itself is elegant and baroque.

the gardener's wife. Others say the name came from the fact that Maximilian "forgot" to build a room for his addled wife, though he did manage to construct a suite for his lover. Today the house is a fine little museum devoted to Indian folk medicine. The botanical garden contains a multitude of traditional herbs and curatives used then and now by the locals. Open daily.

The striking compositions show a pronounced Japanese influence. The figures exhibit a flatness, strength of line and authentic costuming that suggest an oriental-trained artist, possibly even an eye-witness to the events portrayed.

Schools of fanciful sea creatures swim among the boats and around the arches of the doorway, lightening the grim imagery of the narrative scenes. These decorative details are certainly the work of a native artist, and would not be out of place in the pages of a prehispanic codex.

The dramatic circumstances leading to San Felipe's untimely end unfold on the walls in vivid detail. We see his arrival on the shores of Japan, the journey by boat and cart to the place of execution, and finally his crucifixion. The graphic source for this cycle of murals may have been the illustrated chronicle *Evangelization of the Philippines and Japan*, published shortly after the event.

But why should the story of San Felipe have been told here in Cuernavaca? By the end of the 16th century, the spiritual conquest of Mexico had been accomplished. The friars then turned their attention to more distant lands. The teeming islands of Asia and the recently explored Philippines presented new evangelical challenges.

The rambling monastery at Cuernavaca became the colonial gateway to the orient, the last staging post between Mexico City and the port of Acapulco. Here the friars prepared for the arduous missionary task, from which some would not return, including perhaps Philip himself. For the Franciscans, Philip of Jesus personified this spirit of selfless sacrifice, whose greatest reward was the martyr's crown.

The venerable stone baptismal font is the oldest remaining artifact of the early Franciscan era in the church and is now installed beneath the choir, in a sunken marble patio. A primitive Gothic wheel vault spans the choir arch above, at whose hub is a quaint relief of Our Lady of the Angels.

—RICHARD PERRY, *Mexico's Fortress Monasteries*

El Castillito (The Little Castle), on Calle Prof. Agustín Guemes no. 1, is the city's photographic museum. Displays include some old interesting photos of historic Cuernavaca. Open daily.

Teopanzolco Archaeological Site in today's Col. Vista Hermosa neighborhood, was built first by the Tlahuicas between 1200-1500, and then the Aztecs added a pyramid around the old one. The earth-covered pyramid was used during the Mexican revolution as a cannon installation. Archaeologists first excavated the site in 1922, and then again in 1957. Human remains have been found nearby. Open daily.

(🍴) For the zany, **Harry's**, at Gutenberg 3, is a wild stop for wild fun. Tell the truth—have you ever *really* seen someone dancing on tables? You might at Harry's. This is a popular Friday spot where people have a good time.

(🍴) Easy and low-key, both **La Parroquia** and **Los Arcos** are favorite stops to sip coffee or drinks at outside tables on the Jardín Juárez.

Modern-Day Diversions
Jungla Magica was formerly named Chapultepec Park and had a zoo and a lake, but it has been magically transformed into a children's theme park. Both young and old seem to delight in the dolphins and a tropical bird show. This is a large park with boating and picnicking.

Cuernavaca is a student city as well as a getaway place for *chilangos*, so the city is filled with diversions. The **Teatro de la Ciudad** (Morelos and Rayon), the **Teatro Ocampo** (*zócalo*), and **Jardín Borda** occasionally offer a major artist in symphony. Watch for posters around town, or ask at the tourist office.

Cuernavaca Highlights

For the Shopper
On Sunday and Wednesday, the market is active at the square in front of the old Dominican Church at Tepoztlán. Locals from small villages in the surrounding hills and valleys come to take part.

¡Música!
Cuernavaca is a city filled with expat students, mostly Americans. So it shouldn't be a shock to anyone that the most popular music is rock. Discos, though not particularly popular in the States, take on a new attraction in Mexico. But it's mostly the low-key places that attract the kids. Traditional concerts on the plaza take place Thursday and Sunday nights.

Special Events
Fiesta for Ometochli/Festival of the Virgin: Every September a festival begins on the eve of the 7th and lasts into the evening of the 8th. Again, one must choose which story he prefers. On the one hand, it is called the fiesta for

Ometochli, the pulque god, but on the other hand it is the festival of the Virgin, Altepehuital. This is an impressive fiesta with an enactment of the baptism of the old king, Tepoztecatl, a *faux* battle between the Moors and Christians, and Indian dancers in fascinating costumes. Spectacular fireworks light up the night sky and the mountains reflect the shadows of time. No doubt, there are those who are paying excessive tribute to the old god of pulque, because lots of it is consumed during this festival.

Special Excursions

Tepotzlán

Though only 20 km away from Cuernavaca, this small, once ignored village sits in the most beautiful spot available, perched in a tiny valley amidst tall craggy mountains with the clearest air in the country. During pre-Hispanic times, the village was the sanctum of Ometochli, god of pulque. In 1538, the Dominicans decided the people should do away with their drunken carousal during celebrations. The monks brazenly knocked over the stone idol and here the story gets twisted. According to one historian, the idol wouldn't break, defying the religious men. Another legend tells that it did indeed break into many

Hacienda de Cortés, Plaza Kennedy, tel. 15-8844, offers 22 suites, a pool, gardens, a grand restaurant, and an awesome history. Originally built by Cortés to raise sugarcane, it has suffered through many reincarnations. All but destroyed in Mexico's revolution, it has been rebuilt as a charming hotel. Expensive.

Hacienda Cocoyoc, near Oaxcapec, tel. (73) 56-2211, fax 56-1212, is an ex-hacienda that has been converted to an elegant hotel. The original hacienda rooms are decorated in a style befitting their history. The food is good, the service is great, and the gardens are most relaxing. The hotel is out of town, but the on-site golf course, swimming pool, and horseback riding keep guests well occupied. Luxury.

A favorite in the luxury class, **Camino Real Sumiya,** just outside of town, offers a little bit of Japan deep in the mountains of Mexico. The heart of this hotel came from Japan years ago, carried across the ocean in pieces under the direction of heiress Barbara Hutton. The original structure contains her outstanding art collection. Add to all of this a pool and a beautiful kabuki theater for special presentations. The new section of the hotel has been built around and in the same tone as the center. The hotel offers 163 rooms and seven suites looking onto acres of oriental gardens and walking paths. The backdrop: twin snowcapped mountains. It's so like Japan, you can almost smell the cherry blossoms.

Along with the usual luxury amenities, business people will enjoy the high-tech support for computer systems. When dining in the signature restaurant you'll find an international menu highlighted by fine Japanese cuisine. For reservations and information, call (800) 7-CAMINO (from the U.S. and Canada). Premium.

Las Mañanitas, Ricardo Linares 107, tel. 14-1466/12-4646, fax 18-3672, is known as one of the best hotels in Mexico. The ambience exudes luxury, with well-appointed standard rooms or suites. The surrounding grounds include verdant lawns, resident peacocks, an elegant swimming pool, intimate terraces, and all the service you can stand. The hotel contains only 22 rooms, so be sure to make reservations. Restaurant and bar, valet parking, no credit cards. Premium to Luxury.

pieces that were hauled victoriously away by the friars, who used them to build a couple of Dominican churches. Regardless, the Dominicans were successful in their efforts to convert the old king Tepoztecatl, and the rest of his followers—followed.

🍴 A pleasant place to dine is **Restaurant La India Bonita,** Morrow #106B, the former home of Ambassador Dwight Morrow, father of Anne Morrow Lindbergh. Morrow lived in the house 1927-1930, and it has been completely renovated and divided into charming dining areas, including the portals and patios. Best of all, it serves excellent regional food. Moderate. Closed Monday.

To get to the archaeological zone around nearby **Tepozteco Pyramid,** you must journey north to the mountains that rise above town. The Tlahuicas used the site as an observatory, and it honored Ometochli, the Aztec god of "pulque or much." From the town it's about three kilometers to the top; experts say an hour and half should get you there. It's a steep climb along a narrow trail that becomes steps part of the way. Wear comfortable shoes, and expect to be on the trek for a good part of the morning or afternoon. The views are stupendous, especially on a clear day.

The old Dominican church and convent in the town were built in 1550, and judging from the remnants, it must have been a magnificent structure in its day. On the northwest corner of the upper level, artist/author Richard Perry points out the friars' "john," complete with a flushing system that released safely beyond the monastery wall. Today part of the church is a museum with a collection of archaeological artifacts.

During the Revolution, the Zapatistas found the small village to be an isolated hideout. Today paved roads bring in many more people than in the past, so who knows how long it will be able to maintain its reputation. Already a few luxurious hotels have established new "hideouts" for the more peaceful getaway. Folks still come on Sunday and Wednesday for the market day on the *zócalo.*

Oaxaca

BY THE TIME CORTÉS ARRIVED IN THE MOUNTAIN VALLEY OF OAXACA, the Aztecs had subjugated the Zapotecs and the Mixtecs. The Zapotecs were the builders of the dramatic pre-Hispanic sites of Monte Albán, Yagul, Mogote, and San José. By AD 800, this group and others in the valley were constantly at war, their civilization began to decline, and they were taken over by the Mixtecs. The Mixtecs also were artists; they created flamboyant jewelry made of copper, amber, and jade; they added color to pottery; and they introduced intricate metalwork. Mixtec daughters married the royal descendants of the Zapotecs, but still the two ethnic groups never quite "merged." Their feuds opened the door that allowed the hovering Aztecs into Oaxaca. Despite the strangulating power of the Aztecs and then the arrival of the Spaniards, the Mixtec and Zapotec have survived. They split up into hundreds of independent village-states and have kept their ancient traditions alive for more than 450 years.

With a choice of all the lands in Mexico, Cortés chose the Oaxaca Valley for himself, and the King of Spain gave him the title Marqués de Valle de Oaxaca. The Spanish systematically baptized the indigenous, promising salvation and a better life. They built churches, convents, Royal Houses, civic buildings, and plazas. Today's Oaxaca city is a blend of elegant Spanish architecture and rich art of the indigenous; added into the "mix" is the culture of many *foreign* artists who have been attracted to Oaxaca from other cities and countries. You can't help but perceive this special spirit, whether you're studying local art, sitting on a park bench under an ancient laurel tree listening to a live Mozart concert, or strolling in the shadow of historic regal structures. Maybe most important of all, this "mix" has inspired Oaxaca as the great art center of Mexico.

Dominican priests and nuns probably comprised the most prominent evangelical force that spread the gospel in this part of the country. Their churches are typically the richest, holding artwork from some of the finest artists.

For the traveler looking for still-thriving indigenous cultures, Oaxaca is second only to San Cristóbal de las Casas. Pocket-villages south of the city stagger weekly market days, making it easy to inspect all of the small villages and their artistic offerings. As the old padres planned, most villages specialize in one craft. Oaxaca's 16 ethnic groups speak numerous languages or variations of dialects. They all come to Oaxaca city on market day, a time of gossip, giggling, and (according to D.H. Lawrence) a time of communion.

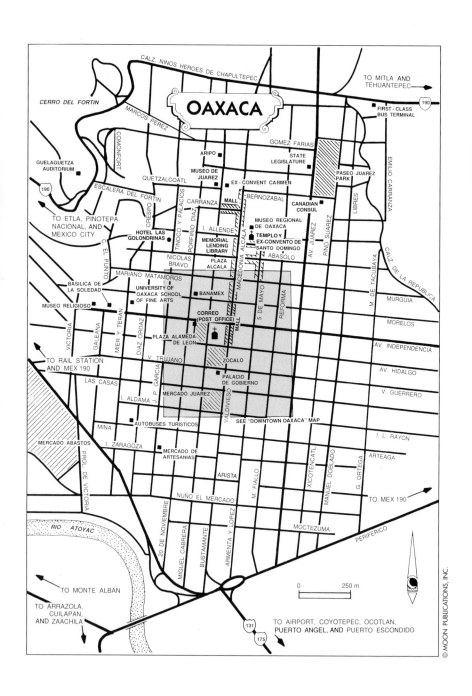

OAXACA

CALZ. NINOS HEROES DE CHAPULTEPEC

TO MITLA AND
TEHUANTEPEC

CERRO DEL FORTIN

MARCOS PEREZ

190

FIRST - CLASS
BUS TERMINAL

GOMEZ FARIAS

COMONFORT

ARIPO

STATE
LEGISLATURE

GUELAGUETZA
AUDITORIUM

QUETZALCOATL

MUSEO DE
JUAREZ

EX - CONVENT CARMEN

PASEO JUAREZ
PARK

EMILIO CARRANZA

190

ESCALERA DEL FORTIN

CARRANZA

MALL

BERNOZABAL

CANADIAN
CONSUL

LIBRES

TO ETLA, PINOTEPA
NACIONAL, AND
MEXICO CITY

CRESPO

TINOCO Y PALACIOS

PORFIRIO DIAZ

I. ALLENDE

MUSEO REGIONAL
DE OAXACA

AV. JUAREZ

PINO SUAREZ

HOTEL LAS
GOLONDRINAS

MEMORIAL
LENDING
LIBRARY

MACEDONIA ALCALA

TEMPLO Y
EX-CONVENTO DE
SANTO DOMINGO

NICOLAS
BRAVO

PLAZA
ALCALA

ABASOLO

C. EL PUNTO

MARIANO MATAMOROS

CALZ DE LA REPUBLICA

BASILICA DE
LA SOLEDAD

UNIVERSITY OF
OAXACA SCHOOL
OF FINE ARTS

BANAMEX

5 DE MAYO

REFORMA

M. DE TACUBAYA

MURGUIA

MUSEO RELIGIOSO

VICTORIA

GALEANA

MIER Y TERAN

DIAZ ORDAZ

CORREO
(POST
OFFICE)

MALL

MORELOS

AV. INDEPENDENCIA

PLAZA ALAMEDA
DE LEON

TO RAIL STATION
AND MEX 190

V. TRUJANO

J. P. GARCIA

ZOCALO

AV. HIDALGO

LAS CASAS

PALACIO
DE GOBIERNO

V. GUERRERO

I. ALDAMA

MERCADO JUAREZ

VALDIVIESO

MINA

AUTOBUSES TURISTICOS

SEE "DOWNTOWN OAXACA" MAP

I. L. RAYON

MERCADO ABASTOS

I. ZARAGOZA

MERCADO DE
ARTESANIAS

ARTEAGA

PROL. DE VICTORIA

ARISTA

M. FIALLO

XICOTENCATL

MANUEL DOBLADO

G. ORTEGA

TO MEX 190

NUÑO EL MERCADO

20 DE NOVIEMBRE

MIGUEL CABRERA

BUSTAMANTE

ARMENTA Y LOPEZ

MOCTEZUMA

RIO ATOYAC

PERIFERICO

0   250 m

TO MONTE ALBAN

TO ARRAZOLA,
CUILAPAN,
AND ZAACHILA

131

175

TO AIRPORT, COYOTEPEC, OCOTLAN,
PUERTO ANGEL, AND PUERTO ESCONDIDO

© MOON PUBLICATIONS, INC.

Once-private and royal residences, churches, and ex-convents are today libraries, business offices, schools, shops, and more recently hotels. Today's Oaxaca, among other things, is the capital of the state, a university city, and a center for foreigners to study Spanish language in several fine schools. Excellent libraries serve the needs of both expats and Mexicans. Museums abound, civil and religious architecture surpasses all expectations, and the city graphically shows respect to Benito Juárez, Porfirio Díaz, and other native sons who made good. Lest we forget, the city is alive with music, gracious plazas, trees, blossoms, and cozy sidewalk cafés.

Oaxaca state contains the most diverse ethnicity in the entire Mexican Republic. Most of the state's three million inhabitants do not speak Spanish as a first language: the population includes 16 distinct ethnic groups, dozens of dialects, and 480 types of traditional costume. That's rather amazing for an area of 94,276 square kilometers (36,400 square miles). Even more remarkable, *most* of them come together at the yearly Guelaguetza dance celebration in July.

Exploring the Streets of Oaxaca

The city was laid out by Alonso García Bravo, who had designed the reconstruction of Mexico City. His design included perpendicular streets radiating from a large central square. Recent engineers have closed off several streets to vehicular traffic, creating a tranquil getaway from the bustle of modern-day traffic. Oaxaca is a comfortable walk-about city with the most historic attractions neatly planned around the **Plaza de Armas**, also called Plaza Principal. In Mexican cities all roads lead to the plazas; this is especially true of Oaxaca.

Early morning coffee at plaza sidewalk cafés is a fine way to start the day. If you're really early, you'll catch a glimpse of the shoeshine men wheeling their blue "packages" to the plaza. Everything folds up—customer's seat, shiner's seat, polishes hidden in separated compartments—all into a neat square package of shiny chrome, enveloped in a fitted blue plastic slipcover, ready to be tipped and rolled on two wheels in and out of the plaza, to and from home: no car or truck needed, thank you. This is one of the great customs on plazas of Mexico, especially popular with Mexican businessmen; it's a time out to relax,

read a paper, have a little conversation, or just meditate while the fast-moving hands of the shine man add a splendid glow to even an old pair of shoes.

If you sit on the plaza long enough, you will see a bewildering slice of Oaxacan life and *lots* of vendors. Anyone who wishes can buy: fried salted *chapulines* (small red grasshoppers—hey, if you like skinny, spicy pretzels give

Cafés shelter under the portales lining the plaza.

them a try); lottery tickets; basil, starfish, and nutmeg from the herbalist; and the pulse-taker can help "cure you of shock and the loss of the soul " by finding your pulse. More ordinary vendors sell torpedo-shaped balloons that the kids blast high in the air, Chiclets, beaded necklaces, and fine little decorated wooden letter openers that really work well. You'll hear fine music on Tuesday, Thursday, and Sunday. Most holidays begin with a cacophonous symphony of church bells; the city is home to 29 churches.

Plaza de Armas is not only the geographic center of the city, but the heart of the tradition that is Oaxaca. On hot sunny days youngsters splash in one or all four fountains. On Mother's Day, people rush by carrying bouquets of roses, and lovers of all ages stroll though the plaza holding hands. The centerpiece of the plaza is the European-inspired wrought-iron kiosk, where the band plays upstairs while kids play down the stairs; hidden underneath the airy structure is a busy little hive of *fondas* selling cold drinks, sandwiches, snacks. In the evening when the band is playing romantic music, women wander through with baskets of aromatic gardenias for sale. Music varies—from the city band to outstanding marimba bands.

The cathedral dominates the plaza.

Schmoozing in an outdoor café is the *in* thing to do on the plaza, no matter the time of day. Tables are always filled with Mexican and foreign students sipping a popular chocolate drink, businessmen in suits and ties making high-powered decisions over strong coffee, stylish young matrons with strollers, and fashion-conscious young businesswomen dressed in sheer stockings and high heels, (Oaxaca boasts one of the highest percentages of up-and-coming professional women in Mexico). Outdoor cafés under the *portales* around the plaza all sort of flow together, with colorful table linens, umbrellas, and lots of people. The food is similar at most of the outdoor cafés, but some have better service, colder beer, spicier sauces, and different specialties; if you're going to be around a while, try them all. Some fine cafés on the second floor of the *portales* offer (limited) balcony seating.

The first printing press in Oaxaca arrived in 1720—brought by a woman!

Oaxaca is one of the few cities in Mexico where you can find a vendor selling real sherbet in the park.

On one side of the plaza stands the immense **Catedral**. Opposite the cathedral on the plaza is the **Palacio de Gobierno**. If for no other reason, visit the Palacio to study the portrayal of history from prehistoric to colonial in different murals around the stairwell.

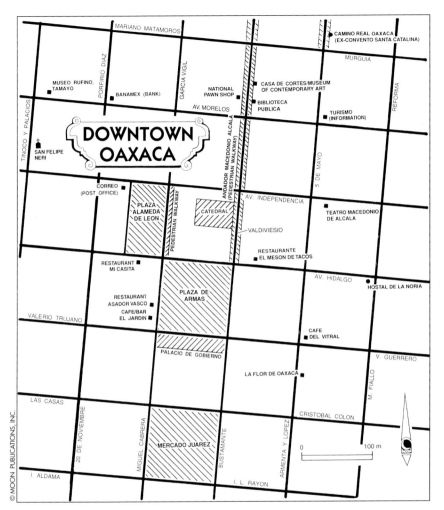

DOWNTOWN OAXACA

The late (native son) Rufino Tamayo, beloved artist of contemporary Mexico, was known for his desire to bring the art of Mexico to the Mexicans. He donated his charming house as well as his collection of pre-Columbian artifacts to the city for a musuem, the **Museo Rufino Tamayo**, on Av. Morelos 503. Tamayo's unique way of looking at his collection was diametrically opposite to what intrigues most archaeologists. He was more concerned with *how* and *why* the art developed in the ancient era rather than with *when*. Tamayo's views of his countrymen were realistic and proud. The artifacts here are presented in this little museum as though he were lecturing on each piece.

In Mitla, as was their manner, the Spaniards built a church in one of the courtyards of the ancient archaeological site. The church continues to serve the locals, mostly Zapotecs, and the fiestas held here flamboyantly combine Zapotec and Catholic ceremonies.

The design of the Teatro Macedonio de Alcala comes from that of late 19th-century Paris.

At the **Teatro Macedonio de Alcala,** Independence 900, year-round entertainment varies from concerts to dance. Check at the tourist office or the sign in front of the building for current attractions. The theater seats about 850, and a fine art gallery and public library also share the building. Much of the art displayed is the work of Miguel Cabrera, a Zapotec Indian who became one of the most "in-demand" baroque artists in all of Mexico in the 18th century. His work is prominent in fine buildings all over central Mexico.

Surprisingly larger than most theaters built during the same era, **Teatro Macedonio de Alcala**, at the intersection of Independencia 900 and Armenta y Lopez, holds more than 850 people. The design typifies the elegant architecture of Paris at the end of the 19th century. Construction was begun in 1903 and finished in 1909, with a striking marble staircase and legends of music, poetry, and the arts displayed in beautifully designed medallions. You can see the building only if you attend a performance. Program schedules are generally posted in front, or check at the tourist office. The theater was opened on 3 September 1909 with a production of Verdi's opera *Aida*.

The 17th-century baroque **Church of San Felipe Neri**, Calle Tinoco y Palacios, was the scene of the marriage between Oaxacan-born President Benito Juárez and Margarita Maza. The main altar and its intricate carved details, all worked in gold, are something to see, along with the church's special architecture.

The **Basílica de la Soledad**, on Av. Independencia, is filled with 16th-century history. Legend says that the Virgin appeared miraculously on the site, and thus a church was built in her honor; she became the patron saint of Oaxaca. A statue of the Virgin is greatly revered, and on special occasions followers place on the statue a crown of gold with 600 diamonds and a large pearl. The church's carved stone façade is covered with columns and niches holding 18 statues. Two domed towers of the basílica are covered with yellow and blue tile. Take a look at the religious museum next door.

Another truly breathtaking colonial building, now the hotel **Camino Real Oaxaca**, was for 300 years the Convento Santa Catalina, founded in 1576. This old building is a close-up study of colonial architecture; for guests it's a stay in an intimate museum. Each stroll to the dining room or down one of the old arched hallways introduces the remains of frescoes, a special turn of an arch, a burnished wooden spindle. While dining under an old portal one can almost feel the whispering presence of the nuns.

The history of the structure echoes the development of the entire country. The Convento Santa Catalina was begun at the end of the 16th century. It was built in phases, reflecting the growth of the religious in Oaxaca. The washing wells in the northeast square of the convent were built at the same time as the convent and remain a rustic touch of the past. The entire village used this fountain to collect water for their daily washing chores. The wells are in a striking octagonal structure built of stone, with an ornate cupola roof covering a series of built-in stone basins. Unique for its time, the ingenious hydraulic system kept the water always running.

Over the years the Convento Santa Catalina (as all Mexico's religious buildings) had its high and low points. After the Reform Laws in 1862 suppressed the nuns, the convent was taken over as the seat of government. Later it became a jail, then an art school, and next a government palace. In the early 20th century, the convent church was used as a movie theater. Finally, in 1972, experts renovated the entire building, artists restored the wall paintings in cells and hallways, and craftsmen reconstructed the original floors. By 1975 it was ready to begin its new "career" as a hotel and has won international honors ever since.

> **Hotel Camino Real Oaxaca** is quite spectacular for those who get a thrill out of stepping into the past. The comfortable rooms conform to the architecture of the colonial era, with substantial walls (some almost two meters thick) and furnishings of heavy dark wood, and all rooms open onto lovely vistas: the pool, a garden, or a patio. Continental breakfast, afternoon cocktails, and hors d'oeuvres are served in a separate club room. Small bars and lounges tucked into hidden corners and patios create a very romantic atmosphere. Strolling musicians, a swimming pool, luscious buffet breakfasts, and 400-year-old artwork still visible on the walls—you get all of that *plus* excellent service. Camino Real Oaxaca is a few blocks from the plaza on a quiet street, Cinco de Mayo 300, tel. (800) 722-6466 from the States. Luxury.
>
> For a classically elegant restaurant, go upstairs (take the door to the left of Café el Jardín) to **Asador Vasco,** Portal de Flores 11. It boasts white linen cloths, crystal, and fresh flowers; a table on the balcony overlooking the plaza is quite romantic. The food is well-prepared, and the menu includes a variety of Spanish-style cookery. The paella is excellent and the steaks are good. A set, four-course dinner is the only meal available on some busy holidays, and if you don't dress up just a little for these special holidays you may end up seated in the back of the room. Live music. Reservations are suggested, and if you desire a balcony table ask a couple of days in advance, if possible. This is a favorite for locals as well as travelers. It's open 1-11 p.m.

Museo de Juárez, Garcia Vigil No. 609, is the house illustrating the early beginnings and the life of Benito Juárez. The late president came from San Pablo Guelatao, a small Zapotec village nearby, and was taken in by Don Antonio Salanueva. First he learned to speak Spanish, and then he helped in the "family" business—book binding. Juárez was the first law graduate from the Institute of Science and Art.

A walk along the **Tourist Andador** from the plaza to the Museo Regional de Oaxaca will bring you past many interesting buildings. **The National Pawn Shop of Oaxaca** started business in the early part of the 1700s, lending cash on personal belongings. Although the first such shop was built in Mexico City, such loans are actually a service begun in Spain in medieval days. In the beginning it was purely humanitarian and no fees were charged, but it was an unstated "rule" that when the owner bought back his belongings he made some small donation to the poor.

The **Biblioteca Publica** (public library) is housed in a lovely old house around small patios. It offers rooms full of books and rooms dedicated to children, not just for reading but for clever puppet shows and other interpretations of literature.

Once Cortés subdued the Indians, New Spain was ready to be shaped and sculpted into a silver-producing machine. Amid the rumblings, jealousies, and accusations of courtly politics, King Charles V decided that he could not choose Cortés to lead the country, but he compensated him instead with an enormous land grant and the prestigious title of **Marqués del Valle de Oaxaca**. Along with the title he was awarded 11,500 square km of land and 25,000 Indians to convert to Christendom, to collect tribute from, and to use on his land as free laborers.

Just next door sits the **Casa de Cortés**, built in the late 1500s. If you step way back, across the street is best, you'll get the best view of the old building. The ground level displays a rich doorway, surrounded by carved stone, and columns. On the second level a wrought-iron balcony offers an even more ornate treatment of the doors, carved Solomonic columns and a Moorish curve. On the third level, above it all, is a shell-decorated niche with a sculpture of Raphael the archangel between two coats of arms.

Every house in the city bears a legend; some believe this one had a rather tenuous connection to Hernán Cortés. They say that after receiving his Oaxaca Valley land grant from the king, Cortés ordered a house befitting a marquesa to be built—but that before he saw it he died in Spain. So the house has no personal attachment—Cortés never walked the old corridors or slept under the roof—even the dates of construction don't jibe with the date of his death in 1547. However, visitors cannot forget the history of the man, his deeds good and evil. Today it is better known as **The Museum of Contemporary Art of Oaxaca**. Works of outstanding contemporary artists past and present are on display and traveling exhibits are brought in frequently.

Once past the modest small Church of La Sangre de Cristo, you cannot miss the tiled domes that herald the enormous compound that at one time made up

the **Templo y Ex-Convento de Santo Domingo,** the powerful seat of the Dominican order in Oaxaca since the 16th century and now the only remaining Dominican residence out of the original 40. The outside of the church is lovely in a simple way, but in no way does it reveal what awaits a visitor to the inside. Today as you walk into the massive structure, it glows with a golden hue. Every surface is opulent, with intricate designs representative of

The relatively simple exterior of the Templo y Ex-Convento de Santo Domingo doesn't begin to hint at the opulence that awaits inside.

God in his glory. Techniques characteristic of the baroque period of Mexican art are displayed: painting, sculpture, woodcarving, plaster relief, color, and above all, gold leaf. "Branches" bloom with small figures of angels, the Virgin, blossoms, leaves—all inlaid with gold leaf and bright colors. Don't miss the **Chapel of the Rosary.** Even more stunning and "golden," it is dedicated to the Virgin of the Rosary. With elabo-

> **Hostal de La Noria,** Av. Hidalgo 918, Centro Oaxaca, 68000 Oaxaca, Mexico, tel. (951) 478-44, fax (951) 639-92, is a fine colonial-style hotel in the center of town. Although it may not be as old as some of the structures in town, it exudes another era. Two stories of archways held up with stone columns and wrought-iron rails surround an open patio filled with umbrella tables and plants on simple tile floors. Classic lanterns create a fine colonial ambience. The food is good, and the hotel is just a couple of blocks from the plaza. The rooms are comfortably fitted with all the modern conveniences. Here the past intersects the present. Moderate.

rately carved and designed gold altars, the chapel is especially ornate with a beautifully painted cupola ceiling. A family tree of St. Dominic himself is a fascinating piece of history. The old church has had its ups and downs, and at one time was used as a stable for horses. Altars were scraped and burned to reclaim the gold leaf; the gold retrieved was infinitesimal, the destruction of the body of artistic work was monumental. The church was restored by the Dominicans in 1938, and totally restored in 1970.

Next door, the **Museo Regional de Oaxaca** is housed in one of the most extraordinary buildings in the city, the Ex-Convento de Santo Domingo. The exquisite old structure has also gone through several reversals of fortune over the centuries, but still maintains its 16th-

To travel into the outlying areas of the city climb aboard one of the *colectivos* waiting at the Mercado Juárez and Mercado Abastos.

century baroque glory. After it was no longer permitted to operate as a convent, it lingered empty. But not for long. The army took it over during the War of Independence and used it as a barracks, and from then it faded in and out of use. In 1972 it became a museum. The museum architecture is typical of the era, with thick walls, high ceilings, stone archways, graceful columns, and central courtyard with a fountain. The museum handles its displays impeccably. Each room tells a story in wonderful exhibits about the history of the state and its people. Upstairs rooms are filled with artifacts and examples of the clothing worn by people from the villages surrounding the city. The exquisite Monte Albán treasure of tomb no. 7, discovered by archaeologist Alfonso Caso in 1932, is displayed here. Though not confirmed by all archaeologists, it appears that in the mid-14th century, tomb no. 7 was created when the Mixtecan people opened an existing Zapotec tomb at Monte Albán and buried a king and his sacrificed entourage. With the bodies were found 500 pieces of jewelry made of gold, amber, turquoise, silver, and conch shells.

After leaving the *andador* and turning left at the corner of the museum, a short walk toward the end of the block will take you past the still existing army barracks.

Oaxaca Highlights

Arts and Artisans

The art of this area encompasses a wide range, more than in any other area of Mexico. Not only does the painter make broad strokes in brilliant colors on his canvas, but she creates textiles in that same manner. Some designs are woven in small patterns, but embroideries are bold representations of nature—perhaps one beautiful flower in heavy embroidery will take up half of a blouse. Entering certain *mercados* is like walking into a still life, only it's anything but still. Fruits and vegetables are displayed with a natural flair for balance, color, and design. More crafts include the pottery, jewelry, wood carvings, leather work, black pottery, *alebrijes*, woolens, embroidered textiles, baskets, and a broad selection of metalwork such as tinware Christmas decorations. The comings and goings of people dressed in bright colors add moving lights to the picture. Festivals and processions present still another form of the Oaxacans' art—artistic placements of people, their jewelry, their clothing, their grace. And what else can you call the gustatory delights of Oaxaca except an art form?

For the Shopper

Real shoppers will uncover small hole-in-the-wall stores tucked in nooks around the city, as well as extravagant large courtyard-shops, their surrounding rooms filled with ceramics, art, and whimsical crafts. Don't forget the *mercados;* several are scattered about town. Oaxaca is well-known for its marvelous selection of arts and crafts. The state's crafters possess a wonderful knack for combining the traditions of the past with ideas of the present. Artists pattern their beautiful jewelry after unique designs of the pieces found in tomb no. 7 of Monte

weaving her wares at the Oaxaca market

Albán. They weave textiles in brilliant colors in both traditional and modern designs on ancient and modern looms. A short list will get you started.

Artesanías Cocijo, Calle Leona Vicario 117, offers native crafts worth a look. **Mercado de Artesanías**, at Zaragoza and J.P. Garcia, is known especially for its rugs and other textiles, but because of its out-of-the-way location, not everyone finds it. Look for good bargains here. Visit a few of the smaller plazas—such as **Plazuela del Carmen** and **Plazuela Lambastida**—for daily street markets. **Aripo**, Garcia Vigil 809, tel. (951) 6-9211, displays crafts from all seven regions of Oaxaca in a lovely old building. Nine rooms plus gardens display the fine work that includes on-the-scene textile weavers working with cotton and wool; others work with leather and chamois, and others with tin-plate Christ-

San Bartolo Coyotepec's famous black pottery

mas decorations. **Galeria Quetzali**, Macedonia Alcala 305, presents art exhibits that change frequently and offers crafts for sale. **Victor**, Porfirio Díaz 111, in a quaint 17th-century building, is a fine shop where browsing and discovering can take time. Oaxaca offers many more but half the fun is discovering something special on your own.

Mercados

For most people fresh produce is a staple food. For the indigenous people of Oaxaca, it's a gathering of color. A bright patchwork quilt of color shouts to shoppers to observe each tomato, melon, or squash displayed in a unique fashion. Go to the **Mercado Abastos**, near the second-class bus station southwest of the plaza. It's a covered building that really comes alive on Saturday, when the people from the surrounding villages come dressed in wonderfully colorful clothes to buy and sell for the coming week. A living art exhibit unto itself is the **Mercado Juárez**; it is quite large and sprawls across an area that's bordered by the streets Senorial, 20 de Noviembre, Mina Arteaga, and Mogon. Again Saturday is especially colorful with people, parrots, blankets, and a huge selection of crafts. You'll find just about anything anyone might want here, from heaps of spices to textiles, tin pots to ceramic *ollas*, serapes to sombreros. If you don't want to buy anything, it's still worth a trip on Saturday to take in the out-of-towners.

To bring home local Mexican coffee—beans or ground—stop by **La Casa de Café** across from the Interdisa Casa Cambio on Valdivieso; let the aroma guide you.

Special Events

Semana Santa

The celebration of Easter Week is the biggie in Oaxaca. Unlike in the U.S., the actual day of Easter is not noticeably celebrated. The events begin with **The Paseos of Lent**. On each Friday night of Lent, 7-9 p.m., young adults (mostly college students) converge on Paseo Juárez Park (called El Llano by the locals), listen to music, and take a *paseo* (stroll) around the park. Young men bring flowers and flirt with pretty girls, presenting their favorites with the blossoms.

On the fourth Friday at noon, the townsfolk celebrate **La Samaritana**, who according to scripture gave Jesus water in defiance of the Roman guards. At the front entrance of all churches, altars are set up and decorated with flowers, and flavored water is dispensed to all who bring their own container (free of course). This symbolic gesture has gained in the translation, and you have a choice of exotic water flavors: *chilacayota,* pumpkin with brown sugar and lemon rind; *horchata,* cinnamon and almond; or prickly pear, tamarind, melon, pineapple, jamaica, and so on.

In the afternoon of Good Friday, the sixth Friday of Lent, dances are held at different schools, another *paseo* is held at the Plaza Alameda, and the nearby Juárez market is jammed with people; the specialty for this day is a vegetable tamal.

Guelaguetza Festival

On the **Feast Day of the Virgen del Carmen,** 16 July, the town comes to life, especially around the Carmen Church on Garcia Vigil. The feast day marks the lead-in to the Guelaguetza Festival. Guelaguetza means "offering" or "gift," and each of the seven regions of Oaxaca "gives" not only a wonderful exposition of brilliant costumes and dances, but some dancers actually throw their "gifts" to the audience. This celebration, which lasts more than a week, is one that all "Mexicophiles" should attend at least once.

On the Sunday night before the Guelaguetza, university students present a program at the Plaza de la Soledad that explains the history of the Guelaguetza through music and dance. Arrive early for a seat. The lively fiesta, which begins the next day, is a centuries-old celebration also called Lunes del Cerro (Monday on the Hill). It's held in the immense amphitheater on Fortín Hill overlooking the city. On the two Mondays following the 16 July feast of the Virgen del Carmen, the dancers dress in *típico* costumes and present traditional ceremonial dances, including a depiction of the arrival of the Spaniards. It's a circus atmosphere with people wearing bright costumes and vendors selling drinks, snacks, and souvenirs; the sound level is awesome, not just from the live music, but from the excitement of the crowd. At the closing of the pineapple dance, performed by the women from the *papaloa-pan* region, the dancers toss whole pineapples into the audience and the people go wild!

If you want a reserved seat up front (with a chance to catch a pineapple), it will cost US$25 or US$35, or you can sit in the back sections free. Tickets are sold at the tourist office and other places around town (ask at your hotel). The production begins at 10 a.m. and is usually finished by 1:30 p.m. If you plan to sit in the free section (much larger than the reserved), you had better get there 8-8:30 a.m. or earlier to guarantee a seat. Even if you have a paid ticket, get there early for the best seats.

The Guelaguetza~ An Ancient Celebration

We can only imagine the original Guelaguetza celebration. We know it was a ceremony honoring the gods of the Mixtecs, Zapotecs, and Aztecs and performed at a place the Spaniards later named Cerro de Fortín. Anthropologists say the ceremony was dedicated to beseeching the gods for rain, good crops, prolific families, and a fruitful year. When the friars arrived they attempted to convert the celebration into a Catholic feast day honoring the Virgin Mary; they officially eliminated the holiday altogether in the 1880s. But that didn't stop the Indians from "unofficially" gathering in the same place on the same dates each year in observance of their sacred day. Eventually, in the early 20th century, the Guelaguetza celebration became a general celebration of dance similar to today's event. Only with the opening of the amphitheater in 1974 and the performance of the regional dancers did it reach its present magnitude, attracting people from all over Mexico and beyond.

Lots of people end up standing for the entire performance. This is a summer event, and the amphitheater is wide open, so bring protection from the bright sun and a thirst quencher. This yearly event brings thousands of people from all over (the amphitheater holds 10,000). The town is packed and hotel rooms without reservations are almost nonexistent. For exact dates of this movable holiday and more information contact your nearest Mexican Government Tourism Office.

Blessing of the Animals
Not nearly so flamboyant as most of the other celebrations is the blessing of the animals (mostly pets) on 31 August. Dogs, cats, burros, birds, and pigs are cleaned and dressed in flowers, feathers, ribbons, straw hats—whatever the owner's imagination can come up with—and then taken at 5 p.m. to La Merced church, where the priest blesses each pet and its owner, who's usually a child.

Day of the Dead
Day of the Dead is a big celebration in Oaxaca. Officially the dates are 1 and 2 November. But it really starts on 30 and 31 October (or sooner) when crowds jam the stalls in the markets. Selling and buying is at a feverish pitch with people

🍴 An exquisite choice for dining in Oaxaca is the **Café del Vitral,** Guerrero 201. The food is beautifully presented by waiters in the finest European style. The setting—a stately ex-mansion—displays elegance and taste, from the impressive staircase to the flamboyant stained glass. The menu offers a wonderful mixture of nouvelle/regional with continental specialties; excellent wine list. This is not the place to go if you're on a budget. It's open daily 1 p.m.-11 p.m.; reservations suggested.

🍴 The following restaurants serve some really outstanding traditional dishes, such as *sopa de garbanzo, manteles, tinga,* and other less frequently encountered but very tasty dishes. Try: **El Biche Pobre,** Calz. de República 66 and also at Rayon 1136, inexpensive; **El Meson de Tacos,** Hidalgo near the plaza, inexpensive; **Mi Casita,** Hidalgo 616, up a flight of stairs, moderate; **Playa del Carmen,** Zapata at B. Dominguez, north of the Pan-American Highway, moderate; **La Flor de Oaxaca,** Armenta y Lopez 311, inexpensive; and **Doña Elpidia,** Miguel Cabrera 413, inexpensive.

In the Centro district, several streets are closed to vehicles: three blocks of **Macedonio Alcala,** going north and south between Morelos and Allende, all four streets around the *zócalo,* and two blocks of **Cinco de Mayo** going north and south between Murguia and Constitución. This creates a couple of convenient corridors for walking to and from the several plazas from the surrounding streets, where there are many hotels, restaurants, museums, churches, and colonial buildings. Progress marches toward more pedestrian-only streets.

searching for flowers, candles, and special foods to prepare on the feast days. Everywhere you look you'll see *cempasuchil,* a marigold look-alike, candies fashioned into anything to do with death—skeletons and skulls, special *pan de muerta* (bread of the dead) formed into unusual shapes and tasty with the sweet spicy flavor of anise. Celebrants set up altars and make offerings. But the place to be on 31 October for a moving, colorful celebration is the cemetery of **Xoxo** village. It's recommended that you go with a group arranged through a travel agency, such as the Hotel Camino Real Oaxaca Travel Agency. Make hotel reservations well in advance.

Radish Festival

This unusual holiday, held on 23 December, is also called the Night of the Radish. From outlying areas, families come to town with carvings from giant radishes. The carvings can be people, structures, flowers, or a hundred other things. Artists are armed with spritz-bottles of water to keep these works of art damp and fresh for the judging. The Radish Festival is just one of many celebrations leading up to the busy Christmas celebration. One of the best parts of this night is the *buñuelos* (a sweet pastry) sold on every corner, and even more fun, you're expected to break the bowl after you consume the confection. It brings good luck, so break it!

Regional Food

The cuisine of Oaxaca is without comparison, with unusual spices and herbs, and its special cheese is famous all over the country. Very popular in Oaxaca and on many restaurant menus is the *platillo de botanas,* also called *botana surtida* and *platillo de Oaxaqueno.* All are a variety of snacks on a large platter, often just small versions of regular local specialties; this is the best way to sample new Oaxaqueno flavors.

You must sample the excellent *moles.* In fact, Oaxaca is referred to in Mexican culinary circles as the "land of seven *moles.*" *Mole* is a sauce that can be served with chicken, turkey, enchiladas, and many other dishes. And though most people automatically think of thick brown chile sauce heavily laden with chocolate when they hear the word *mole,* only one of the Oaxacan *moles* has chocolate in it. Oaxacan *mole* is really a brewed mixture of herbs, spices, various chiles, fruits, and tomatoes. They come in all colors. One *mole* is made with *pipian* (pumpkin seeds) and is a pale green; you'll also see red *mole* and a black *mole.*

Other great Oaxacan dishes are not to be missed. *Sopa de garbanzo,* served cold, is an agreeable blend of mint, onion, and pureed chickpeas. Another dish to try is *tostadas de tinga. Tinga* is a *picante* (spicy) stewlike mix with sausage, onions, *chipotle* chiles, tomatoes, and spices. Pile all of this on a crisp tortilla with lettuce and beans. A common style of meat is *tasajo* (meat dried with chile), and *cecina enchiladas* (made with pork chile) are delicious. If you've never had a quesadilla filled with cheese and a *flor de calabaza* (squash flower), try it. *Manteles,* another exotic dish, is simmered beef with chiles, herbs, pineapple, and bananas. Oaxaca white cheeses are special, and a rich variety of tamales steamed in banana leaves come in spicy, tangy, and sweet. The alcoholic beverage called mescal is the accepted accompaniment to all regional food.

In Oaxaca you can find some of the best meal bargains in the country. That's not to say the prices are dirt cheap, but some of the finest meals are quite affordable. Don't be surprised if instead of a conventional menu you are handed a list of food choices and an order blank to fill in. Make sure you specify how many of each item you want. Many restaurants open only for breakfast and lunch; lunch is still the big meal of the day and it goes on from about 1 p.m.-5 p.m. However, with the influx of students and foreigners the restaurants have adjusted their customs, and you can even buy breakfast all day at some cafés.

Special Excursions

One of the "must-dos" while in Oaxaca City is to visit one or all of the surrounding villages that have great market days. Whether by plan or happenstance, market days are spread over different days of the week. Of course these days, like everything else in Mexico, are subject to change. And granted, it can be busy with busloads of tourists during the high season, but it's well worth the trip to discover really good folk art, whether it be weavings, ceramics, carved wooden figures, or masks. In most cases, the towns specialize in one particular craft. Though not all the villages have market days, almost all the craftspeople leave their villages and bring their crafts for the biggest of all the markets on Saturday in Oaxaca. Others, such as the animal carvers, don't have to bring their wares to the city; they can barely keep up with the orders from their city outlets.

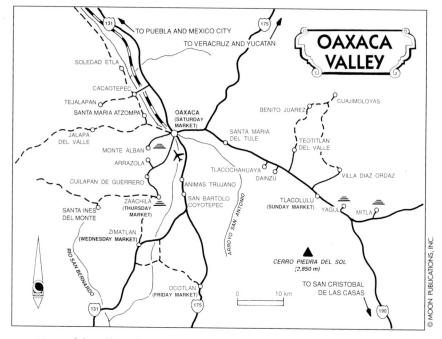

Many of the villages lie down narrow, sometimes dirt, roads that turn off Hwy. 190; others lie off Hwy. 175. The way to see the most villages is by driving your own vehicle, but if that's impossible, take a bus trip, or hire a car and driver. The villages are scattered about, so study the map for a plan of attack. Most of these villages are reasonably close to Oaxaca city, though a few are much longer drives.

Santa María Atzompa

Atzompa is the home of green-glazed pottery. Artisans create huge pots with wonderful raised decorations. It's mesmerizing to watch them as they work. Atzompa lies at the foot of Monte Albán.

Arrazola

Arrazola is well-known for *alebrijes*, brightly painted whimsical animals carved from copal wood. The first village carver to really let his imagination run wild in this present genre was Manuel Jiménez two decades ago. He and his entire family work on the often-very-tall animals painted in bright colors. A giraffe can stand as high as three feet tall or an "alien" animal only two inches tall; all are painted pink, or orange, or blue, or—who knows?—with polka dots and fine geometric designs. Some carvers build their animals to come apart for shipping. Pointed ears, tails, and other projecting pieces slip out of holes, to be returned once you're home. These eclectic little *alebrijes* are on display in the artisans' own homes and in many shops all over Mexico.

San Bartolo Coyotepec

San Bartolo Coyotepec was the home of Doña Rosa Nieto, who invented a popular art form by mistake in 1934. It is said that Doña Rosa accidentally "discovered" ebony-hued pottery when a young lad who worked for her in her family-operated "factory" mistakenly closed the lower vent on her kiln. The lack of oxygen turned the entire batch of ceramics coal-black. Although her first inclination was to toss the heap, her practical side influenced her to take just one piece to market. The rest of the story is history—customers were intrigued with the unusual color, and Doña Rosa began a popular industry.

You can still visit the factory that belonged to Doña Rosa before her death some years back. Her family (and many others) continue to make the black pottery in unique designs, and visitors are shown how the pottery is made and fired. It's just one of the many factory/shops where you can buy the black pottery; a local artisans' market displays the unique beauty and originality of all the artists in town. San Bartolo lies 12 kilometers southeast of Oaxaca off Hwy. 175.

Teotitlán del Valle

Teotitlán del Valle is the place to go for Zapotecan wool rugs and textiles. It is the oldest town in the Oaxaca Valley, and almost every home has a domestic hand loom. The wool is frequently colored with natural dyes made from indigo, moss, and the cochineal insect that lives in the cacti growing all over the area. Teotitlán del Valle lies 28 kilometers east of Oaxaca.

Ocotlán

Ocotlán villagers produce green-glazed pottery. In Ocotlán you can also bargain for and buy prisoner-made baskets, cages, and lamps (all from reeds) right through the prison bars close by. Do stop at the pottery workshop/home of Josefina Aguilar, another Ocotlán gem. Ocotlán is also famous for its Friday market, where you'll get dizzy trying to decide which of the wonderful crafts to buy. You have a choice of myriad pottery designs, regional candles, fine embroidery, and a selection of cutlery including machetes, knives, letter openers, daggers, and swords.

Tlacolulu

Adventurers driving vehicles on offbeat roads will see small *ranchitos,* maybe even primitive mescal stills, where mules turn immense solid rock wheels to crush the maguey hearts into the pulp that is then fermented in large wooden vats before it's distilled. Tlacolulu has long been a big producer of mescal, and it appears that production methods are modernizing. The small town boasts one of the oldest churches around; it was built in 1531. Visit the church to see its stone pulpit and the collection of wrought-iron locks from the 16th century. Tlacolulu is a gathering place for Indians on market day. They excel in producing pottery, serapes, rugs, baskets, all shown outside the village's 16th century church. Tlacolulu lies 30 kilometers east of Oaxaca.

Zaachila

Zaachila was the last capital of the Zapotec empire. If you stroll through the archaeological site here, you'll see that one tomb bears a tantalizing name: "Men From Hell." Doesn't that whet your curiosity? The most famous find here was a polychrome pottery cup with a three-dimensional figure of a blue hummingbird perched on its rim. Most of the villagers today are artists, and it would seem they come by their talent very naturally. The town is noted for good restaurants and its Thursday market. Zaachila lies five kilometers beyond Cuilapan de Guerrero.

Morelia

MICHOACÁN WAS THE PRE-COLUMBIAN CENTER of the Purépecha/Tarasca people, described by the earliest Spaniards as tall and handsome. These powerful warriors controlled most of western Mexico and managed to keep the Aztecs at bay. Their accomplishments were due in part to superior copper weapons made in the Michoacán area. Because of their animosity toward the Aztecs, they were unwilling to join Moctezuma as an ally against Cortés, nor did they wholeheartedly resist the Spaniards' intrusion. In the end they not only succumbed to the foreign invaders, they joined their ranks and fought against the Aztecs.

Founded in 1541 by the first viceroy of New Spain, Antonio de Mendoza, the city was named Valladolid in honor of Mendoza's Spanish birthplace (the name was changed to Morelia after Independence, when all links with Spain were severed). In the late 1540s the seat of power was moved from Pátzcuaro to Morelia. The entire area of what is today the state of Michoacán flourished under the fair leadership of Bishop Don Vasco de Quiroga. Both Indian and Spanish historians report that he was a remarkably gentle, fair, and intelligent man who arrived in the New World in 1531 and in Michoacán in 1533.

After hearing of the cruelty of some conquerors, especially in the western half of the country, the Spanish crown tried to find better people to take charge. When Quiroga arrived in New Spain he was ordained a priest and immediately became a bishop in Michoacán—all very late in his life. His first see (religious headquarters) was in Tzintzuntzán (on Lake Pátzcuaro), but only for a short while until it was moved to Pátzcuaro. Quiroga recognized the talents of the native craftsmen and set about enhancing and simplifying their work. He taught easier agricultural methods and introduced handicrafts from Spain (such as lace worked in the Andalusian style). He encouraged individual villages to excel in a single occupation; everyone was trained and expected to work for the community. Many of the outstanding artisans in the villages in Michoacán

Romantics say that when the Spaniards arrived and the Purépecha Indians submitted, the Indian rulers gave the Spaniards their daughters in an effort to mollify them. Thereafter, the Indians used the term for son-in-law, *tarascue*, to address the Spaniards; the Spaniards mispronounced the term, calling themselves Tarascans, which is what they've been called ever since.

Beltrán Nuño de Guzmán, who followed Cortés to western Mexico, surpassed the cruelties of the Indians with atrocities of his own. He conquered and destroyed most of the Tarascans; under his tyranny their numbers fell from 60,000 to 20,000.

MORELIA

DETAIL

DR. MIGUEL SILVA

SERAPIO RENDON

TO BOSQUE PARK, THE AQUEDUCT, AND CONVENTION CENTER OF MORELIA

VICENTE SANTA MARIA

A. SERDAN

BARTOLOME DE LAS CASAS

CASA DE LAS ARTISANIAS

HUMBOLDT

ANTONIO ALZATE

MARIANO ELIZAGA

JUAN RUIZ DE ALARCON

MERCADO INDEPENDENCIA

OBREGON

PLAZA VALLADOLID

AV. MADERO ORIENTE

VASCO DE QUIROGA

E. ZAPATA

PINA SUAREZ

V. DE MENDOZA

MUSEO CASA DE MORELOS

L. SOTO Y SALDANA

CASA DE CULTURA

PLAZA DEL CARMEN

AV. MORELOS NORTE

AV. MORELOS SUR

LOS COMENSALES

HOTEL DE LA SOLEDAD

CATEDRAL

PLAZA DE LOS MARTIRES

GARCIA OBESO

BENITO JUAREZ

PALACIO FEDERAL

BENITO JUAREZ

IGNACIO ZARAGOZA

VALLODOLID

MUSEO CASA NATAL DE MORELOS

ALDAMA

IGNACIO ZARAGOZA

GUILLERMO PRIETO

MUSEO DEL ESTADO

MELCHOR OCAMPO

HIDALGO

ABASOLO

PLAZA SAN AGUSTIN

SEE DETAIL

AV. MADERO PONIENTE

CONSERVATORIO DE MUSICA DE LAS ROSAS

NIGROMANTE

GALEANA

MUSEO REGIONAL MICHOACAN

HOTEL VIRREY DE MENDOZA

CENTRAL BUS STATION

MERCADO DE DULCES

V. GOMEZ FARIAS

I. LOPEZ RAYON

ALLENDE

CORREGIDORA

COLEGIO DE SAN NICOLAS

NIGROMANTE

LEON GUZMAN

QUINTANA ROO

MADERO

EDUARDO RUIZ

SANTIAGO TAPIA

GUADALUPE VICTORIA

TO TRAIN STATION

NICOLAS BRAVO

PALACIO CLAVIJERO

TOURIST OFFICE

V. GOMEZ FARIAS

150 m

0

© MOON PUBLICATIONS, INC.

are still noted for their particular specialties and excellent quality. Quiroga taught the villagers by example, side by side, and he asked of them nothing that he did not demand of himself. He was well-loved and respected, and the Indians addressed him with the affectionate title Tata Vasco. Quiroga was a true friend to the Indians, but when he was gone, life continued much the same way that it had before his arrival; the Purépecha people, like most of the Indians in Mexico, were mistreated.

In 1828, after independence from Spain, the capital city's Spanish name, Valladolid, was changed to Morelia in honor of Independence hero Morelos. Today it is the sixth-largest city of the republic, modern and upbeat, a high-tech city ready for the 21st century. Yet it proudly carries its stamp of the past, its Indian roots and colonial splendor. Morelia is a lovely city and most visitors find it takes more than a one-day stop to cover it all.

Michoacán has produced many free thinkers, and one of the most famous was home-grown President Lázaro Cárdenas. Morelia has been a university town for centuries and its students have sustained the community's aura of idealistic curiosity; the city has been, and still frequently is, the scene of high-powered dissent against the government. Cárdenas, who served first as governor, in 1928, and then as president of the country 1934-1940, served as benefactor to the peasants of Michoacán. Of Purépecha descent, Cárdenas made massive land transfers, breaking up the large, rich haciendas and distributing the land among the campesinos (peasants); about 45 million acres were shuffled. The move wasn't always successful and in many cases agricultural output slowed down because of the Indians' lack of farming experience.

Exploring the Streets of Morelia

The delicate-pink quarrystone structures of Morelia, the "Aristocrat of Colonial Cities," are as majestic today as they were in the 16th century; all are still in use and adapted to modern-day commerce. It's a tribute to those who designed the city; they had an eye to the future as they laid out the streets in a perfect grid with many wide boulevards. The most Spainlike of all the colonial cities (except maybe for Mexico City), Morelia has a certain air of elegance; UNESCO has designated it a World Heritage Artistic Site.

The heart of Morelia lies at the *zócalo*, called the **Plaza de los Mártires** (Plaza of the Martyrs) in memory of citizen defenders who were executed for taking part in the War of Independence. You'll find its history ensconced in the splendid buildings surrounding this large square. It's a fine way to spend a day—or two, strolling around the plaza from one historical era to the next. This is all flat ground and easy walking. A shady bench is always available if you wish to take a break—or chat with the young Chiclets vendor who will more than likely join you.

Constructed of quarrystone, the **Catedral**, on the plaza at Portal Allende 267, gives off a pink glow. Its two ornate towers soar 200 feet. The cathedral was begun in 1660 and completed 84 years later. Architecture aside, one of the outstanding attractions of this church is its massive pipe organ with 4,600 pipes, a joy to see as well as to hear. Its classical tone would do justice to a New York production of *Phantom of the Opera*. If you can find someone with a

Catedral

key you may climb into one of the two tall spires. Taking pictures is permitted in the exterior areas only.

The **Conservatorio de Música de las Rosas**, on Santiago Tapia, several blocks northwest of the plaza, was established in 1590 as the Dominican Convento de las Monjas. In the late 1700s it was adopted for use as a music school for boys. Today it is still a music school and the center for the internationally known Boy's Choir of Morelia. If you have an opportunity, go to one of the choir's performances. If you can't see a performance, quietly slip into the conservatory and listen to a practice. The building is simple with a rather unusual design as seen from the street. Take a look at the nearby baroque church and garden, formerly part of the Dominican Convent.

Vasco de Quiroga founded **Colegio de San Nicolas** in Pátzcuaro in 1540; it was moved to Morelia in 1580. One of the oldest institutions of learning in the Americas, it was the precursor of what is now the University of Michoacán. Several future patriots attended school here in its earliest days: Miguel Hidalgo, José María Morelos, and Melchor Ocampo.

Conservatorio de Música de las Rosas

Named in honor of Jesuit leader Francisco Clavijero, **Palacio Clavijero**, at the southern end of Mercado de Dulces, was completed in 1660 as a Jesuit college (short-lived since the Jesuits were booted out of Mexico in 1767). Today it serves as the University of Michoacán's public library. Take a look around, and don't miss the immense patio with its center fountain and graceful arches. The structure connecting the former Church of San Francisco and the library is today used as an art gallery as well as the tourist information center.

The **Museo del Estado**, Guillermo Prieto 176, is one of the smallest museums in the city. The building was formerly the home of Ana Huarte, who later married Agustín

Hotel de la Soledad, Calle Zaragoza 90 and Calle Ocampo, tel. 2-1888, is a *posada* housed in an ex-mansion built about 1700. The old pink quarrystone structure has a long history of use; it housed the first stagecoach depot in the city, and a convent lurks in its past. A beautiful courtyard accommodates archways and bright bougainvilleas; it's very Mexican. *Most* of the rooms are spacious, and some overlook the courtyard dining area, but others have no view at all. So either take a look first, or request a room with a view of the patio. The food was just okay but recent reports are glowing. Moderate to Expensive.

de Iturbide (he became the "Emperor" of Mexico for 10 months after the execution of Maximilian). You can trace the timeline of the state of Morelia through the exhibits. The ground floor shows pre-Columbian history through figurines, and displays the use of copper, gold, and silver; the second floor has a pharmacological display from the 18th century, regional clothes, and some very fine murals of the 19th century. Note the lovely wooden shelves and design that house the apothecary jars. Ask about different activities held on Wednesday at 7:30 p.m.; the programs change and include art exhibits, regional dances, and other cultural events.

For a real step back into colonial Mexico, see **Hotel Virrey de Mendoza,** Av. Madero Pte. 310, tel. 12-0633, 12-4940, the ex-mansion of Antonio de Mendoza, first viceroy of Mexico. This lovely, completely renovated 17th-century home preserves the opulence of old royalty while providing the comforts of the present. It's sumptuously furnished with antiques: chests, crystal chandeliers, gold rococo mirrors, paintings, and everywhere lovely fresh flowers. The beautiful staircase and stained glass canopy are striking. The bedrooms offer modern bathrooms, rather firm but comfortable beds, and hiding inside lovely armoires are modern television sets. This is a delightful hotel. Moderate.

Restaurante Fonda las Mercedes, Galvan 47, tel. (451) 12-6113, is a lovely patio restaurant; the most charming old courtyards abound in this city, and many are occupied by restaurants. While enjoying the excellent food you can admire the murals, the flowers, the plants, and the colorful birds. Try one of the unusual pasta dishes. It's closed Sunday, open 1 p.m.-1 a.m. Moderate.

An eternal torch burns at the **Museo Casa Natal de Morelos,** Corregidora 113, in memory of native son/hero José María Morelos. He was born here on 30 September 1765. The house was built about 1650, and now is a national monument and a museum with a public library and well-used auditorium. Many rooms display remnants from Morelos's past that somehow bring him to life. Free cultural events take place every Friday night; ask about the schedule at the tourist office.

Museo Casa de Morelos, Av. Morelos Sur 323, was the home of the hero as an adult from the time he bought it in 1801. The second-story addition was built under his supervision. This museum provides a personal history of Morelos and information about the War of Independence and his part in it.

The **Museo Regional Michoacán,** Allende 305, was originally built for Isidro Huarte. One of its most interesting displays is the mural by Alfredo Zalce showing the "haves and have nots" (people who have helped Mexico, and those who have not). Exhibits include pre-Columbian artifacts, ceramics, colonial arms, and contemporary and colonial paintings. One section is used as a public library, including a library for children. Check out the message board; international films are shown in the museum auditorium on Saturday and Sunday at noon.

Museo Regional Michoacán

the Aqueduct

Bosque Park on the edge of town is the largest park in Morelia and is officially called Bosque Cuauhtémoc Forest. It's a pleasant place to take a walk, away from the sounds of the city. In the small **Plaza Morelos** (on the northeast side of the Bosque), note the proud statue of Morelos on his steed. The **Aqueduct** bordering the park was at one time the primary means of getting water to the city and these days continues its path over the landscape, ending at the **Tarascan Fountain**. The graceful arches once stretched for eight kilometers, supplying 30 public fountains where people hand-dipped their water for home use. Today there are 253 arches, with the highest at 7.5 meters.

Modern-Day Diversions

Bosque Park is bordered by several other sites of importance. The **Museum of Contemporary Art**, Calle Acueducto 18, is housed in another ex-mansion built in the early 19th century. You'll find contemporary art by local and international artists. Three salons exhibit artwork in a variety of media, from oils to acrylics, photography, and lithography. These displays are changed each month, so it's always a surprise. The **Museo de Historia Natural**, Av. Ventura Puente s/n, was inaugurated in 1986 under the auspices of the University of Michoacán. It is devoted to the protection of the state's natural resources and it documents investigations and the growth of the ecological movement in the state.

The **Benito Juárez Zoo**, on Av. Juárez and Av. Camelinas, about three km south of the *zócalo*, is a place to relax, be outdoors, enjoy children (yours or those of others), and observe the habits of a variety of animals. A small lake offers rowboats for rent, a nocturnal display, reptiles, a minitrain that cruises around the park, restaurants, shops, a children's play-

If you want to stay in an upscale inn with beautiful surroundings and a great view several kilometers away from the bustle of town, and if money is no object, the place for you is **Villa Montaña,** Patzimba 201, Col. Vista Bella; write Apdo. Postal 233, Morelia, 58090, Michoacán, Mexico, or call (451) 14-0231, fax 15-1423 in Mexico, or (800) 223-6510 in the States. This hotel is not only well thought of in Morelia, but it is ranked as one of the finest small hotels in Mexico. Don't expect to walk to the Plaza de los Mártires from here (in the Santa María Hills south of town); if you don't have your own car (rentals are available at the airport), expect to take a taxi. The huge, flamboyant villas are decorated with beautiful antiques and surrounded by well-kept, well-landscaped gardens. The gardens are filled with impressive statuary, much of it from the pre-Columbian period. The dining room is famed for its gourmet food. On the grounds are a pool and a tennis court; golf is five minutes away. Reservations are suggested, and rates vary depending on the villa you choose; all include a full breakfast. Premium to Luxury.

ground, a picnic area, and a fine ecology program. Animals come from five continents.

The **Convention Center of Morelia** offers a complex that includes a modern planetarium, the House of Orchids (called the Orchidarium), and the Morelos Theater. The **Planetarium** programs are presented on Sunday at 6 p.m. The dome brings the stars and planets closer to the waiting audience. The **House of Orchids** is a great adventure for both professional and amateur horticulturists or anyone who enjoys lovely flowers. The variety of flora and colors is impressive, and if you're there at the right time of the blooming season, the aroma is marvelous. **Teatro Morelos** is an oversized modern theater used in a grand style for cultural events. The schedule is available at the tourist office. Take the yellow *combi* going east on Calle Santiago Tapia to 20 de Noviembre. Remember to check the hour it stops running; it's a *long* walk back to the center of town. However, taxis are around.

From Plaza Chica the walk to Lake Pátzcuaro is just a little under two kilometers; a local bus leaves about every 15 minutes from Plaza Chica or any bus or *combi* marked **Lago** goes to the docks. Lake Pátzcuaro is well-known for its whitefish, and almost every café near the dock serves this specialty.

Morelia Highlights

Arts and Artisans

The colors, textures, and imagination of the indigenous are resplendent in all of Michoacán. This creative energy has established an economic boon for artists from small villages who just 30 years ago lived a poverty-level existence engaged in subsistence farming. Certainly they are not rich, but tourism has given these people a lift. Visitors spend hours browsing in stores from trendy to stall-like, in state-run workshops, public *mercados*, and upscale galleries. The state's beautiful arts and crafts live on, feeding on the success of its art.

In Morelia the **Casa de las Artesanías**, at the Ex-Convent of San Francisco on Plaza Valladolid, is not just a museum of state crafts, but a workshop and sales floor. You'll find some of the best-quality crafts from the famous surrounding towns. In many rooms you can observe artisans working. The quality here is excellent and the pieces are accordingly priced.

While visiting the **Casa de la Cultura**, Av. Morelos Norte 485, look at the fascinating exhibit of traditional masks used in ceremonies from all over Mexico. Check out the woven modern-style table linens in bright colors. It's open 9 a.m.-8 p.m.

More and more beautiful furniture is coming from Morelia. It *looks* handcrafted, and the carving is lovely and it *is* handpainted. On headboards and desks, wardrobes and chairs, you'll find interesting artwork in subtle pastel colors, designed in the shapes of fruits, vegetables, or geometric patterns. Many companies ship. Check out **Exportationes Guare,** Av. Heroes de Nocupitaro 421, tel. (451) 3-7946, fax 2-5763.

The following shops are always worth looking through if you're interested in Morelia art: **Artes Michoacanas Cerda,** Ignacio Zaragoza 163; **Artesanías del Centro,** Portal Hidalgo 197; **Casa de las Artesanías,** Fray Juan de San Miguel s/n (near the ex-convent of San Francisco); and **Cerámica Morelia,** Tomas Alba Edison 113.

For the Shopper

All sweets-lovers should stroll through Morelia's **Mercado de Dulces**, a delightful "sugar" market on the west side of the Palacio Clavijero. It's always fun. If you've never tasted *ate*, this is a good place to do it. It's a confection made of fresh fruit turned into a pastelike substance in many natural fruit flavors. Making candy was a grand tradition of the colonial era, handed down by European nuns who in turn passed on the tradition at schools for girls. Don't miss the second floor, where artisans exhibit their crafts.

Any place you look in the historic center of Morelia has fine or funky shops. Antiques collectors will delight in finding precious minutiae from the past and ancient religious articles that still circulate. Other shops specialize in local crafts. Michoacán ranks high as an all-round good state for major shopping. The variety of arts and crafts is huge, from copper *everything* (made in Santa Clara de Cobre) to woolen garments and beautiful, brilliantly colored, modern-day woven table linens that are perfect for decorating the table of the new millennia. You'll find intricately wrought silver filigree, woven straw, embroidery, and lovely lacquerware with inlaid gold that rivals that of Asia. In many of the communities you can watch the art as it's created.

¡Música!

Morelia offers more than the plastic arts. It's a musical city; New Spain's first conservatory of music was built in 1743. Today it is home to one of the largest organs in Mexico and a boy's choir of international fame, the **Boy's Choir of Morelia**, based at the Conservatorio de Música de las Rosas on Santiago Tapia, several blocks northwest of the plaza. This group of youngsters travels to the major capitals of the world giving concerts. If you're interested in seeing a performance, ask at the tourism office for the choir's schedule. Musical students continue to study here and to perform.

During the dark days of the Reform, the cathedral was used for many purposes that had nothing to do with religion (including the storage of grains).

Take any opportunity to attend the folkloric dances—especially famous in this area is the **Danza de los Viejitos.**

Musical events are becoming very popular in Morelia. In March listen for the International Guitar Festival; in May, the International Organ Festival at the cathedral; and in June, the International Festival of Music.

Special Events

Those looking will find fine entertainment at the Casa de la Cultura, Av. Morelos Norte 485. Each month it prints and distributes a calendar of events that informs visitors about dances, music, drama, art exhibits, holiday functions, and lots more. While you're here, look at the fascinating exhibit of traditional masks used in ceremonies from all over Mexico.

Regional Food

The state of Michoacán is noted for its tamales and sweets (among many other things). The tamales made here vary from sweet to meat to *picante;* one of the most famous is the *curunda.* Puffy and triangular, it is wrapped in fresh corn leaves rather than dry husks, which changes the flavor entirely. The *uchepos* are really different, made with fresh corn cut off the cob and ground with a little sugar and other spices. Fresh corn husks are used in this dish too and again result in a different flavor, especially after you spoon on chile sauce and sour cream.

The Spaniards were and are great sweets lovers, and so another traditional food they brought to Mexico was *pan dulce.* These sweet breads come in great varieties; some are made from slightly sweetened yeast dough with only the imagination to limit the melange of additional ingredients: candied fruit, sweet crumbs baked into the bun, cream fillings, and, and, and . . .

On certain days special pastries take on a party flair. Celebrations of the Epiphany (6 January, Feast of the Three Kings) include buns decorated with candied fruit; hidden inside

Sweet Morelia

Morelia is known for its sweets, many made from fruit. Before sugarcane was introduced into the country, candy was sweetened with coconut, honey, and fruit. *Dulces* (sweets) are still made with those ingredients, but now with sugar added. *Ate* is popular all over Mexico, but especially in Morelia. It's a simple fruit paste, made from a huge variety of fruits, with sugar and water added; it's then kneaded and formed into cubes. *Cocadas* are made with coconut, and, in Michoacán, are bite-sized and slightly cinnamon flavored.

Wherever you are in Mexico, as the Day of the Dead holiday approaches (31 October to 2 November), you will see sugar skulls with bright colored eyes, as well as caskets and skeletons. Look through the **Mercado de Dulces**, Av. Madero Oriente, s/n., which displays dozens of varieties of candy from all over the country.

one bun is a tiny doll of the baby Jesus. Whoever finds the doll wins the honor of hosting the Candlemas fiesta on 2 February.

Look in the street for the *churro* man, frying a long coil of dough in his big metal wok-shaped pan. Once out of the fat the *churro* is drained, broken into longish strips, and sprinkled with sugar; you only wait until it's cool enough to handle before you eat it. Really good, much like a doughnut, but somehow more delicate.

Buñuelos are a big favorite, especially at Christmastime, when they are served with hot chocolate. The *buñuelos* are puffy tender fritters, made from a sweet dough and then quickly fried in hot oil. While hot, either sprinkle with sugar or pour on a cinnamon and orange syrup. Forget the calories; they're delicious.

At the **Mercado de Dulces,** educate the "sweets-lover" within you. *Dulces* include crystallized fruit, especially figs, pineapple, mangos, and tamarinds. Whole glazed limes are stuffed with shredded coconut; brittles are made from an assortment of nuts, but also from sesame seeds and pumpkin seeds; chunks of candied cactus, pumpkin, and sweet potatoes are common. From this tiny preview, make major discoveries on your own.

Special Excursions

Butterfly Sanctuary

Millions of monarch butterflies make the yearly migration that takes them 5,000-8,000 kilometers from Canada and the central and northern U.S. to Michoacán. If you're here at the right time of the year, Nov.-Feb., visit the **El Rosario Butterfly Sanctuary.** The trip meanders to the forests, where the monarch butterflies cling to the trees in masses. Angangueo and Ocampo, villages at the base of sanctuary, provide public access to the sanctuary.

You start seeing butterflies at the small, unpretentious village of El Rosario. A sanctuary guide escorts all visitors through this high forest, and for about an hour you'll walk along steep mountain paths in the midst of a world that becomes black and orange. The monarch butterflies shroud the branches of the tall green *oyamel* trees and hang on each other for a winter of semi-snoozing, creating a vivid mass of fluttering orange and yellow that is one of nature's most extravagant displays. Have you ever heard the flutter of butterfly wings? If it's a warm day you will hear the flutter of millions. Expect to huff and puff a little; this is high-altitude hiking. The sanctuary is open daily 10 a.m.-5 p.m.

The simplest way to make this trip is with a tour operator. **Operadora Monarcha** in Morelia is a good specialist. The package includes transport, entrance fees, guide, and lunch. The trip takes you through Ocampo and Angangueo and into the beautiful mountains of the Eje Neovolcanico at 3,100 meters. For more information contact Gisela Medina at Av. Madero Oriente 635, C.P., Morelia, 58000, Mich., Mexico, tel. (43) 13-3571, fax 12-0075.

Pátzcuaro

Pátzcuaro is an enigma, a colonial-rich town that dates to a pre-Christian era, still one of the most indigenous cities of the country, and growing. If you can visualize the orderliness of Morelia, imagine just the opposite here. Pátzcuaro was drawn well, but no one colored within the lines. Whitewashed houses with red tile roofs climb up uneven, curvy, hilly streets; lush trees are shrouded in disorderly vines. Then it all falls into place when at the edges of this disarray the smooth green water of lovely Lake Pátzcuaro mates with the shore and drifts off dreamily to the horizon. Today the city is easygoing and laid-back, but it has known its share of violent and political history.

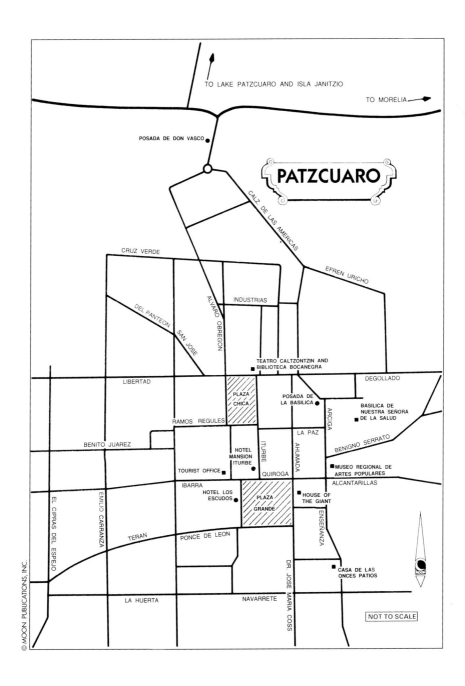

TO LAKE PATZCUARO AND ISLA JANITZIO

TO MORELIA

POSADA DE DON VASCO

PATZCUARO

CALZ DE LAS AMERICAS

CRUZ VERDE

EFREN URICHO

DEL PANTEON

SAN JOSE

ALVARO OBREGON

INDUSTRIAS

TEATRO CALTZONTZIN AND
BIBLIOTECA BOCANEGRA

LIBERTAD

DEGOLLADO

PLAZA
CHICA

POSADA DE
LA BASILICA

BASILICA DE
NUESTRA SEÑORA
DE LA SALUD

ARCIGA

RAMOS REGULES

LA PAZ

BENITO JUAREZ

AHUMADA

BENIGNO SERRATO

HOTEL
MANSION
ITURBE

ITURBE

MUSEO REGIONAL DE
ARTES POPULARES

TOURIST OFFICE

QUIROGA

IBARRA

ALCANTARILLAS

HOTEL LOS
ESCUDOS

PLAZA
GRANDE

HOUSE OF
THE GIANT

EL CIPRAS DEL ESPEJO

EMILIO CARRANZA

TERAN

PONCE DE LEON

ENSEÑANZA

CASA DE LAS
ONCES PATIOS

DR. JOSE MARIA COSS

LA HUERTA

NAVARRETE

NOT TO SCALE

🏠 The **Posada de la Basílica**, Arciga 6, tel. (434) 2-1108, across from the basílica on a little hill, provides a fine view of the town. The pleasant, simple rooms are in a very old colonial mansion—and close to loud church bells in the morning. The restaurant on the premises also possesses a lovely view. Eleven rooms adjoin an open patio. Inexpensive.

🏠 Just one of several old mansions that have been renovated to serve as hotels around the plaza areas, **Hotel los Escudos**, Portal 73, west side of Plaza Grande, tel. 2-0138, has 30 rooms with carpeting and satellite TV; some have fireplaces. A TV might be considered an asset in a town that closes up at 8 p.m. Inexpensive.

🏠 Many consider the 17th-century **Hotel Mansión Iturbe**, Portal Morelos 59, tel. 2-0368, on the north side of the plaza, to be the nicest on the Plaza Grande. Guests enjoy the colonial decor, heavy wood furniture, lace curtains, and a gentle ambience of the past. It has 15 rooms; the restaurant is open all day. Inexpensive.

Hotel rooms in Pátzcuaro run to simplicity. Be sure to bring sleeping-woollies in the winter since very few hotels provide heat, even though they may claim to—a single electric wall heater in a room with a 3.5-meter ceiling is almost a joke.

This was Vasco de Quiroga's city of choice and where he wished to establish his bishopric. His most needy parishioners, the Indians, lived here. A "bishop's" city benefitted from many financial perks in that era, and he began the building projects typical of a bishop's city. Quiroga wanted only the best for the Indians, and he planned a grandiose church for Pátzcuaro. It was going to be bigger than the Cathedral of Notre Dame in Paris. However, the politics between Valladolid (Morelia) and the church were rife, and Morelia's wealthy and powerful insisted on moving the center of Michoacán away from Pátzcuaro to their more aristocratic city.

The **Casa de los Once Patios** is one of the favorite stops for tourists; this centuries-old hospital-then-Dominican-Convent structure has many patios (but good luck finding eleven!). Visitors (shoppers) spend hours in the labyrinth of small workshops where craftsmen create their wares. Don't miss any of them; Michoacán's reputation for quality crafts is well-earned. You'll find a series of doorways that lead to weavings, woolen sweaters, table linens, silver jewelry, modern coffee sets, ceramics, and remarkable lacquerware with gold inlay—incredibly beautiful work. Note that none of the men doing the intricate lacquerware wears glasses, amazing when you consider the poor lighting and the close-up nature of the work. As one artist said, "When the work comes from the heart, the eyes follow."

The center of Pátzcuaro lies about a mile from the lake; much of the town is built on the side of the hill. But the very heart of the city is flat and easy walking. **Plaza Grande** is officially named Plaza de Vasco de Quiroga, with the statue of the beloved priest in the middle of this large, peaceful center of town. The plaza today is edged with restaurants, shops, all in lovely buildings built centuries ago. Only a block away lies **Plaza Chica**, the "other center of town"; its official name is Plaza Gertrudis Bocanegra. (She, her Indian husband, and their 10-year-old son fought on the side of the independence. After her family died in battle, she became a martyr for the cause and was shot in neighboring Plaza Grande while tied to an ash tree.) From Plaza Chica the *mercado* extends off the

west side. The Friday morning Indian market in the plaza features a
plethora of ceramics, woodcarv-
ings, lacquerware, copper, woven
goods, and even furniture, though
the market really bustles all week
long.

The **Basílica de Nuestra Señora
de la Salud**, which stands on the
little hill east of the center of town,
is a striking building. Of special interest is the statue of the Virgin en-
cased in glass. Tarascan craftsmen
created the statue from corn paste
and wild orchids in 1547. It's much
beloved, and on the Virgin's special
feast days, 8 December and 8 May,
pilgrims come from miles around

(¶) Visitors don't come to Pátzcuaro for the
gourmet food (this is blasphemy), not even for the
whitefish, which is highly overrated. Because it is
becoming increasingly scarce, it is becoming increasingly expensive (commonly about US$10-13
for an a la carte plate), and for the same money
you can get a lot of good Mexican food made with
masa, sauces, chiles, beans, etc. This is not to say
you can't find quality food in Pátzcuaro; several
pleasant places serve good hearty food at reasonable prices. One favorite is **Dany's**, open all day,
and equally good for breakfast, lunch, and dinner;
it occupies a rather oddly shaped two-story dining room, with the kitchen on the third floor. You'll
find it on the street between the two plazas.

(¶) **Posada de Don Vasco,** Av. De Lazaro Cardenas, serves tasty Mexican food in a charming
colonial setting. Check out the adjacent gift shop
and look at some of the "X-rated" scenes inside the
ceramic pots.

to salute the Virgin of Good Health. Two stairways lead to
the back of the Madonna. Here the people come to pin
the tiny *milagros* (metal images of arms, legs, hearts, and
heads). They also leave notes to either request favors or
to thank the Virgin for granting favors. Some make drawings and paintings; others leave crutches, even braids of
hair. Note the huge framed collage using thousands of
these *milagros.*

Quiroga built the first Colegio de San Nicolas in 1540
(when the bishropic was moved to Valladolid); it now
houses the **Museo Regional de Artes Populares**, at Calle
Ensenaza, one block east of Plaza Grande. Displays illustrate the crafts of the region, including those that occupied the Indians before the Spaniards arrived and the fine
arts the Indians learned from the Spanish artisans. Along
with crafts, an exhibit explains everyday life for these
early people.

In **Teatro Caltzontzin**, go to the upstairs hall and
look at the murals, which graphically tell the history of
Michoacán from the first meeting between Tarascan

The hilarious **Dance of the
Little Old Men** is a popular
folk entertainment created
shortly after the conquest to
poke fun at the Spaniards.
Each dancer wears a carved,
painted wooden mask—
pink-faced, with white bushy
eyebrows, a hooked nose,
and a smiling mouth.
Throughout, the dancers
remain bent over in an
arthritic posture, creating a
delightful rhythmic clatter
with their wooden boots and
canes. The whole thing is a
spoof; the young men
behind the masks must be
very limber to move the way
they do! Ask around
Pátzcuaro; the dance is
usually performed in several
cafés. In the Hotel Posada de
don Vasco, Av. De Lazaro
Cardenas, the show begins
about 9 p.m. Wednesday
and Saturday.

ruler Tangahxuan II and the Spanish conquistadors in 1522 until and including the reign of native son Lázaro Cárdenas in 1940. **Biblioteca Bocanegra** was
formerly the Church of San Agustín. You will find a number of English-lan-
guage books in the rear of this public library. Look for the fine mural by artist
Juan O'Gorman.

The **House of the Giant,** on the east side of Plaza Grande, is also referred to as the Casa del Gigante. The lovely colonial structure was named for its bigger-than-life-size statue of a soldier. His sword at the ready, he stands guard over the second-story living quarters of this 18th-century mansion. The building is well-preserved with colorful blue and white tile floor, graceful arches and columns, and wrought iron railings. Don't miss a walk through if you have the opportunity. Casa del Gigante was built by an unnamed count and is one of the older structures in Pátzcuaro.

Lake Pátzcuaro

Lake Pátzcuaro is one of the highest lakes in Mexico—and the world—at 2,210 meters. Small villages nestle on the shores of Lake Pátzcuaro, and on the right day the view of the lake is an artist's delight with blue sky, white puffy clouds, calm green water, and the famous butterfly nets of the Pátzcuaro fishermen. Like gossamer wings, the nets give a look of grace to the bulky wooden boats as they glide across the water. However, you seldom see the butterfly nets anymore; most fishermen have progressed to more modern means of fishing. But they still catch whitefish and then rush their catch to nearby restaurants. From the dock to nearby Isla Janitzio the boat ride takes about

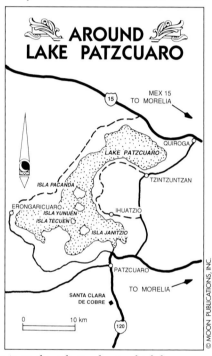

20 minutes. The most economical way is on the *colectivo* boat, which leaves as soon as it's filled; you seldom have to wait more than 15 minutes. Check the ticket office at the dock for other excursions available around the lake.

Isla Janitzio and Day of the Dead

Probably more people go to Isla Janitzio on the Day of the Dead holiday than at any other time. But on an ordinary day, a two- to three-hour day-trip is enough time to see just about everything you wish to on the small island. Add another hour for a fish lunch, and if you're so inclined, poke around the shops, which mostly sell gewgaws found anywhere. A path leads up to the enormous statue of patriot José María Morelos. The statue is 40 meters tall; a climb into the interior of the statue brings you to a mural that tells the story of Morelos's life. Further climbing, into the fist, brings you to an exit onto a terrace where the view is breathtaking, or it would be if you weren't already out of breath after the climb.

Often, when there are many tourists on the island, visitors will glimpse the butterfly boats performing.

On Day of the Dead many visitors travel to the island. On the evening of 1 November the panorama is dramatic. Traveling between the Janitzio dock and the Pátzcuaro dock are the famous butterfly boats, all the fishing boats, and shuttle boats, all lavishly decorated with candles and orange flowers. By nightfall the lake looks as if it's dotted with busy fireflies. The boats are crammed with people going and coming, singing chants, surrounded with puffs of incense. Once they're on the island, visitors fill the dock; people hurry along small paths carrying orange flowers, blue pots filled with tasty food, and candles wrapped in a scrap of paper. Day of the Dead is almost a bigger holiday in Mexico than Christmas. By 6 p.m. the church bells have begun to "summon the departed" from the land beyond; tolling bells and hundreds of candles help guide the deceased back and keep them from losing their way. The bells continue to ring until the sun rises. This is not a sad time; it's a happy vigil when families feel closer to their departed than at any other time of the year. It's almost a party, as a wake is a party.

Commuter boats run frequently between the Pátzcuaro shore and Isla Janitzio; the trip takes about 20 minutes.

The town of **Quiroga,** known as Cocupao in the pre-Columbian era, is another Tarascan center. After the arrival of Vasco de Quiroga, the name was changed in his honor. Today it seems to exist on its pottery business and its string of craft centers. A remarkable number of shops flourish in the small town, selling an immense variety of crafts. In July, the townsfolk celebrate the **Feast of the Blood of Christ** with a fiesta and torchlight parade, featuring a cornpaste statue of Christ made years ago by the Indians.

A walk through the crowded cemetery, with the heavy smell of candle wax mixed with the earthy aroma of marigold-type flowers called *cempasuchiles,* evokes private memories. At each grave people are busy beautifying the site, placing flowers all over the graves; the flowers are outnumbered only by candles. Each grave is different—photographs of the departed, a cherished toy, liquor, pots of fresh cooked favorite foods, a cigar, a preferred hat, all manner of things that were special to those dear people—the worldly "things" are intended to lure them back once each year on 1 and 2 November. This is a two-day celebration; the first night is especially for the dead children. The celebration is very old. Though today some people associate it with Christianity's All Saints' Day and All Souls' Day, or even Halloween, it was also part of the "death" ritual in the Aztec tradition. The ceremony began at the moment an individual died; rich offerings of food and other artifacts were intended to help the deceased make the journey to the other world. It was an easy transition for the Indians; with the introduction of Catholicism, two cultures merged.

Years ago on Isla Janitzio, the Day of the Dead was such a pristine, sincere celebration that it began attracting tourists from all over the world. Today it becomes so crowded with foreigners that it's almost hard to take a photo without capturing at least two or three outsiders in each pic. So be forewarned. If you can look beyond the outsiders (of course we would all like to think that we are not outsiders) and feel the real essence of the occasion, good. However, some visitors complain that the locals have made it a tawdry display. In reality, the locals are doing what they have been doing for centuries, experiencing their attachment to the dead in their own way, which as it happens dates back to pre-Christian days—it is *we* who have turned their private ceremony into a massive photo-op. By the way, don't take photos without asking permission first, and if refused, so be it.

If you want to tour the villages around Lake Pátzcuaro, and you're not driving your own vehicle, there's a bus available that stops at all the little villages. Also (check the sign at the Pátzcuaro dock), tour boats convey passengers to several villages on the lake. Each tiny community exudes a unique personality; some display nothing else.

As you drive from village to village one thing becomes very clear; Lake Pátzcuaro, like Lake Chapala, is obviously polluted. Indiscriminately dumped trash washes into the lovely lake with every rain. Plastic debris is becoming almost as common as wild grasses along the lakeshore. Conservation groups are beginning to crack down on offenders.

Santa Clara del Cobre

From Pátzcuaro it's convenient to take day-trips to many extraordinary small towns and villages along the lake, most with a variety of artisans. **Santa Clara del Cobre,** 20 kilometers south of Pátzcuaro, has been a center for copper work since before the Spanish arrived. At one time, copper was mined from the surrounding hills, though these mines are now coppered out. However, the town is still the copper center of Michoacán. The copper museum whets the appetite of the collector. Small shops and factories all over town produce traditional and modern sleek napkin rings, graceful flower vases, pitchers, miniatures, and whatever you might have in mind; special orders are made by request. A lovely copper roof shelters the kiosk in the Santa Clara town square. Lots of small shops border the main street across from the kiosk, all with copper crafts for sale.

At a local factory (one of about 50 in town), where a giant foot-operated bellows keeps the fire at a high pitch, visitors can watch while a fat red ingot is pulled from the fire. Three or four strong men beat in rhythm with 50-pound sledgehammers until the copper is cold, black, and flat. The craftsmen use every bit of scrap copper they can get their hands on. It's amazing how they manage to shape the metal using such methods.

The **Copper Fair** is held each August for a week.

Tzintzuntzán

At one time Tzintzuntzán was the center of Tarascan power. An easy drive, it's about 15 kilometers from Pátzcuaro on the northeast edge of the lake. An ancient people built a network of five unusual round structures called *yácatas*, which are believed to have been burial centers for their leaders. Down the hill from the unusual archaeological zone, a Franciscan monastery remains from the 16th century. The aged olive trees on the monastery grounds are said to have been planted by Vasco de Quiroga (before the crown banned the planting of grape vines or olives to maintain Spain's monopoly).

The town is filled with shops selling its well-known, dark green-glazed, primitive-style pottery. When you buy the pottery, consider what it will be used for, and ask if lead was used and whether its lead content is within the limits of safety (probably not). But the pottery is lovely for flowers or just to look at.

The Day of Dead Celebration is quite dramatic and colorful in Tzintzuntzán. The cemetery and the next-door *yácatas* are covered with hundreds of candles and thick paths of orange flower petals as the friends and families of the dead gather to talk, sing, and pray together. The souls will find their way to the special foods and drinks, including sugar skulls and skeletons and *pan de muerto* (a special bread of the dead), that are placed all over the graves or mounds, transforming them into altars. Great feasts of favorite foods are ultimately enjoyed by the friends and families left behind.

Wandering around the town will bring you to open markets displaying carved wood pieces, some almost life-sized, including saints, animals, crucifixes, and large chests and armoirs. The town's artisans also weave straw into a multitude of things beyond hats and toys.

Seeds of Independence

N othing is perfection, whether in politics, in love, in daily living, even in nature. And so it was in Nueva España, the rich New World. In the 16th century, a religious fanatic Spanish king (Philip II) used Mexico's gold and silver to fight religious wars in Europe. In the 18th century, political indifference to the descendants of Mexico's first settlers added to the brewing problems of Europe. When an Austrian monarch was brought in to rule, patriotism bloomed. Provincial cities spawned gatherings of disgruntled people who explored their disillusionment with Spanish leadership. The avant-garde spoke out, the strongest rose up; it was time for the country to fight for its independence from Spain. The cities of independent thinkers possessed some common denominators. Each gave birth to brave men and women who were willing to give their lives for what they believed in; in the end they all gave their lives. These "freedom fighters" came from all walks of life: soldiers, priests, civic leaders, and women opened the door and invited independence. In 1821, 11 years after that first invitation, independence arrived. These cities are as beautiful as any other, the old streets are still lined with old stone façades, but there's more—a lingering pride of accomplishment. Each of these cities is affluent, developed, bustling with the activity of the coming century, but each carefully keeps one foot in the glorious past.

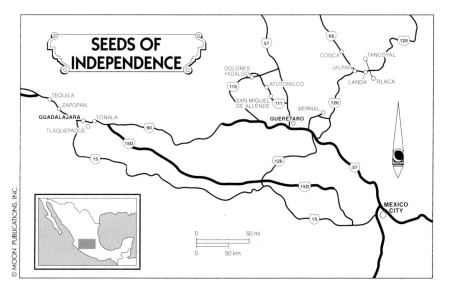

San Miguel de Allende

Between the northern coast and the province of Mechuacan, there are a certain people and town that they call Chichimecas; they are barbarians and less reasonable than the people of other provinces; I am sending 60 horsemen and 200 foot-soldiers, with many friendly natives, to find out the truth about that province and people.

From the Fifth Letter of Affairs,
signed September 3, 1526, by Hernán Cortés.

THE EXPEDITION CORTÉS WRITES OF WAS LED BY Captain Nicolas de San Luis Montanez, who was a converted Otomi chieftain from the borders of the wild Chichimec territory. The Chichimeca village he challenged would eventually become San Miguel de Allende.

By the mid-16th century many mines were producing quantities of silver. Mining was the most lucrative business in New Spain. Many of the areas that did not have mines were swept into the silver legacy because of the needs of the miners, muleteers, and wagon loads of men that traveled long distances between the mines and Mexico City. San Miguel fell into this category.

After the discovery of silver and gold in the central highlands, mule trains were used to carry the precious metals to Mexico City. These trains had to pass through territories controlled by the independent Chichimecs, and frequent battles occurred between the Indians and the muleteers, with many deaths on both sides. The Spanish viceroy decided the Chichimecs must be "evangelized" and that soldiers were needed to help guard the "royal" road. A Franciscan friar named Fray Juan de San Miguel soon had in place a thatched-roof adobe church, the beginning of Mission San Miguel in the center of Chichimeca territory, with a complement of Royalist soldiers stationed as the guards.

While the missionaries taught Catholicism to the indigenous people, the village offered a safe stopover for mule trains carrying freight or silver to Mexico City, and it was a logical place to buy supplies. As more silver trains passed through, haciendas grew and prospered in the surrounding area, and San Miguel became the local market center. Here *hacendados* bought and sold cattle, made equipment, machetes, harnesses, knives, spurs, stirrups, woven goods, blankets, cloaks, rugs, and woolen stuffs. Whatever was needed, San Miguel would provide. The frontier town thrived; great cattle haciendas proliferated near the market center and entrepreneurs built opulent mansions, churches, and civic buildings in the burgeoning town. Life, for a few, was sweet while the silver flowed past.

But not everyone was satisfied with his place in Mexican society. Native son Ignacio Allende joined Miguel Hidalgo of Dolores and played a vital part in the initial uprising of what would eventually become a successful fight for independence. Allende was killed early in the campaign and retribution for spawning one of the primary conspirators came in the form of mass executions and the destruction of local industries; the town barely survived the 11-year war. Once independence was achieved, Ignacio Allende's good name was restored.

Today's Bellas Artes was the Royal Convent of the Conception in 1755.

The name of the town had changed through the years, depending on the era. At first it was called San Miguel de los Chichimecas, and then San Miguel el Grande to differentiate it from the innumerable other villages called San Miguel. In 1826, its name was changed to San Miguel de Allende to honor its war hero, and the town rose to the status of a city.

After the war, much of Mexico went into a slump. Mines were neglected or destroyed, the elegant concentrations of Spanish splendor were abandoned, declined, and decayed, and so it was with San Miguel. Far removed from the bustle of Mexico City, and without the all-important mining operations, the town drifted into a sleepy state. While other cities grew, San Miguel snoozed —and became very poor. No modern buildings rose and no enterprise thrived on the cobbled streets. At the time it was tragic, but in fact the depression placed the city in a cocoon, a small time capsule that was destined for discovery someday.

In 1926, 100 years after San Miguel became a city, the federal government declared the community a Mexican National Monument. This declaration served to further limit modern construction and is responsible for keeping San Miguel and its rich old buildings safe from runaway development. As a result, the city still looks like something straight out of the 1700s (that is if you ignore the automobiles).

Culturally, San Miguel has something interesting going on almost every night. Check out the **Bellas Artes** at Hernández Macías 75 for a list of activities that can include classical concerts, poetry readings, and drama. A block away the **Teatro Angela Peralta** may be screening something to suit your mood. The tourist office can give you dates for the annual **Winter Music Festival** and the **Chamber Music Festival.** Art exhibitions are always fun here, with interesting people and often avant-garde renderings. And last but not least, the **Biblioteca Pública** has a great message board and *everything* visitors and expats are interested in will be here. You can pick up the English language paper *Atención*, with all of its listings, at the library as well.

SAN MIGUEL DE ALLENDE

CALZ. DE LA LUZ

TO DOLORES HIDALGO

CALZ. DE LA PRESA

ORGANOS

HIDALGO

RELOJ

LORETO

Quinta Loreto

SAN ANTONIO ABAD

VOLANTEROS

INSURGENTES

HERNANDEZ MACIAS

SEE INSET

BIBLIOTECA PUBLICA

MERCADO DE ARTESANIAS

CHURCH OF NUESTRA SEÑORA DE LA SALUD

MESONES

ORATORIO OF ST. PHILIP NERI

CHURCH OF THE CONCEPTION

CANAL

TO BUS STATION AND DOLORES HIDALGO

CHURCH OF SAN FRANCISCO

JUAREZ

SAN FRANCISCO

APARICIO

UMARAN

POST OFFICE

CORREO

QUEBRADA

ZACATEROS

CAFE DE LA PARROQUIA

SEE DETAIL

EL RINCON ESPAÑOL

CHIQUITOS

BARRANCA

PEDRO VARGAS

PILA SECA

JAIL OF THE INQUISITION

CUÑA DE ALLENDE

CASA DE SIERRA NEVADA

HOSPICIO

HOUSE OF THE INQUISITOR

CUADRANTE

HACIENDA DE LAS FLORES

CODO

JESUS

ALDAMA

DIEZ DE SOLLANO

RECREO

MONTES DE OCA

TENERIAS

TERREPLEN

HUERTAS

HUERTAS

VILLA JACARANDA

PIEDRAS CHINAS

ANCHA DE SAN ANTONIO

INSTITUTO ALLENDE ART AND LANGUAGE SCHOOL

DIEZMO

TO MEXICO CITY

CARDO

TO GUANAJUATO

MOON

0   150 m

INSET

DETAIL

RELOJ

HIDALGO

MESONES

BELLAS ARTES

CENTRAL

POSADA SAN FRANCISCO

SAN FRANCISCO

CASA DEL MAYORAZGO DE CANAL

HERNANDEZ MACIAS

CASA DE LOS PERROS

PLAZA PRINCIPAL/JARDIN

CORREO

MUSEO DE SAN MIGUEL DE ALLENDE

PARROQUIA DE SAN MIGUEL ARCANGEL

TOURIST OFFICE

The city remained in the shadow of various wars, changing governments, and economic ups and downs. "Ups" quietly began when as early as the 1930s foreigners discovered San Miguel and its low-key lifestyle, the "true" Mexican ambience. A few at a time began to move in. But not until the end of WW II and the advent of the U.S. GI Bill did the city become a real haven for Americans from north of the border. Many former GIs found the schools of San Miguel ideal, and a great number of men who had originally arrived as students never left. About 3,000 U.S. expats live here today. They find this "artist's colony" the perfect place to spend the rest of their lives.

Amazingly, in many ways life continues pretty much as it has for the past several centuries. It would be a lie to say that the city hasn't been changed by the influx of "foreigners." True, transportation now moves on wheels instead of clopping hooves, milk comes in cartons, tortillas are made by machine, and high-tech generators quickly restore electricity during bad storms. None of this, however, has anything to do with the important traditions of this small city. In fact, maybe the foreigners who come here to live change more than San Miguel changes. These outsiders are protective of their adopted town, they love the look and the feel of the town, they appreciate its beauty. And don't forget the *light,* perfect for the artist.

Exploring the Streets of San Miguel de Allende

Those coming to San Miguel should be aware that the city is hilly and steep. As in most colonial cities, some of the most desirable hotels occupy antiquated buildings; hence, no elevators.

A stroll through downtown San Miguel de Allende will take you past staid colonial buildings, houses with hand-wrought brass trim adorning tall carved wooden doors, and extravagant patios of great beauty filled with fountains, trees, flowers, and antique carvings. Around the square artists with easels and paint-spattered palettes try to capture the essence of the city. The striking centerpiece of the town is the neo-Gothic Parroquia Church, its façade supposedly crafted by an Indian artisan copying an image from a postcard. Wear your walking shoes; the streets are steep, narrow, and abrupt. Inside aristocratic 300-year-old mansions you'll find thriving businesses, trendy boutiques, intimate hotels, and gourmet restaurants.

San Miguel is protected by a number of patron saints, and there seems to be a church, and a small story, for every one. The architecture is unique; in most cases, the churches still display the glory of many centuries ago.

The beautiful **Parroquia de San Miguel Arcángel** towers over the *jardín,* (main square). The *parroquia* (parish church) was originally built

> ¶¶ A coffee with your morning paper at **Café de la Parroquia,** Jesús 11, is *de rigueur* in San Miguel. It's open till 3 p.m. every day except Sunday, when it closes at 1 p.m.

in 1683 by architect Marco Antonio Sobrarias, and it received a facelift in 1880. Contrary to what many think, this is not a cathedral. The legend is that the pseudo-Gothic façade was the work of Zeferino Gutiérrez, an Indian artisan of no training but great imagination. He patterned his work after the image of a French cathedral captured on a postcard. Most visitors find the results incredibly beautiful. A few trained students of architecture are more critical, sniping that the church should be considered "Gothesque," rather than Gothic. You can see the church spire for miles, especially when it's lit at night. The interior is typical, with chapels beside and behind the main altar. The crypt vault contains the remains of Felipe Gonzalez and Gen. Anastasio Bustamante, both heroes of the War for Independence. A sculpture of St. Michael the Archangel, namesake of the town and church, is displayed on the main altar.

Parroquia de San Miguel Arcángel honors the town's patron saint.

Church of San Francisco was constructed from 1779 to 1799, financed by local wealthy families and (so the story goes) proceeds from bullfights. It was called the Church of Saint Anthony until Anthony was deposed by Francis. The design is believed to be the work of Don Francisco Eduardo Tresguerras (1765-1833), who designed numerous churches throughout the highlands during the early 19th century. The church features the ultimate in Churrigueresque design. The ceilings are notably high, and a lovely natural light filters through the high windows. The church is filled with many paintings from well-known artists, interesting statues, classic Ionic and Corinthian columns, and doors and windows of carved stone. The **Chapel of the Third Order,** in the small square of San Francisco on the corner of Benito Juárez and Calle San Francisco, was completed and dedicated in 1713 by the Franciscans. It's a church of great simplicity, almost primitive, with bare walls and simple doorways. Compared to nearby churches it's quite stark.

The church of **Nuestra Señora de la Salud** (the Church of Our Lady of Health), which faces the open-air market, offers another bit of local history. The front door is covered with elaborate wrought-iron work; the dome is covered with yellow and blue tile; above the entrance is an enormous enveloping shell of beautiful carved stone. Just below the shell are life-size statues of the Virgin, St. Joachim, and St. Anne, each in a carved niche. Flanking the entrance are St. John the Evangelist and the Sacred Heart. This church was originally part of the Colegio de San Francisco de Sales next door. Here, Father Juan Benito Díaz de Gamarra taught Cartesian philosophy. This priest was well-educated and possessed a very open mind. He encouraged liberal thinking and organized public debates putting down the scholasticism of the period. Díaz de Gamarra instituted literary gatherings, unusual for the time. His thoughts were assembled in a philosophy manual later used as a text by the University of Mexico. The patriots Don Ignacio Allende and Don Ignacio Aldama, who fought in the war of 1810, were graduates of the College of St. Francis de Sales.

The Churrigueresque Church of San Francisco took 20 years to build.

The **Oratorio de St. Philip Neri** illustrates a tale of deceit and deception. The Indians of San Miguel built a simple church soon after they were converted in the 17th century, calling it Ecce Homo Chapel. In 1712 a visiting priest from Pátzcuaro fell in love with the town of San Miguel. Don Juan Antonio Pérez de Espinosa arranged a transfer to the town, and he was given the authority to build a new church. He chose the site occupied by Ecce Homo, decreeing the old Indian church must come down. He managed to convince all the inhabitants of the town, except the Indians, who had built the church

The oldest bell in the church was cast in 1732. Several wealthy families donated gold jewelry for melting; other metals enliven the sound.

Locals gave the church bells a name: the largest bell is **St. Michael,** another is dubbed **St. Peter,** and the oldest and the sweetest is known as **La Luz.** Together they broadcast a unique melody. It's a nice sound. You had better like it, because this town boasts more than 100 bells that can start ringing early in the day.

Church of Nuestra Señora de la Salud

with their labor *and* money. They didn't have a chance, of course, and through clever legal shenanigans the Indians were soon forced to give up their church. In the end the Indians graciously accepted their fate, and they were ordered to build the new church. To this day the Oratorio St. Philip Neri retains a back entrance where the Indians were allowed to exit and enter.

🏨 Central Mexico has an abundance of hot springs, resulting in many spas throughout the countryside. **Hacienda Taboada** is one of the nicest. The lovely white stucco and red tile rooms have balconies covered with bougainvillea blossoms or patios opening onto well-kept lawns and pools. The rooms are pleasant, though a little dark, with heavy colonial wooden furniture. Each bathroom includes a double-sized tub you can fill with natural spring water. The several pools on the grounds are of differing temperatures—the water comes from the ground at 44° C (112° F). The water is rich in minerals and very soothing. Besides the pools, the hotel offers colorful gardens and tennis courts. The dining room serves excellent food as well. The hotel provides a shuttle service to and from San Miguel, 10 km away. For more information, write to 747 Third Ave., New York, New York, 10017-2847 U.S.A., or call (800) 447-7462, (212) 223-2848, fax (212) 644-6840; in Mexico call (415) 2-0888, fax (415) 2-1798. Expensive.

🍴 A typical five-course dinner at **Casa de Sierra Nevada**, Hospicio 35, tel. 2-0415, fax 2-2337 for reservations, might consist of Atlantic shrimp with avocados and a tender vegetable salad; corn soup with fresh mintfoam; asparagus and tomato ragout in herb cream sauce; roast lamb chops with fresh herbs and homemade fettuccine; and a sinful surprise dessert. The price is worth it. Open for breakfast, lunch, and dinner. This is a jacket and tie establishment; the restaurant will furnish you with both.

The Oratorio features many domes in myriad shapes. Some are tall and slender, others are broad, rounded, crenellated, and multi-lanterned. All are quite impressive. The Indian builders used remnants of their old church, including the pink stone of the eastern façade and the figure of Our Lady of Soledad. The Indian artisans of the highlands always managed to inject a certain mystique into their work; the feeling of the early Indians is very strong in this church. The old leather altar screen brought over from Cordoba, Spain, features antiquated Renaissance detail embossed in gold. Thirty-three oil paintings offer vignettes of the 16th-century life of St. Philip Neri. From the Oratorio, you can enter the **Capilla de la Casa de Loreto** (Chapel of the Holy House of Loreto) through a magnificent entrance with elaborate twisted columns at each side. Manuel Canal and his wife, María de Hervas de Flores, founded and financed the construction of the chapel in 1735. Two niches contain statues in an attitude of prayer. These are said to represent the benefactors; below the niches lie their tombs. The gravestones bear the family coat of arms. The chapel is supposed to be a replica of the famous Holy House in Loreto, Italy, which in turn is said to be a copy of the original home of Mary in Nazareth. The ornate chapel is covered with glazed tiles from China, Spain, and Mexico, gilded rosettes, plaster angels in relief, stars made of mirrors, and a fine golden cloth blanketing the walls. An archway inscription claims "This is the home in which the Son of God was conceived." The chapel is usually closed, and you may have to ask to see it. In the octagonal *camarin* a reclining wax figure of St. Columbano is said to contain the saint's bones. If you study the floor tiles, you'll discern the coat of arms of the Canal family.

The **Church of the Conception**, on Hernández Macías, was begun in 1755. This major building project was supported by funds from the Canals' daughter and other wealthy villagers. The dome, one of the largest in Mexico, was not finished until 1891. The design is said to have been influenced by a picture of *Les Invalides* (in Paris), and many suspect it is the work of Zeferino Gutiérrez.

Two stories high, it has Corinthian columns on the botton and pilasters above. The gilded altarpiece is marvelous. The church has a massive wall and atrium which become more obvious as the street descends toward the church, finally ending in an archway.

Casa del Mayorazgo de Canal, on the west side of the plaza, was a beautiful mansion that still belongs to the descendants of Manuel Tomas de la Canal and is often referred to as "the count's house," though Canal was never a count. It was a mansion in the true sense of the word: the original entry exhibits Corinthian columns, the family coat of arms, heraldic symbols of both husband and wife, and a niche holding an image of Our Lady

Casa del Mayorazgo de Canal

of Loreto. The two-story façade and arched porch is one of the best examples of colonial architecture in Mexico. The grand old house has been completely restored and is used as a bank, but it is open for the public to view changing art exhibits.

Old-Home Tours, departing from the Biblioteca Pública every Sunday promptly at 12:15 p.m., are home and garden tours of some of the city's lovely homes. This is a great opportunity to see inside some of these ancient buildings and observe how occupants have adapted lovely old architecture to modern lifestyles.

Museo de San Miguel de Allende, beside the Parroquia and opposite Plaza Allende on Calle Cuna de Allende, is Ignacio Allende's birthplace. Another solid structure still showing neoclassic design, it now houses a historical museum. The museum illustrates the history of the area from the pre-Columbian to the period of Independence. Ignacio Allende is a beloved Mexican hero and the town is proud of its native son. Local historians are quick to point out that it was Allende who urged Hidalgo into the fight for independence. One of the few trained military officers involved in

The **Posada San Francisco,** Plaza Principal 2, tel. 2-0072, is an 18th-century restored mansion and really quite lovely. On the *jardín*, it offers 19 rooms and 13 junior suites. Guests enjoy a pleasant courtyard, coffeeshop, and convenient location on the plaza. Moderate.

the insurrection, Allende quickly became a leader and general, with only Hidalgo outranking him. In 1811, very early in the war, Allende was captured and executed.

Bellas Artes, Hernández Macías 75, in 1755 was the Royal Convent of the Conception; today it's operated by the government and associated with the Palacio Bellas Artes of Mexico City. Though it's called El Centro Cultural el Nigromante and Centro Cultural Ignacio Ramírez, most refer to it simply as Bellas Artes. It is the cultural heart of the city. This big impressive cloister is a must-see, especially the immense patio. Both stories house classrooms for art students and art exhibits of all persuasions.

> 🍴 **El Campanerio,** Canal 34, offers a sedate ambience and classic menu in one of the loveliest patios in town. Green tablecloths pick up the green of the lush plants, all surrounded by old stone arches. Good Mexican food.
>
> 🍴 For a slower-paced evening, try **La Fragua** at Cuña de Allende, a combo dinner/music club. It's a nice place to eat in an old colonial house, where Mexican music is king.
>
> 🍴 At **Rincón Español,** Correo 29, dancers perform flamenco most nights.

A fine example of the work from the muralist Siqueiros adorns the **Jail of the Inquisition,** Calle Hernández Macías and Calle Cuadrante. It sits across from the **House of the Inquisitor,** which was the office of the churchman who presided during the period of horror called the Inquisition. The Jail of the Inquisition is where the victims were housed until their fate was decided. On the building is the green stone cross with blue tiles that designated the Inquisitor's office. Now occupying the building is El Centro de Crecimiento, a center for handicapped children.

Casa de los Perros, Umarán 4, means "House of the Dogs." Note the carved *perros* at the main balcony. Formerly the home of another hero of the Independence, Juan de Umarán, this lovely building is now home to the Galería Mafuele.

San Miguel de Allende Highlights

Arts and Artisans

San Miguel has become an art center, attracting many foreign artists as well as fine Mexican artists. Several good schools offer instruction in all phases of art, from drawing to stone sculpture to weaving. Those who count these things claim San Miguel has the highest ratio of art galleries per capita of any city in Mexico; it's called the Montmartre of Mexico and compared to the art enclaves of Carmel, Key West, and Santa Fe. Art openings at galleries are one of the city's big attractions and occur frequently. **Galería San Miguel** is renowned for its contemporary art, and **Galería Atenea** is famed for national and international artists. The air of San Miguel is clear, attracting numerous *plein air* artists. Because art is so important in San Miguel, you can almost always find an art exhibit or two; shows take place year-round. Check with **Bellas Artes,** Hernández Macías 75, and **Instituto Allende,** Ancha San Antonio 4, or obtain more information at the **Biblioteca Pública** (public library), Insurgentes 25, two blocks north of the Plaza Principal. A local hangout for American and Canadian expats, this is a great library with a large selection—14,000 books in English. The patio is a pleasant place to sit and read; there's a bulletin board with daily info. The library is open Mon.-Sat. 10 a.m.-2 p.m. and 4-7 p.m.

The **Instituto Allende Art and Language School,** one of the town's most popular art schools, is a beautiful old building with a rich legacy on acres of land in the center of San Miguel. At one time the property belonged to the Canal family; when the institute bought the property in 1949, much reconstruction was necessary to restore the building to its original splendor. An image of the Madonna of Loreto, patroness of the Canal family, still stands in the main doorway niche. Remains of old frescoes adhere to the walls of the chapel, while a native-style Christ occupies the altar. The campus features gardens, extensive classrooms, studios, two galleries, a theater, a library, a coffeeshop, and many courtyards. This is a lovely old building, and if you ask the institute will arrange to let you take a look.

The institute offers classes varying from three Master of Fine Arts programs to straightforward conversational Spanish courses. Art classes include multimedia sculpture, silverwork and jewelry, enameling, traditional Mexican weaving, textile design, printmaking, painting and drawing, and ceramics. The faculty is augmented by a roster of well-known visiting artists

Villa Jacaranda, Aldama 53, tel. (415) 2-1015 or 2-0811, fax (415) 2-0883, in the U.S. (800) 532-0294, is one of "Mexico's Romantic Hideaways." A few of the 15 spacious rooms and suites include private patios. The central patio contains a "Roman plunge" pool and solar-heated hot tub. Credit cards are accepted. Open year-round. The hotel is known for its fabulous food and lovely dining spots, indoors and outdoors. Reservations are a must for dinner. Premium.

Hacienda de las Flores, Calle Hospicio 16, tel. 2-1808, is a small and elegant hotel with a colonial personality. The Las Flores is just two and a half blocks from the *jardín* and La Parroquia. At one time an old *quinta*, it now offers 11 rooms, a heated pool, and electric blankets. Rates include two meals. Ask if you're interested in prices without meals. Premium.

La Puertecita Boutique'otel, Santo Domingo 75, Col. Los Arcos, San Miguel de Allende, 37740, Gto., Mexico, tel. 2-2275, fax 2-0424.(800) 336-6776, is one of the newest and nicest small hotels in the city, sitting on the crest of a hill overlooking the town. The rooms are filled with a warm Mexican ambience, offering hand-painted sinks, woven bedspreads, and red tile floors. Services include 24-hour room service, a jacuzzi, a spa, a heated pool, a billiard room, fireplaces, and in-house massages. No smoking. Great cuisine is available here, or a hotel van will take you down the hill to the restaurant of your choice. Call or write for more information. Premium to Luxury.

and scholars from throughout the world. It's also a campus abroad for the Rhode Island School of Design, School of the Art Institute of Chicago, Pennsylvania Academy of the Fine Arts, and Canada's Ontario College of Art. For more information, call Mon.-Fri. 9 a.m.-noon and 3-6 p.m., tel. (415) 2-0190, or write to Instituto Allende, San Miguel de Allende, 37700, Gto., Mexico.

El Centro Cultural el Nigromante/Bellas Artes, also called the **Centro Cultural Ignacio Ramírez**, Hernández Macías 75, tel. 2-0289, offers art and music classes.

San Miguel Photography Workshops are held in a zealous little school summer and winter; tel. 2-1846.

Perhaps because of the eclectic collection of artists in San Miguel, you must look to find local art. But the overall collection here is really inspiring, as is the gathering of artists and art students.

For the Shopper

San Miguel is a shopper's paradise. Quality is high, and originality is unsurpassed. San Miguel has long been known for its metalwork; tin, brass, bronze, copper, wrought iron, and the precious artwork of talented silversmiths. Excellent traditional art, weavings, pottery, paintings, and sculpture are available as well. And anyone looking for folk art and local crafts will find terrific selections in many trendy shops. Arts and crafts are not limited to Mexican art; look around and see art from all over Latin America. Remember to visit the Instituto Allende for some imaginative original art for sale from the artist. As a rule of thumb, shops open about 9 a.m., close for lunch 2-4 p. m. and open again until 7 p.m., Mon.-Saturday. A few shops open on Sunday for a brief time. Many accept credit cards; however, not many will accept American Express. Most will take dollars and you usually get a good exchange rate with a purchase. Some shops will pack and ship to the U.S. or Canada.

Mercados

A good place to start looking for fine buys is the **Mercado de Artesanías**, in a little alleyway between Colegio and Calle Loreto. **Joyería David**, Zacateros 53, produces extraordinary silver art. **Casa Cohen**, Reloj 18, lives up to its reputation for cast brass and bronze as well as stone carvings. **Izquinapán**, Hidalgo 15, creates handwoven linens as soft as silk. Notice the Huichol masks. **Casa Maxwell**, Canal 14, offers folk art from all over Mexico and Latin America.

¡Música!

Besides the plastic arts, you'll find a concentration of musicians. The **International Music Festivals** occur throughout the year. During the first two weeks of August the annual **Chamber Music Festival** is held at the Bellas Artes. Contact your local Mexican Government Tourism office, or the San Miguel Tourist Office, tel. (415) 2-1747. Each year San Miguel sponsors a **Chamber Music Symposium**, and Bellas Artes offers special classes in dance and music.

Special Events

Feast of San Antonio de Padua: On 13 June, the Feast of Saint Anthony is celebrated throughout Mexico. In San Miguel, however, the festivities are a bit kinky. Saint Anthony is considered a cupid, and many young petitioners demand that he deliver them spouses or sweethearts. In San Miguel these pleas take the form of men dressing preposterously as women, while the women whimsically dress themselves as their favorite characters or don duds designed to poke fun at politicians.

Mexican Independence Day: Another important day of celebration is 16 September. Shades of Pamplona—the bulls run the streets; it's party time, with dancing, parades, fireworks, and flags.

The days before and after Christmas and Easter are filled with celebrations of a religious bent, lots of fun and tradition. Make reservations well in advance.

Regional Food

Salsas in different parts of Mexico can be very similar, or not. They usually look the same, and will contain certain ingredients that never change: tomatoes, chiles, garlic, and onions. That's just the beginning. Depending on the area,

> The lovely **Casa de Sierra Nevada,** Hospicio 35, San Miguel Allende, 37700, Gto., Mexico; tel. (415) 2-0415, fax 2-2337, in the U.S. (800) 223-6510, is a member of the prestigious Small Grand Hotels of Mexico and Europe's Relais y Chateau. The inn encompasses 18 suites in five ex-mansions on a cobblestone street near the cathedral and town square. Each beautifully furnished suite has its own personality and decor. Some have private terraces and many feature fireplaces. The warm atmosphere and attentive staff make this a world-class vacation spot. Guests will find safe deposit boxes, laundry service, room service, an in-house masseuse, a large heated pool, a spa, and one of the best restaurants in Mexico. Reservations suggested. Write for a brochure. Luxury.

the salsa might be all fresh vegetables, or it might be cooked. Tomatoes are always used fresh, sometimes quickly roasted to remove the skins. A peanut salsa is made with ground peanuts and chiles and served on rice. In the Yucatán Peninsula, just a bit of sour orange is added; it gives the salsa a delicious citrus thrust. Some salsas are made with the *tomatillo,* added after its brown paperlike husk is removed. The small, light green fruit is tart, and really isn't a tomato at all, but the flavor blends beautifully with the other ingredients. A rich salsa might include cubed avocado. Herbs and spices vary from chopped

cilantro to cloves, marjoram, oregano, and bay leaf.

Salsas are sauces, and though many think of them as something to dip chips into while waiting for the rest of the Mexican dinner, that's just one way of eating them. In Mexico, salsa is added to eggs, meat, sandwiches, marinated vegetables, fish, and of course tacos and enchiladas.

San Miguel de Allende, city on a hill

Special Excursions

Santuario de Atotonilco

Many people come to Atotonilco to see this lovely church with its fine display of art created by the indigenous people. Father Luis Felipe Neri de Alfaro founded the building as a sanctuary and place of spiritual retreat. Begun in 1740, the main section was completed eight years later, and additions continued for decades. The church boasts fine chapels and courtyards; small rooms decorated with murals, canvases, and sculptures; vaults, domes, and dome lanterns. More than in many churches, this one possesses some excellent examples of authentic Mexican folk painting; the walls are alive with color and fantasy. The church was the site of the marriage between the national hero Ignacio Allende and María de la Luz Agustina, widow of Don Benito Manuel de Aldama.

Hot springs are scattered all about the countryside. If you're really into unusual spas, contact the San Miguel tourist office and ask about **La Gruta** hot springs, which is in a cave. It's rather a far-out experience to soak in mineral water in the depths of the earth. It's close to the village of Atotonilco. Another spa, **Parador del Cortijo**, lies nine km from San Miguel along the same road to Dolores Hidalgo.

The curious traveler might want to check out the activity at the sanctuary, where the beautiful architecture and sculpture almost seem lost in the presence of people milling about the church wearing crowns of thorns and flagellating themselves with seven-tailed whips (called *disciplinas*). The Vatican outlawed this kind of thing many years ago, but the practice is still alive and thriving in parts of Mexico.

And it's big business. As many as 3,000 people a year stay here in small stone cells, sleeping on the floor. Businesses throughout the country operate like travel agents, organizing pilgrimages to Atotonilco, where people come to meditate, pray, and practice their "religious exercises" in the privacy of their cells. Vendors in front of the church sell crowns of mesquite thorns and multi-tailed whips of varying sizes.

On certain holidays, the dusty roads near the church are filled with penitents dressed in their best clothes, bringing arts, crafts, produce, or a hen or two to sell. The devout file into the church wearing crowns of thorns. Cannons roar during the night to frighten away bad spirits, while women and men (during separate weeks) slip behind the walls of their private retreat. These retreats go on year-round.

Dolores Hidalgo

The village of Dolores was just an Otomi hamlet called Cocomacán until 1570, when Viceroy Enrique de Almanza arrived and declared the town the Congregation of Our Lady of Sorrows. This became the viceroy's *encomienda*, as was the custom. The small village was a distance from Mexico City and pretty much ignored until 1710, when finally a priest was sent and a church was built.

In 1804, Father Miguel Hidalgo y Costilla, punished for not conforming to the rules, was shipped to the tiny village church of Dolores. And though this was not where he thought he should be, he was genuinely interested in the well-being of his impoverished Indian parishioners—in turn they held him in great esteem. Hidalgo founded a pottery and tile shop in an effort to help the people economically. The pottery industry thrived, and the town today is still a popular ceramic and tile center fast catching up with Puebla.

Hidalgo introduced silkworm farming and raised grapes; the latter was a big transgression. Wine making was forbidden in Mexico by the Spanish crown, which feared it would jeopardize wine importation from Spain, a big money-maker for the king. Hidalgo encouraged the formation of a musical band; historians say he loved to dance. Hidalgo was a rebel priest and he had a hard time accepting church rules that made life difficult for the peasant. More than 50 years before the U.S. abolished slavery, Father Hidalgo demanded the Mexican government do away with this barbarous practice. Today he would be called a liberal. Then, he was called criollo. Though his parents were pure-blooded Spanish, he soon realized that because he was born in Mexico he would never be considered for a plum position in the fine big cities of Mexico. Many priests of the day were rich, richer than some government officials. But Hidalgo knew this would not be his luck, and he, along with many other criollos, was fomenting a plan for revolt at a time of severe discontent. After months of secretly plotting a way to take over the Spanish government peacefully, Hidalgo was awakened by a frantic accomplice who arrived on horseback in the middle of the night to announce the plot had been discovered. After hours of confusion, they decided that since they were discovered they must either put a plan in action or face arrest. So in the hours before dawn on the morning of 16 September 1810, Hidalgo sounded the bells, bringing the townspeople to the church steps. The only part of his speech clearly remembered is his incendiary Grito de Dolores (Cry of Dolores), a cry calling for the people to revolt against their Spanish oppressors. It's still a stirring moment when, before midnight every 15 September in every town and city in the country, Hidalgo's cry is repeated by Mexico's president, governors, and city officials.

Criollos, mestizos, and Indians were inspired by the hometown padre and took up whatever arms were at their disposal—shovels, clubs, rocks. This was the beginning of what would become a bloody 11-year war. The agitating conditions were undeniable—the mestizos (mixed Indian and any other blood) were without hope, the criollos envied the power of the *peninsulares* (also called royalists, those born in Spain), and the Indians were slaves. The people could no longer tolerate the royalists; they had reached the breaking point. But Hidalgo's moments of glory would be short-lived.

At first Hidalgo and the rebels had the element of surprise on their side and did quite well taking towns with little or no fight, but Hidalgo was not a soldier. He was drunk with the power of success.

Hidalgo was excommunicated by the Catholic Church shortly after inspiring the revolt on 13 October 1810. But in the time he had left, this wild-eyed priest did what he thought was right. The people had found a leader with a heart, one willing to sacrifice his life for their cause. However, in less than a year Father Hidalgo was dead. He and his three leading *compañeros* were executed, their heads hung on a Guanajuato granary as a warning to other wayward thinkers wanting freedom. But this only provoked the people to fight harder against the Spaniards. Eventually the people won; the Spaniards returned to their homeland in 1825.

This sunny village, once called Dolores, has officially been designated the "Cradle of Independence." As such it's a popular destination for Mexicans interested in their country's history. Little is here to attract most foreign tourists except that it lies on the road between San Miguel de Allende and Guanajuato in the central part of the state. However, it vibrates with history, and those with curiosity enjoy a stroll through the town, a chance to stand on the church steps where Hidalgo gave his determined speech for independence, and the opportunity to visit Hidalgo's modest former home. Stop by the museums, the church, maybe have lunch, and investigate the ice-cream cone salesman on the plaza (with some of the unusual flavors that are popular and taste quite good, such as corn, chiles, avocado, *chicharrón,* cheese, and some unusual tropical fruits!). Try it before you deny it. And if you're wary of eating from a vendor, on each corner around the plaza are ice cream shops that all try to outdo each other with the most outrageous flavors possible.

Exploring the Streets of Dolores Hidalgo

The **Plaza Principal** is a large tree-shaded plaza and the centerpiece is a statue of Miguel Hidalgo. Growing here is a tree that legend says is a sapling from the Tree of the Noche Triste, the tree under which Cortés wept after his army was forced out of Tenochtitlán by the Aztecs.

The **Museo Casa Hidalgo** a block or two away is in Father Hidalgo's simple home of 1804-1810. The house has a small patio, one bedroom, and within

The Museo Casa Hidalgo in Dolores Hidalgo displays the famous priest's few possessions.

the building there's plenty of room to display his documents, furniture, eyeglasses, saddle, and the flag he used the night he urged his fellow citizens to take up arms and fight. He had few material belongings. Historical paintings that belonged to or depict the criollo priest are on display as well. The **Church of the Grito** is the parish church built 1712-1778. Its official name is Parroquia de Nuestra Señora de Dolores. With pink twin towers and an intricate façade, it's easily the largest building on the plaza. The bell used the night of 15 September to summon the townsfolk is kept in the National Palace of Mexico City, but here in the *parroquia* a replica of the bell hangs in the belfry. The church interior contains remnants of lovely baroque art and unusual paintings. Open daily.

The **Museo de la Independencia Nacional** near the plaza chronicles the horrific events that led to the War of Independence. Displays graphically illustrate the shocking behavior of the Spaniards, who destroyed the lives of millions of Indians. The atrocious details of their lives as slaves make clear the reasons the Indians so readily joined Hidalgo in his fight for freedom. They were filled with a powerful zeal, they so badly wanted him to succeed—most of the rebels from Dolores died before the fight really got started. The museum is open Mon.-Fri. 9 a.m.-2 p.m. and 4-7 p.m., Sat.-Sun. 9 a.m.-3 p.m.

Padre Hidalgo began a pottery school for the Indians in Dolores Hidalgo. He taught them how to improve their own styles, and taught the craft of Talavera pottery making. Today, Dolores is becoming a very popular place to buy ceramics of all kinds. A visit to the **Artesanías Vázquez Factory**, Puebla 56, will show how the craftsmen create their lovely pieces. It's a learning experience —from wrestling the clay to forming on a wheel to delicate painting to firing.

Guadalajara

GUADALAJARA WAS THE WESTERNMOST CITY IN SPAIN'S NUEVA ESPAÑA. The activity was not nearly as great in Western Mexico after the Aztec empire fell as around the "new" city at Tenochtitlán (today's Mexico City). However, a few Spanish explorers traveled through the area, hoping to repeat Cortés's conquest. Nuño de Guzmán, a lawyer, was appointed in 1527 to the Audienca, the governing body of Mexico representing the Spanish crown in Mexico City. This was the low point of royal history. Guzmán, a long-time enemy of Cortés, jumped into action with the conqueror's absence in Spain. Guzmán's treatment of the Indians is legend; he and his soldiers managed to wipe out entire communities of indigenous people with his brutality and intense greed. He forced them to labor long and hard in the gold and silver mines. His siege of brutality lasted until 1529. During that period, Franciscan bishop Juan de Zumárraga was appointed "Protector of the Indians" and sent to Mexico. It didn't take him long to see Guzmán for what he was: a cunning man who succeeded in keeping his actions a secret from the crown in Spain. Guzmán was guilty of corruption and extreme injustice toward both Indians *and* Spaniards. After many attempts and at great risk to his life, the bishop was able to smuggle a letter out of the country. The Spanish royalty was shocked at Guzmán's actions. Ever the wily manipulator, he was informed secretly of this exposé, and he quickly headed west in search of new lands to conquer—hoping to regain his place in the good graces of the Spanish court. Now in a much more isolated area, Guzmán continued to savage the Indians until in 1538 he was ordered to return to Spain—permanently. For the next 20 years he was a prisoner of the court, but because of his birthright, he was treated as a "noble" prisoner.

All the while, Spanish colonists continued to arrive in Mexico looking for the promised lands described to them in their homeland. They came with their horses, cattle, oxen, and other farm animals, tools, and the African slaves they bought as they passed through Cuba. Adventurers had grand ideas and were looking for large plots of ground on which to establish impressive estates; many of the early groups succeeded. Under Guzmán, the area began to develop. He envisioned his own "country" and called it "Nueva Galicia." He named its capital Guadalajara.

When the Spanish were still exploring the territory, Guadalajara became an important link in the chain. As an important supply center it began to grow;

today it's the second-largest city in Mexico. Dozens of Spanish explorers were equipped by and departed from Guadalajara. In 1692, Sebastían Vizcaíno left Guadala-

jara on a journey that would lead to the discovery of Monterey Bay in California. Gaspar de Portola and Father Junípero Serra with 12 Spanish soldiers and 40 Christian Indians made the difficult journey (on horseback and by foot) that eventually led to Portola's discovery of Drake's Bay and San Francisco Bay and Father Serra's establishment of San Diego and all the California missions.

The state of Jalisco and its capital, Guadalajara, managed to remain politically independent of Mexico City for decades and became almost as rich as the capital. It has witnessed dramatic historical moments, such as the abolition of slavery in 1810, the brief establishment of the Reform government of Benito Juárez in 1858, and the occupation of the city by the French army from 1863 to 1866. A serious Catholic center, nearby Los Altos erupted into the war of the Cristero (1926-1929) in its efforts to recover the liberty and privileges that had been withdrawn from the Catholic Church by Mexico's 1917 Constitution.

With its universities, museums, modern buildings, and prosperity, Guadalajara continues to dispense an air of independence and modern sophistication. Agriculture has always been a leading moneymaker in the state. Today Jalisco is Mexico's leading producer of beans and corn, which are marketed all over the country. It's sometimes referred to as *la granadita* (the granary) of the country because of its high-tech foodstuff storage and shipping facilities.

Today's Guadalajara is as modern as pink hair and derriere-hugging miniskirts. Yet the city is a bastion of tradition. High-tech sounds in the centuries-old Degollado Theater enhance musical productions, from opera to bolero to rock. Sleek new hotels mix with a skyline of aged domes and towers. Where you find young people living in the fast lane, you'll also find traditional *dons* and *doñas* living amid the ageless grace of Colonial Mexico. A tour of the city is indeed a shuffle between the old and the new.

Exploring the Streets of Guadalajara

Dozens of colonial plazas are scattered about the city, many with fine old churches. Actually, Tapatíos will tell you that if you try, you can find 100 plazas, all graced with a profusion of trees and flowers. Each of the few vouched for here is worth a visit. Every plaza is different; architecture includes Moorish, Tuscan, Mudejar, Gothic, Byzantine, and Corinthian. The **Plaza of the Mariachis** is noisy and fun-filled, in contrast with the **Jardín de San Francisco,** a quiet spot ideal for meditation. This spectrum adds a special depth to the texture of the city. Keep wandering and you'll find them all.

Visualize Centro Guadalajara as a giant cross-shaped area that includes four large plazas facing a series of colonial structures. Adjacent to the cathedral on

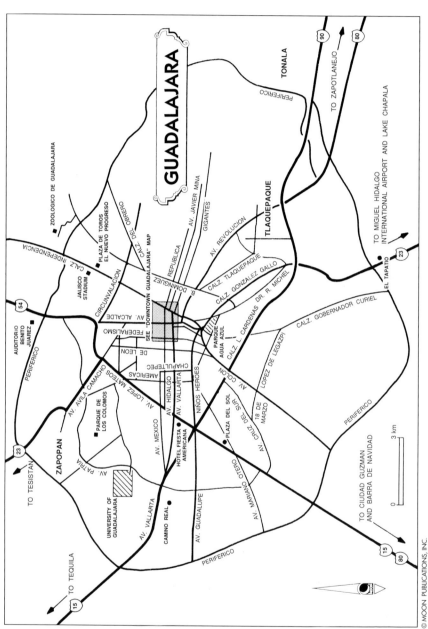

© MOON PUBLICATIONS, INC.

four sides are **Plaza de los Laureles, Plaza de Armas, Plaza Tapatía**, and the **Plaza de la Liberación** with its long waterspout canal. The Centro district attracts crowds of locals as well as visitors. You really don't *need* a reason to visit the center; it's a grand experience to be in the pulsing center of this delightful city. Several times a year Guadalajara puts on large-scale celebrations.

Construction on the monumental twin-towered **Catedral de Guadalajara** was begun in 1561 and it was consecrated in 1618, though it was not really complete by then. As with most large projects of the period, it was in process for centuries. This is a collection of architectural styles all lumped together: baroque, Byzantine, Greek, Moorish, Churrigueresque, Gothic, neoclassical. The lovely sculpture inside the cathedral called *Our Lady of the Roses* was given to Guadalajara by King Carlos V (ruler of Spain 1520-56). The towers of the cathedral were rebuilt after earthquake damage in 1848; the new ones are much taller than those they replaced. Eleven elegant altars were presented to the archbishop of Guadalajara by King Ferdinand VII of Spain. Take a look in the sacristy (ask and an attendant will let you in); the painting *The Assumption of the Virgin* was painted by Bartolome Murillo in 1650.

Bullfights are held most Sundays at 4 p.m. at the **Plaza de Toros el Nuevo Progreso**, Calz. Independencia Norte. Tickets range from cheap in the sunny *(sol)* section to as much as US$70 on the shady *(sombra)* side. Ask at your hotel or the tourism office for special dates for bullfights, and remember, you want the shady side of the arena. You can buy tickets in advance at the Plaza de Toros.

Fútbol (soccer) is undoubtedly one of Mexico's favorite sports, maybe even more popular than the *corrida* (bullfight). Check with your hotel for the schedule at the **Jalisco Stadium**, across from the Plaza de Toros, on Calz. Independencia Norte, and join the often 70,000 shouting fans.

The huge Catedral de Guadalajara represents a conglomeration of architectural styles.

Governors have used the Palacio del Gobierno since the days of Nueva Galicia.

The name gives it away —**Plaza de los Laureles**. This park in front of the cathedral is filled with Indian laurel trees. Look to the north side and note the **Presidencia Municipal**, where a mural depicts the founding of Guadalajara. This city hall is one of the few "newish" buildings in the historical center; it was built 1949-1952.

By creating pedestrian-only walkways, combining plaza areas, re-stoning old walkways, and adding *more* fountains, the city has turned **Plaza Tapatía** into a wonderful gathering place for everyday living as well as an impressive sight for visitors. In the midst of this central plaza, where clusters of historical buildings, monuments, and museums lie within easy reach, you'll find lovely old hotels, shady parks, shops, and innumerable restaurants. The government has been working on the central district with many plans to modernize the infrastructure and to preserve the old colonial structures.

Palacio del Gobierno sits on the east side of the pleasant **Plaza de Armas**. The two-story baroque/Churrigueresque structure was built in the mid-1600s and used as headquarters for the early governors of Nueva Galicia. The governor of Jalisco still uses the offices. Stone gargoyles drain water from the roof, and stone cannons continue to protect it from attack. The entire building is worth a study of the various art forms. The front entrance is bordered by heavy Doric pillars; take a look at the sundial in the central patio. Most visitors connect this impressive building with a comparatively modern man, native son and artist José Clemente Orozco. But perhaps its greatest historical moment came in 1810, when Independence hero Miguel Hidalgo proclaimed the abolition of slavery in Mexico (50 years before the U.S.). On the staircase of the palace, Orozco's mural of the event (painted in 1937) is powerful and invokes the heavy symbolism of an overwhelming church, the cruelties of the Spanish invasion, and a profusion of confused people led by an angry image of Hidalgo brandishing a torch with one hand and holding his other fist high. You'll find this immense work to the right of the large central patio in a deep stairwell.

The **Plaza de Armas** is a rest stop. After a visit to the Palacio del

Hotel Fiesta Americana, Av. López Mateos Sur 2500, tel. 631-5518 or 631-5566, was designed by someone whose heart was pure Mexican. You'll be dazzled by good food, a pool, lovely grounds, and decor from the colonial era. Luxury.

Gobierno and the Cathedral of Guadalajara, sit on a shady bench or have your shoes polished in Guadalajara's main square. A longtime tradition of the state band is to play music in the plaza on Thursday and Sunday at 6:30 p.m. North of the cathedral, the **Rotundo de los Hombres Ilustres** offers an unusual per-

fountains on the plaza

spective on some of Jalisco's more famous men. While these sculptures would never be called caricatures, they certainly have brought to life each of the men's characteristics in a down-to-earth way. The men represented are buried within this handsome circular monument surrounded by graceful columns in a tree-lined park between Hidalgo, Alcalde, Independencia, and Liceo Streets. The small park was built in 1954 and contains the remains of 17 men of arts, letters, and science, and (only) two military men.

An easy walk from Plaza de Armas, the **Museo Regional de Guadalajara** is another old building with an impressive history. The baroque structure is two stories high with a pleasant inner courtyard. Building began in 1696, and for 163 years it served as the Seminary of St. Joseph. In 1810 it served temporarily as a prison for captured Spanish soldiers during the War of Independence, and in 1918 it was converted to a museum. On the first floor, displays include exhibits of pre-Hispanic artifacts, pottery figures, and jewelry said to be more than 1,000 years old. Take a look at the replica of a 780 kg (1,715 pound) meteorite that fell on Zacatecas in 1792. Upstairs you'll find paintings from several eras, an ethnography area, and a peek into what life has been like in Jalisco since its colonial beginning.

> **Hotel de Mendoza,** Venustiano Carranza 16, tel. 613-4646, is another conveniently located old downtown structure with an interesting history. The hotel used to be a convent to the church (still in service) next door, Santa María de Gracia. Nearby on the other side is the Teatro Degollado. The hotel is quite nice, with 104 clean, modern rooms. Amenities include a swimming pool, parking, a restaurant, a bar, and a choice of room or suite. Moderate.

The **Plaza de la Liberación,** also called locally Plaza de las Dos Copas, stretches from the rear of the cathedral east to Teatro Degollado and is the commercial end of the plaza. On both sides of a long, narrow waterway fed by arching water spouts, a large number of shops and restaurants are open to the public. A statue of Miguel Hidalgo holds a broken chain to symbolize his call for the end of slavery in 1810.

Another neoclassic-style building, the **Teatro Degollado** was designed by Jaliscan architect Jacobo Galvez; it was begun in 1855 and completed in 1866. The first performance, on 3 September 1866, was the opera *Lucia de Lammermoor,* performed by Angela Peralta, beloved Mexican soprano of the Grand Italian Opera Company. The inside was renovated and now has a high-tech sound system for the entertainments presented, which include operas, classical concerts, rock concerts, jazz, bolero, and plays. Try to attend a performance of just about *anything,* but if it's impossible, take a tour. Note the classic dome and the proscenium. The multilevel interior accommodates more than 1,400 people in a plush elegance often compared to La Scala Opera House in Milan, Italy. You'll see murals everywhere inspired by Dante's *Divine Comedy,* painted by architects Galvez and Gerardo Suárez. The building sits in Plaza Tapatía with a high shooting fountain in front. On the triangular façade above the entrance, Apollo and the Nine Muses are portrayed in heavy relief. The back of the building is embellished with a stunning bronze mural filled with nine-foot figures depicting the founding of the Atemajaco Valley.

Instituto Cultural Cabañas, on the eastern end of Plaza Tapatía, is a beautiful example of neoclassic architecture; the institute was founded to provide a home for men, women, and children who were crippled, poor, old, abandoned, or orphaned. Built in 1810, the orphanage was the pet project of Bishop Juan Cruz

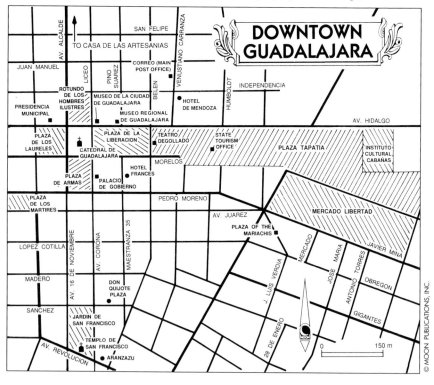

Ruíz de Cabañas, who financed it. Gradually the number of children grew until it was strictly an orphanage; as many as 3,000 children lived here at one time. Into the early 1970s children were cared for, educated, and given good medical and dental care by Jaliscense volunteers, mainly from Guadalajara. In 1983, the children were moved to a more modern building in the city, and the Cabañas was renovated to be used as a cultural center. The Cabañas is one of the largest colonial buildings constructed in the

> The **Hotel Frances,** Maestranza 35, tel. 613-1190, has been around a long time and has a special colonial charm. Originally built in 1610 as a simple inn, it has a long, colorful history of hosting guests that include politicians, revolutionaries, Hollywood movie stars, and tourists from around the world. Many changes and renovations have taken place over the centuries, progressing from an era when an inn provided stables for horses to the present, when guests expect color TV, tubs, and showers. This historic inn continues to be a favorite right down to the antiquated elevator. The hotel is centrally located and within walking distance of parks, colonial buildings, the cathedral, and the central plazas. The inn has 60 rooms, a lovely lobby with a bubbling fountain, bar, and live music. Inexpensive to Moderate.

Americas; it covers six acres and has 23 patios. Tourists come to see the collection of powerful murals by José Clemente Orozco, painted from 1938-1939. Don't miss the chapel and the dome where one of his finest works, *El Hombre de Fuego*, portrays Hidalgo as a sinister man of fire. Aside from the murals, visit the

museum with its large collection of Orozco drawings and paintings. Note the magical bronze sculptures of artist Alejandro Colungas. Each piece depicts a magician transforming himself into a sofa or a chair, and everyone is welcome to rest a while in these whimsical creations. Today, young and old alike find kindred spirits interested in music, dance, painting, sculpture, and film; marvelous dance festivals are held year-round. At the entrance you'll find a small bookstore that sells a number of titles mostly concerned with the history of Guadalajara; a few are in English.

In 1992, the 450th anniversary of the founding of the city was celebrated by the inauguration of the **Museo de la Ciudad de Guadalajara.** To the east of the Rotundo de los Hombres Ilustres, it's in a lovely old building that at one time

detail of José Clemente Orozco's mural in the Palacio de Gobierno

was part of a convent built in the 17th century. The various rooms of the museum will lead you through the growth of the city from the time of the early settlers until today. Just before Christmas visitors are invited to come to hear singing and have the special *posada* drink of the holiday.

Founded in 1791, the **University of Guadalajara** offers a good education to its students for very little money and has a fine international reputation. The main administrative offices are on Av. Juárez, and the rest of the university schools are scattered about the city.

Modern-day Diversions

The **Parque Agua Azul**, Independencia Sur, Cinco de Febrero, and Dr. Michel Streets—the oldest and largest park in the city—isn't just for nature lovers. Something is always going on: free Sunday shows, free Saturday art lessons, a flower market, an artisan's center, swimming pools, swings, slides, and a small zoo. Also, the **Museo de Arqueología del Occidente de Mexico**, part of the University of Guadalajara, displays a small collection of pre-Hispanic artifacts. Other attractions of Parque Agua Azul include an orchid house, an aviary, and a butterfly sanctuary. This green-year-round complex is a must-see for a peaceful afternoon. Redesigned in 1991, the park is separated by Calz. Gonzalez Gallo but is connected by a bridge. Wandering the walkways, it's easy to see what's going on in the outdoor theater and to check out the crafts in the **Casa de las Artesanías** ("House of Crafts"). This is the site of many activities of the Fiestas de Octubres.

Guadalajara Highlights

For the Shopper
Casas de las Artesanías

These two arts and crafts stores are operated by the state of Jalisco and are well worth a look around. You never know what the inventory will be for any given day, since the stock is whatever the craftsmen from around the state bring in. Frequently you find high quality with a little browsing. Both stores lie within walking distance of the town center; north, Av. Alcalde 1221, and south, Calz. Gonzalez Gallo 20 (near the Parque Agua Azul).

Mercado Libertad

This large public market, all under one roof, was built to replace the old market, where an entire street was devoted to a single product.

At first it's confusing getting around, but let your senses direct you; the heady aroma of leather directs you to shoes and saddles. You'll soon catch sight of artistic fruit peddlers who carve mangoes into yellow roses and display slabs of watermelon like round red tiles. Masses of traditional pottery are stacked and perched like fragile logwood. This is a hustling-bustling center for day-to-day living, bargaining, and picking up souvenirs from Jalisco.

¡Música!

Taking a break and having a cold beer on the **Plaza of the Mariachis** is a noisy, fun-filled musical experience, especially on Sunday, when dozens of mariachis give "free auditions" for which they do expect a tip of a few U.S. dollars. The music originated in the state of Jalisco not too far from Guadalajara during the occupation by the French. The word mariachi is a variant of the French word for wedding, *mariage*. During the occupation, guitarists and other musicians were recruited to make music for wedding parties and soon it was common practice to have a mariachi band for *any* party or celebration. A mariachi band generally consists of at least one each of a guitar, violin, and trumpet, along with stringed instruments from ukelele-size to a very fat, broad guitar. The music is happy, romantic, emotional, and lighthearted, and the players are highly respected. In the beginning the bands were just a few men who enjoyed playing and they wore whatever they chose. Today the mariachis are usually dressed in sharp-looking, traditional Mexican suits with short jackets over ruffled white shirts. All costumes are liberally decorated with silver. On their feet the mariachis wear pointed boots, and on their heads heavy, broad-brimmed felt sombreros with embroidered designs and silver trim. Some of these men are fantastic musicians with classical training, and some groups have as many as 20 men. Other groups are just friends who like to sing and play.

The Teatro Degollado is the home of the **Guadalajara Philharmonic Orchestra** (several American musicians play in this marvelous orchestra). Every Sunday at 10 a.m., the **University of Guadalajara Folkloric Ballet** puts on what is considered the most magnificent folkloric ballet in all of Mexico.

Special Events

Fiestas de Octubre: Crowds of people visit during this time, when parties are held everywhere on the plazas, and outstanding musicians, actors, and dancers come to perform in the Teatro. This is a colorful time to visit the city if you like action.

Another colorful, busy, but low-key time to visit is during Christmas holidays. A life-size crèche is displayed in the Plaza Tapatía, entertainment is provided for the kids (and the young at heart), and sidewalk vendors offer a collection of Christmas "specials" to the holiday crowds. Ask at your hotel or the tourism office where and when a *posada* for the public takes place.

Rodeo with a Tapatío Twist

The *charreada* is a kissing cousin of the U.S. rodeo; the biggest difference at a *charreada* is the dress of the participants; *charros* (male riders) and *charras* (women riders) wear elaborate costumes adorned with silver. Both men and women know horses well and show off their exceptional riding skills while doing much the same thing U.S. rodeo riders do: rope, throw, and tie calves and bulls, but with more emphasis on style and less on speed and competition. *Charreadas* are happening all the time—check with your hotel or the tourism office for the current schedule. A performance is regularly held on Sunday at noon at the **Aceves Galindo Lienzo** rodeo ring, east of Parque Agua Azul, tel. (36) 19-3232.

Regional Food

The chile peppers of Mexico are legend. Even though Columbus misnamed them, thinking he had found the pepper of the Orient, no matter. They contribute to some of the best food in the world. Specialists who are supposed to know say that all chiles have been derived from only five wild chiles. Now the number of chiles in Mexico is supposed to be in the range of a hundred, and all are members of the *Capsicum* genus. Mexican gourmets use both dried and fresh chiles, depending on the flavor they're trying to achieve. Certain dishes would be flat if it weren't for the chiles; *mole* is an example.

Cortés and his men were astounded at what they saw at the first market day in Tlacteloco. They could not believe the variety of fruits and vegetables, and it wasn't long before the myriad chiles became an important part of their diets.

Usually the first thing someone wants to know is how hot, or *picante*, a chile dish is. If this worries you, and you have no Spanish, ask your waiter, "¿Picante?" He'll try to pinpoint the degree for you; Mexican waiters are accustomed to visitors who cringe at the thought of *aiyeyayeye picante*. Remember, in most cases, it's the seeds that are the blasters.

A couple of the most common chiles in Mexico are the jalapeño and the smaller serrano, both mildly hot and found in uncooked salsas (among other things). The habanero is probably the hottest of all. The poblano is used in many Mexican dishes and is one of the mildest; it's commonly used for chiles rellenos. These are just a few of the common fresh chiles found in the market.

Big open burlap bags line the walkways of the *merca-do* filled with dried chiles—wrinkly-skinned red to maroon to all shades of brown—in sizes from half an inch to five inches long. A *chile ancho* is the dried version of the mild poblano. The *chipotle* is a light brown smoked version of the jalapeño. *Cascabel* is smallish, round, and the seeds rattle when you shake it; it offers a nutty flavor. The *guajillo* is long and thin and means "old dried thing." It's generally soaked and ground and added to stews and soups, and it is very hot. Anyone who decides to cook with the hot chiles should wear rubber gloves; the owner of a finger that goes from the center of a cut pepper to scratch an eye will regret it for many long hours.

A tequila bottling plant attracts visitors who (no surprise) are fond of Mexican tequila. The main activities on the tour of the **Sauza** bottling plant, Av. Vallarta 3273, are seeing how tequila is bottled and then "testing" it. Lots of people come here for the tour offered Mon.-Fri. 10 a.m.-1 p.m. Some folks just skip the tour and come to "test." If you're genuinely interested in how tequila comes to fruition, from the blue-green agave plant to a taste in a paper cup, take a trip to the town of **Tequila,** about 38 km east of Guadalajara, where there are a couple of distilleries.

Special Excursions

Zapopan

Zapopan is a small community that dates from pre-Columbian history as an important Indian village. It's now a suburb of sprawling Guadalajara, easy to get to by bus from Centro. Zapopan is best known for **The Corn-paste Virgin of Zapopan**, a small statue made of corn. Each June, the 10-inch corn-paste statue is taken from Basílica de Zapopan (her home church) to visit 200 churches in Jalisco. Pilgrims from surrounding villages and mountain communities come to the large *basílica* (built in the 1600s) to celebrate her 12 October return. People have great faith that this replica of the Virgin is responsible for saving many people from area floods. Her followers pray for special favors and in return make physical "restitution." The formal procession begins about dawn after mass at Guadalajara's downtown cathedral. It continues with about 13,000 followers, including dancers in traditional costumes, along the eight-kilometer (five-mile) route. Even Pope John Paul II visited this well-known *basílica* in 1979. Forty years ago, thousands walked great distances to get to the *basílica*. Today, many arrive jam-packed in trucks; the statue is even carried in its own car for part of the parade. A million people come to Zapopan every year for this party. The large churchyard is filled with families that have set up housekeeping for the duration of the fiesta, part of Fiestas de Octubre. Brightly colored squares of cloth make impromptu shelters in the large yard, small braziers are set up to cook the tortillas, portable *fondas* just outside the church gates sell red, green, and orange sugar water, mariachis play music, and it wouldn't be a fiesta without fireworks. On the day the statue is returned, beginning in the wee hours, pilgrims "walk" on their knees from great distances, a kilometer or two to the *basílica* (often as a thank-you for some special favor granted during the year). Young boys and girls, dressed in white shirts and pants and wearing a Red Cross band on one arm, scurry around to tend to those who've fainted or have bloody knees. Other Samaritans on the sidelines fold serapes and place them in front of the pilgrims, making a pathway of soft cloth to lessen the trauma to the knees. It's a very important and moving event for Catholics from all over the country. While at the *basílica*, go next door and look into the **Museo Huichol**, a combination museum/shop where the Huichol Indians display their intricate, colorful designs in both yarn and beads; all for sale. This shop benefits the artisans' co-op.

Tlaquepaque

At one time Tlaquepaque was an out-of-town destination, but the capital city has spread out to meet the small village. It takes about 15-20 minutes to reach Tlaquepaque from the center of town by taxi or a 30-cent local bus ride. A community has been living on this site since before the coming of the Spaniards. Legends tell us that these people were industrious craftsmen who created imaginative pottery using good local clay.

Over the years, Tlaquepaque village has gradually changed into a trendy little town. It took many twists and turns along the path to the 21st century. When tourists first began coming to the pottery and glass factories, quality was good. Somewhere along the way the quality of the art began to falter under the pressure of fame. Many more tourists with seemingly limitless amounts of money appeared ready to buy whatever was there. The temptation to succumb to the get-rich-quick mentality stalled artistic progress and Tlaquepaque began turning out commercial mediocrity—but only temporarily.

The true artists have now come up for air. Quality and tradition have been revived. Tlaquepaque has regained its reputation for producing stellar original art. Many well-respected artists are found in the small city, bringing new ideas, reintroducing old methods, and maintaining a deep interest in preserving the crafts of the past.

Along with the rediscovery of quality, the old mansions that line the street are being renovated one by one and restored to their original beauty. They make a wonderful backdrop to display modern or folkloric art.

Take a look at **El Dorado Galería,** Independencia 145, if you're looking for hand-loomed fabrics, tapestries, or bronze. The shop also carries some excellent modern ceramics. **La Casa Canela,** Independencia 258, tel. 635-3717, is chic and classy, and it's fun to browse in this 260-year-old *finca*. It's still owned by the original family. You'll find exquisite Mexican art, furniture, and antiques here. It's open Mon.-Saturday.

By now, many folks are familiar with the fanciful ceramic work of **Sergio Bustamente,** Independencia 236, tel. 639-5519. His eclectic papier-mâché and ceramic pieces vary from animal to human shapes.

Visitors find as much adventure in the shop-structure as in the products being sold. It's a delight to study the antiquated buildings with two-meter-thick walls, handpainted tile, black iron gates, great carved stone fountains, and often a sprawling display of antiques. Bring a lot of new pesos; today's artist recognizes his value and charges for his work accordingly.

During the colonial era the town became a get-away village for the rich merchants of Guadalajara. At that time people believed that Tlaquepaque was safer from earthquakes than Guadalajara.

Since the early 1970s the area in the center of town has been a pedestrian walkway, which makes it a delight to stroll and explore the small town. Visitors come in droves to wander through the countless shops that offer a huge selection of pottery, glass, textiles, wood carvings, furniture, paintings, jewelry, and metalwork; interior decorators go into feeding frenzy here. The town has a relaxing little plaza, El Parian, featuring music and excellent restaurants for a long late Mexican meal. Visitors drive, taxi, or hop a bus to Tlaquepaque for the day for a real "shop-till-you-drop" sort of vacation.

> (**Y**) A visit to Tlaquepaque would be incomplete without a stop at the most musical spot in town, **El Parian,** built circa 1800. Under the circular roof you can relax in *equipales* (barrel-design chairs traditionally made of rattan and leather) in sidewalk cafés, listen to lively mariachi music, drink cold *cerveza*, snack on traditional dishes including *birria* (goat or lamb), and have a good time. Sunday is the big party day for local color.

In Tlaquepaque getting around is simple; most of the high-powered shops are along the pedestrian walkway in the center of town (no vehicles here). The older, more popular places are within this center. Wander out to some of the peripheral streets (where cars still drive) and you'll find more shops and factories.

Tlaquepaque is a town of tradition as well as a visual feast of color and pattern. Some of the families have lived here several generations. The local museums hold some fascinating historical data. Stop and look at the **Regional Ceramic Museum**, Independencia 237, before shopping to get a quick education about Jalisco pottery, including regional designs. Fascinating displays date from the days of the Huichols up to and including today's fascinating trends. The old kitchen set up in the museum is charming. It's open Tues.-Sat. 10 a.m.-4 p.m., Sunday 10 a.m.-1 p.m.

Sanctuario de Nuestra Señora de la Soledad is the centerpiece of Tlaquepaque. The plaza and wrought-metal kiosk is right by the village church, a beautiful neoclassic structure built in 1878. **La Casa de Cultura** is in a renovated old building called El Refugio (The Refuge) that once operated as an insane asylum for women. Stop here to learn about the history and customs of the city.

For the Shopper

Shopping is the city's primary attraction. Most shops are open daily 10 a.m.-2:30 p.m. and 4-7 p.m. On Sunday many of the shops are open only a short while (10:30 a.m.-2:30 p.m.) to pick up the shopping traffic from (nearby) Tonalá's immense Sunday market. The rest of the week, plan on a nice leisurely lunch in Tlaquepaque between 2:30 and 4 p.m., when most of the stores close. You'll find shops and workshops in vast price ranges—one will fit your budget. Remember, the finer the quality the larger the price. The stores (except perhaps the very tiniest ones) accept U.S. currency and traveler's checks, and many accept credit cards; the stores will also pack and ship products to your home. It's always a good idea to use a credit card when you have things shipped. If things don't arrive or arrive broken, the credit card company will usually replace the goods or cancel the charge. In most cases things come through beautifully.

Many of the shops have their workshops attached, such as **La Rosa de Cristal**, the glass factory across the street from the ceramic museum on Independencia 232. You are welcome to observe the craftsman. If you travel during the summer, be sure you get to the glass factory in the morning; it's cooler then, and observers can't help but catch a bit of the "heat fallout" around the work space. The blowers don't work beyond 2:30 in the afternoon, and because of the excessive summer heat, they sometimes quit early. Note the lovely pitchers, plates, and figurines. If you want something special made to order, just ask the *patrón*. It's fascinating to watch the craftsman and his young apprentices working with molten glass. Visitors are welcome to watch on this busy patio. Just watch out for the long poles.

Tonalá

In the Nahuatl language, Tonalá means "Place of the Sun," and in the pre-Hispanic era, it was the seat of an Indian monarchy. Today, most inhabitants make their living from art. Almost next door to Tlaquepaque (15 minutes farther from Guadalajara Centro), Tonalá has become another well-known (though not as trendy) craft center. For years these factories have been manufacturing pottery to ship all over Mexico. The best days to come to Tonalá are Thursday and Sunday; the town becomes one big street market that shows off many artists in residence. This is becoming a primo place to find pieces worked in gesso, blown glass, ceramics, all types of metals, and handwoven textiles. Among other things many factory ceramic seconds are for sale, and with careful study you can get some terrific bargains. A few outstanding artists/potters have shops (most in their homes) in Tonalá.

At the **Guacamayas Restaurant**, Av. Tonalá 269, tel. (36) 683-0423, the sign says, "comida and crafts," and that's just what you get at Guacamayas. Stop for breakfast or lunch in the garden dining room, and then peek into the **Tropiche Workshop**, where you can watch craftsmen create whimsical papier-mâché figures. And of course, they're all for sale. It's op en daily 10 a.m.-8 p.m.

While you're wandering around town, walk up the "Queen's Hill," where you'll find a statue of the Indian Queen **Tzihuapilli** and a great view of the entire valley. Close by you'll find the **Church of Our Lady of Guadalupe. Museo Nacional de la Cerámica**, Constitución

110, tells the history of the popular arts in exhibits. It's open Tues.-Sat. 10 a.m.-4 p.m., Sunday 10 a.m.-1 p.m., free. For information, stop by the **Tourist Office**, Morelos 180, tel. (36) 683-0971.

Tequila

An indigenous group of Nahuatl speakers lived in this region and discovered the beverage now called tequila. The fermented agave plant has been popular for many years and has become the favored drink of Mexicans as well as people from many parts of the world. Tequila would probably be a unknown sleepy farm town if it weren't for the drink's popularity. The town has been the site of distilleries since the 17th century. Acres and acres of land surrounding the town are covered with a type of blue-green maguey plant, giving the countryside a blue-green glow. This particular agave is supposedly the *best* plant for the liquor and grows only in this area. Jaliscienses are proud of their agave and say that the liquor distilled in Tequila is the only "real stuff." The big distilleries in town are **Sauza** and **Cuervo**. Both give tours of their factories (yes, they include free samples). If you've never been to a distillery it's enlightening to see the process. Workers strip the swordlike fronds from the plant, exposing the "heart," which looks like a giant pineapple without its crown of leaves (the heart of these plants can

Ken Edwards's shop/ studio, Morelos 184, tel. (36) 683-0313, fax 683-0716, offers some fabulous modern creations, including lovely traditional stoneware and some exceptional "collectors items." It's well worth visiting while you're in town. Also visit the shop at the **Blown-Glass Factory,** Av. Tonalá 161, tel. 683-2624. Ask to see the "silver" blown glass, made from recycled glass one piece at a time. The shop carries fine Talavera tile from Puebla and the ceramic "tree of life" from Metepec (state of Mexico).

The town of Tequila is famous for its namesake drink.

rounding up the maguey

get very large, more than 100 pounds). Next they roast the heart and cook it in oversized copper kettles. Toward the end of the tour, you'll walk over immense tanks that hold what looks (and smells) like a witch's brew. Visitors become "experts" once they taste the standard (non-aged) clear tequila against the well-aged tequila gold. Notice the mural at the Sauza factory—it's a real Bacchanalian look at life. This small community leads the nation in tequila production, making more than 15 million gallons yearly. Exports go mainly to the U.S., Germany, and England.

Sauza Family Home is a deserted old *quinta* belonging to the family that began the Sauza Distillery. Ask at the plant to tour the building. A stroll through the old grounds is a wonderful step into the past and what must have been a gracious lifestyle. While visiting the age-covered structure, deserted gardens, chapel, great rooms, stone carvings, and reflecting pool, it's not unusual to find an exuberant teacher with a class of young children sitting with sketching pads and pencils. It's easy to get to Tequila by bus. The town is a primary bus stop on Highway 15 from Guadalajara and buses depart Guadalajara every 20 minutes from the old bus station on Calle Los Angeles or the Nueva Camionera. The trip takes about 30 minutes.

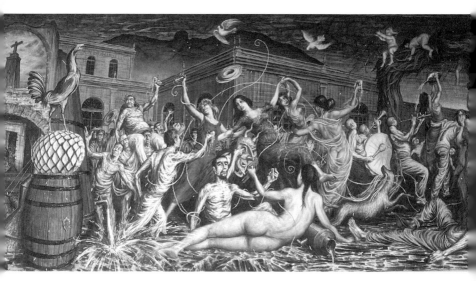

distillery art

Querétaro

IN 1531, AFTER THE CONQUISTADORS VANQUISHED THE OTOMI INDIANS, Querétaro was founded and called Pueblo de Indios de Santiago de Querétaro. Soon after the conquest, the Spaniards began the search for gold and silver—eventually they were overwhelmingly successful. The Royal Highway was constructed at the end of the 16th century and a squad of Spanish soldiers was stationed in Querétaro to guard the road and guarantee safe passage of the precious metals from the rich mines in the north to Mexico City. The presence of the soldiers did *not* always succeed, as proved by the proliferation of *bandidos* (highwaymen).

Querétaro's building boom began when the Franciscans arrived and built their headquarters and mission center in the mid-1700s. By the 18th century the political pot began to bubble with discontent between the Spanish crown and the *criollos,* (pure-blooded Spaniards born in Mexico). And even though Querétaro later witnessed many important events: the execution of Maximilian, the takeover of the city by U.S. troops, the signing of the Treaty of Hidalgo (giving thousands of square miles of Mexico to the U.S.A.), and eventually the signing of the 1917 Mexican Constitution, these incidents all stand in the shadow of the event most revered—the drama of Doña Josefa Ortíz.

Querétaro will forever shine in national fame, since this is where a cabal of free thinkers began plotting the overthrow of Spanish control. It was a time of unrest, conspiracy, and planning right under the noses of the viceroyalty. The machinations of Querétaro's historic players are quite provocative. Locals love to relate the story of collusion involving men and a woman, patriots who secretly plotted at candlelit meetings under the guise of a literary club. The intrigue grows more delicious when the woman, Doña Josefa Ortíz de Domínguez, wife of the mayor, dramatically rescues the overthrow plan while imprisoned in her own room in her own house. These were the movers and shakers who in the end played a big part in the Independence of Mexico.

Querétaro, capital of the state, shines with the aura of a comfortable living standard. As always, though, the Indian populations in the rural, mostly undeveloped regions are the last to feel the economic benefits of rising urban incomes.

Querétaro is a mountainous state; the Cerro el Gallo at 3,350 meters (10,990 feet) is the highest peak.

Rich in many precious minerals, the hilly state is a source of fine opals, amethysts, topaz, and silver. If you collect these valuables, you're safest buying only from reputable stores. Sidewalk "specialists" often try to sell you questionable gems.

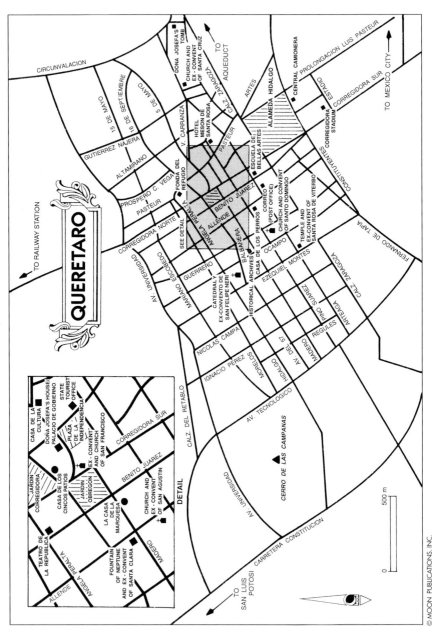

QUERÉTARO

CIRCUNVALACION

TO RAILWAY STATION

TO AQUEDUCT

TO MEXICO CITY

15 DE MAYO
15 DE SEPTIEMBRE
16 DE SEPTIEMBRE
5 DE MAYO
GUTIERREZ NAJERA
ALTAMIRANO
PROSPERO C. VEGA
PASTEUR
CORREGIDORA NORTE
AV. UNIVERSIDAD
MARIANO ESCOBEDO
GUERRERO

DOÑA JOSEFA'S TOMB
CHURCH AND EX-CONVENT OF SANTA CRUZ
V. CARRANZA
HOTEL MESON DE SANTA ROSA
PASTEUR
CALZ. ZARAGOZA
ARTES
ALAMEDA HIDALGO
CENTRAL CAMIONERA
PROLONGACION LUIS PASTEUR
ESTADIO
CONSTITUYENTES
CORREGIDORA STADIUM
CORREGIDORA SUR

FONDA DEL REFUGIO
SEE DETAIL
ESCUELA DE BELLAS ARTES
ANGELA PERALTA
BENITO JUAREZ
ALLENDE
CORREO (POST OFFICE)
CHURCH AND CONVENT OF SANTO DOMINGO
TEMPLE AND EX-CONVENT OF SANTA ROSA DE VITERBO

CATEDRAL Y EX-CONVENTO DE SAN FELIPE NERI
BALBANERA
CASA DE LOS PERROS
HISTORICAL ARCHIVES
OCAMPO
EZEQUIEL MONTES
CALZ. ZARAGOZA
FERNANDO DE TAPIA

NICOLAS CAMPA
IGNACIO PEREZ
MORELOS
MADERO
AV. DEL 57
HIDALGO 57
PINO JUAREZ
REGULES
ARTEAGA

AV. TECNOLOGICO

CALZ. DEL RETABLO

CERRO DE LAS CAMPANAS

AV. UNIVERSIDAD

TO SAN LUIS POTOSI

CARRETERA CONSTITUCION

500 m
0

DETAIL

CASA DE LA CULTURA
DOÑA JOSEFA'S HOUSE/PALACIO DE GOBIERNO
STATE TOURIST OFFICE
PLAZA DE LA INDEPENDENCIA
EX-CONVENT AND CHURCH OF SAN FRANCISCO
CORREGIDORA SUR
BENITO JUAREZ
JARDIN CORREGIDORA
CASA DE LOS CINCOS PATIOS
JARDIN OBREGON
LA CASA DE LA MARQUESA
CHURCH AND EX-CONVENT OF SAN AGUSTIN
TEATRO DE LA REPUBLICA
FOUNTAIN OF NEPTUNE AND EX-CONVENT OF SANTA CLARA
ANGELA PERALTA
ALLENDE
MADERO

© MOON PUBLICATIONS, INC.

Today Querétaro is a city of well-ordered plazas, flower-filled gardens, ornate structures—but more important—this is a city of powerful history. Everywhere you look you find reminders of this history. It lurks in every monument, mansion, and monastery. The city buzzes with historical events as well as whimsical hearsay, *chucherias,* (important and not-so-important) bits of gossip from the past. If you want more than just the dry historical facts, find a guide. Querétaro guides are inspired.

Today Querétaro is a 20th-century city totally in control of its destiny but with great respect for its history. Modern factories, clean, well-kept roads, and high-tech businesses thrive *almost* to the center of the city, and running through the middle of it all is the 1700s **aqueduct.** The towering stone monolith is the most grandiose "antique" in the city.

In its day it was a remarkable feat of engineering. Water was scarce in this arid countryside and during times of epidemic it was unhealthy. Don Juan Urrutia, the Marquesa de la Villa del Villar del Aguila, came up with the idea for the aqueduct. At first it was called "Don Juan's Folly," but the gentleman had great determination. Despite a total lack of cooperation by any of the other rich men in town, Don Urrutia continued the perilous construction that wound into the mountains eight kilometers to La Cañada, where copious springs spewed quantities of water. Twelve years later, the project was finished, complete with majolica ceramic tubes to carry the water cleanly to an ornate fountain in the middle of Querétaro village. The aqueduct was soon filling 10 public

some of the aqueduct's 74 arches

and 60 private fountains in the city. With 74 arches (some 22 meters high), it is said to be the seventh-largest aqueduct of its style in the world. Today it stands securely and placidly—in the center of modern-day telephone poles and rushing traffic—a graceful reminder of the past.

Exploring the Streets of Querétaro

The heart of the city is the oldest part. Narrow alleys, substantial buildings, and numerous plazas beg for discovery. It's small enough that the easiest way to get around town is on foot; the pedestrian walkways make it pleasant. Most visitors are delighted at the architecture and legends of these historical buildings, squares, and plazas. The streets reflect the era when strolling or horses and buggies provided transportation. In recent years, with the influx of more

The tourist office offers a free escorted walking tour of the most important sights of the city, with an historical overview thrown in. This is a great opportunity and the price is perfect; free. It begins daily (except Sunday) at 10 a.m.

and more automobiles, the narrow roads became dangerous traffic lanes that really hindered pedestrian traffic. So the city fathers closed a few boulevards to vehicular traffic and now more people than ever enjoy strolling around the "old" town via the *andadores* (walkways or alleys). What a difference it has made—in just a few years businesses have dressed up and multiplied. Inviting benches are scattered here and there amidst plants and tree-lined walkways. Small sidewalk cafés are filled with people chattering, in all languages. A good walker will find Andadores Paseo de la Corregidora (goes north and south); Cinco de Mayo, Libertad, and 16 de Septiembre (go east and west) and Vegara and Madero. These alleys are lined with two- and three-story structures. Many have been converted to museums, shops, hotels, cafés, and many gift shops selling the local arts and crafts. On Avenida Manuela Ancuna the vegetable markets create a brilliant patchwork. Spots of color and designs are created by stacks of orange mangos, green limes, red pomegranates, and displays of black avocados and bright orange squash blossoms—each a gastronomic delight of area cuisine.

And plazas! Plazas and parks are everywhere. It was the custom for the richest and finest houses to be built around a plaza. The churches all had large

The Ex-Convent and Church of San Francisco has served many roles: fort, barracks, and now a museum.

plazas as an extension of the church. In the heart of Querétaro the **Plaza de la Independencia**, also called Plaza de Armas, is a small but beautiful plaza with elegant cooling fountains. **Jardín Obregón** lies close to the Regional Museum. The centerpiece of the park is a bronze statue of the Greek goddess Hebe. **Jardín Corregidora** is another small park that was created in the memory of Josefa Ortíz; even the statue of the celebrated woman expresses her undaunting way of looking at life—through all eternity. Don't hesitate to explore the walkways that fan out from these plazas. You'll make remarkable discoveries.

Construction of the **Ex-Convent and Church of San Francisco**, on the corner of Corregidora and Cinco de Mayo, began in 1540 and continued for more than two centuries. One of the most important convents of Nueva España, it was the arena of several historical events. Under Maximilian it was turned into a fort; in 1867 U.S. troops used it as a barracks. Only in 1936 did it become the Regional Museum. The architecture is a lovely collection of broad archways, domes, and stone columns. Note the cupola on the church is covered with shiny Talavera tile. Its history is as rich as its architecture. The museum in the ex-convent houses a collection of artifacts and trivia from the city's early years. Most of the artifacts are on the first floor, and the upper floor displays an immense gallery of 17th- and 18th-century art.

From Jardín Obregón, the pedestrian walkway (going east) takes you past many small shops and cafés to the Plaza de la Independencia. Along the way, Indian women from small villages on the fringes of town sell, among other things, handmade embroidered cloth dolls. These ladies are almost always accompanied by their beautiful children—usually peeking out of a rebozo on mom's back. In the midst of this miniplaza, you'll see a statue of the **Marquesa de la Villa del Villar del Aguila**, benefactor of Querétaro and builder of the aqueduct. On the east side of the Plaza de Independencia another flamboyant old house, **Casa de Ecala**, displays the nouveau-Hispanic baroque style from the 18th century. Don Tomas Lopez de Ecala was governor in the 18th century and it was very important to him to exhibit his affluence to the world. He wanted the biggest and the best. Note on the façade an unusual window treatment; the intricate carving in stone resembles the folds of a pulled-back curtain. The building today houses offices of the state government.

Now used as the Palacio de Gobierno, **Doña Josefa's House** is more formally called Casa de la Corregidora and is one of the original Casa Reales, (Royal Houses); it was completed in 1770. Doña Josefa Ortíz de Domínguez lived here with her husband Corregidor (mayor) Don Miguel Domínguez. Most people are interested in seeing the legendary room above the entrance where Doña Josefa was locked under suspicion of being a traitor. Although the Palacio

---

Hotel Mesón de Santa Rosa, Pasteur Sur 17, Plaza de la Independencia, tel. (42) 14-5781, fax 12-5522, occupies a delightful old colonial structure converted into a 21-suite hotel with swimming pool, restaurant, and bar. The comfortable rooms still exude the aura of the colonial era, including arches and stone walls. An old fountain cools and brightens the inner courtyard. Before its rescue, it had decayed to the level of a slum with 70 "squatter" residents living on the premises. Moderate to Expensive.

La Casa de la Marquesa sits at Madero 41, tel. (42)12-0092, fax 12-0098. Each room is unique— and who knows what famous (or infamous) personality occupied it in the past. Emperor Don Agustín de Iturbide and President Don Eulalio Gutierrez were one-time houseguests. The rooms and bathrooms are decorated in colonial-era style, but since the hotel's renovation, they possess the luxurious amenities of today. The hotel is listed as one of the "Small Luxury Hotels of the World." Dinner at La Casa de la Marquesa is beautifully served in the sumptuous old dining room, and, more important, the food is very tasty. The menu includes continental and Mexican dishes. Luxury.

Even a governor has his moments. A popular story relates how Don Tomas Lopez de Ecala and a neighbor feuded over the property line while remodeling their houses; each tried to outdo the other. Ecala ended up the winner, gaining the freedom to enlarge and finish his unique house as he wished.

de Gobierno is the on-going seat of state government, visitors are welcome to visit the building, daily 7 a.m.-9 p.m., but not always the "fateful" room since it is often used for government business. The Palacio is on the north side of the Plaza de la Independencia, about a block east of Jardín Obregón.

Monument to La Corregidora, in the Jardín Corregidora on Av. Corregidora one block north of Jardín Obregón, is a dignified statue of Doña Josefa with a slightly Roman look; it was dedicated on 13 September 1910 to commemorate the National Independence Centennial. Querétaro is indeed a town that takes its history very seriously. Doña Josefa is the only Mexican woman to have her image on a coin.

When **Doña Josefa's Tomb**, another monument to the heroine of Querétaro, was built next to the Ex-Convent of Santa Cruz, it was designed to remember the

Doña Josefa was not the only person incarcerated in the Palacio. In the back quarter of the building, tiny cubicles served as prison cells; a one-meter by five-meter cell housed 15 convicts. The prisoners existed (just barely) on bread and salt water. Their jailers hoped that the salt would cause dehydration and that the prisoners would die on their own. However, if prisoners clung to life too long, they were taken to the back patio and hung until they died.

Doña Josefa's Arrest Starts a War

First, Doña Josefa tapped the heel of her shoe on the wood floor, attracting the attention of a loyal servant, Ignacio Perez. Through the keyhole of the locked door Josefa whispered her instructions. Perez immediately stole away into the night on horseback, heading to San Miguel and the home of Ignacio Allende. By a stroke of bad luck, Allende was gone. The quick-witted Perez took the message of Josefa's arrest to Juan de Aldama, another important player in the plot. De Aldama immediately made his way to the village of Dolores, and found Allende already there with Father Miguel Hidalgo. Between them they agreed that the discovery of their nonviolent plan for the overthrow of the Spanish Crown placed them all in jeopardy. The decision the three patriots made that night would affect thousands of lives over the next 11 years—and beyond. In the wee hours of the morning, Hidalgo tolled the church bells, wakening the small village. Then, from the church steps, Hidalgo gave a short impassioned message to his people, ending with his Grito (shout)—"Death to bad government!" Thus began the War of Independence.

many famous people of Querétaro. However, the main memorial is for Doña Josefa. Her tomb at the pantheon's center contains the remains of both Josefa and her husband, Don Miguel.

On the hill known as Cerro del Sangremal the Otomi Indians surrendered to the Spanish. And as the story goes, the Indians were encouraged in this peaceful move by the miraculous appearance of St. Santiago. In respect for the saint and the Indians who laid down their weapons, the **Church and Ex-Convent of Santa Cruz**, on Independence St. at Manuel Acuna, was begun on the hill in 1654. In the convent the first College of Apostles of Fide Propaganda in America began instructing the Indians in Christian teachings, and it is still a parochial school. Historically prominent men have walked these corridors: Junípero Serra (California missions) and Fray Antonio Buenaventura (who founded the mission that ultimately became the city of San Antonio, Texas), but probably the most famous resident was Emperor Maximilian of Hapsburg (the Austrian archduke who for three years became the emperor of Mexico, supported by Napoleon III). For a short time in 1867 he used the convent as a fort; later, after his capture, he was kept in one of its cells as a prisoner before he was executed. Visiting this museum is well worth a visit, with demonstrations of what everyday living was like in that time: cooking methods, water storage, naturally cooled refrigeration room, friars' cells, and the cell occupied by Maximilian as he awaited his execution.

Yet another tale about Doña Josefa tells of her background. Orphaned at an early age, she was raised by an elderly aunt in a very cloistered atmosphere. At 16 she broke loose and married don Miguel Dominguez. Was it love? No one knows, but hearsay claims that one of the dedicated patriots involved in sparking the War of Independence was her lover—and, perhaps, her motivator? Before anyone could find out they were all killed.

The Church and Ex-Convent of Santa Cruz was built to honor an Otomi Indian surrender.

The convent is open free to the public, and it covers a large area; the best way to see it is with a guide who will explain all of its charming aspects, legends, and history. Check at the bookstore for guide service in English and Spanish; a tip for the guide is expected (usually the guide is one of the brothers and the tip is really a donation to the convent). Expect a 15- to 20-minute walk from the plaza. Once there you have a wonderful view of the city and especially the aqueduct.

Built as someone's beautiful home in 1770, the colonial ex-mansion **Mesón de Santa Rosa** sits across from Plaza de Armas. For many decades it was a home for a large family. However, at some point it was abandoned (as so many of these homes were when the rich were forced to share their property) and for more

🏨 On the way from Mexico City to Querétaro, you'll come across another ex-hacienda, the **Hotel la Mansión Galindo,** about two hours into the trip. On the grounds visitors find beautiful old halls, a multitude of arches, wood-carved balustrades, stone fountains, tile walkways, lots of shade trees, grass, flowers, and blossom-covered stone walls. Guest rooms are spacious and furnished in an elegant conservative style befitting an antique building that flourished hundreds of years ago. The dining rooms are beautiful, with oil paintings, linen and crystal table settings, and excellent service; open to the public for breakfast, lunch, and dinner. Golf can be arranged. Write for more information, Carretera a Amealco Km 5, San Juan del Río, 76800, Qto., Mexico. Expensive.

La Casa de la Marquesa, where an emperor and a president once stayed

than a hundred years it functioned in a variety of ways, even as a hotel. The passage of time and lack of upkeep contributed to its decay; at one point it became a tenement. In 1992 the governor rescued the once-lovely old structure from an untimely end. Talented hardworking craftsmen renovated and gave it new life but left its original colonial design intact. Where once the blacksmith tended the horses of the house, there's a bar; where the horses were stabled, there's a swimming pool; the pine lintel that spans the original doors is more 200 years old. The best of the era remains, and it is now one of the loveliest hotels in the city.

One of the largest viceregal buildings in the city, **Casa Don Bartolo** on the Plaza de la Independencia exhibits unique architecture and ornamentation from the 17th and 18th centuries. No one knows the exact construction date, the original builder, or its history before it became the home of Don Bartolo Sardanetta, Marqués de Rayas (one of the wealthiest men in colonial New Spain). The architecture is unique both inside and out. Note the corner balcony and you can't miss the building's bright color. Today it is used as the office of the state's Ministry of Education.

At **Casa de los Cincos Patios** (House of the Five Patios), two blocks west of the Plaza de la Independencia on Corregidora, the graceful architectural design is simple baroque. Moorish arches and columns separate the broad patios, which are colored a delicate peach with deep sienna and white trim. It was built between 1742 and 1781 for Don Pedro Romero de Terreros, Count of Regla (another mining mogul of the times). It now houses the Language Center of the Mexican Culture Institute.

The **Teatro de la República,** on the corner of Juárez and Angela Peralta a block north of Jardín Obregón, has served as the backdrop of important historical events. Within the decorative columns, multistoried box seats, and velvet drops, the powers-in-place in 1867 pronounced Maximilian's death sentence, signed the Constitution of 1917, and in 1929, politicians met here to establish the principles of the PRI party—still the political force of Mexico in the 20th century. Construction began on the theater in 1845 and was completed in 1852. In 1922, the name was changed from Gran Teatro Iturbide to Teatro de la República. For some time it was the seat of the legislature. Today, it's used for cultural events and state ceremonies. Visitors are permitted Mon.-Fri. 10 a.m.-3 p.m. and 5-9 p.m.

The **Fountain of Neptune**, on the corner of Madero and Allende, one block west of Jardín Obregón, looks just as most would expect. The stone statue portrays a well-muscled man clutching his trident, ready to protect his minions while standing tall over the denizens of the sea. The fountain was

The hills surrounding Querétaro are filled with ex-haciendas. Most have gone the way of abandonment, but many have not. A few survivors of the bad years have become hotels. For those wanting to stay in a hacienda or just see one, visit for breakfast, lunch, and dinner. **Hotel Hacienda Jurica,** just 16 km north of Querétaro, tel. (42) 18-0022 or 18-0001, fax 18-0136, is a 17th-century ex-hacienda covering 10 hectares with lovely gardens and inviting walkways. The structures still reflect the beauty of their beginnings, with three-meter-thick stone arches and stucco walls. Some of the spacious rooms have tiled patios. An old horse buggy rig is on the grounds. The hacienda lies about a 15-minute taxi ride from Querétaro. Premium.

Strolling along the pedestrian-only walkway in the historical district near Corregidora, you'll find several charming sidewalk cafés, including the **Fonda de la Refugio.** This is a favorite for any time of the day. It's open 7:30 a.m.-10:30 p.m. Moderate-expensive.

constructed in 1797 and designed by Don Francisco Eduardo Tresguerras, one of the most famous architects in neoclassic design.

The **Ex-Convent of Santa Clara**, one block west of Jardín Obregón, is a few steps from Neptune's statue. Built in the 17th century, only the church remains. At one time this was part of a very large religious complex that stretched over several blocks and accommodated 8,000 Clarisa nuns. No matter how many church towers or cupolas you see, each has its own personality. Note the door of the anteroom to the sacristy as well as the interesting forged grating that crowns the same. Tresguerras is believed to have designed the main altar of the church.

Construction of the **Church and Ex-Convent of San Agustín**, at Allende 14 Sur, began in 1731. The moderate baroque style of the

the Fountain of Neptune, built 1797

façade is carved from quarry stone. The dome, on the other hand, is a lovely example of a more Mexican baroque. Life-size angels wielding carved musical instruments surround the dome with outstanding detail. The cloister here is quite pretty with highly decorated arches, subtle pinks and deep siennas, and a richly carved fountain in the center. The **Museum of Art of Querétaro** is in the cloister of San Agustín ex-convent. After the monks left in the 1800s, it was ignored and left to decay. However, the "bones" of this antiquated structure were really sturdy, and during Porfirio Díaz's regime it was renovated and used for

government offices. Almost one hundred years later it became the museum of art. The museum is well-run and displays a fine collection of works by various Querétaran artists and many Latin American and European artists from the 16th to the 20th century. Locals are encouraged to participate in choosing exhibits and workshops and in raising money (from auctions and concerts). The bookstore is well worth a browse, especially if you read Spanish.

The **Historical Archives** building on Ocampo 70 was constructed at the end of the 18th century in the neoclassic style, and the building alone is worth a look. It has had many uses over the years. One of its notable lives was as the National Palace and state government build-

The Ex-Convent of Santa Clara once was home to 8,000 nuns.

ing. Today it contains memorabilia of the colonial era: old periodicals and newspapers, ancient birth certificates and marriage licenses, property transfers, old deeds, and all other historical records.

The Count of Regla, Pedro Romero de Terreros, had the good fortune to inherit large amounts of money from several relatives. And, being a wise man, he invested in an engineering project that revived one of the richest mines in the state of Hidalgo, Real del Monte. The rejuvenated mine made him the wealthiest man in the country (after Cortés)—so rich that he lent King Charles III a million dollars. Even more impressive, he designed and paid for the construction of a man-of-war ship that he graciously bestowed upon his King. The beautiful three-decker cedar and mahogany ship was built in Cuba. If you travel around Mexico much, you'll run into Regla-built homes in many cities of New Spain.

The **Casa de los Perros** at Allende 16 is a unique but simple old house occupied by owner/architect Ignacio Mariano de las Casas until he died in 1773. Undoubtedly, it gets its name from the doglike gargoyles on the baroque façade. In the center of the courtyard note the fountain supported by winged sphinxes. The imagination of the designers in the 17th century continues to amaze. In one corner of the house is a small "for repentence" spot. Today the house is a kindergarten school.

Maximilian of Hapsburg and his generals Miramón and Mejía were executed by a cadre of sharpshooters on 19 June 1867 on **Cerro de las Campanas**, the Hill of Bells. A small memorial to Max sits in the midst of a cool green park on the rise of the small hill. A guide will no doubt tell you the legend in which Max gave each of his executors a gold coin to shoot straight and not at his head. Depending on which historian you read: yes, they shot him in the heart; no, despite the gold they shot him in the head. Also on the hill is a large statue of Benito Juárez. Many think this site on the west side of the city is worth the half-hour walk from the town center.

La Casa de la Marquesa was once the palatial home of the wife of Don Juan Urrutia. The intricately carved portal door has been admired for years, since well before the entire house was renovated. Each carved door in the house has a different look—some in the baroque, many designed with exquisite Moorish details. The interior of the house sings with bright colors, vivid tiles, and unusually carved wood. It's truly a house fit for a king, or in this case, a queen. Built in 1756, it was totally renovated and long-forgotten details were rediscovered and refurbished, such as wall paintings that once had been covered with something more modern. The building served as the Office of Foreign Affairs under the regime of President Venustiano Carranza. This was a house of great luxury; today it continues as a luxurious hotel.

Everywhere you look in Querétaro you see old churches; many are no longer religious structures and have been converted to other needs. A few still conduct masses, and you'll know this at sundown, when the bells of the various churches ring out in a lovely symphony. The front of the 1786 **Catedral y Ex-Convento de San Felipe Neri** is unusual, with its brick façade covered with columns and ornamentation that lean more to the austere neoclassic. Pope Benedict XV raised its status to cathedral in 1921. The property is known as Palacio Conín (dedicated to the prominent Indian named Conín before his conversion). It is now a state government office. The **Church and Ex-Convent of Santo Domingo** dates from 1692. Planned and built by architect Ignacio Mariano de las Casas, it's a large simple structure on the corner of Guerrero and Pino Suárez. Still another that was planned by architect Mariano is the **Temple and Ex-Convent of Santa Rosa de Viterbo**, built in 1752. This unusual design features jutting curvatures unlike any seen in the city. The interior of the church is another shining example of Churrigueresque combined with its own brand of baroque. Many artistic sights, large and small, will catch your

the unusual façade of the Temple and Ex-Convent of Santa Rosa de Viterbo

eye, but in particular note the pulpit with its inlaid wood and ivory design.

Modern-day Diversions

Queretanos enjoy a modern park, **Querétaro 2000**, with facilities for sports and recreation including an open theater and library. Even if you're not in the

According to legend the tree with cross-shaped thorns in Santa Cruz sprouted from the walking stick of a saintly priest who spent his last days in the patio of the ex-convent.

A legend is whispered about one of the richest men in the city, Don Bartolo. Before he made his millions, in a moment of despair, he made a deal with Satan—trading his soul for all the riches man could desire. He achieved great power and wealth. But, in the end, emotionally desolate, he ended his life with a bullet.

mood for sports, visit the remarkable sculpture of life-sized pre-Columbians playing an ancient ball game, stone ring and all. Another venue for active modern citizens, **Corregidora Stadium** is an arena that will comfortably hold 41,673 people and that offers parking for 6,700 cars. The structure was designed so that it could be emptied of all people in 10 minutes. All soccer fans welcome!

With two universities, Autonoma and Tecnologico, the town is filled with students—and something is almost always going on at night. Check at the **Universidad Autonoma de Querétaro** for evening cultural entertainments sponsored by various classes of fine arts. For the most part these entertainments will be in Spanish, but if you're having fun, you're understanding a universal language. For those into classical music, the **Escuela de Bellas Artes** music department offers classical concerts every Friday evening at the corner of Independencia and Juárez Sur beginning at 8 p.m. At the same place on Sunday at 6 p.m. there's a popular get-together with sing-alongs and a variety of popular music; it's free. **Casa de la Cultura** sponsors frequent entertainment such as dance, drama, art, or other cultural performances, at Cinco de Mayo 40. The tourism office offers a two-hour tour of the city.

Aficionados of the *corrida* (bullfight) will find that **Plaza de Toros Santa María** southeast of the city is one of the finest bullrings in Mexico. Built in 1963, it holds 10,000 people. The season begins each year in November and continues until February. Querétaro attracts some of the most courageous matadors and bulls. Occasional *corridas* are held out of season for special holiday events. The tourist office has schedules and other information.

Querétaro Highlights

Regional Food

In the public market the tortilla stall is always the busiest place. Folks line up to buy two, four, or six kilograms of tortillas every day. The staple of the Mexican diet, they are still made by hand in many homes, but a large percentage of people buy them for a reasonable price, saving hours of work on the *metate* (grinder) and the *tomal* (griddle). One could spend 20 minutes observing the whole operation: 50-pound plastic sacks of shucked corn kernels (called *nixtamal* after soaking in limewater) stacked in a corner of the stall, the machinery that grinds it, the pale yellow or white dough, the unsophisticated conveyor belt that carries the dough across the live-flame cooking surface, the patrons who patiently line up for the fresh results, and let's not forget the baker, who hands the traveler several tortillas hot off the fire along with a friendly smile. If you're looking for a shop along the streets, they're most easily found off the main historical center; look for the sign that says *tortilleria*.

Absolutely the best-tasting tortillas are handmade. Nothing beats starting from scratch, soaking the kernels in limewater, grinding them by hand, and then cooking them over a *tomal* (metal or ceramic). However, they take lots of time and effort, and as in households all over the world time is a precious commodity. In some bigger, more affluent cities, the "breadman" still delivers lumps of *masa* all made and the cook (whether the lady of the house or the hired cook) might pat the tortillas out by hand, or use a tortilla press; the press can be either wooden or cast iron. If that still takes too much time, or there isn't a delivery man, then there's the market or small neighborhood *tortilleria*. The price of tortillas is controlled by the government.

Are you wondering why **Cerro de las Campanas,** the Hill of Bells, is called so? Behind the small chapel on the left side, you'll see several large boulders. Pick up a rock and hit one of the boulders; instead of a dull thud, the sound is melodious, like a metal bell.

The magic nights for plaza music are Saturday and Sunday evenings, when there's free music for everyone. The state band plays at **Jardín Obregón** beginning at 6 p.m. On Saturday evening at 6 p.m., the **Plaza de la Independencia** comes alive with magic, music, and mimes.

Bernal Dulces, Pasther Sur 70, is a great little shop run by the family of Pedro Montes Dorantes in the lovely city of Bernal. Here the homemade *polvarones* (cookies), *buñuelos* (sweet buns), and a variety of candies including *natias* and *queretanas,* lure the sweet-lover into a look around.

Special Excursions

Bernal

This charming small town off Highway 120 is either very crowded (on weekends and holidays), or completely deserted. Along the old streets a couple of small simple hotels, a couple of restaurants, gift shops that specialize in wool vests, and the terrific little **Bernal Dulces** invite all. The *buñuelos* are fantastic. Bernal has a popular festival to celebrate the **Feast of the Holy Cross,** 3-4 May. Artisans come from the surrounding areas to sell at the market; they set up stalls with woven goods and semiprecious stones: opals (common in this area), quartz, amethysts, and some carved stones.

Sunday is a popular day in Bernal; many visiting climbers come, lots of them. Most of the pilgrims come to climb the **Rock**; also called Bernal, it's just minutes outside town. The rock is immense, a monolith second in size only to Ayers Rock in Australia. The town is 2,100 meters high, and the rock is 2,500 meters high at its crest. The view from the top is spectacular on a clear day. If you visit on a cool winter day, you almost think you're in a rustic town in the Swiss Alps. The big basalt rock looming in the background looks like sandstone with a lot of lichen; in the fall the lower half is dabbed with blue and red wildflowers, really quite lovely. A small "chapel" sits about halfway up, though the local priest is too old to say mass there anymore. The chapel is about as far as most amateur hikers get. Beyond that, you need special skill and equipment,

Just outside the town of Ezequiel Montes, on Hwy. 20, **Cava Antonelli Winery,** tel. (467) 7-0049, invites visitors to tour its complex. Open since 1968, the winery produces about one million liters yearly. It's an interesting tour because so much of the work is done by hand. For instance, the bottles are turned by hand daily, the wires and corks on the champagne (called *spumoso* in Mexico) are placed by hand, and 12 workers wash and fill the bottles. Grapes are harvested in October. Antonelli produces chenin blanc and traminer whites, plus cabernet, merlot, and burgundy reds. It also makes small quantities of sherry and champagne. Recently the winery began making vodka from grain alcohol and apple cider vinegar. It doesn't have wine-tasting rooms as in the United States. However, if you want to throw a party there, you're invited to buy wine (at a good price) and bring your friends. To tour the winery you must make reservations.

or at the very least good boots and gloves to protect your hands. Someone has driven pitons into the upper rock to assist the climber. Figure about an hour to get to the chapel. At the base of the rock a small free campground (rather dirty) has tables, benches, and a "loo." For information, write to Villa San Carlos, Ezequiel Montes, Barrio La Capilla, Bernal, Querétaro, Mexico.

The Rock in Bernal is the world's second-largest monolith.

The Sierra Gorda Missions

It's really best to have a vehicle to take this long detour, but for adventurers interested in history, missions, and low-key architecture, it's worth the time and effort. Before Father Junípero Serra embarked on his famed mission trips north to California, he and Father Francisco Palou made their way into often rugged regions of the Sierra Gorda. Here, five missions, founded in 1744 by Don José de Escandon, were constructed and organized by these two priests. Amazingly, the state has restored many of the buildings and even operates a few small hotels in the area, conveniently near archaeological zones as well. Don't rush this trip. The roads are not freeways; allow at least three full days.

Father Junípero Serra was born in Mallorca and came to Mexico with the Franciscans to teach and evangelize in the New World. Father Serra spent seven years in the central plateau of Mexico. His California missions are famed worldwide, but those in Mexico are just beginning to gain renown. The last mission Serra supervised was the Mission Dolores in San Francisco. Junípero Serra is buried in Carmel, California.

All five of these churches are architectural masterpieces, each with the same floor plan. As you face the front, the bell tower stands to the left of the main door, with the attached convent and priest's quarters farther to the left. All are Romanesque, containing a dome with a cupola to cover the top. The combination of baroque with the cultural design of the people who built them gives each a special personality, yet they have a certain commonality. And while the façades of these missions are ornate, the inside of each is quite simple. Most of the churches are

> ❤️ A good restaurant in Jalpan is the **Restaurant Jacarandas.** The food is tasty, though portions might be a bit small for a healthy young hiker. "Enchiladas Huasteca" is kind of a make-your-own taco consisting of tortillas, cheese, sauce, marinated beef, avocados, and sliced tomatoes—roll it all up in the tortilla; US$5. Breakfast *chilequiles* are good; US$3.50.

believed to have been built within the years of 1750-1768, although historians still debate exact dates.

For more information about the Sierra Gorda region write to **Probaditur,** the state promotional office: Prespero C. Vega 31, Querétaro, 76000, Qro., Mexico, tel. (42) 12-1241, fax 14-0997.

Misión de Santiago

This lovely church in Jalpan is 210 kilometers northeast of the city of Querétaro. The façade exhibits ornate sculptures in individual niches. Where today the clock resides there was formerly a statue of Santa Santiago. Jalpan is the largest of all the mission towns. The **Museo Historica de La Sierra Gorda** is across from the plaza on Calle Fray Junípero Serra 1. It details Serra's life and the history of the area. All exhibits of course are explained in Spanish.

Misión de Santa María de la Purísima Concepción del Agua

This mission in Landa stands about 231 kilometers northeast of Querétaro and

21 kilometers beyond Jalpan on the same road. The façade of this church is probably the most ornate of the five with multiple statues of saints (mostly all life-size), angels, curlicues, carved curtains, stone columns, and topped with Michael the Archangel beating the dragon. This church was the last to be built. Its dome was destroyed by an earthquake 100 years ago and 50 years passed before it was replaced. The Indians participated more in the construction of this mission than in that of the other missions.

Misión de San Miguel Arcángel

This mission is in Conca, 48 kilometers from Jalpan, and this church façade has a different look. It's covered with bunches of grapes, is a different color, and is the smallest of the five. You really feel the influence of the Indians in these designs, since many themes are of nature rather than of saints and angels. Take time to study the front of this building; you will discover many interesting forms. The elevation is lower here, and you can feel the difference in the climate, which is very tropical and a little warmer. Although you see cactus, much of it is entangled with vines and a great variety of butterflies flutter about the plants. On the way from Jalpan you pass the Río Santa María where it converges with the Río Ayutla. Downhill from the mission is the Río Santa María; note the banks, where sugarcane, oranges, peanuts, and corn grow. The rural area appears more as it must have been in Serra's time. Locals say puma, jaguar, and white-tailed deer live in the area, but no one has really seen any of them for some time. Wildflowers are beautiful here in May and June.

Misión de San Francisco de Asisi

To reach this mission, turn off Hwy. 120 at Lagunitas; the mission lies in Tilaco, 16.5 km beyond Lagunitas. Not too many years ago, the only way to the mission was on foot or mule/horse. Apparently cars (or visitors) are still a novelty. Tilaco is a migrant town (as is Landa). Because there's so little work in the area, many of the men migrate to the U.S. for seasonal farm jobs and return in December—it's a 12-hour drive to the Texas border. Not much of a commercial nature is here, only a small *tienda* (store). Although again the façade of the mission is ornate, the overall look of the church is not nearly so lovely as the first two. You'll see traces of the original paint if you look carefully. Wander about the grounds and inside the church for a real feeling of the era.

Misión de Nuestra Señora de la Luz

This mission lies in Tancoyol, 262 kilometers from Querétaro. Just north of the turnoff to Tilaco is the turnoff to Tancoyal. The drive meanders along a canyon whose walls are covered with tall straight cactus, which looks like a forest of telephone poles (pretty green ones). Despite the busy baroque design of the church, the first thing you notice is an empty niche above the front entrance. At the rear of the church is a beautiful dome. Note the extravagant

carved wooden outer doors. On the inside, like the others, everything is simple terra-cotta and white with a large courtyard in front. Built on a hillside, this
town is second in size to Jalpan. An old spring-fed aqueduct that was built at
the same time as the mission still stands at the edge of town. Today the people
use water from a well closer in.

MAYA
COUNTRY

Cortés and his crew became aware of Maya Country at Isla Cozumel, their first sighting of land after leaving Cuba. The next stop on the Yucatán Peninsula was on the coast of today's Tabasco, where they were attacked. Cortés's superior firepower defeated the Indians, and his agile tongue persuaded the chief of the glory of the Spanish king and the Christian God. Before the Spaniards were on their way, the Indians presented Cortés and his men a gift of 20 young maidens. The one called Marina, or Malinche, would be his greatest asset as interpreter, traveling companion, and lover. The coastal cities on the Gulf became important trade centers, where ships filled with treasure were attacked by pirates from around the world. Most of the colonial cities were founded near the grand ceremonial centers of the Maya. Explorers found the Maya tough warriors, and difficult to bring under control. Over the years, the Maya managed to stay to themselves and to keep their culture relatively pure. Even today near busy resorts, groups of Maya have changed very little since the time the Spanish arrived. But a union between ancient Maya beliefs and Christianity has survived, the people have learned the value of their crafts, and more than ever they find it profitable to mingle with visitors.

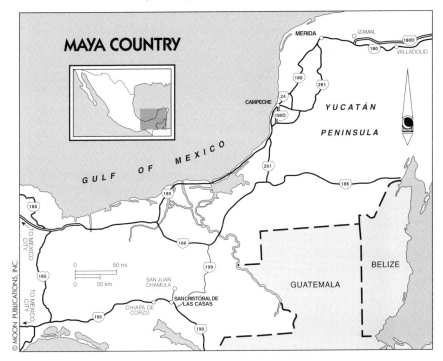

Campeche

CAMPECHE'S PRE-COLUMBIAN PAST IS RICH IN MAYA LEGEND, and its colonial past is steeped in pirates' lore. During pre-Hispanic times the Campechean coast bore the title of La Ruta Maya (The Mayan Route); it was a main artery for traders traveling by land and on the sea in their sturdy canoes. Until 22 March 1517, when the first Spaniards arrived here, the Maya people had never seen people that were so different. It took 25 years of both Spanish and Indian bloodshed to end Maya power in Ah Kim Pech (Campeche). Despite the difference in arms (Spanish guns versus Indian lances), a deadly determination to repel the intruders motivated the Maya to resist for an entire generation.

Once the Spaniards gained control of Campeche harbor, the financial attention of Spanish viceroy Francisco Hernández de Córdoba and explorer Juan de Grijalva enabled the city to blossom into the major seaport on the Yucatán Peninsula. Campeche was on its way to becoming a jewel of Spanish colonial development as the country's riches were channeled to Spain from the port. Tales of this great treasure drew the attention of those who resented Spain's hold on the fabled riches of the New World. Pirates and buccaneers Laurent Graff "Lorencillo," Brasiliano, John Hawkins, William Parck, Diego el Mulato, Barbillas, James Jackson, and Pie de Palo "Pegleg" came all the way from England, France, Portugal, and Holland—determined to get "their" share—and more.

From 1558, for almost two centuries the city of Campeche was harassed, burned, and sacked by buccaneers who'd taken up permanent residence on the Island of Tris, today's Ciudad del Carmen—only 208 km away. On 9 February 1663, the corsairs joined forces, gathered their ships on the horizon, and launched a furious attack. They completely wiped out the city, killing men, women, and children—the worst massacre in Campeche's history. Finally, after so much misery and so many deaths, the Spanish crown agreed that the city needed protection. City leaders formulated a plan and quietly the work began. On 3 January 1686 builders laid the cornerstone of the new walled city. The wall that surrounded Campeche was of stout stone construction, from three meters thick with four gates placed strategically around the city. The builders, in an effort to make this bastion impregnable, extended the wall into the sea, with huge gates that allowed ships to swiftly unload their cargo into the protected fort, often with a brigantine in pursuit. Though finishing touches weren't made until 1704, the completion of the sturdy bastion finally gave

*the original
sea gate*

Campecheans a security that would ultimately end the era of invasion. Still, isolated attacks upon the coastal cities south of Campeche continued from the pirates' notorious island base. In 1717, determined to wipe the bandits out, Captain Don Alonso Felipe de Aranda led a sneak attack that routed or killed all the pirates and burned their ships. Once and for all, peace reigned over the Gulf coast. The Puerta de Tierra (Land Gate) was built in 1732.

Campeche spent the next 200 years developing a peaceful society, including the growth of an economy not dependent on the shipment of silver and gold. Even after the Independence in 1821, Campeche, isolated from much of greater Mexico's turmoil, suffered from its own problems of development.

Before the Mexican revolution, Campeche city was inhabited almost exclusively by descendants of colonial Spaniards. During the early glory days after the wall was built and the pirates were vanquished, life was good for the landowners. The Indians were slaves and suffered the same indignities as their fellows in the rest of the land. In the 1820s, with the coming of Mexico's independence, slavery was abolished. Campeche soon settled into an era of humble existence, an oblivion that brought few changes for decades. For years Campeche was part of an alliance with Mérida, but several years after the Caste War in 1842, it seceded and became part of the Federal Republic of Mexico as the independent state of Campeche.

Exploring the Streets of Campeche

The old city within the ramparts of the ancient wall is well-laid out, and once you figure out the numbering system for the 40 square blocks, walking is a piece of cake. The streets that run southeast to northwest, perpendicular to the sea, are odd-numbered from 51 on the north to 65 on the south. Streets running northeast to southwest are even-numbered beginning with Calle 8 on the west

Campeche Trolley takes visitors on a tour of the city daily at 9:30 a.m., 6 p.m., and 8 p.m. *Sometimes* this trip is given by a bilingual guide, but even if you don't *comprende* Spanish, you'll get a great overview of the city just by going along.

In Chompoton (south of Campeche), **San Antonio Redoubt** marks the place of the Moch Cohuch, an early Maya victory that forced the Spaniards to retreat to their ships.

through Calle 18 on the east. Most of the more popular sights and services lie within these ancient boundaries, set off by the seven remaining *baluartes* (bastions) built by Spanish settlers. This old part of the city is surrounded by Circuito Baluartes on three sides, and by Av. 16 de Septiembre on the seaward side (a filled-in area). The city outside the wall is creeping ever outward toward the mountains, north and south, up and down the coast. Campeche has a good bus system covering the entire city, inside and outside the wall.

Near the sea, Campeche's **Central Plaza** is bordered by Calles 8, 10, 55, and 57. This charming spot provides a resting place between walking tours around the city. Park renovations in 1985 added contemporary wrought-iron fences and benches. But even with its modern gazebo in the center, the plaza's feeling of antiquity is overwhelming. Campeche is endowed with the charm of 1700s architecture, and the city has recently been involved in revitalizing the oldest buildings, renovating old stone façades, painting where needed, bringing back its colonial charm. The central plaza is bordered on one side by **Catedral la Inmaculada Concepción,** one of the oldest Christian churches on the Yucatán, constructed 1540-1705. On Calle 10, the plaza faces **Los Portales,** another aging structure with a graceful façade and arcaded passageways.

The **Regional Museum of Campeche,** on Calle 59 between 14 and 16, is housed in a lovely old building with a colorful history. Its exhibits are a combination of colonial and archaeological/anthropological artifacts. Among other things, you'll see the famous jade mask from Calakmul. When Mexican archaeologists found the mask years ago it was in many pieces; it has since been put together. On display upstairs are many of the arms used in the days of the marauding pirates. Small admission.

The **Mansion Carvajal** is another old mansion that has been restored to its original beauty, and is perhaps even more beautiful now. Formerly owned by a rich family named Carvajal, it was used as Hotel Senorial until the mid-

The Catedral la Inmaculada Concepción took more than a century and a half to build.

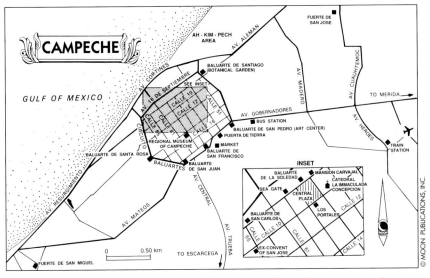

1970s. Today it houses the government offices. It's well worth a visit; note the Moorish-style architecture.

Many remnants of the city's bastions remain more or less intact. Though neglected for years, even with parts destroyed to make way for trolley tracks, the remaining ramparts have managed to survive modern architects and violent storms and to lend a wonderful old-world ambience to Campeche. What was formerly the seawall and shipyard within the gate was filled in some years back to make way for a wide avenue and new buildings on the modern waterfront. You can visit seven of the eight original bastions—Soledad, San Carlos, Santa Rosa, San Juan, San Francisco, San Pedro, and Santiago—now used as public buildings. The Circuito Baluartes is the trail where once the wall stood—a bus tour circles the old city and takes you to each bastion.

Baluarte Nuestra Señores de la Soledad, easy to find near the waterfront on Calle 8 across from the central plaza, is the site of many stelae found in Campeche, now in a hall called Dr. Roman Pina Chan. Many of the carved stones are said to be 1,000 years old. This is the largest bastion on the city's seaward side. See the Maya fountain close by.

Baluarte de San Carlos, on the west corner of Circuito Baluartes between Calle 8, the Progress Fountain, and Av. 16 de Septiembre, was one of the first fortresses built; today it's flanked by the Palacio de Gobierno, the modern square glass building near the waterfront with the colorful mosaic, and the state Congressional Hall, the concrete building that resembles a flying saucer. The *baluarte* now contains a city museum, with photographs, drawings, and models of the city's development. It's open daily 9 a.m.-2 p.m., 4-8 p.m.

Unless otherwise noted, all museums in Campeche are open Tues.-Sat. 9 a.m.-8 p.m., Sunday 9 a.m.-2 p.m., and are closed on Monday. They charge admission every day except Sunday.

At **Baluarte de Santiago**, on Av. 16 de Septiembre near the waterfront, you'll find the **Jardín Botánico Xmuch Haltum**, a small garden with many species of plants native to the arid plains in the north and the green jungle of the wet

the restored Mansion Carvajal

southern region. This walled garden is a short but worthwhile trip. The eco-tourism offices are here, and they would be worth checking out if you are touring the state. Each of this garden's ancient gates is a wonder of architecture that shouldn't be missed.

From **Puerta de Tierra** visitors experience how the forts and walls protected the city parameters. This inland wall, a long stone fortification, seems impenetrable even today. If someone is minding the fort you'll get an escorted tour atop the stone walls, from where you can spot the corresponding wall across town that protects the city from the sea.

Fuerte de San José, one of Campeche's two remaining forts, complete with cannons and rifle slits and thick walls, houses a museum that shows the arms used during the pirate era.

Campeche's first lighthouse was built on the front of the Ex-Convent of San José.

Ex-Convent of San José, on Calle 10 at 65, was the first lighthouse in Campeche, raised in 1864 and built on the front of this former church. The original part of the structure, the ex-convent, was built by Jesuits in 1700; the adjacent building, a Jesuit college, was constructed in 1756. The baroque church, impressive with its quixotic Talavera tile façade, provides an artisans' exhibit and shop. The history of the building is as varied as that of the city of Campeche: it's gone from church to army post to warehouse to art museum. The paintings on display present a striking contrast: two giant religious murals are placed next to a modern artist's violent portrayal of what was wreaked upon the Maya in the name of God.

The 18th-century **Fort San Miguel**, 2.5 km southwest of town, includes moat and drawbridge. You can feel the terror that motivated inhabitants to build such sturdy protection—so sturdy that it has survived 200 years. This fort houses Campeche's archaeological museum, or as the tourist office refers to it, the Maya Museum. The collection here is not large, but you'll get just a small taste of the fine pieces found on Isla Jaina, which apparently was used as the cemetery of the noble Maya. To get to the fort, follow the coastal road south until you come to the large statue of a man with a raised arm, a work titled *The Resurgence of Campeche*, and then follow the signs.

Campeche Highlights

¡Música!

Sunday concerts are held in the plaza; the band looks as if it stepped out of a Norman Rockwell painting, black shiny-brimmed hats and all. Don't be surprised to hear an oompah band—with French horns, flutes, violins, and bassoons—blaring forth with the excitement of a great orchestra. The plaza is the heart of the city: families gather, friends meet, and children run and play.

Special Events

Sound and Light Show: The show takes place at the Puerta de Tierra, Calle 59 at Av. Gobernadores, every Friday evening at 8:30 p.m. The 30-minute show transports visitors back into the past via lights, music, and drama. The presentation tells of the romance and the tragedy of the Indians, the pirates, and the Spaniards. Who knows whether it is historically accurate, but attending is a good experience; US$3 admission. For more information, check at the tourist office or at your hotel.

Regional Food

Remember that this is seafood country, so take advantage of it. Try the shrimp, excellent though expensive, the stone crabs, or the fish specialty of the day, which is usually sweet and fresh. Try other regional dishes, including Pan de Cazon, a dish of layered baby shark, beans, and tortillas. This is a favorite of the region and on most menus.

For the budget gourmet, the public market at Calles 39 and 20 is a good source of quick and inexpensive tacos, tamales, *tortas,* and fried fish.

on the streets of Campeche

Mérida

SPANIARDS ARRIVED ON THE YUCATÁN PENINSULA IN THE EARLY 1500s. They found a large Maya ceremonial center called T'ho, or Ichcansiho, depending on which chronicler you read. The city was built with ornate stone structures that reminded them of the Roman ruins in Spain's city of Mérida—hence the name. Mexico's Mérida was founded 6 January 1542 by Francisco de Montejo "El Mozo" (The Younger) to celebrate his victory over the Indians after 15 years of conflict (begun by Francisco de Montejo The Elder). The Maya, when defeated, became slaves of the Spanish invaders and were forced to dismantle their temples and palaces and to use the materials to build homes, offices, cathedrals, and parks that they were not permitted to enjoy. Mérida became the capital and trade center of the Peninsula, the seat of civil as well as religious authority. The Spaniards lived in fine houses around the central plaza in downtown Mérida, while Indian servants lived on the outer edges of town. For centuries *centro* Mérida maintained its colonial appeal: narrow streets lined with elegant stone houses and churches around lovely plazas.

Mérida's citizens were isolated from the rest of Mexico. It was easier to reach Louisiana (by ship from Progreso) than to get to Mexico City. While Nueva España was organizing itself, scurrying around to find gold and silver, the priests of Mérida concentrated on saving the souls of the Maya and continued to build churches and monasteries. The war of Independence in the 1800s lightly touched the Meridanos, unlike the Caste War, which nearly wiped them out in the 1840s. In the three years between 1864 and 1867, Maximilian and Carlota left their imperial European touch on Mexico. And with the reign of Porfirio Díaz 1876-1911, Mérida was even more influenced by the Europeans. During that period henequen fiber became a major export for the region. And the large haciendas switched from raising grains and foodstuffs to raising thousands of acres of henequen. Quantities of money flowed into the sheltered city and haciendas grew to immense proportions, and *hacendados'* townhouses became bigger and better mansions, all with the touch of Europe. Designers built the boulevard Paseo de Montejo wide and tree-lined, much like the Champs Élysées in Paris. To this day, the colonial capital of the state of Yucatán displays the appeal and grace of old Europe.

Exploring the Streets of Mérida

Mérida is a Mexico that clings to its past. It embraces intriguing prehistoric archaeological sites and an ancient history well displayed in fine libraries and museums; some are at the sites themselves. Today's visitors come to bathe in the light of this antiquity, to climb the old stone pyramids, to study the intricate architecture of elegant old colonial mansions-turned-inns, to sit in shady plazas and listen to marimbas near domed churches, or to spend a few nights in a henquen hacienda while experiencing the lifestyle of a rich *hacendado*. However, don't be misled. The Yucatán is no longer isolated and its largest city, Mérida, is modern and high-tech with hotels and attractions to match. Take several days to investigate the many museums, old churches, beautiful government buildings, monuments, and shady, tree-lined plazas everywhere. The longer you stay, the better you'll like this city of contradictions.

Downtown is the heart of the historic city; standing here are the remnants of the first buildings built under Spanish rule. In most cases the structures were created by European-trained Indians—and as a bonus, behind each façade is an intriguing story.

For centuries Mérida maintained its colonial appeal; elegant stone mansions lined its narrow streets. However, it was inevitable that time would take its toll. Many of the once beautiful old homes began to deteriorate from the

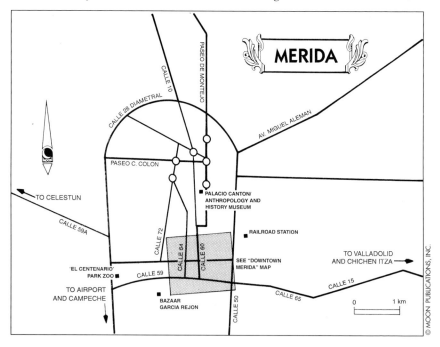

inside; outsiders were unaware. Eventually some buildings were abandoned. Few families were able to keep up the old houses, and they could not afford the staffs of servants that families enjoyed at the time these immense homes were built. Those with money wanted shiny, new, and modern houses and moved to the suburbs on the outskirts of the city. Little by little the carved stone began to chip and crack; façades fell into disrepair. Many more homes were abandoned.

The last five or 10 years have brought an epiphany. The government realized that visitors, Mexican and otherwise, *enjoyed* the old architecture and perhaps the aura of "what-once-was." Owners who could afford it jumped on the construction wagon and have been improving the buildings and in many cases turning them into hotels, banks, malls, or restaurants. Tourism soared.

Sidewalk cafés do a lively business, as do dozens of pushcarts selling drinks, *tortas* (sandwiches), *elote* (corn on the cob), tamales, and sweets. In the evening some families take in the cinema; others meet with friends, listen to the music, and chat. The one disheartening aspect of Mérida is the traffic in the narrow streets. Unlike

view from a calesa

so many colonial cities, Mérida is so far unwilling to close off traffic to create pedestrian walkways. However, the city is so charming that it's possible to overlook the rush of cars and buses—it's really one of the loveliest old colonial towns on the Peninsula.

The large green **Plaza de la Independencia** is an oasis surrounded by aristocratic buildings in the heart of this busy city. Friends and strangers gather here all day and late into the night. This is a city where people stroll the streets after dark and feel safe and comfortable. In the old custom, sweethearts sit on *confidenciales* (S-curved concrete benches) allowing intimate tête-à-têtes—oh, so close!—but without touching. White-sombreroed men gather early in the morning; visiting mestizas from outlying villages in colorful *huipiles* sit in the shade and share lunch with their children, excited by the sights of the big city. Busy sidewalk cafés edge the park, and in the cool of evening locals and tourists enjoy the musical nights.

Built 1555-92, the cathedral sits on the east side of the plaza. Across from that is the Palacio Municipal, built in 1735; on the south edge is Casa de Montejo, built in 1542 by the conqueror Francisco Montejo, and occupied by his family into the 1900s. On the north side is the Palacio de Gobierno, built in 1892. These few buildings took up most of the area where today streets have been cut in.

The most prominent building on the plaza is the **Catedral San Idelfonso**. Built with stones taken from Maya temples on site, it's one of the largest churches on the Peninsula and one of the oldest buildings on the continent. Visitors search for the occasional stone with a Maya glyph still visible, and the architecture prevalent in late 16th-century Spain is reflected in the Moorish style of the

two towers. Surprisingly, the interior is stark in comparison to some of the ornately decorated churches in other parts of Mexico— during the Caste War and then again during the revolution of 1910, the church was stripped of its valuable trimmings. Note the impressive painting of the meeting between the nobles of the Maya Xiu clan and the Spanish invaders in 1541. This solemnly portrays the Xiu tribe joining the Spaniards as allies—a trust that was violated, and the beginning of the end of the Maya regime. (A few descendants still carry the Xiu name in the area around Mama outside of Mérida.)

On the right side of the church as you enter is a small chapel that houses an honored image of Christ called El Cristo de las Ampollas (Christ of the Blisters), carved from a tree in Ichmul that is said to have been engulfed in flames but remained undamaged. Reportedly the wooden statue then went through another fire in a church,

The Spanish built the Catedral San Idelfonso with stones taken from Maya temples.

this time developing blisters as living skin would. Though the statue is honored with a fiesta each fall, every Sunday the devout crowd around to touch the statue and sigh a brief prayer.

Just south of the cathedral facing the plaza is the **Palace of the Archbishop**. This once-elaborate building was the archbishop's home. After the reform, when the church's power was restricted, the large structure housed the local military post. Today, it houses the Museo Macay, and an assortment of small shops offer a variety of souvenirs from art to clothing.

Facing the south edge of the central plaza is the **Casa de Montejo**, now the Banamex Bank building. Francisco de Montejo "El Mozo" built the home in 1542 using talented Maya craftspeople and recovered stone. The unique carvings of Spaniards standing at attention with their feet planted firmly on the heads of the Maya remain in place today—a blatant reminder of their dominance at the time. These works of art were also rendered by Maya slaves. According to Mexican art experts, this is one of the very few structures that has maintained completely its colonial façade. It's said that 13 generations of Montejos lived in the house before

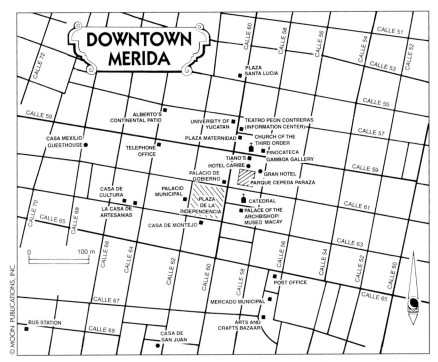

it was sold to Banamex in 1980 and completely renovated inside. Today the bank takes up the entire structure, including a large second floor. You can see the enormous patio during business hours (9 a.m.-1 p.m.).

Opposite the northeast corner of the central plaza is the **Palacio de Gobierno**. Striking abstract murals painted by Fernando Castro Pacheco in 1978 decorate the interior walls and upper galleries. In a style unlike that of some of the other famous muralists, he used subtle colors represent the birth of the Maya, gods of wisdom, sale of slaves, and other social commentaries. This is the seat of government offices for the state of Yucatán; it's open daily to the public. The **Palacio Municipal** (City Hall), is on the west side of the central plaza, a gracious building dating from 1543. Architecturally charming with its tall clock tower, it was renovated in the mid-1800s.

Casa de Lagarto (house of the alligator), a private home on Calle 61 between 62 and 64, has a wild history. It was built by wealthy members of the Montejo family, who also owned many acres of hacienda land in a swampy Campeche region. At some point, it is said around 1937, a visitor came from the hacienda

A bank inhabits the former home of "El Mozo" Montejo.

🏨 The **Casa Mexilio Guesthouse,** Calle 68 #495, (99) 21-4032; in Mérida fax 28-2505, or in the States (800) 538-6802; fax (303) 674-8735, offers a charming collection of eight eclectic rooms in an old colonial residence. It's owned and operated by hosts who speak English, Spanish, and Maya and who are dedicated to providing personal touches and the warm coloful decor of Mexican and Guatemalan folk art. Guests mingle in the second-floor living room, complete with piano. Cool off in a tiny swimming pool, soak in a jacuzzi, or simply sit amid lush plants in a shady patio of the one-time colonial townhouse. Breakfast included. Moderate.

🏨 The **Hotel Caribe,** Calle 59 #500, tel. (99) 24-9022 or (800) 826-6842, fax 24-8733, is ideally located with a delightful history that dates to the Convent of San Idelfonso. On Parque Cepeda Peraza, it's near everything and just one block from the main plaza. This old colonial structure has been renovated with tranquil colors, colonial furniture, and a swimming pool on the third-floor roof. Dine next to the center garden, or at the lively El Mesón, the hotel's outdoor café on the Park. Graceful archways and the winding staircase are reminders of another century. Budget to Inexpensive.

in Campeche and brought two baby alligators for the señora of the house. They were very tiny and cunning, and she, being an animal lover, fed them by hand; by day they lived in the garden of the house, by night in the basement. One of them died, but his brother grew well beyond what the señora must have expected, and the family called it Toot, short for Tutankhamen. By now the remaining aligator was very large, though tame, and a great playmate for the children and grandchildren of the family. One of the grandchildren remembers how he and his brothers and sisters would ride the alligator like a horse. Toot continued to grow, and one day the family realized that it was necessary to change *his* name to *her* name; Tutankhamen became Nefertiti. During a violent hurricane, the city streets flooded, as did the basement that was Nefertiti's inside shelter. As the water rose in the basement, it raised the gator to the level of the open window and she managed to swim out into the street. Locals were terrified. From here the story gets hazy: was Nefertiti captured by the local gendarmes? Or was she rescued by the family? It is certain that *National Geographic* picked up on the story and came to interview reptile and owner. Nefertiti lived in the Casa de Lagarto 1937-1970.

The **Parque Cepeda Paraza,** also called Parque Hidalgo, is a popular plaza for marimba music, crowded outdoor cafés, and events that attract visitors and locals from all over the area. Sunday of course is the busiest day of all. At one time, the park and most of the buildings were part of the Convent and Colegio San Idelfonso. The entire complex included the cathedral and what is now the City Museum on the south side of the plaza, and Parque Cepeda Paraza (cut apart with the addition of the streets). Construction began on the convent (originally called Plazuelo de Jesús) in 1560. By 1592, all the buildings were complete, including the Catholic College. Most of the old buildings still maintain their colonial character, with renovations coming yearly. In the **Gran Hotel,** what was once a grand lobby with a graceful curved stairway has been cut up and a dining room added. But the rest of the hotel is a gem of nostalgia.

The **Teatro Peón Contreras,** at Calles 60 and 57, built in 1908 during Mérida's moneyed period, was patterned after a European design. A lovely old building of enchanting beauty, it continues to offer a variety of concerts and other entertainment. It's worth visiting just to see the classic interior with its marble staircase and elegant dome. During the busiest seasons (winter and spring), colorful folkloric dances are presented every Tuesday night, and admission is free. Frequently a list of attractions is posted in the theater lobby. Or check at the tourist information center on the corner of the theater building. All along the side of the building is a small outdoor café with tables and umbrellas, snacks and drinks; remember this isn't a gourmet stop.

One of the most outstanding renovated structures beyond the center of town on Paseo de Montejo is the **Palacio Canton.** This lovely rococo-façade building was built 1909-11 for Gen. Francisco Canton Rosado, a former governor of Yucatán. It was designed by the architect who built

The museum in the Palacio Canton displays ancient Maya artifacts and a history of Yucatán.

the Teatro Peón Contreras on Calle 60. The building served as the official state residence 1948-60. Today it is a fine museum administered under the auspices of the National Institute of Anthropology and History. Even for those not into haunting museums, the building alone is worth the trip. The museum offers a permanent exhibit that includes ancient artifacts of the Maya culture and a history of Yucatán. Other displays include such intriguing treasures as antiquities brought up from the sacred well at Chichén Itzá.

The large **Museum of Popular Art**, behind the Mejorada Church on Calle 59 between 48 and 50, introduces the Maya way of life and style of dress in and around the city as well as in the entire state. A small shop offers a selection of some of the area's finer crafts. The **Pinacoteca del Estado/Juan Gamboa Museum/ Gottdiener** museum, Calles 59 and 58, houses a collection of Yucatecan art and sculptures. Many paintings are antique and the collection includes sculptures by Gottdiener, well known in the Yucatán. The museum seems to be known by all three names, but between those three you should find it. At the **City Museum**, Calle 61 at 58, visitors

> 🍽 When you order a cold beer in the middle of the afternoon, you'll be served tasty snacks (a more than ample lunch!). **La Prosperidad,** Calle 53 #491, attracts daily crowds of Méridanos and visitors into the large café for drinks, snacks, and good live music. Try it either for cold beer or for a large *típico comida corrida* (typical meal of the day), including a variety of dishes: *pollo pibil, panuchos, pollo escabeche,* tortillas, *rellenos,* cold chicken, and avocado—a big meal for a reasonable price.

⊞ Staying at a hacienda surrounds you with the gracious atmosphere of Mérida's past. **Hacienda Tanil,** tel. (99) 25-9194, fax (99) 25-3646, is about 10 km south of town through the rural countryside. Its history shares the intrigues of all of these old properties. The present owners can trace the history of the hacienda to 1607, when it was owned by Diego Solis Osorio, mayor of the Yucatan Province (long before there were states). His wife was the granddaughter of Francisco de Montejo the elder (an important player in settling the area). Originally an ordinary farm, the hacienda later specialized in cattle. When the Independence of Mexico was finally settled, it became a prosperous henequen plantation. This is a lovely place to spend a few days relaxing—the rooms are comfortable, the architecture is typical with thick walls, broad archways open onto a lovely courtyard, and guests are pampered.

Up a flight of stairs the original chapel is still in use; this is where many of the family were baptized and married. There are three rooms, a swimming pool, beautiful horses, and the owners are delightful. The food here is delicious, with tortillas homemade by the village ladies who take care of the kitchen. If you yearn for something different, a change of pace as you whiz through the Yucatán Peninsula, stop at Tanil. Ask about the weekend special. Moderate.

The Hacienda Tanil, now a hotel, has been around since 1607.

find some excellent photographs of old Mérida. **Museo de Historia Natural,** Calle 59 at 84, offers a look into Yucatecan wildlife.

At the **Museo de la Canción Yucateca** within the Casa de Cultura, Calle 63 between 64 and 66, musicians and nonmusicians alike enjoy the displays of music and instruments, some very old, that give you an insight into the culture of Yucatán. Mérida continues its wonderful tradition of bringing music to its people. In the Palace of the Archbishop, **Museo Macay,** Calle 60 next to the cathedral, offers a permanent exposition of Yucatecan artists. The **Museo Numismatico de Mexico,** Calle 60 between 53 and 55, is something a little different. Take a quick whirl around and you'll discover a comprehensive *Exposición de Monedas* (coin collection).

Several art galleries are scattered about the city. **Teatro Peón Contreras** frequently offers exhibits in the lobby of the lovely theater, and usually these art shows are free.

The narrow streets were originally designed for *calesas* (horse-drawn buggies). You can still ride the *calesa* through the old residential neighborhoods and see beautiful old mansions built at the turn of the century or earlier. A major section downtown surrounding the central plaza is closed to vehicular traffic on Sunday 9 a.m.-9 p.m. This is the ideal day to tour the city in a *calesa*. Like taxis, the horse-drawn buggies are not metered, so arrange your fee and route before starting out: average price is about US$12 per hour. On Sunday a downtown ride through the quiet streets will cost a little less. The *calesas* follow regular routes for their one-hour tours, including a ride along the Paseo Montejo Drive, Old Mérida neighborhoods, Centenario Park, and Park of the Americas.

Mérida Highlights

Arts and Artisans

Hammock weaving is one of Mérida's practical arts. Yucatán's hammocks are touted the best in Mexico and available in many colors. Embroidered *huipiles* are another great indigenous art form. The white *huipil* is decorated around the square neckline and the hem with a three- or four-inch strip of lovely thick embroidery. Colors can be brilliant primary colors, or they can be subtle pastel hues. Some of the nicest are crisp white cotton *huipiles* with white embroidery and drawn work.

Many fine artists in Yucatán make excellent reproductions of Maya artifacts. Some of the best were produced under the supervision of the late artist Wilbert González in Ticul. González used Maya techniques to create his pottery. His work is so extraordinary and authentic that it fooled police, who accused him of stealing original art. He sat in jail for three months while the "expert archaeologists" studied the pieces and found them to be "original" Maya art. Only when his friend Victor Manzanilla Schaffer (ex-governor of the state of Yucatán) returned from an extended trip to Japan was the matter clarified and González released. He shrugged the incident off with a smile and the comment, "That's my Mexico." After that incident he began inserting a hidden code or a dime in each piece to protect himself. For years González created his art in the small town of Ticul, where he also instructed students in the style of the ancient Maya under the auspices of the government. The gallery and workshop, called **Arte Maya**, continues to do business in González's style in the city of Ticul. Note the striking wall of Maya reproductions designed by González in **La Casa de Artesanías**, on Calle 63 between 66 and 64.

La Casa de Artesanías center for arts and crafts displays items from all over the state of Yucatán. You'll also find silver, gold, leather, ceramics, onyx, and typical clothing from the 31 states of Mexico. The selection of folk art in this restored monastery is excellent, and the back courtyard has been turned into a gallery featuring rotating art and folk art exhibits. **Bazar Garcia Rejon** is on Calle 65 and is another fine place to find something "special."

The *huipil* is a lovely garment—first used by mestiza women at the insistence of hacienda *patrones* to designate their Indian ethnicity—edged with bright-colored embroidery around the squared neck and hem, with a lace-finished petticoat peeking out below the dress. The similar *terno* is a long, more elaborate dress than the *huipil* but with the same ornate embroidery; it's worn at fiestas and celebrations and always with lovely gold chains around the neck.

Yucatecan men wear the *guayabera* in place of a white shirt with tie and jacket. This shirt is perfectly acceptable for any dress occasion you may encounter in Mérida or any other part of Mexico. The most common color is white, but they're also available in pastel tones. They're found in most shops, but check out these two popular places to buy or order the popular Yucatecan shirt: the **Camisería Canul** at Calle 59 #496B, or **Guayaberas Finas Cab** at Calle 60 #502, tel. 2-85127. Prices range from about US$18 up to US$75 for made-to-order. Visitors on tour buses are brought to these shops so they're apt to be crowded, but both have very large selections and a great variety of sizes.

For the Shopper

Mérida offers interesting shopping at the **Mercado Municipal**, Calles 56 and 67. You'll find a selection of quality crafts from all parts of Yucatán. Even those not interested in a shopping spree should take a trip through the busy *mercado* for a wonderful social and cultural experience. You'll see many women from the rural villages of Yucatán state wearing *huipiles*.

Along with the euphoric pleasures of color—bundles of brilliant flowers and rainbows of neatly stacked fruit and vegetables—watching the steady stream of people makes a visit to the bustling market a diverse entertainment. Here are foods of all description: cooked tamales, raw meat, live chickens, and pungent odors from mounds of unusual-looking herbs, spices, and fruit. The candy man offers delicate sugar flowers, shoes, and skulls for just a few pesos.

The *tortillería* is probably the busiest stop of all. Upstairs, a series of tiny fast-food windows serve the cheapest regional meals in the city: tacos, tamales, *tortas*, and *licuados*.

Chattering merchants invite you to inspect (and bargain for) their colored woven hammocks, huaraches, and gleaming chunks of clear, amber copal (incense), in use since the days of the Maya. Narrow little "gold stalls" hold thousands of dollars worth of gold earrings, along with charms and bangles of every description, stored in their small glass cases. You'll see the common and the uncommon, the ordinary and the extraordinary. Some things you may not want to see, such as *mecech*, jeweled lapel beetles—the crawly kind outlawed in the U.S. The ordinary seems always in demand: straw baskets of every shape, pottery bowls for every use, Panama hats in the final stages of manufacture on a metal stand with a live flame, *guayaberas* (wide-lapel, pleated cotton shirts), and white *huipiles* with thickly embroidered flowered borders in every color. All-

Hacienda Katanchel is a gracious spot with 741 acres to roam and enjoy. An abandoned henequen hacienda (for more than 35 years), it became a gathering place for hundreds of bird species. Recently it was renovated and miraculously returned to its original splendor. Built in the 17th century as a cattle ranch, it was used to raise henequen in the 19th century. Henequen ranchers realized huge profits for decades and took pleasure trying to outdo themselves in the grandeur of their haciendas. Nothing lasts forever, and when nylon was developed, the henequen market took a big plunge. Many of these fine old haciendas were deserted, and many have fallen into complete decay. Katanchel has been brought back to life.

The 39 suites today cater to travelers who delight in this historical grandeur. While exploring the property, owners Anibal Gonzalez and his wife, Monica Hernandez, discovered a pre-classic astronomical observation site dating from the 3rd century. While clearing the jungle they found the platforms of what were once 33 workers' dwellings. These have been transformed into stunning deluxe pavilions for guests.

A hacienda was a "little city." Each had a *casa de maquina* (machine house) where the henequen was processed; today at Katanchel it is a wonderful dining room. Each possessed a chapel and a combination general store and pay office called a *tienda de raya*. Today the *tienda* is a boutique featuring crafts, herbs, and souvenirs with striking antique furniture. The main house and its public rooms are beautifully decorated, there's a swimming pool, and guests can explore the many villages scattered about the countryside. In the States call (800) 223-6510, or U.S. toll free fax (888) 882-9470, or write Tixkokob, 97470, Yucatán, Mexico; email: hacienda@mail.mda.com.mx. Expensive cotton, hand-embroidered garments are available, but you must search them out and the cost is much higher. The thick embroidered designs are often symbolic to the woman who made them. If the price of the hand-embroidered garment discourages you (US$150 and up), shop around for good-quality machine work (US$45). In fact, most *huipiles* are machine embroidered nowadays, and the quality varies greatly.

Most Mérida women are fashion-conscious and vitally into the clothes of today. *Huipiles* are worn almost exclusively by women who have come to market for the day from small rural villages surrounding Mérida, or for special celebrations throughout the year. The *huipil* is a unique remembrance to take home and a cool *típico* garment to wear in warm weather. Try the *mercado*, the small shops that line the streets around the plazas, or hotel gift shops such as the boutique at the **Casa del Balam**, Calle 60 #488. Also try **Casa de Artesanías Crafts Center**, Calle 63, between 64 and 66. Here many are cotton, but seldom hand embroidered.

Open-air tour buses from the **Discover Mérida** company depart from Parque Santa Lucía daily at 10 a.m. and 4 p.m. For a two-hour city tour call (99) 27-6119 for information. A new tour will probably be in motion by the time you read this. A city tour will show you the city, and will also take you to some of the outlying haciendas in the area; lunch is included. This is a great tour, an opportunity to wander through the lovely old haciendas and get a whiff of lifestyles of the rich, 19th-century style

Special Events

Domingo en Mérida: Sunday is family day in Mexico, and Mérida is no exception. Domingo en Mérida emphasizes that Sunday is a wonderful day here. The

How to Buy a Hammock

Yucatán is noted for producing the best hammocks in Mexico. Street vendors try to induce tourists to buy them, which is okay as long as the buyer knows what to look for. Many shops sell them, including **La Casa de los Jipis**, Calle 56 #526, and **Hamacas el Aguacate**, Calle 58 #604. Don't hesitate to ask the vendor to stretch out the entire hammock while you inspect it carefully. To judge whether a hammock will be long enough for you, hold one end of the *body* of the hammock to the top of your head and let it drop. The other end of the body of the hammock (not the strings) should be touching the floor and then some for you to be comfortable. Ask what it's made of, and don't be afraid to bargain. The finer the weave (the more strings) the stronger the hammock.

tree-shaded parks are popular for picnics, playing ball, buying giant colorful balloons, and just doing what kids do. The music goes on all day and you have your choice of marimba, classical, or folkloric. Everyone in the city (or so it seems) dresses in his or her Sunday best and comes downtown. Closed-off streets, as well as around the plaza, are filled with strolling people. Loud, smelly cars are gone for the day and a glorious freedom turns the clock back to a more gracious period.

If the Hat Fits

If you're in the market for a hat, look for a local *jipi* shop and pick up a Panama hat. They're made in several towns in the states of Yucatán and Campeche, and the finest are made of the *jipijapa* fiber; ask for *finos* for the most supple hat. The best ones can be folded and stuffed in a pocket to pop back into shape when needed. But buyer beware: many cheaper "palms" are used as well and these will not survive that kind of treatment. Browse around **La Casa de los Jipis**, Calle 56 #526, where you'll see the hat in many degrees of quality. Ask questions; the shopkeeper will educate you about Panama hats. Not cheap here, the *finos* may cost US$65 and up, but if you want classic design and the best quality that should last forever, it's worth it. For a simple straw sun hat, street vendors in nearly every plaza wear a stack of them, and you'll also see them at the entrances of many hotels—haggle!

Tiano's on the park presents a full-out Mexican fiesta with marimba musicians playing through the afternoon and evening, and festive banner and piñatas hung above the outdoor tables. It serves well-prepared Mexican and regional dishes and first-rate margaritas. Unlike the other restaurants around the park, Tiano's serves drinks only with meals.

An antique and crafts bazaar in the **Plaza Santa Lucía** bustles, followed by typical Yucatecan music performed by a band, often the well-known Mérida Police orchestra. Sellers bring worn books, antique bric-a-brac, old stamps, furniture, typical clothing, and lovely artwork—good browsing! A large handicraft market with a good selection of crafts sets up on Sunday at 11 a.m. in the **Plaza de Principal (Independencia)**. Visit **Parque Cepeda Paraza** (also known as Hidalgo Square) for live marimba music at 11:30 a.m. Or visit the Hall of History on the second floor of the **Palacio Municipal** at 1 p.m. for a concert and performance of the mestizo wedding dance.

On Sunday festivals are held at **El Centenario Park Zoo** and **La Ceiba's Park** at 11 a.m., and at **Mulsay's Park** at 6 p.m. Here children (and parents) are entertained by magicians, clowns, puppets, and theater groups. All take part in organized games that include even the smallest child and offer prizes to winning participants. See artists and their paintings, sculpture, and crafts, and—to add a little zing—chess instructors go knight to rook with students. The Mérida zoo is outstanding and a popular stop for both children and adults.

Also on Sunday at the **Plaza Maternidad**, children take part in drawing classes and play chess. In every city of Mexico there is a statue of a mother and children called the Plaza Maternidad in honor of all mothers everywhere. Each statue is similar; it's usually always of white stone and there's always a baby included.

On Good Friday, what appears like the entire population of the city walks along specific closed streets to the cathedral in the city center. What's unusual is the total lack of sound—this is the "walk of silence." It's quite a moving event to take part in.

Mérida is a musical city. Heady Latin rhythms and the latest disco steps share billing with Maya and Spanish folkloric songs and dances, along with good American swing. Free nightly concerts and other cultural gatherings throughout the week are well attended by local citizens as well as outsiders.

Regional Food

According to ancient legends, the gods made several attempts with different materials to make humans before they finally created man using the *masa* of white and yellow corn. So, not only has corn been the main staple of the ancient Indian people from 4500 B.C., but corn has been an integral part of the Maya doctrine of the universe. When the Spanish arrived they found the simplest people lived almost entirely on corn, beans, and squash. Corn in a variety of forms continues to be an important part of the diet. The most common daily item is the tortilla, made from ground corn, baked in the form of a thin round pancake. But that's just one way the *masa* is used. There are *sopes, panuchos*, quesadillas, tamales, and soups with added lumps of *masa*; that's just the tip of the you-know-what.

Alberto's Continental Patio, at Calle 64 #482, serves Mexican, Continental, and Yucatecan-style dishes. For a refreshing supper, try the Lebanese salad: mixed greens covered with a light blend of olive oil, vinegar, a hint of garlic, and a smidgen of fresh chopped mint leaves—perfect for a warm tropical evening. Delightful atmosphere, moderate to expensive prices. The building dates from 1727. Five-foot-thick walls weathered to an "ancient" hue surround the patio, with plants and vines providing dappled shade. Here and there are astounding pieces of ancient stonework and antique furniture.

On Parque Hidalgo, a delightful outdoor café **Giorgio,** Calle 59 #498, offers heaping platters of pasta, good pizzas, and sandwiches stuffed with ham, salami, and cheese, in front of the Gran Hotel.

Restaurante "La Cava," Km. 12.5 Carretera Mérida—Chichén Itzá, is a must for an authentic Yucatecan meal in a magnificently restored hacienda: *Poc-chuc*, pork marinated in chiles, sour orange juice, and *achiote*, and then grilled; *lomitos de Valladolid*, another Valladolid pork favorite; and *Cochinita pibil*, pork wrapped and cooked in banana leaves with herbs and spices. It's open Tues.-Sun. noon-6 p.m

Casa de San Juan, Calle 62 #545A, tel. in the States (800) 555-8842, in Mexico (99) 23-6823, is a delightful small bed and breakfast in an old house a few blocks from the Mérida plazas. The rooms are spotlessly clean, with lovely crisp linens, an old-fashioned dining room, and a courtyard where guests can relax. Touches of old Mexico grace each room. Some of the rooms contain private baths, others share. Fan cooled. Continental breakfast is fresh fruit, coffee, teas, juices, and fresh *pan dulce*. This is probably one of the best bargains in Mérida. Inexpensive.

Certain spices are associated with the Yucatán Peninsula, such as achiote (a yellow/red paste made from annatto tree seeds). This distinct flavor *says* Yucatán in such dishes as *pollo pibyl*, chicken originally wrapped in banana leaves along with spices and then baked in an underground stone-covered pit lined with more leaves. Today the dish is still popular, but seldom cooked underground.

At dinner parties, it's common for the hosts to serve a wonderful simple *botana* (appetizer) of chunks of jicama and oranges sprinkled with ground chile *piquin*. This is a vibrant combination of flavors and textures—sweet oranges, crunchy jicama, with the buzz of *picante* chile—it goes well with almost any drink. Another local favorite is a hearty breakfast called *huevos motulenos* built from the plate up with a tortilla, refried black beans, a fried egg or two, another tortilla and the whole thing topped with a zingy tomato sauce, chopped ham, and green peas. This dish first gained popularity in the town of Motul, not too far from Mérida.

Special Excursions

Izamal

The original Maya city of Izamal was an important pilgrimage site for the Maya. They called it Itzámna (variously translated as "City of Hills" or "Dew from Heaven"). Arriving Spaniards were determined to alter the importance of Izamal as a religious destination. Led by Friar Diego de Landa, they lost no time in tearing down most of the religious Maya ceremonial centers; to add insult to injury, they used the same stones to construct their own city buildings and churches.

Izamal is a fine old colonial town (pop. 13,500) with Maya origins. The most imposing structure in the small town is the yellow **Convent of Saint Anthony**, a church-convent complex built on what looks like a broad hill. Actually, the hill is the base of what was once a Maya temple, Popul-Chac, destroyed in the 1600s. The immense base measures 180 meters long and stands 17 meters high. The current church was designed by Fray Juan de Mérida; construction began in 1533. Wander through the church grounds, and in one of the stark stone cells you'll see a huge cauldron, metal tools, and a hanging rack still used to make candles for church use. The buildings surround a grassy court-yard (8,000 square meters, the largest in Mexico) with 75 arches. The church glows with yellow-gold paint and the courtyard is well-maintained. A steady stream of visitors tour the church.

The grounds of the Convent of Saint Anthony feature 75 arches.

The town plaza isn't as beautiful as some, but it is surrounded by buildings all of the same color, condition, and arched design, with massive porticoed stone archways and sheltered walkways. During the colonial period the city must have been a shiny jewel in New Spain's showcase. Because most of the structures in Izamal are the same yellow, it's often referred to as Ciudad Amarilla (Yellow City).

Itzámna was already an ancient city when the Spaniards arrived. Although the archaeologists date it from the Early Classic period (A.D. 300-600), pottery carbon-dated to 1000 B.C. has been found. When standing on one of the stone stairways on the grounds near the church, you have a good view of a Maya temple called **Kinich Kakmó**, dedicated

the Saint Anthony altar

to the sun god. Years ago when you tried to track it down from street level, the structure mysteriously eluded you, even though the site is only two blocks northeast of the main plaza! Now it is well-signed, or ask at the Visitor's Center. One of the tallest pyramids in the Western Hemisphere, it has been only partially restored. If you decide to climb to the top, be aware that the upper stairway is not completely reconstructed. Once on the peak, you'll have a striking view of the surrounding brush-covered landscape. Looking east, you can see for 50 km to Chichén Itzá. Archaeologists continue to reconstruct the buildings and hope to find the burial chamber of an honored ruler.

You need look no further for evidence of Izamal's "discovery" than the lovely **Parador Turística** (Visitor's Center) at the entrance to town. Built in the style of a Yucatecan hacienda, with arches and a yellow façade, the center incorporates a large central plaza, a cultural center and museum, a restaurant area, handicraft shops, and restrooms. It's a wonderful addition for this little city that only a decade ago didn't even have an acceptable place to eat, much less a shiny new tile restroom. The center will become a cultural hub for the community as well as for visitors, providing a community meeting place as well as an official entryway to the colonial city. It is indeed the hub of visitors who come from Mérida aboard the "tourist" train for a daylong tour of Izamal.

At any hour of the day, you'll find a queue of *calesas*, which serve as taxis for the townspeople, parked in front of a broad stairway leading to the church and courtyard. These tiny, horse-pulled buggies do an active business carrying locals (often whole families) around town. The *calesas* are not impractical bits of nostalgia for the tourists to admire (though all will); they're the only transportation some families have.

Valladolid

The Maya were successful fighting off conquistador Francisco de Montejo when he attempted to capture the city in 1544. However, Francisco "El Mozo" (The Younger) was tougher. After finally conquering the city 15 years later, he built large churches in Valladolid as a reminder to the indigenous people that the Spanish were now in control and would not let up until they totally crushed the people's ancient beliefs—just as they had already crushed many of their temples. It looked as though the Spanish accomplished this, but anyone who has the opportunity to witness a religious event will recognize that the Maya didn't give up their beliefs—they just blended them with the Catholicism forced upon them.

Valladolid played an important role in the events that led to the beginning of the War of Independence. One eager young priest named Miguel Hidalgo was ordained in 1778 in Mexico City, and immediately left for Valladolid to teach at the College of San Nicolas Obispo. However, by the turn of the century the free-thinking priest had put himself in the spotlight of the Office of the Inquisition. His orthodoxy was suspect. Although no one knows what was rumor or what was fact, he indulged in gambling, loved to dance, challenged the infallibility of the pope, the virgin birth, and questioned whether sexual relations outside of marriage were sinful. Probably his two biggest "failings" were his attacks on the Spanish king and his taking a mistress (María Manuela Herrera). No one could ever prove these allegations; however, the charges were filed away and they were added to his dossier, which would come into play later. He accepted a position in the small village of Dolores Hidalgo in 1803, and the die was cast.

Valladolid is gaining popularity with tourists as an alternative to staying at the Chichén Itzá ruins or in Piste. It's an easy bus or car ride to Chichén Itzá, restaurants and hotels are less expensive, and you get the advantage of staying in a traditional Mexican town. Shopkeepers and hoteliers are responding to the attention by sprucing up their properties and providing more tourist services. If you're en route between Chichén and Cancún, consider spending a night here.

In the provinces, the criollos were restless. The more sophisticated criollos in Mexico City certainly held their private thoughts about the tougher demands from an unstable government and the alarming economic picture. They were also wise enough to consider that a rebellion against the crown would end the rich Spanish traditions they so enjoyed. Those in the more isolated provinces began meeting to discuss their options (under the guise of literary clubs). In 1809 one of these groups was exposed and the clergy, military officers, and Indians who were discovered were imprisoned for a short time and then released. More was to come and all of those exposed would be involved again later.

Valladolid was captured by Miguel Hidalgo (its former parish priest) in October of 1811. Native son Agustín de Iturbide supported the crown and became a local hero in the war despite the fact he fought on the side that lost. The small jewel of the Yucatán Peninsula faded into obscurity for many years while the infant republic tried to gain its balance. Its rather isolated position in the Yucatán kept life simple.

Even today this once-important city centers its social life around the downtown *zócalo*. Young couples and whole families enjoy the cool shade on a Sunday afternoon while the kids play hide-and-seek amid the trees; this is a great place to meet the friendly Valladolidans. During fiestas, such as Candelaria Day, the park comes alive with music, and the cool walkways are lined with stalls selling balloons, pottery, leather goods, and all manner of prepared goodies straight from local kitchens. Because Valladolid is the center of an agricultural district, cattle-raising is becoming more popular as well as profitable. Note all the leather shops in the city—they're great places to pick up belts, sandals, even a saddle! The people of the city, though not rich, appear to enjoy a good life.

Valladolid has many churches. Some are no longer used for services, but instead offer exhibits on the city's history (San Roque for instance, Calles 41 and 38). Most of the ornate decorations that once lined the altars were removed during either the Caste War or the revolution. The architecture of these structures is graceful, powerful, and quite remarkable. The most well-known are the **Church of San Bernardino de Siena** and the **Ex-Convent of Sisal**, built in 1552. Among the oldest churches in the Yucatán, they're on Calle 41A, three blocks southwest of the *zócalo*. Also check out the following churches if you're into old architecture: **Santa Ana**, Calles 41 and 34; **La Candelaria**, Calles 35 and 44; and **Santa Lucía**, Calles 27 and 40.

Cenote Zaci on Calle 36 still attracts tourists, local and national. This particular lake always has a green scum on the surface, which the Mexicans call lake lettuce (supposedly excellent feed for ducks and chickens). You see few gringos swimming in this water. The cave itself is dark, very large, and littered —a sign of tourism. When climbing back up the often-slippery stairs, stop at the museum (small thatched huts, which house interesting exhibits of the area). You'll find a café and bar on the grounds. It's open 8 a.m. till dark.

San Cristóbal de las Casas

IN 1528, LIFE DRASTICALLY CHANGED FOR THE INDIANS who had settled in the Hueyzacatlan Valley centuries before. On 31 March of that year Diego de Mazariegos founded the city called Villa Real de Chiapas (today's San Cristóbal de las Casas). It began a conflict of cultures that still has not been resolved. But by 1538 life had moved on, a neat grid of streets had been cut into the hilly valley, and the Spaniards had taken over. They quickly built Christian churches and houses of authority around a central plaza, and one-story red-tile-roofed houses with wrought-iron fences grew along narrow streets. Spanish padres took seriously their task of preaching the gospel and proselytizing Indians who also took *their* gods seriously. The city was laid out with barrios in the corners and on the edges of the growing town, each with a church and a priest who looked after the souls and bodies of his flock. In 1544, Bishop Bartolomé arrived and he was shocked at the way the Indians were used by the rich and powerful. He tried to make humane changes, and though he succeeded to a point, in the large picture he was but a leaf flying into the wind.

Reaching 2,200-meter-high San Cristóbal de las Casas by car takes time. The roads are continuously being improved. Only 45 years ago you could figure a trip from Tuxtla Gutiérrez was 12 hours by mule. Today it's a one-and-a-half-hour drive on a good road. But be prepared for steep, winding, hairpin curves with many switchbacks and dramatic canyon drops. From Villahermosa expect the drive to take about five to six hours through the beautiful green forest, with spectacular views of the valleys below from Highways 190 and 195. From Palenque to San Cristóbal, figure about five to six hours, especially if you plan to stop along the way.

Villa Real de Chiapas was the most important city in the highlands and became the state capital—until 1892. After that it stumbled along in anonymity, growing and changing very little. In 1943 the city name was changed to San Cristóbal de las Casas in honor of the patron of the Indians. In the early days under the friars, barrios were industrious centers of specific industries. **Barrio Cerrillo** was known for its blacksmiths, **Barrio Guadalupe** for its carpenters; **La Merced** was the candle-making center; **Santa Lucia** was a center for handcrafts; and **San Felipe** was the laundry center. Today it's not quite so segmented, but each barrio still has its church and plaza and the barrios all celebrate their feast days with parties that continue through the night with loud explosions of fireworks, and music, dancing, and traditional food.

The Spaniards introduced wheat growing into the area and for centuries it was a common crop on the outskirts of San Cristóbal. From the 16th century and into the beginning of the 20th century wheat mills sat near the mouths of the great rivers in the valley. These haciendas became important centers of life. Eventually high-tech methods took over and most of the mills disappeared. Just a few remnants survive; northeast of the city on the Río Amarillo are the mills of **Utrilla** and **Los Arcos**. More are scattered about, but none are functioning.

In Chiapas more than other areas, the Indian groups—Chamulans, Zinacantecans, and others—have held onto their ancient beliefs; each group is different, each with its own color, traditions, and mystery. And though most of their villages lie on the outskirts of San Cristóbal, the heart of the city draws them together, bolsters their conviction for a separate

Chiapas Indian Groups	
Olmecs	Tzotzils
Choles	Tzeltals
Lacandóns	Chamulans
Tojolabales	Zinacantecos
Chiapanecans	Oxchuqueros
Mames	San Pedranos
Zoques	

existence. Despite the intrusion of the Pan American Highway after WWII bringing outside influences and the seduction of material temptations from visitors from all over the world, San Cristóbal remains the ship that carries these ethnic groups through centuries of change—*unchanged*. In the new millennium will there be a "chicken in every pot?" or more to the point, electricity in every hut? And will major life-changes take place with the addition of television and computers, changes that were resisted for nearly 500 years?

Perhaps those interested should visit San Cristóbal's Indian culture now while it remains the vibrant Indian center of the Mexican highlands. Each year finds more and more people on the narrow streets, more outvillagers turned vendors-of-something. Tourism officials continue to talk about building an airport nearby, and if it comes to pass, even more people will come to explore.

San Cristóbal is an appealing old town. The pastel buildings lend a special charm. For centuries, behind unadorned paint-deprived walls antiquated colonial buildings held hidden courtyards filled with plants and flowers, bits and pieces of another life, memories of the past—many in a state of decay. But now, as more and more tourists discover San Cristóbal, the wonderful old buildings are opening up. The dramatic architecture is almost as breathtaking as the businesses within: art galleries, restaurants, trendy malls selling beautiful clothing, crafts, and antiques. They attract visitors by the droves.

Despite the influx of tourists, little change has taken place here. You'll still find no high-rise hotels, no Denny's, but always thousands of traditional Indians, bustling to the rhythm of San Cristóbal's public market. Okay, you will find a few variations in the lifestyle of the indigenous people: more men wear factory-made straw cowboy hats or even baseball caps, and among city-dwelling mestizos polyester clothing is becoming popular. The people in the outlying villages such as San Juan Chamula and Zinacantán still make flat-crowned hats but seldom wear them; the women still use the backstrap loom to weave the colorful fabric for clothes for most of the family.

Exploring the Streets of San Cristóbal de las Casas

The official name of the main square is **Plaza de 31 de Marzo**. Green iron benches are scattered along the wide walkway under tall shade trees. The centerpiece is a two-story kiosk with tables and umbrellas where cold drinks and snacks are served; but only tourists visit there. The square has had many faces; during the colonial era a large fountain supplied water for the village, it was the public market, and it was the site of horrific punishment during the years of the Inquisition. More recently, the Zapatistas rebelled against poverty and governmental neglect. Today it has resumed its tranquil appearance, though often crowds of indigenous people displeased with things governmental stage peaceful demonstrations in front of the governor's palace, Palacio Municipal, and spill out onto the square. And it's the gathering place for fiestas, especially for Christmas and the Fiesta of San Juan.

If you decide to sit a while in the square, expect to be inundated by Chamulan women and children selling woven bracelets and belts, small wooden Zapatista dolls in all sizes, and Chiclets gum. Young entrepreneurs, boys 9-10

SAN CRISTOBAL DE LAS CASAS

years old, carry boxes of candy and lollipops, younger brothers sell newspapers, and older teens hawk amber of questionable origin. Most of the women carry babies in their rebozos, many of the children are unkempt with skin rashes, women and children are dirty, and most of them chew on big brother's candy. Of all the Indians from the outlying villages, the Chamulans seem to be the ones who need help the most, the ones who seem to be stuck in a private time warp.

Look for the very aged leather-faced man who uses a long palm frond to sweep and clean one long side of the stone-lined walkway before he moves to the next side of the square.

Across from the plaza, **Casa Sirena**, the oldest house in town, was constructed about 1555. It is

view from the shady Plaza de 31 de Marzo

a lovely old building, and still visible is a stylized version of what looks like two serpent women, and over the corner of the building, a carving of a sea nymph that gives the house its name. Look for the carved lions, an indigenous craftsman's interpretation from some medieval representation. The insignia on the coat of arms over the door has been destroyed, so although the house is most often ascribed to be the original home of Luis de Mazariegos (the conqueror of Chiapas), some believe it may have been built by another, Andres de la Tobilla.

The **Palacio Municipal**, on the west side of the main square, is a good example of 19th-century civil architecture. It has been rebuilt many times since the first stone was laid in 1885. The previous building was burned to the ground in 1863 by rebel troops led by Juan Ortega. When construction of this building began, the city was still the capital of the state and the plan included a much larger edifice, but before it was finished fate stepped in and San Cristóbal lost its rank. Construction was halted with only 25% of the building completed. It's a lovely neoclassic design, with columns painted a pale blue. The columns and lower arches present a show of dignity due a structure that takes care of state business. Frequent demonstrations take place here, and this building bore the major damage during the Zapatista uprising in 1994. Behind the palace lies a plaza where civic ceremonies are held.

The main plaza of the **Catedral** was constructed in 1528 on the north side of the main square. Originally dedicated as the Nuestra Señora de la Anunciación, it was rededicated a few years later to San Cristóbal. The

Visitors to San Cristóbal should know that the Chamulans, Zinacantecans, and Lacandóns do not like to be photographed, and they like it *even less* when you produce a camera inside their churches. In Chamula you can buy a permit at the city hall to take pictures in the square as long as it isn't a special holiday. You can ask permission from your subject, and if he/she asks for payment—well, that seems fair. Just don't expect too much cooperation.

Work on the cathedral began in 1528, the year the Spanish arrived.

the Palacio Municipal

façade is a standout, its bright yellow-ocher contrasting with 17th-century white mortared niches and geometric designs. Some call it austere, but the simplicity of it presents an outstanding backdrop for the hordes of colorfully dressed Indians and tourists who constantly crowd into the church plaza. On the inside, note the elaborately carved wooden pulpit. Those interested in religious art will see much from the colonial era. The church and church plaza come to life during festivals, especially the celebration of the feast day of Corpus Christi.

The **Law School Auditorium** is another old building with a fanciful history as the ex-church and monastery of the Jesuits. At one time it was an exclusive school, San Francisco Javier School. After the Jesuits were expelled in 1767, the school no longer functioned and it was converted to the Tridentine Seminary of Nuestra Señora de la Concepción, which it housed until the beginning of the 19th century. Today it houses the Universidad Autonoma de Chiapas Law School, and the old structure of the church serves as the auditorium.

Anyone curious about the ethnic history of the Mexican Indians will enjoy a visit to the **Sergio Castro Museum.** This is a private museum and not open all of the time, but you can arrange a visit with just a phone call. Sergio Castro is an intelligent, well-educated gentleman who knows the ethnology and anthropological history of all the communities in the Chiapas highlands. Along with the display on the history of clothes that play an important role in the "togetherness" of each village, he tells anecdotes and legends of the people. He will answer your questions, not always with the answer you want, but you will come away feeling that you have seen the highlands through experienced eyes and understand a little better the People of the Bat (Zinacatecan). Call or go to the Office of Tourism in the Palacio Municipal on the square for more information about entrance to the museum.

DOWNTOWN SAN CRISTOBAL DE LAS CASAS

NOT TO SCALE

© MOON PUBLICATIONS, INC.

Another out-of-the-ordinary museum to visit is **Na Balom Museum and Research Center**, originally the home of late Swiss-born Gertrude Duby Blom and her husband, Danish archaeologist Frans Blom. They arrived in the 1920s in San Cristóbal to excavate Moxviquil, Maya ruins outside of town. Frans had been involved over the years with the archaeology of the Maya in several Yucatán Peninsula locations, including Bonampak (Lacandón land). Both Frans and Trudy became very interested in the highland Lacandón Indians and worked to preserve their culture and the rainforest; Trudy continued her work with them for many years after Frans's death. The Bloms' San Cristóbal home (cum museum/research center/library/guesthouse) is named Na (House) Balom (Jaguar), from the Tzotzil language. The entire

Hotel el Paraíso, Calle Cinco de Febrero #19 close to the plaza, tel. and fax (967) 8-0085, opened in 1993—it only looks as if it originated in the colonial era. Heavy wood beams and textured ochre and blue walls reflect the regional traditions, and glass skylights cover corridors filled with sculptures and plants. The 13 rooms boast sloping wood ceilings, wood-framed windows facing the courtyard or street, and colorful Guatemalan textiles. Inexpensive.

house (and garden) is a museum of Maya artifacts. An old chapel and several rooms offer extraordinary exhibits showing life in the jungle. The gardens cover a large area and include vegetables, trees, flowers, and plants of the area. At one time, thousands of sapling trees were grown here from seed and given to the Indians to encourage them to replant areas of rainforest destroyed over the years by logging and slash-and-burn farming.

Although the Lacandón did not allow anyone else to photograph them, they posed for thousands of pictures for Trudy. Over the years she exhibited the photos on tours to raise money to help the Indian group. Marvelous black and white portraits of these people are displayed throughout the house. The extensive library has books and articles covering all of Central America and attracts social scientists and students who come every year to intern at Na Balom. Na Balom is open for individual guided tours or a more involved group tour that includes a film on Trudy's work with the Lacandón. About a dozen rooms are available for guests, though it's rare to get a room without a reservation.

A random stroll through the streets of the city takes visitors past many churches—some are more than 400 years old. In 1547, the first **Santo Domingo Church** was a simple adobe. The present church is probably the most impressive of the many churches in the city. Santo Domingo offers a baroque façade that glows a delicate rose in the sun. The structure is covered with ornamented mortar with intricate carvings, Solomonic columns, statues tucked into ornate niches —and that's just the outside. The interior houses a sensational pulpit with gold carvings everywhere. You'll see many nostalgic religious paintings frequently offered in place of money donations, or in thanks for favors; the painters were *not* professionals. It's not unusual to find an Indian healer (often a female *curandera*) performing rituals in the Catholic environment: touching the stricken pilgrim with flowers, surrounding him with smoking copal, murmuring incantations in the guttural Maya language while passing burning candles over and around the "patient"—all in front of the church altars. These ceremonies spring from a mix of Maya and Catholic rituals. In the Ex-Convento Santo Domingo a fine museum offers examples of the Maya culture on three floors. Alongside Santo Domingo Church and

Santo Domingo Church

Hotel Santa Clara, Insurgentes #1 Plaza Central, tel. 8-1140, fax 8-1041, on the plaza, is well worth checking out even if you decide you don't wish to stay—it's the former home of conquistador Diego de Mazariegos. The quite simple but lovely hotel displays 16th-century touches such as wooden beams and fascinating old carvings, and all 42 rooms can get as cold as any old castle in the winter. The hotel boasts a pool and courtyard tables with umbrellas, and a restaurant and bar on the premises. Remember, this building is going on 500 years old. Inexpensive.

neighboring Church of la Caridad clusters of Indian artisans set up tables or on rugs to sell their crafts. This is larger than some "regular" markets.

Up many steps, high on a hill looking over the entire town, the **Church of San Cristóbal** opens just once a year, July 17-25, during the celebration of the feast of St. Christopher, patron of the city. During this celebration, pilgrims stream up and down the steps to the church; a road approaches the rear of the church as well. Built in the 17th century, it now has a neoclassical façade.

The **Church of la Merced** was the first convent established by the order of Our Lady of Mercy in the New World in 1537. In the 19th century it was converted into military quarters; today it houses the municipal jail. The building façade today represents the neoclassical era. Note the polychrome arch in the sacristy; it's obviously the work of indigenous artists of the time. Included are striking motifs and imagery: the sun and the moon, flowers and fruits, faces with feathered headdresses, and two-headed eagles. It is still the custom to request that a prisoner be released from jail during the celebrations for the Virgin, and the request is usually granted.

The **Church of San Francisco** was once part of a Franciscan monastery that was done in long ago. It has been reconstructed at various stages and at one time marked the southernmost limits of the city. The church has a single nave roofed by wooden beams and clay tiles. The main altar is Churrigueresque style and the church contains many colonial art treasures. The simple façade is of painted plaster crowned with two squat towers; it stands on a small square with a baptismal font. This is a good example of the neoclassical influence on San Cristóbal's popular architecture in the late 19th and early 20th centuries.

Church of San Francisco

Church of Santa Lucía was reconstructed during the 19th century in typical neoclassical style. About the middle of the 1600s, it served as a small hospital. Today it's surrounded by many modest cafés, which are very busy during the patron saint's feast on 13 December. It's large for a neighborhood church. The Gothic style predominates in the interior with a circular dome. Small towers cap the centerpiece of the painted plaster façade.

Church of El Carmen was the church of San Sebastian from the end of the 16th century; in 1930

The charming **Hotel Palacio de Moctezuma,** Av. Juárez #16, tel. 8-0352, fax 8-1536, is just two blocks from the center of town. This cozy lodging contains 42 rooms, mini-courtyards, greenery, fresh flowers everywhere, and intimate salons. Old, but modern and clean, the hotel offers pleasant vistas with arched entrances, tile floors, and a delightful dining room with a fireplace and good food. Rooms are small and carpeted—some recently added, others remodeled with modern bathrooms. Most rooms are equipped with telephones and one or two double beds. Inexpensive.

> **ⓧ El Fogon de Jovel,** 16 de Septiembre #11, is a delightful place to spend an evening over dinner and often live entertainment. Waiters wear *típico* outfits in this lovely old mansion, where candlelight and linen napkins set the scene. The menu offers a wide selection of choices from regional to continental.

it was dedicated to El Carmen. It was part of the Encarnación convent, which served to "take in women who did not marry and desired to live modestly and withdrawn." The "la Torre" bell tower has a Moorish shape but is much simpler without all the ornamentation. The tower was added during the late 1600s and is supposedly the only one of its kind in the Americas. Note the statue of San Sebastian that most likely dates from the 17th century. Today this church is the hub of a new urban complex called the **El Carmen Cultural Center.**

The **Church of San Nicolas** was established in the 1600s (next to the cathedral facing the plaza). It is probably the least modified of all the city's historical monuments. Small cylindrical towers top the sedate baroque main entrance. The tile-covered eaves, with their strong wooden beams, extend on each side of the church creating a play of light and shadow. On the inside are two outstanding Guatemalan sculptures: one of the Señor de la Misericordia and the other the Virgen de los Dolores; below the choir are two murals attributed to the indigenous artist Andres de Mazariegos.

San Cristóbal Highlights

Arts and Artisans

Weaving is spectacular in the state of Chiapas because of the dense population of indigenous groups. Each village boasts a particular style and design, and to the weavers these have traditional meanings. To the outsider it's simply beautiful work, brilliant color, and desirable designs woven on a *típico* backstrap loom.

a village weaver at the San Cristóbal market

The Larrainzar women add colored bits of yarn to the warp and weft of their looms to create special designs. One product is the brocade, in which the designs are woven directly into the cloth. The ancient designs portray gods, animals, flowers, fertility symbols, and the Maya vision of the cosmos, incorporating traditional symbols such as the snake, diamond, flower, and the "trickster monkey," popular in Maya mythology. The symbols tell a story that's handed down from mother to daughter.

The Zinacatecan women create unique textiles noted for colorful embroidery over woven designs. They work outdoors in a family yard with most of the women attached to a waist loom. These particular designs are woven in flamboyant reds, pinks, cerise, purple, and navy blue. They create tablecloths, bedspreads, and place mats to sell to visitors. The traditional men's tunic is woven with red and white thread, giving it a pink color. Over the top of the pink weave, the women embroider flamboyant colored flowers.

Occasionally visitors will come across a Zinacatecan wedding gown. Mostly white, the open-weave fabric is lighter and more delicate than most, but not quite sheer. On the top of the *huipil*, a small cross is embroidered just below the neckline. But the really unusual part

Zinacatecan women wear their art.

is the bottom third of the dress, embroidered with lovely white feathers (usually chicken feathers) trimmed in rather subtle colors. Historically, the Aztecs used the feathers in their weaving, but this group obviously was exposed to this tradition early on, perhaps by the Tlaxcaltecans that accompanied Mazariegos when he conquered the Chiapas highlands in the 16th century.

Shoppers and browsers find excellent regional crafts at **Sna Jolobil** (in Tzotzil Maya, it means House of Weaving), at the ex-Convento de Santo Domingo at 20 de Noviembre. This co-op is made up of 700 weavers from 20 Tzotzil- and Tzeltal-speaking villages in the highlands of Chiapas. The creation of Sna Jolobil encouraged a revitalization of Maya art and gave a new dignity to preservation of the ancient designs. The women study old textiles and give and take classes in the ancient art of natural dyes. The younger generations are motivated to study old methods of dyeing wool and cotton as well as ancestral weaving techniques. Each weaver creates her original designs with unique symbols and values related to her ancestors. Sna Jolobil is also a study center for the technique of

A favorite is **Hotel Rincón del Arco,** Ejercito Nacional #66, tel. 8-1313, fax 8-1568, about a 10-minute walk from town center. The easiest way to get here the first time is by taxi. Once a private home, the building has been in the same family for several generations. The original structure was built in 1650, with some additions and renovations over the centuries. The architecture is stunning, with lots of tile, brick-arched doorways, white stucco, wooden beams, and greenery-filled inner patios. Each room boasts a unique clay fireplace, stocked with wood to light on a cold night. The rooms are modern and comfortable with carpeting, tile, and spotlessly clean bathrooms. The upper rooms offer terrific views of the city and its churches. Inexpensive.

brocade. This is a true incorporated profit-sharing co-op (Sociedad Civil) run by Tzeltal and Tzotzil craftspeople. Outstanding textiles are displayed with set prices, most of which are quite moderate for the work each piece requires. (Outside of Santo Domingo you can bargain, but not in here. Credit cards are accepted in Sna, but not outside).

The Chiapanecan artist also produces pottery. Again, each village specializes in something different. Tzeltal potters from the village of Amatenango del Valle create extra-large jars and graceful doves from very small to huge (about 3-4 feet tall). These are formed without a wheel. The pottery is "fired" on an above-ground open-flamed "kiln."

You'll find more Maya craftsmen and their work at Taller Lenateros, Calle Flavio A. Paniagua 54, an award-winning press where Maya men and women produce beautiful handmade paper. Along with art cards, notebooks, photo albums, etc., limited editions of children's books, poetry, art, and a wonderful

Amber

Amber formed from the resin of several kinds of pine trees that forested various regions of the earth 40 or 50 million years ago. Natural catastrophes entombed many forests of these now-extinct varieties of conifers. Among those classes of trees buried was the succinifer pine, which, judging by the size of some pieces found, secreted great quantities of resin, which was gradually transformed into amber by the eon-spanning process of petrification.

Amber is hard and brittle, and it emits a unique aroma when it is burned. It is generally yellowish, but with many variations of tint, such as white, pink, red, wine, brown, or black, among others. It can be opaque or transparent, or, on occasion, marbled, all depending on its degree of purity.

Archaeological evidence shows that many primitive civilizations attributed magical properties to amber. For this reason, historians tie their theories about the commercial routes of Maya traders across Central America in ancient times to the distribution of amber.

Evidence shows that Indians in the state of Chiapas knew of amber's existence as far back as 250 B.C. Until the arrival of the Spaniards, they principally used amber to make adornments such as nose and lip rings, earrings, and beads for necklaces. Subsequently they traded and bartered it throughout the Yucatán Peninsula, Oaxaca, and what is now central Mexico by two Maya tribes of southern Mexico, the Zoques and Zinacantecos. In the Mendocino Codex, amber is mentioned among the tributes paid to the Aztecs by the inhabitants of the Soconusco, the southwest coastal region of the state of Chiapas.

The first amber mines to be worked were found near Simojovel, a small town in the north of Chiapas. Throughout the years new veins have been discovered. Unfortunately for the amber miners the deposits are consistently found in hard-to-reach places possessing a constant danger of landslides.

guide to natural dyes are all for sale here. This is a Maya cultural center in action, and it helps the individual artists come into their own while preserving this fragile old culture. Free English/Spanish tours are given daily except Sunday; ask for Andrew, Ambar, or Doña Mari.

For the Shopper

The public market, **Mercado José Castillo** on Av. Utrilla, is large but mostly devoted to the needs of the locals. This is a lively gathering spot for the *indigenes* every morning except Sunday, which is the day that most of the outlying villages have their own markets. It's at these village Sunday-markets that visitors see outstanding woven textiles and leather goods. Market days are perfect people-watching days.

Guatemalan textiles are in great supply, with piles of shirts, shorts, and pants of Guatemalan fabrics and rows of leather and fabric belts. Guatemala is

To find amber deposits, miners begin by searching for layers of coal, a highly risky job because of the condition of the loose, shaky terrain. Once they find coal, they drill a tunnel and cut away large blocks of coal until they find the "hearth of amber."

Generally the raw amber is sold to the artisans of Simojovel, who use sandpaper and files to polish each piece to a beautiful lustre. Then, inspired by the amber's luminous shine, the artisans create a great variety of pieces in imaginative forms, including vine leaves—which were a motif even before the Spanish conquest—as well as feet, hands, hearts, crosses, and other amulet designs clearly influenced by silver medals. Also carved from amber are red currant berries, feathers, raindrops, fangs, triangles, leaves, flowers, and tears. Amber is also set in earrings, rings, bracelets, and necklaces, in multifaceted pieces that look like geometrically carved gems.

Sometimes a chunk of amber contains trapped insects, which raises its value considerably. By studying these preserved creatures entomologists have classified almost 75 insect species that lived during the Tertiary or Cretaceous periods. One advantage of studying insect specimens preserved in amber is that the insect's molecular structure remains intact, without a substitution of minerals for its organic tissues. These specimens offer excellent study conditions to biologists and archaeologists.

In Chiapas, tradition has endowed amber with magical properties. Certain Maya groups put bracelets hung with small pieces of amber on their children to protect them from the "evil eye." With the passage of time, the mestizo population adopted this custom and added the more modern attribute of "good luck" to the wearing of amber.

Amber has been given many names. The Greeks called it *electron* because of its capacity to accumulate electricity. Because of its resinous origins the Romans called it *succo* or juice and, because of its similarity to water bubbles with the reflection of sun rays within them, the Aztecs called it *apozonalli,* or water foam.

woven goods on display at the town market

close, sharing a border with Chiapas. Some real treasures are to be found in the various markets if you look hard enough.

Note: Be careful with your camera if you are in one of the outlying villages, where people strongly object to having their photos taken.

¡Música!

Anyone who has spent any time in San Cristóbal or Tuxtla, or just in a plaza or an outdoor café, is familiar with the sound of the Chiapa marimba; this is *tropical* music! The marimba appears to have originated in Chiapas with the dense settlement of Spaniards in Chiapa de Corzo. It is believed that a small version of the instrument was originally brought from Africa's Angola with the slaves accompanying the Spanish. In no time the instrument was adopted and adapted by Mexicans and Central Americans. A change here, an adjustment there, and Chiapas produces some of the finest marimbas in the country. In Chiapa de Corzo area, it is constructed from the "singing" wood, *hormiguillo,* which gives the marimba its brilliant sound. Sticks made from the strong but flexible *guisisil* wood are wrapped at one end with natural rubber to make mallets that fly across the keys. The marimba is no longer the step-sister of concert instruments; it lacks only two octaves to equal the range of a concert piano. More and more excellent music is being written for the marimba by classical and popular musicians all over the world.

The Nandayapas from Chiapa de Corzo are an extended family of extraordinary musicians. They are creators of the country's finest marimbas, still patterned from the 100-year-old templates of the first generations of the Nandayapa family. The keys function like the parts of a string quartet, says the elder Zeferino Nandayapa. You hear a violin, second violin (contralto voice), the viola, and the cello. The Nandayapas play Bach, Mozart, Sanbas, Sones, and lively Mexican music. Their marimbas come in all sizes, but their "concert" marimba can be up to eight feet long, waist high, and can range up to six and a half octaves.

If you're lucky enough to attend a concert of the Nandayapa Orchestra at Carnegie Hall in New York, you're apt to hear selections such as Franz Liszt's *Rhapsody #2* or Manuel Falla's *Fire Dance,* both played as you've never heard them before. Marimba music is an art form, an art form that lives in the heart of Mexicans, especially the Chiapanecans. Award-winning Mexican poet Oscar Oliva said, "In all religious and sacred ceremonies, the marimba is there. With music from the marimba, we bury our friends, our parents, our brothers." The marimba is the soul of Chiapa life, at birth, at death, in happiness, in sadness.

Special Excursions

San Juan Chamula

Indian children begin learning their life's work at an early age. As infants they're carried around in their mothers' rebozos until they can walk or until there are other infants to take their places. It's not much longer before they begin trailing after mom or dad. Mom and kids usually look after their small flocks of sheep grazing on empty hillsides. The animals are well-cared-for, their flesh is *never* eaten, and they are shorn regularly. All little girls learn the art/craft of cutting wool from the sheep, carding, spinning, weaving, and embroidering. Each community is trapped by tradition into a certain design and type of clothing; so far only the rebels (and outside influences) try to change the system.

Visitors to San Cristóbal will recognize Chamulan women by their white *huipiles* with simple flowers embroidered around the necklines and black or brown wool skirts with red belts and sky-blue wool rebozos wrapped around their shoulders; there's almost always a baby tucked into the folds of the shawl. These garments are not only handwoven on a waist loom, but they are generally made of wool that has been carded by the women from animals raised on the family plot. Chamulan men wear long white woolen tunics and the village leaders wear black

The Lacandón

Though usually associated with archaeologist Frans Blom and his wife, Trudy, the Lacandóns first gained notoriety after a visit in 1933 by French anthropologists Jacques and Georgette Soustelle. Jacques Soustelle told the world of the Indians' hunting techniques, which involved the use of bows and poison-dipped arrows. They generally hunted monkeys, wild pigs, and wild turkeys. More intense contact with the outside world began in the last half of the 20th century, when loggers began harvesting the local mahogany trees and floating the logs downriver to Tenosique. The Lacandón worked for the loggers, earning money for the first time; logging continues in the area. The Lacandón men still wear the traditional white dress and long black hair. (Amazingly, some of the oldest Lacandóns show no sign of gray in their black tresses.)

tunics. Generally there are three outfits in an Indian's adult life: wedding outfit, fiesta, and everyday. A man also wears a special official "outfit of authority" during the time he fulfills his obligation to help run the government. His political year is spent living in Chamula, serving in the parliament or as a policeman (there are seven villages in the municipality of Chamula). During that time the rest of his village helps to keep his milpa (family corn field) watered and cared for while he leaves his barrio and lives near the city hall.

Men have little choice. All seven districts of the highland Indians know this is a civic duty that is expected of them, and it generally involves the whole family one way or another. Another duty is to donate a year as caretaker of a *santo* (patron saint.) They wash the saint's statue and its clothes, change it from everyday to fiesta clothing, make offerings of candles and *posh* (Indian brandy made from sugarcane). It is their responsibility to pay for fireworks and food and to see that there is music at the appropriate times. In recent years, especially with the coming of Protestant evangelists, Chamulan families have refused this obligation on economical and moral grounds; to finance these practices when they barely have enough money to sustain themselves does seem ludicrous to most outsiders. As a result a whole community of Chamulan people has drifted away one by one; they now house together along the *periférico* of San Cristóbal.

Exploring the Streets of San Juan Chamula

Visitors are welcome in Chamula as long as they understand the *rules* set forth by the villagers. One of the favorite attractions is the colorful blue and white **St. John the Baptist Church** and the huge plaza in front. To go inside, get the necessary permit at the government building catercorner from the church on the side of the plaza (there's a small charge per person)—hang onto it because you will be asked to produce it. Remember, the permit is an agreement that stipulates no cameras in the church. Don't even carry a camera where it can be seen; tuck it in your backpack, purse, pocket, hide it somewhere—and if you use it, you lose it—literally! They mean business and **will** do bodily harm if the contract is broken!

Visitors must get a permit to enter St. John the Baptist Church in Chamula.

The large plaza is the center of life outside the church. On Sunday huge crowds come for market day. Theatrical celebrations mark feast days. This is a busy intriguing place to observe the Chamulan people in their natural surroundings. Large green crosses nearby have special meanings and play an important part in ceremonies.

Visiting St. John the Baptist Church is always an experience. An exotic aroma greets you as you walk in the door of the church: a mixture of fresh pine, flowers, incense, and candles. You may witness people prostrated before their favorite icons. During special celebrations, groups of two or three musicians dressed in colorful ancient garb are scattered about the church adding a low-pitched tintinnabulation of ancient sounds on unusual harps and violins. Hundreds of tapers placed reverently on the floor in front of each penitent glow in the dim light, and families kneeling together reverently pray—pausing now and then for a swig of *posh* (sugarcane brandy) or Coke. Visitors are expected to come to church only to pray. Strangers are requested to stay at the back of the church and not to disturb the congregation. Seventy-five thousand Chamulans from these hills consider the church their own.

The church is a precious space for villagers. This is no longer a Catholic church; there are no clergy and haven't been for many years since the Chamulans kicked all mestizos out of their village. The rituals used today are the Indians' interpretation of old Catholic rituals mixed with their original beliefs. The floor is covered with pine needles; fresh bundles are carried from the forest every Saturday. The statues of the saints are dressed in many layers of brilliantly flowered clothes with mirrors hung around their necks. Most of the statues are now kept in glass boxes because villagers in the recent past occasionally sought revenge when a request to a saint was not fulfilled. It wasn't unusual for them to break off a finger, turn the statue backward to face the wall, or even to take the statue outside and stick its head in the ground. The Chamulans do not think of the statues as statues, but rather as real people with whom they can interact. Beware the wrath of the believer! Some anthropologists say that the innermost layer of clothing on the statue is woven with secret symbols of the ancient Maya.

On the top of the hill overlooking the village are the remains of an early Catholic church. Built in 1526, it was destroyed by the indigenous people later in the 16th century. The Chamulans were quite set in their notion of keeping outsiders away even then. Today the old structure is surrounded by a cemetery and is often filled with people tending the graves of their families. The building itself is just a brooding skeleton of old stone.

The Chamulans destroyed this early Catholic church in the 16th century.

Special Events

Carnaval: Chamulan holidays are a scene to be experienced, especially during Carnaval. This is one of the biggest celebrations in Chamula and goes on for a week. Shrove (or fat) Tuesday, the day before Ash Wednesday, is especially colorful. Ceremonies take place on the days leading up to it, and the final event takes place around the church atrium and central plaza. It includes the men from three Chamulan barrios, San Juan, San Sebastian, and San Pedro. The men gather into their three groups, much like army platoons preparing to attack. They dress in special costumes, including "rooster foot" (high-backed huaraches), knee-length pants, red-tasseled white scarves around their necks, brilliantly striped cummerbunds, and tall cone-shaped hats. The hats, covered with monkey fur, strap around their chins like beards and are topped with colorful ribbons springing from the point of the cones. Some carry a cane made from the penis of a bull; others wave flowered cloth banners on tall poles. Tooting horns and clouds of incense signal the time to run. Little boys join the festivities, running behind the men and learning their futures. At an unseen signal they stop, slowly wave the banners over the incense and then begin running again. The *casiques* (head men) of the different villages crowd together on a second-floor balcony of the government building wearing straw, flat-crowned, beribboned hats, each holding under his arm a silver-headed cane (a sign of his authority). What a colorful scene, and you can't take even one picture! The whole week is filled with intriguing events, and Good Friday brings another time of great ceremony.

Chiapa de Corzo

Many years before the Spanish conquest, Chiapa de Corzo was inhabited by Indians from Nicaragua. The settlement was on the Kandelumini River (today called the Grijalva River). The Chiapanecos were courageous warriors and only after two invasions did the Spaniards get them under control. Conquistador Luis Marin led the first foray in 1524. His troops were forced to turn back in failure. In 1528, Diego de Mazariegos attacked and was brutally successful conquering the Indians. On 3 April of that year, the town was named Villa Real and dedicated under a large ceiba tree. Like most Spanish settlements in those early years, it was given as an *encomienda* to the conqueror Mazariegos. This lifestyle made vassals of the Indians who built the new city under the direction of the Spanish. Years later, Bishop Bartolomé de las Casas managed to institute changes, and by 1552 the *encomienda* was dismantled. Las Casas became the Indians' hero. The city was then called Villa Real Corona. The name of the settlement continued to change as it grew; it was called Chiapa Español and then Chiapa de los Indios. According to legend it was always named for the *chia*, a small fruit filled with tiny flavorful seeds that once grew abundantly in the region. The city's present name, Chiapa de Corzo, was given in 1888 in honor of the president of the municipality, Ángel Albino Corzo.

Exploring the Streets of Chiapa de Corzo

The centerpiece of the small city is **La Pila,** the largest colonial fountain in the state. Set regally under an elegant Moorish-style brick structure in the center of a grassy park, it illustrates the strong Moorish influence over the Catholic kings of Spain. The fountain was built by Fray Rodrigo de Léon in the middle of the 16th century and was completed in 1562. This was not just the village water supply. It was a gathering place where women did their laundry, collected water in *calabasas* for drinking, but maybe more important, the gathering was a social event: even the animals had their own water troughs. The striking building is made of red bricks cut in unusual three-dimensional diamond shapes in a typical Muhadin style, or as some say, as a replica of the Spanish king's crown. La Pila is in the center of the grassy town plaza, and a variety of small shops and businesses lie across the road: a pharmacy, an *escrito publico* (the town letter writer), and at least one shop that sells the locally made wooden masks and other crafts.

> The nicest hotel is **La Ceiba,** three blocks west of the plaza. It has an old world look but with the shiny flavor of New World products: pool, parking garage, lobby bar, a/c, a dining room that serves fine local specialties, and 42 rooms with private bath. Budget.

 Santo Domingo Cathedral, is a large, though simple, white building next to the town soccer field. Its huge bell was cast in gold, silver, and copper in 1576; they say when it tolls it can be heard for miles around the countryside. Vendors set up shop near the church and among other things sell "black" and "white" *pozol* in large (maybe a liter), round-bottomed tin cups. This thick drink is made from hominy, chocolate, and cinnamon. It serves as a "fast-food" lunch for workers on the go in Chiapas. Eat your heart out, McDonald's. One family drives up in a truck every morning and unloads tables, buckets, and everything needed to prepare the

La Pila reflects the Spaniards' Moorish heritage.

pozol. This same family has been selling *pozol* from this corner under the trees for more than a decade. Some diners make the trip all the way from Tuxtla to lunch or breakfast on this tasty *pozol.* Nearby you'll find women selling pottery from Amatenango, and across the street the flower lady always has a glorious display of colors; you'll first notice the sweet aroma and then the splash of color.

 The **Ex-Convent of Santo Domingo-Cultural Center** was built in 1554 in the usual design of the friars, with thick walls and broad archways edging once-lovely patios. Tile floors and wooden stairways lead to a multitude of rooms. Wandering through the old convent is worth the time to see the graceful old architecture. The Spaniards really knew how to build to last. Some of the old walls are eight feet thick. No matter how hot the day, it's always cool in the shadows of the arched corridors. As museums go, it's not large, but the exhibits are fascinating. Displays focus on quality antique lacquerware, a precision craft—everything from tiny, delicate jewelry boxes to enormous wooden chests, each covered with bright colors and intricate designs. Artist Doña Martha Vargas puts on a lacquer-painting demonstration *almost* every day; if this is important to you, ask the tourism office about her schedule. Her work is amazing. Also displayed in the museum are wooden masks depicting the Spanish conquistadors with those vivid blue eyes, as well as a lonely burnished wood or two.

It's a short walk from town center to the *embarcadero* (city dock), where passengers board launches to go up the Grijalva River through Sumidero Canyon. The docks are a bustling hub; try one of the outdoor *palapa* cafés for a cold beer or snack with a good view of life on the river. Chugging along in one of the small boats gives you the opportunity to view the steep canyon walls from the level of the river. This awesome waterway was formerly a roaring series of mighty rapids that literally cut their way through massive towering stone. In 1960 it took a team of surveyors nine days to travel through the hazardous, rushing white water of the canyon. In 1981 the water was harnessed with construction of the **Chicoasén Dam**, one of Mexico's largest. As a result, the tranquil riverway serves as a favorite recreational area for locals and visitors alike. A trip in a launch to the dam and back takes about three hours. The boats pass interesting rock formations, caves (some large enough for a small boat to pull into), waterfalls (during the rainy season), and an ever-changing vista of plants and trees clinging to the face of the cliffs.

A walk through the ruin of **San Sebastián** shows enough to indicate that it was obviously a grand building in its 17th-century days of glory. Built on the hill of San Gregorio, it illustrates once again a history of great wealth and the one-time importance of the city of Chiapa. The church had three naves, and the remaining walls echo the influence of the Muhadin, Renaissance, and baroque architecture. The structure has been used in a variety of ways over the centuries. During the battle of 21 October 1863, it served as a fort. Not a great deal is left today, just a few walls and fine arches, and many memories—but the view takes in the urban development that covers the landscape below.

Special Events

Festival of St. Sebastian: Come to a fiesta! Imagine an army of wooden-faced (real wood), blue-eyed Spaniards wearing mustaches and bright bushy yellow hair—many of them only three feet tall, others man-size; this is the beginning of a great fiesta in Chiapa. On 15 January the biggest celebration of the year is held in the park around *la pila* (the fountain). A favorite legend tells about a rich Spanish woman, María de Angulo, living in Central America with her crippled son. She prayed to St. Sebastian and searched for the special doctor who would cure him. After many false leads, she was told of a powerful herbalist in Namandiyugua near Chiapa de Corzo; she moved to the village as soon as possible. The herbalist carefully examined the boy and then instructed her to bathe him in a small lagoon called Jaguey ("where the wild pig swims"). She continued to bathe him in the lagoon for many weeks (all the time praying to St. Sebastian just in case.) The boy was cured, indeed a miracle. She gave credit to both the herbalist and St. Sebastian. The herbalist suggested the boy needed a little fiesta to help him recuperate and cheer him up. Doña Angulo organized her servants, who put on costumes with wooden masks, serapes, and whips. And so the first Parachico (*para* for, *chico* small one) celebration was born. Of course, it made sense that the celebration be held on the feast day of St. Sebastian—just in case.

Over the years the Parachico costume evolved into today's colorful representation. It consists of a headdress of a bushy, yellow fiber (like an old-fashioned scrub brush) and an artfully painted wooden mask. This blond, blue-eyed (with real-hair eyelashes), pink-skinned Spaniard carries a rattle and wears pants and shirt of "good" quality, a belt of richly embroidered satin, and brightly colored serape from the city of Saltillo. Women and girls wear the typical dress of embroidered tulle (in honor of Doña Angulo). The design of this costume is prescribed and they faithfully adhere to it. Parachico is the biggest event of the year in Chiapa de Corzo.

Purists and some historians disagree with the accuracy of this version of the legend, and so the argument continues—but so does the celebration. Whatever the origin, if you happen to be in the area, visit on 15 January to take part. Shoppers, note: these quality masks are handcrafted by special artisans in Chiapa de Corzo and though you'll see the masks all over Mexico, this is one of the major originating points and you will find them in gift shops around the city.

APPENDICES

Cities of Colonial Mexico

Acapulco, State of Guerrero

ALTITUDE: Sea level
CLIMATE: It's hot and humid year-round.
DISTANCE FROM MEXICO CITY: 418 km south
GEOGRAPHY: The coastal city is backed by the Sierra Madre, which drop
   dramatically to the sea.
POPULATION: 1.5 million
PRONUNCIATION: ah-kah-POOL-koe
TELEPHONE AREA CODE: (74)

Tourist Information
The Secretaría de Turismo, 187 Costera Miguel Alemán, tel. (74) 85-1049,
is open Mon.-Fri. 8 a.m.-3:30 p.m., Saturday 10 a.m.-2 p.m.
   The State of Guerrero Department of Tourism, tel. (74) 84-7050, is in the
convention center; it's open Mon.-Sat. 9 a.m.-3 p.m. and 6 p.m.-9 p.m.

Transportation
Air
The airport is a 25-minute drive from downtown Acapulco. Upon arrival buy a
ticket near the entrance of the airport for the *colectivos*. Taxis are more costly, close
to US$20 trip (for three people). At your departure, an airport shuttle service
(US$16) is available but you must make reservations the night before. Ask at your
hotel.

Bus
Travelers will find the Estrella Blanca station on the northwest side of town at Av.
Ejido 47. From here you can board luxury service (most of these lines have the
word "plus" in their names), first class, and second class buses. The station is
pleasant and very clean. Services include clean restrooms, luggage lockers, and
a long-distance telephone service.

Campeche, State of Campeche

ALTITUDE: Sea level

CLIMATE: Campeche is typically tropical—hot and humid by day, the same at night, and in the winter an occasional *norte* comes up bringing coolish winds.

DISTANCE FROM MEXICO CITY: 1,316 km east

GEOGRAPHY: The city lies along the Gulf of Mexico in the southwest section of the Yucatán Peninsula.

POPULATION: 50,000

PRONUNCIATION: kahm-PAY-chay

TELEPHONE AREA CODE: (981)

Tourist Information

The Tourist Information Office is on the Plaza Moch Couoh, Av. Ruiz Cortines, s/n, tel./fax (981) 667-67, 655-93.

Transportation

Air

The Campeche airport is about 20 minutes out of the city. Not a lot of air traffic flies in and out of the city.

Bus

The bus station is four blocks northeast of the city at Gobernadores #289 between Calle 47 and Calle Chile.

Train

The train station is two km northeast of the town center on Av. Héroes de Nacozari.

MAIN ARCHAEOLOGICAL SITES NEARBY

Edzná, Chicanná, Becán, Xpujil, Calakmul

Cuernavaca, State of Morelos

ALTITUDE: 1,538 meters
CLIMATE: Cuernavaca is called the city of eternal spring.
DISTANCE FROM MEXICO CITY: 85 km south
GEOGRAPHY: The city is built in the hills of the Mexican highlands.
POPULATION: 290,000
PRONUNCIATION: qwhere-nah-VAH-kah
TELEPHONE AREA CODE: (73)

Tourist Information

The State Tourism Office is on Av. Morelos Sur 802, tel. (73) 14-3860, fax (73) 14-3881.

An information kiosk is in the Plaza de Armas, open daily 9 a.m.-noon and 3-6 p.m.

Transportation

Air

No large commercial airlines fly to Cuernavaca. The Cuernavaca airport is 25 kilometers from the center of town, and the only way to get there is by taxi. Expect to pay US$8-10 either way. Taxis wait at the airport only while flights are arriving.

Bus

Cuernavaca is close to Mexico City and on the way to several other popular tourist destinations. Many travelers find the bus very convenient; the ride takes one to one-and-a-half hours. Four companies arrive from various places into Cuernavaca, each with a separate terminal; a couple are reasonably close to the center of town.

The Estrella Roja terminal is at Galeana and Cuauhtemotzin, about eight blocks from the city center.

Flecha Roja lets you off at the terminal at Morelos 255. Ask to be dropped off at the central plaza.

The Autobuses Estrello de Oro terminal requires about a 20-minute walk to town. If you don't want to flag a taxi, take a local bus going up the hill on Morelos; you can get off at the city center.

The Autobuses Pullman de Morelos bus terminal leaves you with a two-block walk up the hill on Nezahualcoyotl to Hidalgo; turn right and you'll see the town center. If you know what hotel you're going to, it might make more sense to just hop a cab and let the driver deliver you.

Guadalajara, State of Jalisco

ALTITUDE:1,567 meters
CLIMATE: Guadalajara enjoys a moderate springlike year-round climate, but it's
always good to have a sweater along during the winter.
DISTANCE FROM MEXICO CITY: 535 km northwest
GEOGRAPHY: Guadalajara is in the mountains just high enough to miss the hot,
humid tropics and low enough to have a springlike atmosphere year-round.
POPULATION: three million
PRONUNCIATION: gwah-dah-lah-HAH-rah
TELEPHONE AREA CODE: (3)

Tourist Information

The Tourist Information Office is on Morelos 102 on Plaza Tapatía (walk along
the pedestrian way behind the Teatro Degollado in the building called Rincón
del Diablo; it's open Mon.-Fri. 9 a.m.-9 p.m., Sat.-Sun. 9 a.m.-1 p.m., tel. (3)
658-2222.

If you happen to be strolling on the Plaza de Armas, there's another, smaller
office in the Palacio del Gobierno, open Mon.-Fri. 9 a.m.-3 p.m., 6-8 p.m., Saturday 9 a.m.-1 p.m.

Transportation

Air

The Miguel Hidalgo International Airport is 20 km south of downtown
Guadalajara on the highway to Chapala in the municipality of Zapotlanejo.

Autotransportes Guadalajara-Chapala, a public airline bus, leaves the new
Nueva Central Camionera station on the hour and half hour, and takes 30-40
minutes; fare is little more than a dollar.

From the airport, be prepared to take the Autotransportaciones Aeropuerto,
a *combi*, or a taxi. The *combi* can cost US$12-14, depending on where in town
you wish to go. A taxi will cost approximately US$14-50, depending on your
bargaining skills and where you wish to be taken.

Bus

Central Camionera is a well-organized bus terminal in Tlaquepaque, 10 km
(six miles) from downtown; it's referred to as either La Nueva Central or La
Nueva Camionera. Each terminal serves several bus lines, first and second
class. Central Camionera looks more like a modern air terminal than a bus station; passengers find seven buildings with covered walkways connecting them.
An information kiosk at each one offers a well-informed staff.

To get to the Central Camionera bus terminal from downtown Guadalajara,
go to the parking lot on the corner of Calle Cinco de Febrero and Doctor R.

Michel; a special bus leaves every five minutes 5 a.m.-11 p.m., and the trip takes about 30 minutes. The buses all make the circuit of the station and passengers get off at one of the seven connected buildings. The fare is less than 50 cents until 10 p.m., when it doubles. These buses are traveler-friendly with ample space for luggage.

To save yourself a lot of running around, check with the Servicios Coordinados office on Independencia 254 in downtown Guadalajara for complete information about routes, departure times, reservations, and ticket purchases.

Train

Several trains serve Guadalajara; check at the station at Calz. Independencia for the best information (routes, schedules, and prices). From Centro take the bus marked "Estación." By taxi figure about US$5 from the station to downtown hotels.

Guanajuato, State of Guanajuato

ALTITUDE: 2,020 meters
CLIMATE: The weather is springlike year round; winter evenings can be cold, summer days hot.
DISTANCE FROM MEXICO CITY: 356 km northwest
GEOGRAPHY: Guanajuato is built up and down the mountainous terrain.
POPULATION: 75,000
PRONUNCIATION: gwah-nah-WAH-toh
TELEPHONE AREA CODE: (473)

Tourist Information

Across from the *basílica* on Juárez, the tourist office usually has at least one friendly staff member who speaks English. The address is Plaza de la Paz 14, tel. (473) 2-1574 or 2-0086. It's open weekdays 8:30 a.m.-7:30 p.m., Sat.-Sun. 10 a.m.-2 p.m. Those arriving by bus will find tourist information at the bus station on weekdays 10:30 a.m.-7 p.m., Saturday 10:30 a.m.-2 p.m.

Transportation

Air

Guanajuato city does not have a large airport; the gateway to the state is the modern Bajio Léon Airport, where large carriers come and go. From the airport you either hire a taxi to Guanajuato city (20 minutes), or take the Aero-Plus bus (473) 3-1332, which meets all flights into the Léon Airport.

Bus

Guanajuato's modern bus station is on the southwest edge of town. To get to the town center from the bus station, board the city bus marked "Centro" or hail a taxi.

Train

The station is north of Guanajuato at Calle Tepetapa; usually a taxi meets the train. The train seems to take longer and cost more than bus services.

Mérida, State of Yucatán

ALTITUDE: Slightly above sea level.
CLIMATE: Merida is tropical, hot, and humid, in the winter slightly cooler and when an occasional *norte* comes, it is cold and windy; bring a sweater.
DISTANCE FROM MEXICO CITY: 1,505 km northeast
GEOGRAPHY: Mérida lies on a flat bed of limestone. The entire state of Yucatán has no rivers or lakes and for centuries the state has been dependent on underground rivers and natural wells called *cenotes* (say-NOE-tays).
POPULATION: 600,000-plus
PRONUNCIATION: MAY-ree-dah
TELEPHONE AREA CODE: (99)

Tourist Information

Of several tourist information centers, recommended is the one at the Teatro Peón Contreras on Calle 60; the staff speaks English and gives out lots of good information. It's open daily 8 a.m.-8 p.m., tel. (99) 24-9290 or 24-9389.

Transportation

Air

Mérida has a good airport, and *colectivos* meet the flights. Go directly to the ticket counter near the front door to get your ticket; don't buy a ticket from someone who approaches you.

Bus

The main bus station is on Calle 69 between 68 and 70, tel. (99) 21-9150. The station houses both first- and second-class companies.

The Progreso Bus Station on Calle 62 between Calles 65 and 67 has departures for Progreso every half-hour 5 a.m.-7 p.m.

Train

Mérida's train station is on Calle 55 between Calles 48 and 50. Look for the sign that says "Ferrocarriles Unidos del Sureste."

MAIN ARCHAEOLOGICAL SITES NEARBY

Uxmal, Chichén Itzá, Izamal, Sayil, Kabah, Labná, Xlapak

Mexico City, Distrito Federal

ALTITUDE: 2,240 meters

CLIMATE: Though the city is in a tropical latitude, thanks to its high altitude the searing heat and humidity of the tropics is "gentled" to a year-round spring. Expect summer (May-Sept.) to be warm and springlike by day, cooling a bit in the evening. A definite change of season comes Oct.-April: Dry, daytime temperatures are just slightly cooler than in the summer, but evenings can be cool enough for a sweater or light jacket. Air pollution is worse in the winter because of thermal inversions.

GEOGRAPHY: Mexico City sits in a high valley surrounded by mountains and volcanoes, and frequently suffers a horrendous smog problem. The city is built on an ancient, spongy-soiled lakebed.

POPULATION: Twenty million

TELEPHONE AREA CODE: (5)

Tourist Information

In Mexico City you'll have a choice of several different sources of information. For a complete picture of the city and its many attractions, stop at any of the information offices you happen to pass; it will have many brochures, maps, and magazines with upcoming cultural and sporting events, concert dates, and film events.

At Secretaría de Turismo, most of the material available is in Spanish. The office, Presidente Masaryk 172, is open Mon.-Fri. 8 a.m.-8 p.m., Saturday 9 a.m.-1 p.m., tel. (5) 250-0123.

At the Mexico City Chamber of Commerce (CANACO), Paseo de la Reforma 42, tel. (5) 546-5645, ask for maps, brochures, and pamphlets of the sites in the city and state.

Mexico City Tourism staffs several booths about town: at Amberes 54, Zona Rosa, open daily 9 a.m.-1 p.m., tel. (5) 525-9280; at the International Airport in both the National Arrivals and International Arrivals halls; and at the TAPO bus station.

Transportation

Air

Aeropuerto Internacional Benito Juárez is the gateway to the country and continues to grow and modernize. The airport services carriers from all over the world; most commuter flights originate from Mexico City for ongoing connections.

Bus

Mexico City boasts a powerful bus system and many bus terminals to take you to almost any place in the country, from the smallest village to the farthest coastal resort:

Terminal Central del Norte (North Terminal), Av. de los Cien Metros 1907, tel. (5) 587-1552;

Terminal Central del Sur (South Terminal), Av. Tasqueña 1320, tel. (5) 544-2101;

Terminal Poniente (Western Terminal), Av. Sur 122, tel. (5) 271-0038 or 271-4519;

Terminal Central Oriente (Eastern Terminal), Calz. Ignacio Zaragoza 200, tel. (5) 542-4210.

Deluxe Bus Service: These comfortable buses are a great way to travel Mexico. The costs are higher but the buses and nonstop routes make up for it. Several companies have earned outstanding reputations:

ETN, tel. (5) 273-0251 or 567-3773;

Omnibus de Mexico, tel. (5) 567-7698;

Tres Estrellas de Oro, tel. (5) 587-5700;

Turistar, tel. (5) 587-5377.

Train

The Ferrocarriles Nacional de Mexico is the national railway system; the Central Station is on Insurgentes Norte, in Col. Buenavista, tel. (5) 547-1097. The station is the main hub of the rail service that spreads throughout Mexico.

Though most of the cities in Mexico are fairly easy to figure out, Mexico City is huge and spread out so it has designed a fine train system. The Metro is a series of nine different lines that crisscross the city, linking airport, rail, and bus terminals. The fare is about US$20 cents, and millions of people a day use it to get around. The hours of operation vary slightly according to day of the week and the line, but they're roughly 6 a.m.-midnight, slightly later on Saturday night.

MAIN ARCHAEOLOGICAL SITES NEARBY

Templo Mayor, Teotihuacán

Morelia, State of Michoacán

ALTITUDE: 1,915 meters
CLIMATE: It can be coolish mornings and evenings during winter; the summer is reliably warm.
DISTANCE FROM MEXICO CITY: 315 km west
GEOGRAPHY: Morelia lies in a high fertile valley surrounded by tree-covered mountains, with many lakes scattered about.
POPULATION: one million
PRONUNCIATION: mow-RAYL-yah
TELEPHONE AREA CODE: (43)

Tourist Information

The tourist office is in Palacio Clavijero, corner of Madero and Nigromante; it's open Mon.-Fri. 9 a.m.-2 p.m. and 4-8 p.m., Sat.-Sun. 9 a.m.-8 p.m. Ask about the free guided walking tours of the Morelia city center, tel. (43) 13-2654, fax 12-9816.

Transportation

Air

The Francisco J. Mugica Airport is 45 minutes from downtown Morelia. Taxis meet the flights and cost about US$15 to town; airport bus service is available from your hotel, tel. (43) 15-0218.

Bus

You'll find Central Camionera at Eduardo Ruez and Valentin Gomez, seven blocks northwest of the cathedral. New modern deluxe buses (ETN, Flecha Amarilla) run throughout the day to and from Mexico City.

Train

On the southwest side of the city, the Estación del Ferrocarril ticket office is open 5:30-6:30 a.m., 10 a.m.-noon, 4-6 p.m., and 10-11 p.m., tel. (43) 16-1697.

MAIN ARCHAEOLOGICAL SITES NEARBY
Tzintzuntzán

Oaxaca, State of Oaxaca

ALTITUDE: 1,541 meters
CLIMATE: Summer is warm to hot; winter in these mountains can be cool at night.
DISTANCE FROM MEXICO CITY: 523 km southeast
GEOGRAPHY: Oaxaca City is set in a beautiful high mountain valley.
POPULATION: 850,000
PRONUNCIATION: wah-HAH-kah
TELEPHONE AREA CODE: (951)

Tourist Information
You'll find the tourist office at Av. Independencia 607, tel. (951) 6-0123, and one at Oaxaca's Aeropuerto Juárez.

Transportation
Air
The Juárez Airport is nine km south of the city along Hwy. 175. Transportes Aeropuerto Oaxaca provides transport to and from the airport, tel. (951) 4-4350.

Bus
Central Camionera first-class bus station is at Niños Heroes de Chapultepec.

Train
Just west of Cerro del Fortín on Calz. Madero, you'll find the train station about 16 blocks from the plaza. It's best to make your arrangements ahead of time at the station.

MAIN ARCHAEOLOGICAL SITES NEARBY
Monte Albán, Yagul, Mitla

Pátzcuaro, State of Michoacán

ALTITUDE: 2,200 meters
CLIMATE: It's usually warm by day, chilly in early morning and late at night, especially during the winter. Occasionally the wind blows across the lake; bring a wrap and warm sleeping clothes.
DISTANCE FROM MEXICO CITY: 377 km west
GEOGRAPHY: Pátzcuaro lies alongside one of the highest lakes in the world, Lake Pátzcuaro; high mountains surround the lake.
POPULATION: 100,000
PRONUNCIATION: PAHTZ-kwah-roh
TELEPHONE AREA CODE: (434)

Tourist Information
The tourist office is on Plaza Grande, Ibarra St. 2, tel. (434) 2-1214.

Transportation
Air
The closest airport is in Morelia.

Bus
Buses come and go very frequently from Morelia to Pátzcuaro and take about one hour. The Pátzcuaro bus station is about 1.5 km from downtown on Libramiento Ignacio Zaragoza.

MAIN ARCHAEOLOGICAL SITES NEARBY
Tzintzuntzán

Puebla, State of Puebla

ALTITUDE: 4,343 meters
CLIMATE: The weather is pleasantly warm, but it can be cool on winter evenings.
DISTANCE FROM MEXICO CITY: 130 km southeast
GEOGRAPHY: Puebla lies in the region near the mountain chain called the Transverse Volcanic Sierra. From the city you can see the volcanoes Popocatépatl and Ixtaccíhuatl. The snow-capped mountains are visible only when the air is free of smog.
POPULATION: 1.5 million-plus
PRONUNCIATION: PWAYB-la
TELEPHONE AREA CODE: (22)

Tourist Information

The office of tourism, on Av. 5 Oriente 3, is open daily, tel. (22) 46-1285. It sponsors tours of the city beginning at 10 a.m. and 3 p.m. The microbus travels to Cholula (if enough people sign up). The tours are in English and Spanish and cost about US$17, which includes entrance fees to museums. Check tour schedules; they tend to change.

Transportation

Air

The biggest airport is Hermanos Serdán Airport, about 25 minutes (or more) by taxi to the Puebla Plaza, closer to Cholula or Huejotzingo.

Bus

The large Puebla bus station (CAPU) is north of town. Many buses, including "Plus" buses, travel to destinations all over the country. Look for the bus marked "CAPU Central Camionera-Centro" to get to downtown Puebla.

MAIN ARCHAEOLOGICAL SITES NEARBY
Great Pyramid of Tepanampa

Querétaro, State of Querétaro

ALTITUDE: 1,500 meters
CLIMATE: It's pleasantly warm year-round.
DISTANCE FROM MEXICO CITY: 222 km northwest
GEOGRAPHY: Querétaro state lies near the geographical center of the country. It is mountainous, with the Cerro el Gallo the highest peak at 3,350 meters. This high valley in which the city sits is mainly agricultural and in the hilly region is rich in minerals, especially opals, amethysts, topaz, and silver.
POPULATION: 470,000
PRONUNCIATION: kay-RAYH-tah-roe
TELEPHONE AREA CODE: (42)

Tourist Information

The State Tourist Office, Cinco de Mayo 61 on the Plaza de la Independencia, is open Mon.-Fri. 9 a.m.-3 p.m. and 6-8 p.m., Sat.-Sun. 9 a.m.-2 p.m., tel. (42) 14-5623 or 14-0179.

Transportation

Air

So far no commercial planes fly into Querétaro, which has only a small airstrip.

Bus

Central Camionera, the large busy bus station south of Alameda Hidalgo, is a regional center for buses coming and going to many destinations in Mexico. From here you can efficiently and inexpensively travel to all nearby colonial cities.

Train

Estación del Ferrocarril is about one kilometer north of Centro Querétaro at Av. Héroes de Nacozari. Taxis generally meet incoming trains.

MAIN ARCHAEOLOGICAL SITES NEARBY
Las Ranas, Toluquilla

San Cristóbal de las Casas, State of Chiapas

ALTITUDE: 2,200 meters
CLIMATE: Winter especially is cold at night, coolish by day; summer days are pleasant, but they can still be chilly at night.
DISTANCE FROM MEXICO CITY: 1,177 km
GEOGRAPHY: Surrounded by mountains, the city sits in a high tropical valley.
POPULATION: 90,000
PRONUNCIATION: sahn kris-TOH-bal de lahs KAH-sahs
TELEPHONE AREA CODE: (967)

Tourist Information Office

The local office is on the plaza in the municipal building across from the cathedral; it's open Mon-Sat. 8 a.m.-8 p.m., Sunday 9 a.m.-2 p.m.

The State Tourist Office, or Sedetur, tel./fax (967) 8-6570, is a block away from the Palacio Municipal.

Transportation

Air

So far there's no major air service to or from San Cristóbal de las Casas. The majority of travelers to Chiapas fly into Tuxtla Gutiérrez and drive or take a bus or taxi to San Cristóbal de las Casas; bus service also is available from nearby Villa Hermosa as well as many other cities in Mexico.

Bus

In San Cristóbal several deluxe lines, including ADO Gran Lux and Cristóbal Colón, have headquarters in the Cristóbal Colon bus station on Insurgentes, with first-class and deluxe service. Smaller second-class lines are scattered around the city, and there is talk of a new bus terminal planned for the outskirts of town; check with the tourist office.

MAIN ARCHAEOLOGICAL SITES NEARBY
Palenque

San Miguel de Allende, State of Guanajuato

ALTITUDE: 2,000 meters
CLIMATE: It can be chilly early in the morning and late at night, especially during the winter. Bring warm sleeping clothes and a light wrap. Daytime is usually warm.
DISTANCE FROM MEXICO CITY: 275 km northwest
GEOGRAPHY: San Miguel is a hilly city in a mountain region, surrounded by more mountains.
POPULATION: 61,000
PRONUNCIATION: sahn mee-GEL day ah-YEN-day
TELEPHONE AREA CODE: (415)

Tourist Information

If you spot the La Terraza café, you've found San Miguel's tourist office, left of the *parroquia*. Usually someone in the office speaks English and will distribute literature and maps. It's open Mon.-Fri. 10 a.m.-2:30 p.m. and 5-7 p.m., Saturday 10 a.m.-6 p.m., Sunday 10 a.m.-noon, tel. (415) 2-1747.

The tourist office in Dolores Hidalgo lies on the north side of the plaza, in the municipal building next to the church. Friendly staff will answer questions and dispense a city map. It's open Mon.-Fri. 9 a.m.-3 p.m. and 5:30-8 p.m., Sat.-Sun. 9 a.m.-3 p.m.

Transportation

Air

The nearest airport is in León, two hours away; bus or taxi transportation is available to and from the airport. If you have reservations, some of the nicer hotels in San Miguel de Allende will send a limo to pick you up; some charge extra for this service. It's one-and-a-half hours to the airport in León from San Miguel Allende, by bus a little longer. From the airport you can either hire a taxi to San Miguel or take the AeroPlus bus (473) 3-1332 (US$8), that meets all flights into the Léon Airport. The taxi is considerably more expensive.

Bus

Different classes of buses are available, taking three to five hours to reach Mexico City. The "Plus" (luxury) buses leave from the station on Calle Canal, west of San Miguel.

In Dolores Hidalgo, the Flecha Amarillo bus station is on Calle Hidalgo, two and a half blocks from the plaza, and the Herradura de Plata station sits on the corner of Chiapas and Chihuahua. Buses travel from both stations to many nearby towns and to Mexico City.

San Luis Potosí, State of San Luis Potosí

ALTITUDE: 1,887 meters
CLIMATE: The summer is pleasantly warm, and evenings are nicely cool; however, during the rest of the year, bring a sweater or jacket. In winter the temperature can occasionally drop to 0 degrees. Bring warm sleeping clothes.
DISTANCE FROM MEXICO CITY: 424 km north
GEOGRAPHY: The city is wedged between two mountains in the high rugged plains.
POPULATION: 550,000
PRONUNCIATION: sahn lu-EES poh-toh-SEE
TELEPHONE AREA CODE: (48)

Tourist Information

The State Tourism office, Terranza 325, tel. (48) 12-9939, fax (48) 12-6769, is open Mon.-Sat. 9 a.m.-8 p.m.

Transportation

Air

The airport is about 12 km out of town. Aero Taxi provides bus service to the airport, tel. (48) 11-0165.

Bus

The Camionera Central is on the eastern outskirts of town; from here buses travel to many cities in Mexico. You have a choice of many lines, including the "plus" luxury buses.

Train

Look for the train station opposite Alameda Park.

Taxco, State of Guerrero

ALTITUDE: 1,784 meters
CLIMATE: In the winter it can be chilly at night, but warm by day.
DISTANCE FROM MEXICO CITY: 179 km southwest
GEOGRAPHY: Taxco is a city of hills, surrounded by more hills.
POPULATION: 88,000
PRONUNCIATION: TAHS-koe
TELEPHONE AREA CODE: (762)

Tourist Information
You'll find the State Tourism Office on Av. John F. Kennedy 28,
tel. (762) 2-1525; it's open 9 a.m.-8 p.m.

Transportation
Air
Taxco has no airport yet. The best way to get to Taxco is by bus from your
choice of a gateway city.

Bus
Estrella de Oro and Flecha Rojo bus stations are both on the outer edge of
town; be prepared to take a taxi into town.

Tlaxcala, State of Tlaxcala

ALTITUDE: 2,225 meters
CLIMATE: It can be cool in the early morning and late evening in the winter, pleasantly warm during the day.
DISTANCE FROM MEXICO CITY: 120 km east
GEOGRAPHY: The city lies in the highlands of the Sierra Madre Oriental.
POPULATION: 41,000
PRONUNCIATION: tlahsh-KAH-lah
TELEPHONE AREA CODE: (246)

Tourist Information

At the Tourist Office, Av. Juárez 18, tel. (246) 2-0027, you can pick up maps and brochures, look at photos and displays of Tlaxcala, or hire a guide. The staff is pleasant and professional and eager to practice speaking English.

Transportation

Air

Tlaxcala has no airport.

Bus

Tlaxcala's central bus station is one kilometer from the Plaza de Constitución.

To get here from Mexico City, buses leave frequently from the TAPO (eastern terminal) at Calz. de Zaragoza 200; ADO and AU offer first-class buses for the two-hour ride.

Buses from Puebla leave CAPU throughout the day for the one-hour ride to Tlaxcala.

MAIN ARCHAEOLOGICAL SITES NEARBY
Cacaxtla

Veracruz, State of Veracruz

ALTITUDE: Sea level
CLIMATE: Hot and humid, typically tropical year round; it's not unusual for a
cold *norte* to blow up during the winter.
DISTANCE FROM MEXICO CITY: 430 km east
GEOGRAPHY: It parallels the Gulf of Mexico along Mexico's east coast.
POPULATION: 375,000
PRONUNCIATION: vayr-ah-CREWZ
TELEPHONE AREA CODE: (29)

Tourist Information
The tourism office is on the south side of the Plaza de Armas in the Palacio
Municipal, tel. (29) 32-1999.

Transportation
Air
Heriberto Jara Airport is three and a half kilometers from town. Airport
colectivos meet the arriving flights for transportation into town.

Bus
Both the ADO and Camionera (Díaz Miron) bus services are available to Mexico
City and stops in between. Ask for information about the schedule from Veracruz
to Jalapa.

Train
The train station is on Plaza de la República, near the harbor. An overnight train
leaves Mexico City and includes a sleeping compartment; US$130 RT.

MAIN ARCHAEOLOGICAL SITES NEARBY
El Tajín, Cempoala

Zacatecas, State of Zacatecas

ALTITUDE: 2,496 meters
CLIMATE: Zacatecas can be coolish in spring, cold in the winter, pleasantly
    warm in the summer.
DISTANCE FROM MEXICO CITY: 603 km northwest
GEOGRAPHY: The city lies in arid, mountainous countryside.
POPULATION: 200,000
PRONUNCIATION: zah-cah-TAYH-cahs
TELEPHONE AREA CODE: (492)

Tourist Information
The tourist office, Hidalgo 603, is across from the cathedral; look hard to find
it. It's open 9 a.m.-2 p.m. and 4-7 p.m.
    You'll find another tourist office at the train station, tel./fax (492) 2-9329.

Transportation
Air
The airport is 30 minutes north of town. Aero Transportes vans meet all
flights.

Bus
Although called the Camionera Central, the station is not very central, about 15
minutes (by car) out of town; local buses and taxis to and from the bus station
are available.

Train
The station is almost in the center of town.

MAIN ARCHAEOLOGICAL SITES NEARBY
Chicomóstoc Ruins (La Quemada)

The Hotels of Colonial Mexico

THE HOTELS LISTED IN THIS BOOK WERE CAREFULLY CHOSEN with no concern for price or geographical distribution. Instead, they were chosen for their distinction in one of several areas. In many cases they are hotels that convey the feeling of the colonial era: they may be in aged colonial buildings, turn-of-the-century mansions, or even in new buildings that "feel" like the era. Some were chosen by location because of excellent views or tranquil surroundings, and others were chosen because they capture the spirit of the colonial city. Many are expensive, a few are not, most are comfortable, and in all cases guests will come away feeling that they have visited beautiful Mexico.

Below are summary listings of the hotels that are scattered throughout the text of this book. They use the following price ratings categories, based on high-season, double occupancy:

Budget: under US$35   Inexpensive: US$35-60
Moderate: US$60-85   Expensive: US$85-110
Premium: US$110-150   Luxury: over US$150

Acapulco (special excursion from Taxco)
Camino Real Hotel Diamante, p. 115
Baja Catita, tel. (74) 81-2010, in the U.S. tel. (800) 722-6466.
All the amenities, overlooks the water, pool, dining, free airport shuttle.
Luxury.

Las Brisas, p. 116
Clemente Mejia off Carretera Escenica, in the U.S. tel. (800) 228-3000, fax (74) 85-2748, 84-1650.
A honeymoon favorite, 300 *casitas,* 250 pools, full-service resort, fine dining.
Luxury.

Chiapa de Corzo (special excursion from San Cristóbal)
La Ceiba, p. 301
Near the plaza.
Old World look with New World features, 42 rooms, private baths, pool, dining room. **Budget.**

Cholula (special excursion from Puebla)
Villa Arqeológicas, p. 69
Av. 2 Poniente 601, in the U.S. tel. (800) 258-2633.
Run by Club Med, pool, library, French restaurant. **Moderate.**

Cuernavaca
Camino Real Sumiya, p. 169
In the U.S. and Canada tel. (800) 7-CAMINO.
Japanese-flavored resort, 163 rooms and seven suites overlooking acres of
Oriental gardens and walking paths, all the usual luxury amenities,
international menu, computer hookups. **Premium.**

Hacienda Cocoyoc, p. 169
Near Oaxcapec, tel. (73) 56-2211, fax 56-1212.
An ex-hacienda, good food, great service, relaxing gardens, on-site golf course,
swimming pool, horseback riding. **Luxury.**

Hacienda de Cortés, p. 169
Plaza Kennedy, tel. (73) 15-8844.
Originally built by Cortés, 22 suites, pool, gardens, grand restaurant. **Expensive.**

Las Mañanitas, p. 169
Ricardo Linares 107, tel. (73) 14-1466/12-4646, fax 18-3672.
One of Mexico's best, 22 rooms, pool, terraces, great service, restaurant and
bar, valet parking. **Premium to Luxury.**

Guadalajara
Hotel de Mendoza, p. 229
Venustiano Carranza 16, tel. (3) 613-4646.
Former convent downtown, 104 clean, modern rooms and suites, swimming
pool, parking, restaurant and bar. **Moderate.**

Hotel Fiesta Americana, p. 228
Av. López Mateos Sur 2500, tel. (3) 625-3434 or (800) 223-2332.
Colonial decor, good food, pool, lovely grounds. **Luxury.**

Hotel Frances, p. 231
Maestranza 35, tel. (3) 613-1190.
Built in 1610, now with modern features, near city center, 60 rooms, lovely
lobby, bar, live music. **Inexpensive to Moderate.**

Guanajuato

Casa de Espiritus Alegres, p. 123
In Mexico, write to La Casa de Espiritus Alegres La Ex-Hacienda La Trinidad, 1, Marfil, Guanajuato, 36250, Gto., Mexico; tel./fax (473) 3-1013. In the U.S., write or call Joan Summers, 2817 Smith Grade, Santa Cruz, California 95060, U.S.A.; tel. (408) 423-0181.
A 1700s ex-hacienda, now a bed and breakfast run and decorated by artists, six bedrooms, some fireplaces. **Expensive.**

Hotel Castillo de Santa Cecilia, p. 128
For reservations write to Camino a la Valenciana Km 1, C.P. 36000, Guanajuato, Gto., Mexico; tel. (473) 2-0485, fax 2-0153.
Eighty-eight rooms, excellent service, luxury amenities, dining room, swimming pool, cable TV, a handicraft workshop, parking, entertainment. **Moderate to Expensive.**

Hotel Museo Posada Santa Fé, p. 126
Guanajuato, 36000, Gto., Mexico, tel. (473) 2-0084.
Established in 1862, 50 rooms, TV, private baths, self-serve bars, lobby bar, inside dining, sidewalk cafe, immense fireplaces, attentive staff. **Expensive.**

Hotel San Diego, p. 129
Apdo. Postal 8, Guanajuato, 36000, tel. (473) 2-1300, fax 2-5626.
Former 17th-century convent, great location, private bathrooms, hot water, and shower/tubs, dining room. **Moderate.**

Parador San Javier Hotel, p. 127
Dolores Hidalgo Hwy. on the Plaza San Javier, tel. (473) 2-0626 or 2-0944, fax 2-3114.
Colonial-modern mix, gardens, fireplaces, tile, coffeeshop, dining room, efficient waiters, piano bar, disco. **Expensive.**

Mérida

Casa de San Juan, p. 279
Calle 62 #545A, in Mexico tel. (99) 23-6823, in the U.S. tel. (800) 555-8842.
Bed and breakfast in an old house close to plazas, spotlessly clean, dining room, courtyard, some private baths, Continental breakfast. **Inexpensive.**

Casa Mexilio Guesthouse, p. 272
Calle 68 #495, in Mérida tel./fax (99) 28-2505, in the U.S. tel. (800) 538-6802.
Colonial townhouse, eight rooms, folk art decor, tiny pool, jacuzzi, breakfast included, hosts speak English, Spanish, Maya. **Moderate.**

Hacienda Katanchel, p. 276
Write Tixkokob, 97470, Yucatán, Mexico, in the U.S. tel. (800) 223-6510 or
toll-free fax (888) 882-9470, or e-mail: hacienda@mail.mda.com.mx.
Restored 17th-century hacienda, 741 acres, 39 suites, dining room, boutique,
pool. **Expensive.**

Hacienda Tanil, p. 274
South of town 10 km, tel. (99) 25-9194, fax 25-3646.
Dates from 1607, three rooms, pool, horses, authentic kitchen. **Moderate.**

Hotel Caribe, p. 272
Calle 59 #500, tel. (99) 24-9022 or (800) 826-6842, fax 24-8733.
Former convent, block from plaza, rooftop pool, outdoor cafe. **Budget to
Inexpensive.**

Mexico City
Casa Gonzalez, p. 80
Río Sena 69, in Col. Cuauhtémoc, tel. (5) 566-9688.
Victorian inn, great location, 22 rooms, parlor, dining room, third-generation
family/staff. **Budget to Inexpensive.**

Hotel Colonial Plaza, p. 91
Av. Cinco de Mayo 61.
Very old building undergoing spectacular renovation. Stay tuned. **Luxury.**

Hotel de Cortés, p. 85
Av. Hidalgo 85, in Mexico tel. (5) 518-2181, fax 518-3466, in the U.S. and
Canada, tel. (800) 528-1234.
Former 16th-century convent, 27 archaic but clean rooms, courtyard,
entertainment. **Expensive.**

Hotel Majestic, p. 86
Madero 73, tel. (5) 521-8600, fax 518-3466, in the U.S. (800) 528-1234.
Sixteenth-century building, small rooms, great location, seventh-floor dining
balconies overlook the Zócalo. **Expensive.**

Hotel Marquis Reforma, p. 90
Paseo de la Reforma 465, tel. (5) 211-3600, fax 211-5561.
Full amenities, beautiful rooms, business-friendly, Italian restaurant, two bars,
gym, sauna, jacuzzis. **Luxury.**

Intercontinental Presidente Hotel, p. 80
Av. Campos Elyseos 218, in Mexico tel. (5) 327-7700, fax 250-9130, in the

U.S. and Canada tel. (800) 462-2427.
Restaurants, bars, disco, 660 rooms. **Luxury.**

La Casona Hotel, p. 83
Durango 280, Colonia Roma, Mexico D.F. 06700, fax (5) 211-0871, in the
U.S. tel. (800) 223-5652
Mansion built in 1922, 30 rooms, striking decor, impeccable service, wine
cellar/bar, breakfast included. **Expensive.**

Morelia
Hotel de la Soledad, p. 192
Calle Zaragoza 90 and Calle Ocampo, tel. (43) 2-1888.
Ex-mansion from about 1700, courtyard, most rooms spacious, some with
patio views. **Moderate to Expensive.**

Hotel Virrey de Mendoza, p. 193
Av. Madero Pte. 310, tel. (43) 12-0633, 12-4940.
Ex-mansion of Mexico's first viceroy, opulent, modern amenities, TV.
Moderate.

Villa Montaña, p. 194
Patzimba 201, Col. Vista Bella; write Apdo. Postal 233, Morelia, 58090,
Michoacán, Mexico, or in Mexico call (43) 14-0231, fax 15-1423, in the U.S.
tel. (800) 223-6510.
One of Mexico's finest small hotels, outside town, huge villas, beautiful
gardens, gourmet dining, pool, tennis, golf nearby, full breakfast. **Premium to
Luxury.**

Oaxaca
Camino Real Oaxaca, p. 177
Cinco de Mayo 300, in the U.S. tel. (800) 722-6466.
Colonial building, close to plaza, pool, garden, patio, excellent service, bars,
lounges, cocktails, hors d'oeuvres, Continental breakfast. **Luxury.**

Hostal de la Noria, p. 179
Av. Hidalgo 918, Centro Oaxaca, 68000 Oaxaca, Mexico, tel. (951) 478-44,
fax (951) 639-92.
Center of town, patio, dining, modern rooms. **Moderate.**

Pátzcuaro (special excursion from Morelia)
Hotel los Escudos, p. 200
Portal 73, tel. (434) 2-0138.
Old mansion, 30 rooms, satellite TV, some fireplaces. **Inexpensive.**

Hotel Mansión Iturbe, p. 200
Portal Morelos 59, tel. (434) 2-0368.
From 17th century, colonial decor, 15 rooms, restaurant. **Inexpensive.**

Posada de la Basílica, p. 200
Arciga 6, tel. (434) 2-1108
Colonial mansion, 11 pleasant, simple rooms, restaurant. **Inexpensive.**

Puebla
Hotel Camino Real Puebla, p. 60
Av. 7 Poniente 105, Centro, tel. (800) 996-7325, fax (212) 223-6499.
Former convent from 1593, Talavera tile, frescoes, lovely rooms, all amenities, king beds, TV, telephone, computer hookups, private bathrooms, courtyard, dining, bar. **Luxury.**

Hotel El Mesón del Angel, p. 59
Av. Hermanos Serdán 807, tel. (22) 48-2100, fax 48-7935.
Garden, pools, health center. **Expensive.**

Mesón Sacristia de la Compañía, p. 56
6 Sur 304, Callejon de los Sapos, tel. (22) 32-4513, fax 42-1554.
Antique-filled bed and breakfast, 200-year-old building, nine large rooms, balconies, courtyard dining. **Premium.**

Querétaro
La Casa de la Marquesa, p. 245
Madero 41, tel. (42) 12-0092, fax 12-0098.
One of the "Small Luxury Hotels of the World," colonial-era style, luxury amenities, dining room. **Luxury.**

Hotel Hacienda Jurica, p. 249
North of Querétaro 16 km, tel. (42) 18-0022 or 18-0001, fax 18-0136.
Former 1600s hacienda, gardens, spacious rooms, patios, dining room. **Premium.**

Hotel la Mansión Galindo, p. 248
Write Carretera a Amealco Km 5, San Juan del Río, 76800, Qto., Mexico.
Former hacienda, beautiful grounds, spacious guest rooms, dining rooms, golf by arrangement. **Expensive.**

Hotel Mesón de Santa Rosa, p. 245
Pasteur Sur 17, Plaza de la Independencia, tel. (42) 14-5781, fax 12-5522.
Colonial building, 21 suites, pool, restaurant, bar, courtyard. **Moderate to Expensive.**

Real de Catorce (special excursion from San Luis Potosí)
Abundancia Hotel, p. 156
Former 1800s mint, simple, clean, meals. **Inexpensive.**

San Cristóbal de las Casas
Hotel el Paraíso, p. 289
Calle Cinco de Febrero 19, tel. and fax (967) 8-0085.
Colonial-style, built in 1993, 13 rooms, near the plaza. **Inexpensive.**

Hotel Palacio de Moctezuma, p. 291
Av. Juárez 16, tel. (967) 8-0352, fax 8-1536.
Close to town center, 42 small rooms, modern bathrooms, phones, mini-courtyards, delightful dining room, good food. **Inexpensive.**

Hotel Rincón del Arco, p. 293
Ejercito Nacional 66, tel. (967) 8-1313, fax 8-1568.
Dates from 1650, modern rooms, spotless bathrooms, clay fireplaces, some rooms with good views, 10-minute walk from town center. **Inexpensive.**

Hotel Santa Clara, p. 290
Insurgentes 1 Plaza Central, tel. (967) 8-1140, fax 8-1041.
Former home of a conquistador, on the plaza, 42 rooms, pool, courtyard, restaurant, bar, chilly in winter. **Inexpensive.**

San Miguel de Allende
Casa de Sierra Nevada, p. 219
Hospicio 35, San Miguel Allende, 37700, Gto., Mexico, tel. (415) 2-0415, fax 2-2337, in the U.S. tel. (800) 223-6510.
One of the Small Grand Hotels of Mexico and Europe's Relais y Chateau, 18 suites near cathedral, safe deposit boxes, laundry service, room service, in-house masseuse, large heated pool, spa, fine restaurant. **Luxury.**

Hacienda de las Flores, p. 217
Calle Hospicio 16, tel. (415) 2-1808.
Former *quinta*, 11 rooms, heated pool, electric blankets, near La Parroquia. **Premium.**

Hacienda Taboada, p. 214
In Mexico tel. (415) 2-0888, fax (415) 2-1798, in the U.S. write 747 Third Ave., New York, NY, 10017-2847 U.S.A., or call (800) 447-7462, (212) 223-2848, fax (212) 644-6840.
Spa rooms have balconies or patios, double-sized tubs, mineral water pools, gardens, tennis, dining. **Expensive.**

La Puertecita Boutique'otel, p. 217
Santo Domingo 75, Col. Los Arcos, San Miguel de Allende, 37740, Gto.,
Mexico, tel. (415) 2-2275, fax 2-0424, in the U.S. (800) 336-6776.
New hotel, 24-hour room service, jacuzzi, spa, heated pool, billiard room,
fireplaces, in-house massages, great cuisine, no smoking. **Premium to Luxury.**

Posada San Francisco, p. 215
Plaza Principal 2, tel. (415) 2-0072.
Restored 18th-century mansion, 19 rooms, 13 junior suites, courtyard,
coffeeshop. **Moderate.**

Villa Jacaranda, p. 217
Aldama 53, tel. (415) 2-1015 or 2-0811, fax 2-0883, in the U.S. tel.
(800) 532-0294.
One of "Mexico's Romantic Hideaways," 15 spacious rooms and suites, some
with patios, "Roman plunge" pool, hot tub, fine dining. **Premium.**

Taxco
Hotel Monte Taxco, p. 105
North end of town near Hwy. 95. tel. (762) 2-1300.
Atop a bluff, standard rooms and suites, golf, tennis, restaurants, disco, pool,
horses, steam bath, fitness center. **Expensive.**

Hotel Posada de la Misión, p. 105
Cerro de la Misión 32, tel. (762) 2-0063 or 2-0533, fax 2-2198.
Colonial-style, 150 rooms, private baths, suites with fireplaces, two bars,
coffeeshop, dining room, gardens, views, pool, tennis, golf, parking. **Expensive.**

Tlaxcala
Posada San Francisco/Villa Arquelógicas, p. 45
Plaza de la Constitución 17, in Mexico tel. (246) 2-6022, fax (246) 2-6818,
in the U.S. tel. (800) 258-2633.
Renovated building in city center, run by Club Med, lovely rooms, patio,
pool, dining room, coffeeshop, bar, live entertainment. **Expensive.**

Zacatecas
Hotel Quinta Real, p. 140
Av. Rayon 434, Zacatecas 98000, Zacatecas, in Mexico tel. (492) 2-9104,
in the U.S. tel. (800) 445-4565.
Colonial-style built in 1866, suites superimposed on former bullring's
bleachers, formal dining, all the amenities, marble bathrooms, pool, TV.
Luxury.

Transport Tips

Getting Around Colonial Mexico

If traveling by bus always ask before buying your ticket if it's direct (*directo*), with a few stops, or with more stops (*con escalas*), or no stops (*sin escalas*). If you travel on the deluxe buses, often with *plus* in their names, there will be no stops, but you'll pay higher fares.

Those traveling by car should consider using the new *cuota* tollways. They are much quicker and safer than the older roads; they are well-engineered, especially in the mountain areas, but some of them charge hefty tolls.

Taxi service is good in most cities covered in this book, but always ask what your fare will be before you get in the taxi. Most Mexican taxis are unmetered. Beware in Mexico City. Some dishonest taxi drivers working with accomplices have been robbing passengers. Don't try to save money here. Have the doorman at your hotel procure you a taxi; he'll summon one of the taxis that pay for the privilege of parking in front of the hotels, especially the nicer hotels.

Do not use the green VW bug taxis. If you're in a restaurant, ask the staff to call a taxi and make sure to ask for an ID number.

Shipping Your Packages Home

Shipping goods home might be a necessity if you've come to the colonial cities to shop. One option is to pack light (one suitcase) and carry an extra bag suitable for whatever you plan to buy—most airlines allow passengers two suitcases, and the second case can be a securely wrapped box. However, if you buy large items such as furniture or wood carvings, you'll probably need to ship. Shipping options will cost more than in the U.S. FedEx, UPS, and DHL are available, or you can arrange shipping with the airlines. If shipping, carry copies of your receipts for everything you buy. Many of the nicer shops will pack and ship for you. Check with your airline for its luggage and shipping regulations.

Useful Terms

andadores	walkways or alleys
arabesque	elaborate ornamental pattern of Islamic origin
ashlar	rectangular cut stone facing
atria/atrium	enclosed churchyard or monastery front court, square
baluartes	bastions
baroque	17th-century architectural style using complex forms, strong ornamentation, and dramatic design that juxtaposes contrasting elements to create a sense of movement
basílica	an oblong church with a broad, elevated nave flanked by colonnaded aisles and ending in a semicircular apse; it's also a title of honor that gives a church ceremonial privileges
bas-relief	sculptural relief with a low projection from the surrounding surface
cantera	a local stone used for construction, usually fine-grained and easily worked
capilla	chapel
Casa Reales	Royal Houses
catedral	a church that is the official seat of the bishop of a diocese
centro	historical city centers
Churrigueresque	named for Spain's Churriguera family of architects, it's a late baroque style in neo-Hispanic churches and cathedrals characterized by heavy ornamentation
criollos	pure-blooded Spaniards born in Mexico
dentils	toothlike rectangular blocks used to ornament classical cornices
desiertos	Carmelite monasteries
encomendero	possessor of an *encomienda*
encomiendas	parcels of Indian towns and lands that were distributed to Spanish conquerors as rewards for their assistance in vanquishing the Indians of New Spain
escutcheon	heraldic shield or coat-of-arms

ex-convento	a former convent or monastery
faro	lighthouse
flamboyant	architecture of the French/Flemish High Gothic
fluting	vertical grooves decorating the shaft of a pilaster or column
fresco	technique of painting on wet or dry plaster
granadita	granary
hacendados	owner of a hacienda
Herreresque	named after the architect Juan Herrera
iglesia	a parish church
jardín	main square (garden)
lantern	glazed or non-glazed openings in a roof to let in light and air
lavabo	basin for ritual handwashing
malecón	waterfront boulevard
mercado publico	public market
milagros	miracles or tiny images representing miracles
Mudejar	Spanish architectural style based on Moorish forms
neoclassic	a style of architecture that constitutes or adapts the classical architecture of ancient Greece and Rome
ogee	curved pointed arch
palacios	government offices
parroquia	parish church
peninsulares	those born in Spain, also called royalists
pila	fountain or waterbasin
pilaster	flattened column used as a decorative architectural element
portales	broad covered walkways with wide arches
posada	procession or inn
quinta	fifth of a hacienda
real	royal
recinto	extremely hard and coarse black basalt
renaissance	the neoclassic style of architecture prevailing in Europe during the 14th-17th centuries
retablo	carved and painted wooden altarpiece
santo	patron saint
Solomonic	column with spiral decoration, often in the form of a grapevine, from biblical descriptions of the Temple of Solomon
spandrel	triangular space between an arch and the rectangular surrounding frame

Talavera	a style of tile brought to Puebla from Spain
teatro	theater
tecali	translucent onyx, also called Mexican alabaster
templo	common name for a church
tezontle	porous, lightweight reddish-black volcanic stone
tianguis	marketplace
tienda	store
zapata	wooden roof beam, often decoratively carved
zócalo	main square, often called Plaza de Armas

Spanish Phrasebook

PRONUNCIATION GUIDE

Consonants

c   as c in cat, before a, o, or u; like s before e or i
d   as d in dog, except between vowels, then like th in that
g   before e or i, like the ch in Scottish loch; elsewhere like g in get
h   always silent
j   like the English h in hotel, but stronger
ll   like the y in yellow
ñ   like the ni in onion
r   always pronounced as strong r
rr   trilled r
v   similar to the b in boy (not as English v)
y   similar to English, but with a slight j sound. When y stands alone it is pronounced like the e in me.
z   like s in same
b, f, k, l, m, n, p, q, s, t, w, x as in English

Vowels

a   as in father, but shorter
e   as in hen
i   as in machine
o   as in phone
u   usually as in rule; when it follows a q the u is silent; when it follows an h or g its pronounced like w, except when it comes between g and e or i, when it's also silent

NUMBERS

0	cero	11	once	40	cuarenta
1	uno (masculine)	12	doce	50	cincuenta
1	una (feminine)	13	trece	60	sesenta
2	dos	14	catorce	70	setenta
3	tres	15	quince	80	ochenta
4	cuatro	16	diez y seis	90	noventa
5	cinco	17	diez y siete	100	cien
6	seis	18	diez y ocho	101	ciento y uno
7	siete	19	diez y nueve	200	doscientos
8	ocho	20	veinte	1,000	mil
9	nueve	21	viente y uno	10,000	diez mil
10	diez	30	treinta		

DAYS OF THE WEEK

Sunday — *domingo*
Monday — *lunes*
Tuesday — *martes*
Wednesday — *miércoles*

Thursday — *jueves*
Friday — *viernes*
Saturday — *sábado*

TIME

What time is it? — *¿Qué hora es?*
one o'clock — *la una*
two o'clock — *las dos*
at two o'clock — *a las dos*
ten past three — *las tres y diez*
six a.m. — *las seis de mañana*
six p.m. — *las seis de tarde*
today — *hoy*

tomorrow, morning
  — *mañana, la mañana*
yesterday — *ayer*
day — *día*
week — *semana*
month — *mes*
year — *año*
last night — *anoche*

USEFUL WORDS AND PHRASES

Hello. — *Hola.*
Good morning. — *Buenos días.*
Good afternoon. — *Buenas tardes.*
Good evening. — *Buenas noches.*
How are you? — *¿Cómo está?*
Fine. — *Muy bien.*
And you? — *¿Y usted?*
So-so. — *Más ó menos.*
Thank you. — *Gracias.*
Thank you very much. — *Muchas
  gracias.*
You're very kind. — *Muy amable.*
You're welcome; literally, "It's nothing."
  — *De nada.*
yes — *sí*
no — *no*
I don't know. — *Yo no sé.*
it's fine; okay — *está bien*
good; okay — *bueno*
please — *por favor*
Pleased to meet you. — *Mucho gusto.*
excuse me (physical) — *perdóneme*
excuse me (speech) — *discúlpeme*
I'm sorry. — *Lo siento.*
goodbye — *adiós*

see you later; literally, "until later"
  — *hasta luego*
more — *más*
less — *menos*
better — *mejor*
much — *mucho*
a little — *un poco*
large — *grande*
small — *pequeño*
quick — *rápido*
slowly — *despacio*
bad — *malo*
difficult — *difícil*
easy — *fácil*
He/She/It is gone; as in "She left," "He's
  gone" — *Ya se fue.*
I don't speak Spanish well.
  — *No hablo bien español.*
I don't understand. — *No entiendo.*
How do you say . . . in Spanish?
  — *¿Cómo se dice . . . en español?*
Do you understand English?
  — *¿Entiende el inglés?*
Is English spoken here? (Does anyone
  here speak English?)
  — *¿Se habla inglés aquí?*

MAKING PURCHASES

I need . . . — *Necesito . . .*
I want . . . — *Deseo . . .* or *Quiero . . .*
I would like . . . (more polite)
  — *Quisiera . . .*
How much does it cost? — *¿Cuánto cuesta?*
What's the exchange rate?
  — *¿Cuál es el tipo de cambio?*

Can I see . . . ? — *¿Puedo ver . . . ?*
this one — *ésta/ésto*
expensive — *caro*
cheap — *barato*
cheaper — *más barato*
too much — *demasiado*

TERMS OF ADDRESS

I — *yo*
you (formal) — *usted*
you (familiar) — *tú*
he/him — *él*
she/her — *ella*
we/us — *nosotros*
you (plural) — *vos*
they/them (all males or mixed gender)
— *ellos*
they/them (all females) — *ellas*
Mr., sir — *señor*

Mrs., madam — *señora*
Miss, young lady — *señorita*
wife — *esposa*
husband — *marido* or *esposo*
friend — *amigo* (male), *amiga* (female)
sweetheart — *novio* (male), *novia*
  (female)
son, daughter — *hijo, hija*
brother, sister — *hermano, hermana*
father, mother — *padre, madre*

GETTING AROUND

Where is . . . ? — *¿Dónde está . . . ?*
How far is it to . . .?
  — *¿A cuánto queda . . . ?*
from . . . to . . . — *de . . . a . . .*
highway — *la carretera*
road — *el camino*
street — *la calle*
block — *la cuadra*
kilometer — *kilómetro*

mile (commonly used near the
  U.S. border) — *milla*
north — *el norte*
south — *el sur*
west — *el oeste*
east — *el este*
straight ahead — *al derecho* or *adelante*
to the right — *a la derecha*
to the left — *a la izquierda*

ACCOMMODATIONS

Can I (we) see a room?
  — *¿Puedo (podemos) ver un cuarto?*
What is the rate? — *¿Cuál es el precio?*
a single room — *un cuarto sencillo*
a double room — *un cuarto doble*
key — *llave*
bathroom — *lavabo* or *baño*
hot water — *agua caliente*

cold water — *agua fría*
towel — *toalla*
soap — *jabón*
toilet paper — *papel higiénico*
air conditioning — *aire acondicionado*
fan — *ventilador*
blanket — *frazada* or *manta*

PUBLIC TRANSPORT

bus stop — *la parada del autobús*
main bus terminal
  — *terminal de buses*
railway station
  — *la estación de ferrocarril*
airport — *el aeropuerto*
ferry terminal
  — *la terminal del transbordador*

I want a ticket to . . .
  — *Quiero un boleto a . . .*
I want to get off at . . .
  — *Quiero bajar en . . .*
Here, please. — *Aquí, por favor.*
Where is this bus going?
  — *¿Adónde va este autobús?*
roundtrip — *ida y vuelta*
What do I owe? — *¿Cuánto le debo?*

FOOD

menu — *lista, menú*
glass — *vaso*
fork — *tenedor*
knife — *cuchillo*
spoon — *cuchara, cucharita*
napkin — *servilleta*
soft drink — *refresco*
coffee, cream — *café, crema*
tea — *té*
sugar — *azúcar*
purified water — *agua purificado*
bottled carbonated water — *agua
    mineral*
bottled uncarbonated water — *agua sin
    gas*
beer — *cerveza*
wine — *vino*
milk — *leche*
juice — *jugo*
eggs — *huevos*

bread — *pan*
watermelon — *sandía*
banana — *plátano*
apple — *manzana*
orange — *naranja*
meat (without) — *carne (sin)*
beef — *carne de res*
chicken — *pollo*
fish — *pescado*
shellfish — *mariscos*
fried — *a la plancha*
roasted — *asado*
barbecue, barbecued — *al carbón*
breakfast — *desayuno*
lunch — *almuerzo*
dinner (often eaten in late afternoon)
    — *comida*
dinner, or a late night snack — *cena*
the check — *la cuenta*

HEALTH

Help me please. — *Ayúdeme por favor.*
I am ill. — *Estoy enfermo.*
pain — *dolor*
fever — *fiebre*
stomache ache — *dolor de estómago*
vomiting — *vomitar*
diarrhea — *diarrea*

drugstore — *farmacia*
medicine — *medicina, remedio*
pill, tablet — *pastilla*
birth control pills — *pastillas
    anticonceptivas*
condoms — *preservativos*

Booklist

The following titles provide insight into Mexico, its history, its drama, and its people. A few of these books are easier to obtain in Mexico, but all of them will cost less in the United States.

Calderon de la Barca, Frances. *Life in Mexico.* Berkeley: University of California Press, 1982.

Coe, Andrew. *Archaeological Mexico—A Traveler's Guide to Ancient Cities and Sacred Sites.* Chico: Moon Publications, 1998.

Coe, Michael D. *Mexico, from the Olmecs to the Aztecs.* London: Thames and Hudson, 4th edition, 1994. One of the most readable volumes about Mexico's ancient civilization.

Collis, Maurice. *Cortés and Montezuma—History's Greatest Tale of Adventure and Conquest.* New York: Avon, 1954.

Cortés, Hernán. *Five Letters.* Gordon Press, 1977. Cortés wrote long letters to the king of Spain telling of his accomplishments and trying to justify his actions in the New World.

Davies, Nigel. *The Ancient Kingdoms of Mexico.* New York: Penguin Books. Excellent study of preconquest (1519) indigenous people of Mexico.

Díaz del Castillo, Bernal. *The Conquest of New Spain.* London: Penguin, 1963. History straight from the adventurer's reminiscences, translated by J.M. Cohen.

Esquivel, Laura. *Like Water For Chocolate.* New York: Doubleday, 1992. You'll be wowed by Mexican tradition, pathos, and whimsy—and ready to go directly to a restaurant when you arrive after reading the descriptions and recipes of succulent Mexican cuisine. This isn't a cookbook but a love story.

Fehrenbach, T.R. *Fire and Blood: A History of Mexico.* New York: Collier Books, 1973. Told in a way to keep you reading, this covers 3,500 years of Mexico's history.

Franz, Carl. *The People's Guide to Mexico.* Santa Fe: John Muir Publications, first published 1972. Updated numerous times since its initial publication, this is a humorous guide filled with anecdotes and helpful general information for visitors to Mexico. Don't expect any specific city information, just nuts-and-bolts hints for traveling south of the border.

Greene, Graham. *The Power and the Glory.* New York: Penguin Books, 1977. A novel that takes place in the '20s, about a priest and the antichurch movement that gripped the country.

Heffern, Richard. *Secrets of the Mind-Altering Plants of Mexico.* New York: Pyramid Books. A fascinating study of many substances, from ritual hallucinogens used by the ancients to today's medicines.

Kandall, Jonathan. *La Capital—The Biography of Mexico City.* New York: Random House, 1988. An easy-to-read biography of Mexico City with some of the more juicy tidbits of gossip about its important historic figures.

Meyer, Michael, and William Sherman. *The Course of Mexican History.* New York: Oxford University Press, 1991. A concise one-volume history of Mexico.

Prescott, William H. *The Conquest of Mexico.* New York: Bantam Books, 1964. Another point of view of the Cortés saga in Mexico.

Stein, Philip. *The Mexican Murals.* Mexico City: Editur, 1984.

Stephens, John. *Incidents of Travel in Yucatán.* 2 vols. New York: Dover Publications, 1969.

Index

Acapulco: 11, 111-119
Acuario (Veracruz): 35-36
Acuayematepec: 69
Africam (Puebla): 65
Agua Azul (Puebla): 65
Aguilar, Jorge "Ranchero": 45
Alameda Park (Mexico City): 81-82
Aldama, Ignacio: 213
Aldama, Juan: 122
alebijes: 186
Alemán, Miguel: 33, 36
Alhóndigas de Granaditas (Guanajuato):
    120-121
Allende, Ignacio: 122, 209, 213, 220, 246
amber: 294-295
Anaya: 93, 94-95
Anguiano, Raul: 130
Anthropology Museum: see Museo
    Nacional de Antropología
Aparicio, Sebastian: 61
aqueduct (Querétaro): 243
Aqueducto de Atempa (Tlaxcala): 48
Aranda, Julian: 53
Arches of Hidalgo (Tlaxcala): 46
architecture: 9, 12-14; French influence
    in 14; see also specific place
Arciniega, Claudio: 76
Arrazola: 186
Arte Maya (Mérida): 275
Artesanías Vázquez Factory (Dolores
    Hidalgo): 223
arts and artisans: 15-19; craft specialties
    by city 16; Acapulco 116; Guanajuto
    129-130; Merida 275; Morelia 195;
    Mexico City 85; Oaxaca 180; Oaxaca
    area: 185-188; Puebla 65-66; San
    Cristóbal de las Casas 292-295;

San Luis Potosí 151-152; San Miguel
    de Allende 216-217; Taxco 108-109;
    Tlaxcala 48-49
Atlanga Cattle Ranch: 54
audienca: 8
Aztec Calendar Stone: 89
Aztecs: 2, 5, 6, 13, 15, 28-29, 42, 55,
    73-74, 87, 94, 98-99, 162, 163, 166,
    168, 171, 183, 189

B
ballet: 82
Ballet Folklorico (Mexico City): 82
Baluarte de San Carlos (Campeche): 263
Baluarte de Santiago (Campeche): 34, 264
Baluarte Nuestra Señores de la Soledad
    (Campeche): 263
Bank of Mexico (Mexico City): 83
Barra Vieja (near Acapulco): 119
barrios: 11, 13; see also specific place
Barrio de la Luz (Puebla): 66
Barrio del Artistas (Puebla): 64
Barroso de la Escaloya, Vincenzo: 54
Basílica de la Soledad (Oaxaca): 176
Basílica de Nuestra Señora de Guadalupe
    (Mexico City): 92
Basílica de Nuestra Señora de
    Guanajuato (Guanajuato): 128
Basílica de Nuestra Señora de la Salud
    (Pátzcuaro): 201
Basílica y Santuario de Nuestra Señora de
    Ocotlán (Tlaxcala): 47-48
Bazar del Claustro (Tlaxcala): 49
Bazar Garcia Rejon (Mérida): 275
Bazar Sábado (Mexico City): 85, 96
Becerra, Francisco: 58
beer: 24

Bellas Artes (San Miguel de Allende): 209, 215, 217, 218
Bello, José Luis: 62
bells: 59, 77, 84, 85-86, 213, 223
Beltran, Alberto: 33
Benito Juárez Zoo (Morelia): 194-195
Bernal: 253-254
Bernal Rock: 253-254
Biblioteca Bocanegra (Pátzcuaro): 201
Biblioteca Palafoxiana (Puebla): 59
Biblioteca Publica (Oaxaca): 178
Biblioteca Pública (San Miguel de Allende): 209
Blessing of the Animals (Oaxaca): 183
Blom, Frans: 289-290
Blom, Gertrude Duby: 289-290
Bocanegra, Gertrudis: 200
Bosque Park (Morelia): 194
Boys Choir of Morelia: 196
Brady, Robert: 164
Bravo, Alonso García: 173
Buenaventura, Antonio: 247
bullfighting: 21-23; Acapulco 117; Huamantla 53; Guadalajara: 227; Puebla 63; Querétaro 252; San Luis Potosí 150, 152; Tlaxcala 45; Zacatecas 140
Bustamante, Anastasio: 212
butterflies: 198
butterfly nets: 202

C
Cabrera, Miguel: 39, 176
Cacahuamilpa Caves (near Taxco): 111
Cacaxtla: 43
Caja de Agua (San Luis Potosí): 149-150
Calderón de la Barca, Fanny: 97
Callejón del Beso (Guanajuato): 131-132
Callejón de los Sapos (Puebla): 67
callejoneadas (San Luis Potosí): 152
Camino Real Oaxaca (Oaxaca): 176-177
Campeche: 11, 261-266
Canal, Manuel: 214
Capilla de Aranzazu (San Luis Potosí): 150
Capilla de la Virgen de los Remedios (Cholula): 71
Capilla del Patrocinio (Zacatecas): 144

Capilla del Rosario (Puebla): 60
Capilla del Señor Ojeda (Taxco): 108
Capilla de Santo Cristo del Buen Viaje (La Antigua): 41
Capilla Pocito (Mexico City): 93
Capuchin Church and ex-convent (Mexico City): 92
Cárdenas, Lázaro: 94, 191
Carlota of Saxe-Coburg: 14, 30, 86, 87, 162, 163, 167, 267
Carmelites: 97-98
Carnaval (Cholula): 72
Carnaval (San Juan Chamula): 300
Casa Borda (Taxco): 107
Casa de Artisanías (Morelia): 195
Casa de Azulejos (Mexico City): 81
Casa de Cortés (Oaxaca): 178
Casa de Cultura (Puebla): 59
Casa de Cultura (Taxco): 107
Casa de Ecala (Querétaro): 245
Casa de el Dean (Puebla): 63
Casa de Figueroa (Taxco): 106
Casa de la China Poblana (Puebla): 64
Casa de la Corregidora (Querétaro): see Doña Josefa's House
Casa de la Cultura (Morelia): 195
Casa de la Cultura (Querétaro): 252
Casa de Lagarto (Mérida): 271-272
Casa de la Malinche: 92
Casa del Gigante (Pátzcuaro): see House of the Giant
Casa del la Cultura (San Luis Potosí): 150-151
Casa del Mayorazgo de Canal (San Miguel de Allende): 215
Casa de los Cincos Patios (Querétaro): 248
Casa de los Muñecos (Puebla): 63
Casa de los Once Patios (Pátzcuaro): 200
Casa de los Perros (Querétaro): 250
Casa de los Perros (San Miguel de Allende): 216
Casa del Risco (San Ángel): 96
Casa de Montejo (Mérida): 270
Casa Don Bartolo (Querétaro): 247
Casa Maximiliano: see Museo de la Herbolaría/La Casa del Olvido

Casa Othón (San Luis Potosí): 151
Casa Sirena (San Cristóbal de las Casas): 287
Casa von Humboldt/Museo de Arte Colonia (Taxco): 107
Casas de las Artesanías (Guadalajara): 232
Castillo de Chapultepec (Mexico City): 87-89
Castillo San Juan de Ulua: 34
Catedral (Jalapa): 39
Catedral (Morelia): 191-192
Catedral (Oaxaca): 174
Catedral (San Cristóbal de las Casas): 287
Catedral (San Luis Potosí): 147
Catedral de Guadalajara (Guadalajara): 227
Catedral de la Asunción (Cuernavaca): 164
Catedral de Nuestra Señora de La Asunción see Ex-Convento de San Francisco
Catedral de Nuestra Señora de la Asunción (Veracruz): 33
Catedral de Puebla (Puebla): 58-59
Catedral de Zacatecas (Zacatecas): 137
Catedral la Inmaculada Concepción (Campeche): 262
Catedral Metropolito (Mexico City): 76-77
Catedral Nuestra Señora de la Soledad (Acapulco): 113
Catedral San Idelfonso (Mérida): 270
Catedral y Ex-Convento de San Felipe Neri (Querétaro): 251
Catemaco: 39
Cava Antonelli Winery: 254
Cenote Zaci (Valladolid): 283
Central Plaza (Campeche): 262
Central Post Office (Mexico City): 83
Centro Civico Cinco de Mayo (Puebla): 68-69
Centro Cultural Ignacio Ramírez (San Miguel de Allende): see Bellas Artes
Centro Cultural y Biblioteca Isidro Fabela (San Ángel): 96
Centro de Difusion Cultural del Instituto Potosino de Bellas Artes (San Luis Potosí): 151
Centro de Talavera la Colonial (Puebla): 67

Centro Taurion Potosino (San Luis Potosí): 150
Centro Vacacional Gogorron (Villa de Reyes): 154
Cerro de la Campanas (Querétaro): 253
Cerro de las Campanas: 250
Cervantes, Miguel: 13, 122, 127, 129-130, 132
Cervantes, Ysauro: 52
cerveza: 24; see also specific place
Chamber Music Festival (San Miguel de Allende): 209
Chapel de la Casa de Loreto (San Miguel de Allende): 214
Chapel of San Jeronimo (near San Luis Potosí): 155
Chapel of the Little Well (Tlaxcala): 48
Chapel of the Third Order (San Miguel de Allende): 212
Chapel to Jesús (Puebla): 60
Chapultepec Castle: see Castillo de Chapultepec
Chapultepec Park (Mexico City): 87-92
Charlot, Jean: 17, 81
charreada: Guadalajara 234; Puebla 63
Chiapa de Corzo: 300-303
Chichimeca: 10
Chichimecs: 208
Chicoasén Dam (near Chiapa de Corzo): 302
Chihuahua (dog): 6-7
china poblana: 20, 63, 64
Cholula: 69-72
Christmas: 20; see also specific place
Church and Convent of San Luis Obispo (Huamantla): 53
Church and Ex-Convent of Our Lady of Santa Ana Chiautempan: 51
Church and Ex-Convent of San Agustín (Querétaro): 249-250
Church and Ex-Convent of Santa Cruz (Querétaro): 247
Church and Ex-Convent of Santo Domingo (Querétaro): 251
Church and Viceroyalty Museum of Guadalupe: 145

Church of El Carmen (San Cristóbal de las Casas): 291-292
Church of la Merced (San Cristóbal de las Casas): 291
Church of Nuestra Señora de la Salud (San Miguel de Allende): 212-213
Church of Our Lady of Guadalupe (Tlaquepaque): 238
Church of San Bernardino de Siena (Taxco): 106
Church of San Bernardino de Siena (Valladolid): 283
Church of San Cristóbal (San Cristóbal de las Casas): 291
Church of San Felipe Neri (Oaxaca): 176
Church of San Francisco (San Cristóbal de las Casas): 291
Church of San Francisco (San Miguel de Allende): 212
Church of San José (Jalapa): 39
Church of San Miguel (Taxco): 107
Church of San Nicolas (San Cristóbal de las Casas): 292
Church of San Nicolas Tolentino (Taxco): 108
Church of San Pedro (near San Luis Potosí): 155
Church of Santa Lucía (San Cristóbal de las Casas): 291
Church of Santa Monica (Puebla): 62
Church of Santa Veracruz (Taxco): 107
Church of the Conception (San Miguel de Allende): 214-215
Church of the Grito (Dolores Hidalgo): 223
Church of the Holy Spirit (Puebla): 60
Church of the Immaculate Conception (Real de Catorce): 158
Church of the Santísima Trinidad (Taxco): 108
Churriguera, José: 77
cigars: 36
Citlaltepetl: 40
City Hall: see Palacio del Ayuntamiento
City Museum (Mérida): 273-274
City of Flowers: 38
city layout: 12

Colegio de San Nicolas (Morelia): 192
Columbus: 1, 8, 24
Colungas, Alejandro: 231
comida corrida: 24
Conquest, the: 2-9, 28-29
conquistadors: 1-10; see also specific conquistador
Conservatorio de Música de las Rosas (Morelia): 192
Convention Center of Morelia: 195
Convent of Our Lady of the Assumption see Ex-Convento de San Francisco
Convent of Saint Anthony (Izamal): 280
Convent of San Bernadino (Taxco): 106
Convento Santa Catalina (Oaxaca): see Camino Real Oaxaca
copper (Santa Clara del Cobre): 204-205
Copper Fair (Santa Clara del Cobre): 205
Corn-paste Virgin of Zapopan: 235
Coronel, Pedro: 17, 130, 139
Coronel, Rafael: 17, 141
Corregidora Stadium (Querétaro): 252
corrida see bullfighting
corrida de toros: 21-23 see also bullfighting, specific corrida
Cortés, Hernán: 1-10, 27-29, 38, 41, 42, 51, 55, 64, 70, 73, 81, 92, 102, 162, 164, 171, 178, 208, 259
Corzo, Ángel Albino: 300
Covarrubias, Miguel: 17
Coyoacán: 85, 92-94
Coyuca Lagoon (near Acapulco): 118-119
craft specialties by city: 16
criollos: 11
Cuernavaca: 162-169
Cuetlaxcoapan: 55

D
Dali, Salvador: 130
danzones: 34
Day of the Dead (Oaxaca): 183-184
Day of the Dead (Tzintzuntzán): 205
Day of the Dead (Isla Janitzio): 202-204
de Aldama, Juan: 246
de Almanza, Enrique: 220
de Borgraf, Diego: 58

Crafts

see also arts and artisans for each city
alebrijes: 186
Arte Maya (Mérida): 275
Artesanías Vázquez Factory (Dolores
Hidalgo): 223
Casa Cohen (San Miguel de Allende): 218
Casa de Artisanías (Morelia): 195
Casas de las Artesanías (Guadalajara): 232
Centro de Talavera la Colonial (Puebla): 67
copper: Santa Clara del Cobre 204-205
craft specialties by city 16
Ex-Convento de Santa Rosa/House of
Handicrafts (Puebla): 62-63
glass: Tlaquepaque 236
hammocks: Merida 275
Izquinapán (San Miguel de Allende): 218
Joyería David (San Miguel de Allende): 218
marionettes: 53
masks: Chiapa de Corzo 303

Mercado de Artesanías (San Miguel de
Allende): 218
Museo Nacional de la Cerámica
(Tlaquepaque): 238-239
pottery: Dolores Hidalgo 223; Ocotlán 187;
San Bartolo Coyotepec 187; San Cristóbal
de las Casas 294; Santa María Atzompa
186; Tlaquepaque 236, 238-239
rebozos: San Luis Potosí 151-152; Santa
María del Río 154
reedwork (Ocotlán): 187
Sergio Bustamente: 236
silver: Taxco 102-103, 108-109; San Miguel
de Allende 218
Sna Jolobil weaving co-op (San Cristóbal
de las Casas): 293-294
Talavera tile (Puebla): 65-67
textiles: San Cristóbal de las Casas 292-
294; San Miguel de Allende 218;
Teotitlán del Valle 187

de Córdoba, Andres: 46
de Gálvez, Matias: 87
de Grijalva, Juan: 260
de Hervas de Flores, María: 214
de Iturbide, Agustín: 80-81, 106, 192-
193, 282
de la Asunción, Andrea: 62
de la Borda, José: 102-103, 107
de la Cueva, Amado: 81
de la Gandara, Vicerine Doña Francisca:
153
de la Luz Agustina, María: 220
de Landa, Diego: 12, 280
de las Casas, Bartolome: 8, 284, 300
de la Villa del Villar del Aquila,
Marquesa: 245
de Léon, Rodrigo: 301
de Loayzaga, Manuel: 48
de los Reyes Martínez, Juan José: 121
de los Reyes Pichardo, Fernando "El
Callao": 53
de Mazariegos, Andres: 292
de Mazariegos, Diego: 284, 300
de Mazariegos, Luis: 287
de Mendoza, Antonio: 189

de Mendoza, Hurtado: 12
de Mérida, Juan: 280
de Montejo "El Mozo," Francisco: 267
de Montejo, Francisco: 282
de Ovando y Villavincencio, Agustín: 63
de Palafox y Mendoza, Juan: 46, 52
de Portola, Gaspar: 225
de Quiroga, Vasco: 189, 200, 205
de Rola, Antonio: 72
de Saavedra, Hernando: 56
de San Juan, Catarina: 20
de San Luis Montanez, Nicolas: 208
de San Miguel, Juan: 208
de Umarán, Juan: 216
de Villalpando, Cristóbal: 58
del la Tobilla, Andres: 297
Desert Sanctuary of Our Lady of
Guadalupe (near Mexquitic): 154
Díaz de Gamarra, Juan Benito: 213
Díaz del Castillo, Bernal: 2, 7, 38, 86
Díaz, Porfirio: 14, 16, 63, 79, 81, 82,
157, 267
diseases: 2, 11, 30, 42, 73
dogs: 2, 6-7
Dolores Hidalgo: 220-223

Doña Josefa's House (Querétaro): 245-246
Doña Josefa: *see* Ortíz de Domínquez, Josefa
Don Quixote: 12, 122, 127, 129-130, 132; *see also* Cervantes
Drake, Sir Francis: 30
Dream of a Sunday Afternoon in Alameda Park: 81
Durini, Francisco: 31

E

Easter: 20
Echeverioja, Balthazar: 58
Eiffel: 163
El Caballito: 84
El Carmen Cultural Center (San Cristóbal de las Casas): 292
El Castillito (Cuernavaca): 168
El Centenario Park Zoo (Mérida): 278
El Centro (Acapulco): 113
El Centro Cultural el Nigromante (San Miguel de Allende): *see* Bellas Artes
El Cid: 22
Elias Amador Library (Zacatecas): 139
El Jardín de la Unión (Guanajuato): 122-125
El Parian (Puebla): 66-67
El Rosario Butterfly Sanctuary (near Morelia): 198
El Tajín: 28
encomiendas: 5, 10, 11
Escuela de Bellas Artes (Querétaro): 252
Espinoza Yglesias, Manuel: 62
estudiantinas: 18, 122, 131
events: Campeche 266; Guadalajara 234; Guanajuato 132; Merida 277-279; Morelia 196; Oaxaca 182; San Luis Potosí 152; San Miguel de Allende 218-219; Zacatecas 144
Ex-Convent and Church of San Francisco (Querétaro): 244
Ex-Convent and Church of San Gabriel (Cholula): 71-72
Ex-Convent of San José (Campeche): 265
Ex-Convent of Santa Clara (Querétaro): 249

Ex-Convent of Santo Domingo-Centro Cultural (Chiapa de Corzo): 301-302
Ex-Convent of Sisal (Valladolid): 283
Ex-Convento de San Francisco (Puebla): 60-61
Ex-Convento de San Francisco (Tlaxcala): 46-47
Ex-Convento de Santa Rosa/House of Handicrafts (Puebla): 62-63
Ex-Convento Santo Domingo (San Cristóbal de las Casas): 290-291
Ex-Hacienda El Lencero: 39-40
Ex-Hacienda San Gabriel de Berrera (Guanajuato): 128-129
Ex-Mercado Victoria (Puebla): 60
Ex-Palacio Legislativo (Tlaxcala): 45
Ex-Templo y Bishopric de San Agustín (Zacatecas): 140

F

Fabian y Fuero, Francisco: 59
farming: 11
Feast of San Antonio de Padua (San Miguel de Allende): 218
Feast of St. Francis of Assisi (Real de Catorce): 157, 158
Feast of the Assumption of the Virgin Mary (Huamantla): 52
Feast of the Blood of Christ (Quiroga): 203
Felipe de Aranda, Alonso: 261
Felipe de Jesús: 166-167
Feria del Rebozo (Santa María del Río): 154
Feria Nacional de la Plata (Taxco): 110
Feria Nacional de Zacatecas: 144
Feria Nacional Potosina (San Luis Potosí): 152
Festival de Arte Primavera Potosina (San Luis Potosí): 152
Festival de Música y Danza de la Huasteca (San Luis Potosí): 152
Festival de Virgen de los Remedios (Cholula): 72
Festival Internacional Cervantino (Guanajuato): 132
Festival of St. Sebastian (Chiapa de Corzo): 302-303

Fiesta for Ometochli/Festival of the Virgin (Cuernavaca): 168-170
fiestas: 19, 21 *see also specific festival; specific place*
Fiestas de Octubre (Guadalajara): 234
food: 21, 24; Acapulco 117-118; Campeche 266; Guadalajara 234; Guanajuato 132-133; Merida 279; Mexico City 86-87; Morelia 196-197; Oaxaca 184-185; Puebla: 68; Querétaro 252; San Luis Potosí 152-153; San Miguel de Allende 219; Taxco 110; Tlaxcala: 49; Veracruz: 37-38; Zacatecas 145
Fort of Our Lady of Loreto (Puebla): 69
Fort San Miguel (Campeche): 265
Fountain of Neptune (Querétaro): 249
Fountain of the Baratillo (Guanajuato): 27

France: 30
Franciscans: 8
Fuentes, Carlos: 31
Fuerte de San José (Campeche): 265
Fuerte San Diego (Acapulco): 111, 113-115
fútbol: Guadalajara 227

G
Galvez, Jacobo: 230
gardens: *see* parks, plazas, and gardens
gems: Queretaro 241
glass: Tlaquepaque 236
gold: 2-3, 5, 7, 8, 29
Gonzalez, Felipe: 212
González, Wilbert: 275
Gottdiener museum (Mérida): 273
government: 11

Festivals and Fiestas

Blessing of the Animals (Oaxaca): 183
Carnaval (Cholula): 72
Carnaval (San Juan Chamula): 300
Carnaval (Veracruz): 37
Chamber Music Festival (San Miguel de Allende): 209, 218
Copper Fair (Santa Clara del Cobre): 205
Day of the Dead (Oaxaca): 183-184
Day of the Dead (Tzintzuntzán): 205
Day of the Dead (Isla Janitzio): 202-204
Feast of San Antonio de Padua (San Miguel de Allende): 218
Feast of St. Francis of Assisi (Real de Catorce): 157, 158
Feast of the Assumption of the Virgin Mary (Huamantla): 52
Feast of the Blood of Christ (Quiroga): 203
Feria del Rebozo (Santa María del Río): 154
Feria Nacional de la Plata (Taxco): 110
Feria Nacional de Zacatecas: 144
Feria Nacional Potosina (San Luis Potosí): 152
Festival de Arte Primavera Potosina (San Luis Potosí): 152
Festival de Música y Danza de la Huasteca (San Luis Potosí): 152

Festival de Virgen de los Remedios (Cholula): 72
Festival Internacional Cervantino (Guanajuato): 132
Festival of St. Sebastian (Chiapa de Corzo): 302-303
Fiesta for Ometochli/Festival of the Virgin (Cuernavaca): 168-170
Fiestas de Octubre (Guadalajara): 234
Guelaguetza Festival (Oaxaca): 182
Holiday of the Virgin of Guadalupe (Mexico City): 92
International Music Festivals (San Miguel de Allende): 218
Jornadas Alarconians (Taxco): 110
Mexican Independence Day (San Miguel de Allende): 218
Moors vs. Christians mock battle (Zacatecas): 144
Pilgrimage of Birds (Santa María del Río): 154
Radish Festival (Oaxaca): 184
Semana Santa (Guanajuato): 132
Semana Santa (Oaxaca): 182
Semana Santa (San Luis Potosí): 152
Semana Santa (Taxco): 109-110
Winter Music Festival (San Miguel de Allende): 209

Goya: 23
Great Pyramid of Tepanampa: 69
Great Temple of Tenochtitlán (Mexico City): 79-80
Grito de Dolores: 85-86
Guadalajara: 25, 224-235
Guadalajara Philharmonic Orchestra: 233
Guadalupe: 145
Guadalupe Posada, José: 81, 83
Guanajuato: 9, 11, 120-133
Guelaguetza Festival (Oaxaca): 182-183
Gutiérrez, Zeferino: 212, 214
Guzmán, Nuño de: 224

H
Hacienda de Bledos (Villa de Reyes): 153
Hacienda de la Ventilla (Villa de Reyes): 154
Hacienda Manga de Clavo *see* Ex-Hacienda El Lencero
haciendas: 11
Hall, Charles: 60
hammocks: Merida 275
Hemiciclo de Benito Juárez (Mexico City): 81
henequen: 267
Hernández de Córdoba, Francisco: 260
hidalgo: 12
Hidalgo y Costilla, Miguel: 77, 86, 121-122, 143, 192, 209, 221, 228, 229, 282
Hill of San Pedro: 154-155
Historical Archives building (Querétaro): 250
Holiday of the Virgin of Guadalupe (Mexico City): 92
holidays: 19-20; *see also* festivals and fiestas; *specific place*
Hospicio (Puebla): 64
Hotel de Cortés(Mexico City): 83
House of Forgetfulness: *see* Museo de la Herbolaría/La Casa del Olvido
House of the Giant (Pátzcuaro): 202
House of the Inquisitor (San Miguel de Allende): 216
Huamantla: 52-53
huapangos: 34
Huastec: 40

huipiles: Merida 275; San Cristóbal de las Casas 293

I
Iglesia de Guadalupe: (Puebla): 64
Iglesia del Carmen (Puebla): 60
Iglesia de San Diego (Guanajuato): 128
Iglesia de San Francisco (Mexico City): 81
Iglesia de San José (Puebla): 60
Iglesia de San Juan Bautista (Coyoacán): 92
Iglesia de Santa Cruz (Puebla): 61
Iglesia de Santo Domingo de Guzmán (Puebla): 60
IIndependence Day: 19
Independence Day (Mexico City): 85-86
independence from Spain: 11, 30
Inquisition: 13
Instituto Cultural Cabañas (Guadalajara): 230-231
International Music Festivals (San Miguel de Allende): 218
Isla Janitzio: 202
Izamal: 12, 280-281
Izucar de Matamoros: 66

J
Jail of the Inquisition (San Miguel de Allende): 216
Jalapa: 11, 18, 38-41
Jardín Borda (Cuernavaca): 163-164
Jardín Botanico Tizatlán (near Tlaxcala): 49-51
Jardín Botánico Xmuch Haltum (Campeche): 264-265
Jardín Corregidora (Querétaro): 244
Jardín de San Francisco (Guadalajara): 225
Jardín Juárez (Cuernavaca): 163
Jardín Obregón (Querétaro): 244
Jarochos: 31
Jeronimo de Zendejas, Miguel: 58
Jiménez, Mariano: 122
Jornadas Alarconians (Taxco): 110
José Luís Rodríguez Alconado Exhibition Hall *see* Barrio del Artistas
Juan Gamboa Museum (Mérida): 273

Juárez, Benito: 30; 31-32, 34; 55-56; 68;
89; 135; 147; 157; 176; 177; 225; 251
Jungla Magica (Cuernavaca): 168

K
Kahlo, Frida: 85, 92, 93-95, 164
Kamio, Hiroshi: 36
Kinich Kadmó (Izamal): 281
Klee, Paul: 94

L
La Antiqua: 41
la bamba: 18, 31, 36-37, 84
La Candelaria (Valladolid): 283
La Casa de Artesanías (Mérida): 275
La Casa de la Marquesa (Querétaro): 251
La Ermita del Santa Cristo del Buen
Viaje: 35
Lake Atlanga: 54
Lake Pátzcuaro: 202-205
La Pila (Chiapa de Corzo): 301
La Prueba Cigar Factory: 36
La Santísima Muerte: 81, 83
La Transfiguración del Señor (near
Cuernavaca): 167
Lancandón: 297
Larios, Juan: 59
Latin American Tower see Torre Latino
Americana
Law School Auditorium (San Cristóbal
de las Casas): 288
Lazarillo de Tormes: 12
Lazaro, Diego: 52
Lindbergh, Charles: 164
Lopez de Ecala, Tomas: 245
Lorencez, General: 67
Lorencillo: 30
Los Pinos: 91
Los Portales (Campeche): 262
Lowry, Malcolm: 162
Luis Cuevas, José: 80

M
Madero, Francisco: 81
maguey: 25
Malinche Volcano: 49
Malinche: see Marina

Malintze: see Marina
Malintzin: see Marina
mangos: 117
Mansion Carvajal (Campeche): 262
mariachis: 17-19; Mexico City 84; Puebla
67
marimbas: 296-297
Marin, Luis: 300
Marina: 4, 92, 259
marionettes: 53
masks (Chiapa de Corzo): 303
matadors: Jorge "Ranchero" Aguilar 45;
Fernando "El Callao" de los Reyes
Pichardo 53; Antonio "El Marinero"
Ortega 53
Maximilian of Hapsburg: 14, 30, 38, 55,
67, 86, 87, 127, 147, 157, 162, 163,
167, 245, 247, 248, 250, 267
Maxixcatzin: 51
Maya Museum (Campeche): 265
Mayer, Franz: 82-83
Mercado Emilio Sanchez Piedras
(Tlaxcala): 49
Mercado Gonzalez Ortega (Zacatecas): 139
Mercado Municipal (Acapulco): 116
Mérida: 12, 267-280
mescal: 25
Mesón de Santa Rosa (Querétaro): 247
Metropolitan Cathedral (Mexico City):
see Catedral Metropolito
Mexican Independence Day (San Miguel
de Allende): 218
Mexquitic: 154
Meyer, Michael C.: 9
Miguel de Santa María, José: 60
Mina el Edén (Zacatecas): 142-143
mining: 9-10; 101-102, 120-121, 133-
134, 135, 142-143, 154-157; see also
gold; silver
Ministry of Education (Mexico City): 81
Misión de Nuestra Señora de la Luz
(Tancoyol): 256
Misión de San Francisco de Asisi
(Tilaco): 256
Misión de San Miguel Arcángel (Conca):
256

Misión de Santa María de la Purísima
   Concepción del Agua (Landa): 255-256
Misión de Santiago (Jalapan): 255
Mixtecs: 171, 183
Moctezuma: 1, 3, 5, 27, 29, 42, 55, 70, 77
mole: 68
mole poblano: 62
Momay, Luis: 134

Montejo: 12
Monumento de los Niños Héroes
   (Mexico City): 90
Moors: 15
Moors vs. Christians mock battle
   (Zacatecas): 144
Morado, José Chavez: 39,126, 127
Morales, Ignacio: 63

Museums

Anthropology Museum: see Museo
   Nacional de Antropología
Baluarte de San Carlos (Campeche): 263
Baluarte de Santiago (Veracruz): 34
Casa de Cultura (Puebla): 59
Casa de el Dean (Puebla): 63
Casa de Figueroa (Taxco): 106
Casa del Risco: see Museo Colonial Casa
   del Risco
Casa Maximiliano: see Museo de la
   Herbolaría/La Casa del Olvido
Casa von Humboldt/Museo de Arte
   Colonia (Taxco): 107
Castillo San Juan de Ulua (Veracruz): 34
Church and Viceroyalty Museum of
   Guadalupe: 145
City Museum (Mérida): 273-274
El Castillito photographic museum
   (Cuernavaca): 168
Ex-Hacienda El Lencero (Jalapa): 39-40
Ex-Hacienda San Gabriel de Berrera
   (Guanajuato): 128-129
Fuerte San Diego (Acapulco): 111, 113-115
Gottdiener museum (Mérida): 273
House of Forgetfulness: see Museo de la
   Herbolaría/La Casa del Olvido
Juan Gamboa Museum (Mérida): 273
Maya Museum (Campeche): 265
Mummy Museum see Museo de las Momias
Musem of the Masks: see Museo de la
   Máscara
Museo Alhóndigas de Granaditas
   (Guanajuato): 126
Museo Amparo (Puebla): 62
Museo Anahuacalli/Diego Rivera
   (Coyoacán): 94
Museo Bello y Gonzalez (Puebla): 62
Museo Carrillo Gil Arte Contemporano
   (San Ángel): 95
Museo Casa de la Torre (Cuernavaca): 164

Museo Casa de Morelos (Morelia): 193
Museo Casa Hidalgo (Dolores Hidalgo):
   222-223
Museo Casa Natal de Morelos (Morelia): 193
Museo Colonial Casa del Risco (San
   Ángel): 96
Museo de Antropologia de la Universidad
   Veracruzana (Veracruz): 40-41
Museo de Arqueología del Occidente de
   Mexico (Guadalajara): 232
Museo de Arte Alvar y Carmen T. Carrillo
   Gil: see Museo Carrillo Gil Arte
   Contemporano
Museo de Arte Moderno (Mexico City): 90
Museo de Benito Juárez (Mexico City): 77
Museo de Cuauhnahuac/Palacio de Cortés:
   164-166
Museo de Culturas (Tlaxcala): 49
Museo de Estada/Casa de Alfenique
   (Puebla): 63
Museo de Historia Natural (Mérida): 274
Museo de Historia Natural (Morelia): 194
Museo de Historia Natural Alfredo Duges
   (Guanajuato): 126-127
Museo de José Luis Cuevas (Mexico City):
   80
Museo de Juárez (Oaxaca): 177
Museo de la Alameda (Mexico City): 81
Museo de la Canción Yucateca (Mérida): 274
Museo de la Ciudad (Veracruz): 34
Museo de la Ciudad de Guadalajara: 231
Museo de la Estampa (Mexico City): 83
Museo de la Herbolaría/La Casa del Olvido
   (Cuernavaca): 167
Museo de la Independencia Nacional: 223
Museo de la Máscara (San Luis Potosí):
   147-149
Museo de las Intervenciones (Coyoacán): 93
Museo de las Momias (near Guanajuato):
   133

Morelia: 11, 189-198
Morelos, José María: 192, 193-194, 202
Morrow, Dwight: 164, 166
Mulsay's Park (Mérida): 278
Mummy Museum see Museo de las
    Momias
Municipal Fish Market (Veracruz): 38
muralists: 16-17; Jean Charlot 17, 81;

Pedro Coronel 17; Rafael Coronel 17;
Miguel Covarrubias 17; Amado de la
Cueva 81; Jacobo Galvez 230; José
Chavez Morado 39, 126, 127; Juan
O'Gorman 17, 89, 95, 201; Pablo
O'Higgins 17; José Clemente Orozco
17, 82, 83, 85, 89, 90, 94, 95, 228,
231; Fernando Castro Pacheco 271;

Museo de Rafael Coronel (Zacatecas): 141
Museo de Revolución (Puebla): 63
Museo de San Miguel de Allende (San
    Miguel de Allende): 215
Museo de Santa Monica (Puebla): 61-62
Museo de Taxco Guillermo Spratling
    (Taxco): 105-106
Museo de Templo Mayor (Mexico City): 80
Museo del Caracol (Mexico City): 90
Museo del Estado (Morelia): 192-193
Museo del Pueblo de Guanajuato: 127
Museo Estudio Diego Rivera (San Ángel):
    95
Museo Franz Mayer (Mexico City): 82-83
Museo Frida Kahlo (Coyoacán): 93-94
Museo Galería de la Lucha del Pueblo
    Mexicano por su Libertad: see Museo del
    Caracol
Museo Historica de La Sierra Gorda
    (Jalapan): 255
Museo Leon Trotsky (Coyoacán): 94
Museo Macay (Mérida): 270, 274
Museo Mural Diego Rivera: see Museo de la
    Alameda
Museo Nacional de Antropología (Mexico
    City): 89-90
Museo Nacional de Arte (Mexico City): 84
Museo Nacional de la Cerámica
    (Tlaquepaque): 238-239
Museo Nacional de los Culturas Populares
    (Coyoacán): 93
Museo Numismatico de Mexico (Mérida):
    274
Museo Pedro Coronel (Zacatecas): 139
Museo Regional de Artes Populares
    (Pátzcuaro): 201
Museo Regional de Oaxaca: 179
Museo Regional de Tlaxcala: 47
Museo Regional del Guadalajara: 229
Museo Regional Michoacán (Morelia): 193

Museo Regional Potosino (San Luis
    Potosí): 150
Museo Rufino Tamayo (Mexico City): 90-91
Museo Rufino Tamayo (Oaxaca): 175
Museo Taurino (Huamantla): 53
Museo y Casa de Diego Rivera
    (Guanajuato): 129
Museum of Art of Querétaro: 249-250
Museum of Contemporary Art (Morelia): 194
Museum of Contemporary Art of Oaxaca: 178
Museum of Modern Art (Mexico City): see
    Museo de Arte Moderno
Museum of Popular Art (Mérida): 273
Museum of the Capture of Zacatecas
    (Zacatecas): 142
Na Balom Museum and Research Center
    (San Cristóbal de las Casas): 289-290
National Art Museum: see Museo Nacional
    de Arte
National Puppet Museum (Huamantla): 53
Palacio Canton (Mérida): 273
Parque Nacional Desierto de los Leones
    museum (near San Ángel): 97-98
Pinacoteca del Estado (Mérida): 273
Plaza del Carmen (San Ángel): 96-97
Railroad Museum (Puebla): 65
Regional Anthropology Museum (Santiago
    Tuxtla):
Regional Museum of Campeche: 262
Regional Museum of Tlaxcala see Museo
    Regional de Tlaxcala
Regional War Museum (Puebla) see
    volución
San Diego Fort Museum (Acapulco): 113-115
Sergio Castro Museum (San Cristóbal de
    las Casas): 288
Silver Museum (Taxco): 106
University of Guanajuato museums: 126
Venustiano Carranza Lighthouse
    (Veracruz): 34

muralists (*continued*)
Diego Rivera 16, 77, 81, 82, 85, 89,
90, 93-95, 129, 166; David Alfaro
Siqueiros 17, 82, 83, 85, 89, 90, 95,
97, 216; Gerardo Suárez 203; Rufino
Tamayo 16-17, 90-91; Francisco
Antonio Vallejo 150; Desiderio
Hernandez Xochitiotzin 45, 48
murals: 16-17; Campeche 265;
Cuernavaca 166; Guadalajara 228,
230; Guanajuato 126, 127; Jalapa 39;
Mérida 271; Mexico City 77, 81-83,
85, 89, 90, 91; Morelia 193; Pátzcuaro
201; San Ángel 97; San Luis Potosí
150; San Miguel de Allende 216;
Tlaxcala 48; Zacatecas 137
Musem of the Masks: *see* Museo de la
Máscara
Museo Alhóndigas de Granaditas
(Guanajuato): 126
Museo Amparo (Puebla): 62
Museo Anahuacalli/Diego Rivera
(Coyoacán): 94
Museo Bello y Gonzalez (Puebla): 62
Museo Carrillo Gil Arte Contemporano
(San Ángel): 95
Museo Casa de la Torre (Cuernavaca): 164
Museo Casa de Morelos (Morelia): 193
Museo Casa Hidalgo (Dolores Hidalgo):
222-223
Museo Casa Natal de Morelos (Morelia):
193
Museo Colonial Casa del Risco (San
Ángel): 96
Museo de Antropologia de la
Universidad Veracruzana (Veracruz):
40-41
Museo de Arqueología del Occidente de
Mexico (Guadalajara): 232
Museo de Arte Alvar y Carmen T.
Carrillo Gil: *see* Museo Carrillo Gil
Arte Contemporano
Museo de Arte Moderno (Mexico City): 90
Museo de Benito Juárez (Mexico City): 77
Museo de Cuauhnahuac/Palacio de
Cortés (Cuernavaca): 164-166
Museo de Culturas (Tlaxcala): 49

Museo de Estada/Casa de Alfenique
(Puebla): 63
Museo de Historia Natural (Mérida): 274
Museo de Historia Natural (Morelia): 194
Museo de Historia Natural Alfredo Duges
(Guanajuato): 126-127
Museo de José Luis Cuevas (Mexico
City): 80
Museo de Juárez (Oaxaca): 177
Museo de la Alameda (Mexico City): 81
Museo de la Canción Yucateca (Mérida):
274
Museo de la Ciudad (Veracruz): 34
Museo de la Ciudad de Guadalajara: 231
Museo de la Estampa (Mexico City): 83
Museo de la Herbolaría/La Casa del
Olvido (Cuernavaca): 167
Museo de la Independencia Nacional: 223
Museo de la Máscara (San Luis Potosí):
147-149
Museo de las Culturas (Mexico City): 79
Museo de las Intervenciones
(Coyoacán): 93
Museo de las Momias (near Guanajuato):
133
Museo del Caracol (Mexico City): 90
Museo del Estado (Morelia): 192-193
Museo del Pueblo de Guanajuato: 127
Museo de Rafael Coronel (Zacatecas): 141
Museo de Revolución (Puebla): 63
Museo de San Miguel de Allende (San
Miguel de Allende): 215
Museo de Santa Monica (Puebla): 61-62
Museo de Taxco Guillermo Spratling
(Taxco): 105-106
Museo de Templo Mayor (Mexico City):
80
Museo Estudio Diego Rivera (San
Ángel): 95
Museo Franz Mayer (Mexico City): 82-83
Museo Frida Kahlo (Coyoacán): 93-94
Museo Galería de la Lucha del Pueblo
Mexicano por su Libertad: *see* Museo
del Caracol
Museo Historica de La Sierra Gorda
(Jalapan): 255
Museo Huichol (Zapopan): 236

Museo Leon Trotsky (Coyoacán): 94
Museo Macay (Mérida): 270, 274
Museo Mural Diego Rivera: see Museo de
  la Alameda
Museo Nacional de Antropología
  (Mexico City): 89-90
Museo Nacional de Arte (Mexico City): 84
Museo Nacional de la Cerámica
  (Tlaquepaque): 238-239
Museo Nacional de los Culturas
  Populares (Coyoacán): 93
Museo Numismatico de Mexico
  (Mérida): 274
Museo Pedro Coronel (Zacatecas): 139
Museo Regional de Artes Populares
  (Pátzcuaro): 201
Museo Regional del Guadalajara
  (Guadalajara): 229
Museo Regional de Oaxaca: 179
Museo Regional de Tlaxcala: 47
Museo Regional Michoacán (Morelia): 193
Museo Regional Potosino (San Luis
  Potosí): 150
Museo Rufino Tamayo (Mexico City):
  90-91
Museo Rufino Tamayo (Oaxaca): 175
Museo Taurino (Huamantla): 53
Museo y Casa de Diego Rivera
  (Guanajuato): 129
Museum of Art of Querétaro: 249-250
Museum of Contemporary Art (Morelia):
  194
Museum of Contemporary Art of
  Oaxaca: 178
Museum of Modern Art (Mexico City):
  see Museo de Arte Moderno
Museum of Popular Art (Mérida): 273
Museum of the Capture of Zacatecas
  (Zacatecas): 142
music: 17-19; Acapulco 116-117;
  Campeche 266; Cuernavaca 168;
  Guadalajara 233; Guanajuato 122,
  131; Morelia 196; Puebla 67; San
  Cristóbal de las Casas 296; San Luis
  Potosí 152; San Miguel de Allende
  218; Veracruz 34, 36-37; Zacatecas 143
musical instruments: 18

N
Na Balom Museum and Research Center
  (San Cristóbal de las Casas): 289-290
Nacional Monte de Piedad (Mexico
  City): 77-79
National Art Museum: see Museo
  Nacional de Arte
National Pawn Shop of Oaxaca: 177
National Pawnshop: see Nacional Monte
  de Piedad
National Puppet Museum (Huamantla): 53
Neri de Alfaro, Luis Felipe: 220
Nieto, Rosa: 187
Noriega, José: 147

O
O'Gorman, Juan: 17, 89, 95, 201
O'Higgins, Pablo: 17
Oaxaca: 11, 171-185
Obregón, Alvaro: 95
Ocampo, Melchor: 192
Ocotlán: 187
Old School of Medicine (Mexico City): 81
Olmec: 40-41
Ometochli: 168-170
open chapels: 6
Oratorio of St. Philip Neri (San Miguel
  de Allende): 213-214
Orozco, José Clemente: 17, 82, 83, 89,
  90, 94, 95, 228, 231
Orquestra Sinfónica Nacional (Mexico
  City): 82
Ortega, Antonio "El Marinero": 53;
Ortega, Juan: 287
Ortíz de Castro, Damian: 76-77
Ortíz de Domínguez, Josefa: 241, 244,
  245-247
Othón, Manuel José: 151
Otomi: 52, 241
Our Lady of Loreto (Puebla): 69

P
Pacheco, Fernando Castro: 271
Pachuca mines: 18
Palace of Fine Arts: see Palacio de Bella
  Artes
Palace of the Archbishop (Mérida): 270

Palacio Canton (Mérida): 273
Palacio Clavijero (Morelia): 192
Palacio de Bella Artes (Mexico City): 82
Palacio de Gobierno (Jalapa): 39
Palacio de Gobierno (Mérida): 271
Palacio de Gobierno (Oaxaca): 174
Palacio de Gobierno (San Luis Potosí): 147
Palacio de Gobierno (Tlaxcala): 45
Palacio de Gobierno (Zacatecas): 137
Palacio de Gobierno/Colegio de San
    Ignacio (Puebla): 64
Palacio de Iturbide (Mexico City): 80-81
Palacio de Justicia (Tlaxcala): 46
Palacio de la Cultura (Tlaxcala): 48
Palacio de la Mala Noche (Zacatecas): 137
Palacio del Ayuntamiento (Mexico City):
    79
Palacio del Gobierno (Guadalajara): 228
Palacio Juárez (Tlaxcala): 46
Palacio Municipal (Cuernavaca): 163
Palacio Municipal (Mérida): 271, 278
Palacio Municipal (Puebla): 60
Palacio Municipal (San Cristóbal de las
    Casas): 287
Palacio Municipal (Veracruz): 33
Palacio Nacional (Mexico City): 77
Palafox y Mendoza, Juan: 59
Palou, Francisco: 255
Parish of Saint Ann (Santa Ana
    Chiautempan): 51-52
Parque Agua Azul (Guadalajara): 232
Parque Centenario (Coyoacán): 92
Parque Cepeda Paraza (Mérida): 272, 278
Parque Juárez (Huamantla): 53
Parque Juárez (Jalapa): 39
Parque Nacional Desierto de los Leones
    (near San Ángel): 97-98
Parque Nacional la Malinche (Tlaxcala):
    49
Parque Paseo de Bravo (Puebla): 64
Parque Xochimilco: see Xochimilco Park
Parque Zamora: 34
Parroquia de Nuestra Señora de Dolores
    (Dolores Hidalgo): see Church of the
    Grito
Parroquia de San Agustín (Tlaxcala): 54
Parroquia de San José (Tlaxcala): 45, 46

Parroquia de San Marcos (Puebla): 64
Parroquia de San Miguel Arcángel (San
    Miguel de Allende): 211-212
Paseo Viejo (Puebla): 61
Pátzcuaro: 11, 198-204
photography: 168, 287
Picasso, Pablo: 80, 130
Pico de Orizaba: 40
Pilgrimage of Birds (Santa María del
    Río): 154
Pinacoteca del Estado (Mérida): 273
piñata: 17
Pípila Monument (Guanajuato): 123
Pípila: 121
pirates: 11, 30, 111-112, 260
Plan de Iguala: 106
Playa Pie de la Cuesta (near Acapulco):
    118
Plaza Borda (Taxco): 105
Plaza Chica (Pátzcuaro): 200
Plaza de 31 de Marzo (San Cristóbal de
    las Casas): 286
Plaza de Armas (Cuernavaca): 163
Plaza de Armas (Guadalajara): 227, 228
Plaza de Armas (Oaxaca): 173
Plaza de Armas (Puebla): 56-57
Plaza de Armas (Veracruz): 31
Plaza de la Conchita (Coyoacán): 92
Plaza de la Constitución (Tlaxcala): 43
Plaza de la Independencia (Mérida): 269,
    278
Plaza de la Independencia (Querétaro): 244
Plaza de la Liberación (Guadalajara): 227,
    229
Plaza de la República (Veracruz): 31
Plaza del Carmen (San Ángel): 96-97
Plaza del Carmen (San Luis Potosí): 149
Plaza del la Constitución (Mexico City):
    see Zócalo
Plaza del los Mártires (Morelia): 191
Plaza de los dos Copas (Guadalajara): see
    Plaza de la Liberación
Plaza de los Laureles (Guadalajara): 227,
    228
Plaza de los Trabajos (Puebla): 67
Plaza de Santa Inez (Puebla): 67
Plaza de Santo Domingo (Mexico City): 81

Plaza de Toros (Tlaxcala): 45
Plaza de Toros Caletilla (Acapulco): 117
Plaza de Toros el Nuevo Progreso
  (Guadalajara): 227
Plaza de Toros el Relicario (Puebla): 63
Plaza de Toros Santa María (Querétaro):
  252
Plaza de Vasco de Quiroga (Pátzcuaro):
  see Plaza Grande

Plaza Garibaldi: (Mexico City): 84
Plaza Gertrudis Bocanegra (Pátzcuaro):
  see Plaza Chica
Plaza Grande (Pátzcuaro): 200
Plaza Hidalgo (Coyoacán): 92
Plaza Maternidad (Mérida): 278
Plaza Morelos (Morelia): 194
Plaza of the Mariachis (Guadalajara):
  225, 233

Parks, Plazas, and Gardens

Alameda Park (Mexico City): 81-82
Bosque Park (Morelia): 194
Chapultepec Park (Mexico City): 87-92
El Centenario Park Zoo (Mérida): 278
El Jardín de la Unión (Guanajuato): 122-125
Jardín Borda (Cuernavaca): 163-164
Jardín Botanico Tizatlán (near Tlaxcala):
  49-51
Jardín Botánico Xmuch Haltum
  (Campeche): 264-265
Jardín Corregidora (Querétaro): 244
Jardín de San Francisco (Guadalajara): 225
Jardín Juárez (Cuernavaca): 163
Jardín Obregón (Querétaro): 244
Lake Atlanga: 54
Mulsay's Park (Mérida): 278
Museo de la Herbolaría/La Casa del Olvido
  botanical garden (Cuernavaca): 167
Parque Agua Azul (Guadalajara): 232
Parque Centenario (Coyoacán): 92
Parque Cepeda Paraza (Mérida): 272, 278
Parque Juárez (Huamantla): 53
Parque Juárez (Jalapa): 39
Parque Nacional Desierto de los Leones
  (near San Ángel): 97-98
Parque Nacional la Malinche (Tlaxcala): 49
Parque Paseo de Bravo (Puebla): 64
Parque Zamora (Veracruz): 34
Paseo Viejo (Puebla): 61
Plaza Borda (Taxco): 105
Plaza Chica (Pátzcuaro): 200
Plaza de 31 de Marzo (San Cristóbal de las
  Casas): 286
Plaza de Armas (Cuernavaca): 163
Plaza de Armas (Guadalajara): 227, 228
Plaza de Armas (Oaxaca): 173
Plaza de Armas (Puebla): 56-57
Plaza de Armas (Veracruz): 31

Plaza de la Conchita (Coyoacán): 92
Plaza de la Constitución (Tlaxcala): 43
Plaza de la Independencia (Mérida): 269, 278
Plaza de la Independencia (Querétaro): 244
Plaza de la Liberación (Guadalajara): 227,
  229
Plaza de la República (Veracruz): 31
Plaza del Carmen (San Ángel): 96-97
Plaza del Carmen (San Luis Potosí): 149
Plaza del la Constitución (Mexico City):
  see Zócalo
Plaza del los Mártires (Morelia): 191
Plaza de los dos Copas (Guadalajara): see
  Plaza de la Liberación
Plaza de los Laureles (Guadalajara): 227, 228
Plaza de los Trabajos (Puebla): 67
Plaza de Santa Inez (Puebla): 67
Plaza de Santo Domingo (Mexico City): 81
Plaza de Vasco de Quiroga (Pátzcuaro): see
  Plaza Grande
Plaza Gertrudis Bocanegra (Pátzcuaro): see
  Plaza Chica
Plaza Grande (Pátzcuaro): 200
Plaza Hidalgo (Coyoacán): 92
Plaza Maternidad (Mérida): 278
Plaza Morelos (Morelia): 194
Plaza of the Mariachis (Guadalajara): 225,
  233
Plaza Principal (Dolores Hidalgo): 222
Plaza Principal (Oaxaca) see Plaza de
  Armas
Plaza San Jacinto (San Ángel): 95-96
Plaza Tapatía (Guadalajara): 227, 228, 230
Plaza Xicotencatl (Tlaxcala): 43
Querétaro 2000 (Querétaro): 251-252
San Roque Square (Guanajuato): 127
Xochimilco Park (Xochimilco): 99
Zócalo (Mexico City): 76-80

Plaza Principal (Dolores Hidalgo): 222
Plaza Principal (Oaxaca) see Plaza de
Armas
Plaza San Jacinto (San Ángel): 95-96
Plaza Tapatía (Guadalajara): 227, 228,
230
Plaza Xicotencatl (Tlaxcala): 43
plazas: 13-14; see also specific plaza
Polyforum Cultural Siqueiros (San
Ángel): 97
Pope Alexander VI: 1
Popocatépetl: 163
Porfiriata: 13, 43
portales: 14
Portales de los Evangelistas (Mexico
City): 81
Portales de Miranda (Veracruz): 33
posada: 20
Posada de la Moneda (Zacatecas): 140
pottery: see crafts
pozole: 110-111, 118
privateers: 30; see also pirates
Puebla: 55-58
Puebla Cultural Center: 65-66
Puerta de Tierra (Campeche): 265
pulque: 25
puppets see marionettes
Purépecha/Tarasca: 189
pyramids: Great Pyramid of Tepanampa
69

Q

Quebrada (Acapulco): 111, 113
Querétaro: 10, 11, 241-253
Querétaro 2000 (Querétaro): 251-252
Quetzalcoatl: 29, 45
Quiroga: 203

R

Radish Festival (Oaxaca): 184
Railroad Museum (Puebla): 65
Ramírez Vázquez, Pedro: 89, 90
Rampart of the Shackles: 34
Real de Catorce: 155-159
Rebozo School and Workshop (San Luis
Potosí): 151

rebozos: San Luis Potosí 151-152; Santa
María del Río 154
Recinto de la Reforma (Veracruz): 33
Reform Laws: 8
Reform War: 8
Regional Anthropology Museum
(Santiago Tuxtla):
Regional Museum of Campeche: 262
Regional Museum of Tlaxcala: see Museo
Regional de Tlaxcala
Regional War Museum (Puebla): see
Museo de Revolución
religious holidays: 19-20
Renaissance: 12
Rivera, Diego: 16, 77, 81, 82, 85, 89, 90,
93-95, 129, 166
rodeo: see charreada
Romero de Terreros, Pedro: 248, 250
Rosete-Aranda puppet troupe: 53
Rotundo de los Hombres Illustres
(Guadalajara): 229
Royal Chapel (Tlaxcala): 46
Royal Cities: 10-11

S

Sagrario Municipal (Mexico City): 77
San Ángel: 85, 94-97
San Bartolo Coyotepec: 187
San Cristóbal de las Casas: 284-297
Sanctuary of Saint Michael (San Miguel
de Milagro): 52
San Diego Fort Museum (Acapulco):
113-115
San Felipe de Jesús: 166-167
San Gabriel Monastery (Cholula): 71
San Juan Chamula: 297-300
San Luis Potosí: 9, 10, 146-153
San Miguel Allende: 10, 208-219
San Pedro Gogorron (Villa de Reyes):
153-154
San Roque Square (Guanajuato): 127
San Sebastián (Chiapa de Corzo): 302
Santa Ana (Valladolid): 283
Santa Ana Chiautempan: 49, 51-52
Santa Anna, Antonio Lopez de: 30, 38,
95, 97

Santa Catalina (Puebla): 61
Santa Clara del Cobre: 204-205
Santa Lucía (Valladolid): 283
Santa María Atzompa: 186
Santa María del Río: 154
Santa María Tonanzintla: 72
Santa Prisca Church (Taxco): 105
Santiago de la Laguna: 137
Santiago Tuxtla: 41
Santo Domingo Cathedral (Chiapa de
    Corzo): 301
Santo Domingo Church (San Cristóbal
    de las Casas): 290
Santo Entierro (Taxco): 106
Santuario de Atontonilco (Atotonilco): 220
Santuario de Patrocinio (Zacatecas): 141-
    142
Santuario de Plateros de Zacatecas: 135
Santuario San Francisco Acatepac (near
    Cholula): 72
Sardanetta, Bartolo: 247
School of Mining: 84
Scott, Gen. Winfield: 30
Semana Santa (Guanajuato): 132
Semana Santa (Oaxaca): 182
Semana Santa (San Luis Potosí): 152
Semana Santa (Taxco): 109-110
Serdán Alatriste, Aquiles: 63
Serdán Alatriste, Maximo: 63
Sergio Bustamente: 236
Sergio Castro Museum (San Cristóbal de
    las Casas): 288
Serra, Junípero: 225, 247, 255
Sherman, William L.: 9
sholo: 6-7
shopping: 17; Acapulco 116; Cuernavaca
    168; Guadalajara 232; Guanajuato
    130-131; Jalapa 41; Merida 276-277;
    Mexico City 85; Morelia 196; Oaxaca
    180-181; Puebla 66-67; San Cristóbal
    de las Casas 295-296; San Miguel de
    Allende: 218; Santa Ana Chiautempan
    52; Taxco 109; Tlaxcala: 49; Veracruz
    36; Zacatecas 143
Sierra Gorda Missions: 255-257
Silver Cities: 9-10
Silver Museum (Taxco): 106

silver: 2-3, 5, 7, 9-10, 18, 53, 101-103,
    120-121, 133-134, 135, 142-143
Siqueiros, David Alfaro: 17, 82, 83, 89,
    90, 95, 97, 216
smallpox: 2, 42
Sobrarias, Marco Antonio: 212
Socavon del Rey: 102
soccer: see fútbol
special events: Cholula 72; Mexico City
    85-86; Puebla 67-68; Taxco 109-100;
    Veracruz 37
spices: 23-24
Spratling Ranch Workshop (Taxco): 108-
    109
Spratling, William: 102-103
St. John the Baptist Church (San Juan
    Chamula): 298
Street Lacking Doors or Windows
    (Guanajuato): 127-128
sugarcane: 162
symphony: 82

T
Talavera tile: 65-67
Taller Escuela de Plateria (Tlaxcala): 48-49
Tamayo, Rufino: 16-17, 90, 164, 175
Tarascan Fountain (Morelia): 194
Tarascans: 205
Taxco: 9, 102-111
Taylor, Zachary: 95
Teatro Angela Peralta (San Miguel de
    Allende): 209
Teatro Calderon (Zacatecas): 139
Teatro Caltzontzin (Pátzcuaro): 201
Teatro Cervantes (Guanajuato): 126
Teatro de la Paz (San Luis Potosí): 147
Teatro de la República (Querétaro): 248
Teatro Degollado (Guadalajara): 230
Teatro de la Ciudad (Cuernavaca): 168
Teatro Juárez (Guanajuato): 125-126
Teatro Macedonio de Alcala (Oaxaca): 176
Teatro Ocampo (Cuernavaca): 168
Teatro Peón Contreras (Mérida): 272-
    273, 274
Teatro Principal (Guanajuato): 126
Teatro Principal (Puebla): 64
Teatro Xicotencatl (Tlaxcala): 47, 48

Temple and Ex-Convent of Santa Rosa de Viterbo (Querétaro): 251
Templo de la Santísima Trinidad (Puebla): 61
Templo de San Agustín (San Luis Potosí): 150
Templo de San Felipe Neri (Guanajuato): 128
Templo de San Francisco (Guanajuato): 128
Templo de San Francisco (San Luis Potosí): 149
Templo de Santo Domingo (Mexico City): 81
Templo de Santo Domingo (Zacatecas): 139
Templo del Carmen (San Luis Potosí): 10, 150
Templo Mayor (Mexico City): 79-80
Templo y Ex-Convento de Santo Domingo (Oaxaca): 178-179
Tenochtitlán: 1, 3, 9, 27, 42, 55, 73, 99
Teopanzolco Archaeological Site (Cuernavaca): 168
Tepanampa, Great Pyramid of: 69
Tepatitlán: 25
Tepotzlán: 169-170
Tepoztecatl: 169
Tepozteco Pyramid: 170
Tequila (town): 25, 239-240
tequila: 25, 235, 239-240
The Course of Mexican History: 9
Tizatlán: 51
Tlacolulu: 187-188
Tlahuica: 162, 166, 168, 170
Tlaquepaque: 236-238
Tlaxcala: 42-49
Tlaxcaltecans: 3, 9, 42
Tlaxco: 53-54
Tlayoltehuanitzin, Francisco Miguel: 48
Tolosa, Juan: 135
Tolsá, Manuel: 58, 77, 84, 81, 106
Tomas de la Canal, Manuel: 215
Torre Latino Americana (Mexico City): 83
Totonacs: 18, 28, 40
Tourist Andador (Oaxaca): 177
tree of life: 15

Tresguerras, Francisco Eduardo: 150, 212, 249
Trotsky, Leon: 129
Tzintzuntzán: 205

U
Universidad Autonoma de Querétaro (Querétaro): 252
University of Guadalajara: 232
University of Guadalajara Folkloric Ballet: 233
University of Guanajuato museums: 126
Urrutia, Juan: 243

V
Valencia, Rafael Guizar: 39
Valenciana Church of San Cayetano (near Guanajuato): 134
Valenciana Mine (near Guanajuato): 133-134
Valens, Ritchie: 37
Valladolid: 12, 282-283
Vallejo, Francisco Antonio: 150
Vasco de Quiroga: 8
Vázquez, Don Rodrigo: 120
Venustiano Carranza Lighthouse: 34
Veracruz: 9, 11, 28-38
Verdi: 176
Villa de Reyes: 153
Villa, Pancho: 86, 97, 135
Vizcaíno, Sebastían: 225
voladores: 18, 28
von Humboldt, Alexander: 70

WXYZ
weaving (San Cristóbal de las Casas): 292-294
wine: 254
Winter Music Festival (San Miguel de Allende): 209
witchcraft: 39
Xicohtencatl the Elder: 51
Xicohtencatl the Younger: 51
Xochimilco: 98-99
Xochimilco Park: 99
Xochiquetzal: 51
Xochitiotzin, Desiderio Hernandez: 45, 48

xoloitzcuintli: see sholo
Yucatán: 11
Zaachila; 188
Zacatecas: 9, 135-145
Zapata, Emiliano: 97, 162

Zapopan: 235-236
Zapotecs: 171, 183
Zaragoza Seguin, Ignacio: 56, 67, 68
Zócalo (Mexico City): 76-80
zócalo: 13

Index of Churches and Cathedrals

Basílica de la Soledad (Oaxaca): 176
Basílica de Nuestra Señora de
    Guadalupe(Mexico City): 92
Basílica de Nuestra Señora de Guanajuato
    (Guanajuato): 128
Basílica de Nuestra Señora de la Salud
    (Pátzcuaro): 201
Basílica y Santuario de Nuestra Señora de
    Ocotlán (Tlaxcala): 47-48
Capilla de Aranzazu (San Luis Potosí): 150
Capilla de la Virgen de los Remedios
    (Cholula): 71
Capilla de Santo Cristo del Buen Viaje (La
    Antigua): 41
Capilla del Patrocinio (Zacatecas): 144
Capilla del Rosario (Puebla): 60
Capilla del Señor Ojeda (Taxco): 108
Capilla Pocito (Mexico City): 93
Capuchin Church and ex-convent (Mexico
    City): 92
Catedral (Jalapa): 39
Catedral (Morelia): 191-192
Catedral (San Cristóbal de las Casas): 287
Catedral (San Luis Potosí): 147
Catedral de Guadalajara (Guadalajara): 227
Catedral de la Asunción (Cuernavaca): 164
Catedral de Nuestra Señora de La Asunción
    see Ex-Convento de San Francisco
Catedral de Nuestra Señora de la Asunción
    (Veracruz): 33
Catedral de Puebla (Puebla): 58-59
Catedral de Zacatecas (Zacatecas): 137
Catedral la Inmaculada Concepción
    (Campeche): 262
Catedral Metropolito (Mexico City): 76-77
Catedral Nuestra Señora de la Soledad
    (Acapulco): 113
Catedral y Ex-Convento de San Felipe Neri
    (Querétaro): 251
Chapel de la Casa de Loreto (San Miguel de
    Allende): 214
Chapel of San Jeronimo (near San Luis
    Potosí): 155
Chapel of the Little Well (Tlaxcala): 48
Chapel of the Third Order (San Miguel de
    Allende): 212

Chapel to Jesús (Puebla): 60
Church and Convent of San Luis Obispo
    (Huamantla): 53
Church and Ex-Convent of Our Lady of
    Santa Ana Chiautempan (Santa Ana
    Chiautempan): 51
Church and Ex-Convent of Santa Cruz
    (Querétaro): 247
Church and Ex-Convent of Santo Domingo
    (Querétaro): 251
Church and Viceroyalty Museum of
    Guadalupe: 145
Church of El Carmen (San Cristóbal de las
    Casas): 291-292
Church of la Merced (San Cristóbal de las
    Casas): 291
Church of Nuestra Señora del la Salud (San
    Miguel de Allende): 212-213
Church of Our Lady of Guadalupe
    (Tlaquepaque): 238
Church of San Bernardino de Siena
    (Taxco): 106
Church of San Bernardino de Sienna
    (Valladolid): 283
Church of San Cristóbal (San Cristóbal de
    las Casas): 291
Church of San Felipe Neri (Oaxaca): 176
Church of San Francisco (San Cristóbal de
    las Casas): 291
Church of San Francisco (San Miguel de
    Allende): 212
Church of San José (Jalapa): 39
Church of San Miguel (Taxco): 107
Church of San Nicolas (San Cristóbal de las
    Casas): 292
Church of San Nicolas Tolentino (Taxco): 108
Church of San Pedro (near San Luis Potosí):
    155
Church of Santa Lucía (San Cristóbal de las
    Casas): 291
Church of Santa Monica (Puebla): 62
Church of Santa Veracruz (Taxco): 107
Church of the Grito (Dolores Hidalgo): 223
Church of the Holy Spirit (Puebla): 60
Church of the Immaculate Conception
    (Real de Catorce): 158

Church of the Santísima Trinidad (Taxco): 108

Convent of Our Lady of the Assumption see Ex-Convento de San Francisco

Convent of Saint Anthony (Izamal): 280

Convent of San Bernardino (Taxco): 106

Ex-Convent and Church of San Gabriel (Cholula): 71-72

Ex-Convent of Santa Clara (Querétaro): 249

Ex-Convent of Santo Domingo-Centro Cultural (Chiapa de Corzo):

Ex-Convent of Sisal (Valladolid): 283

Ex-Convento de San Francisco (Puebla): 60-61

Ex-Convento de San Francisco (Tlaxcala): 46-47

Ex-Convento Santo Domingo (San Cristóbal de las Casas): 290-291

Iglesia de Guadalupe: (Puebla): 64

Iglesia de San Diego (Guanajuato): 128

Iglesia de San José (Puebla): 60

Iglesia de San Juan Bautista (Coyoacán): 92

Iglesia de Santa Cruz (Puebla): 61

Iglesia de Santo Domingo de Guzmán (Puebla): 60

Iglesia del Carmen (Puebla): 60

Kinich Kadmó (Izamal): 281

La Candelaria (Valladolid): 283

La Ermita del Santa Cristo del Buen Viaje (Veracruz): 35

La Transfiguración del Señor (near Cuernavaca): 167

Metropolitan Cathedral (Mexico City): see Catedral Metropolito

Misión de Nuestra Señora de la Luz (Tancoyol): 256

Misión de San Francisco de Asisi (Tilaco): 256

Misión de San Miguel Arcángel (Conca): 256

Misión de Santa María de la Purísima Concepción del Agua (Landa): 255-256

Misión de Santiago (Jalapan): 255

Oratorio of St. Philip Neri (San Miguel de Allende): 213-214

Our Lady of Loreto (Puebla): 69

Parish of Saint Ann (Santa Ana Chiautempan): 51-52

Parroquia de Nuestra Señora de Dolores (Dolores Hidalgo): see Church of the Grito

Parroquia de San Marcos (Puebla): 64

Parroquia de San Mituel Arcángel (San Miguel de Allende): 211-212

Sagrario Municipal (Mexico City): 77

San Gabriel Monastery (Cholula): 71

Sanctuary of Saint Michael (San Miguel de Milagro): 52

Santa Ana (Valladolid): 283

Santa Catalina (Puebla): 61

Santa Lucía (Valladolid): 283

Santa Prisca Church (Taxco): 105

Santo Domingo Cathedral (Chiapa de Corzo): 301

Santo Domingo Church (San Cristóbal de las Casas): 290

Santo Entierro (Taxco): 106

Santuario de Patrocinio (Zacatecas): 141-142

Santuario San Francisco Acatepac (near Cholula): 72

St. John the Baptist Church (San Juan Chamula): 298

Temple and Ex-Convent of Santa Rosa de Viterbo (Querétaro): 251

Templo de la Santísima Trinidad (Puebla): 61

Templo de San Agustín (San Luis Potosí): 150

Templo de San Felipe Neri (Guanajuato): 128

Templo de San Francisco (Guanajuato): 128

Templo de San Francisco (San Luis Potosí): 149

Templo de Santo Domingo (Zacatecas): 139

Templo del Carmen (San Luis Potosí): 150

Templo y Ex-Convento de Santo Domingo (Oaxaca): 178-179

Valenciana Church of San Cayetano (near Guanajuato): 134

About the Authors

Chicki Mallan discovered the joy of traveling with her parents at an early age. They would leave their Catalina Island home yearly, hit the road, and explore the small towns and big cities of the U.S. Traveling was still an important part of Chicki's life once she had a bunch of her own kids to introduce to the world. At various times Chicki and kids have lived in Asia and Europe. When not traveling, lecturing, or giving slide presentations, Chicki and her photographer husband, Oz, live in Paradise, California, a small community in the foothills of the Sierra Nevada. Between books she does what she enjoys most, writing newspaper and magazine articles. She has been associated with Moon Publications since 1983, and is the author of Moon's *Yucatán Peninsula Handbook, Cancún Handbook*, and *Belize Handbook*, co-author of Moon's *Mexico Handbook*, and author of Pine Press's *Guide to Catalina Island*. In 1987, Chicki was presented the Pluma de Plata writing award from the Mexican Government Ministry of Tourism for an article she wrote on the Mexican Caribbean, published in the *Los Angeles Times*. Chicki is a member of the SATW, Society of American Travel Writers.

Oz Mallan has been a professional photographer his entire working career. He spent much of that time as chief cameraman for the Chico *Enterprise-Record*. Oz graduated from the Brooks Institute of Photography in Santa Barbara. His work often has appeared in newspapers and magazines across the country via UPI and AP. He travels the world with his wife, Chicki, handling the photo end of their literary efforts, which include travel books, newspaper and magazine articles, as well as lectures and slide presentations. The photos in *Colonial Mexico* were taken during many visits and years of travel in the vast country. Other Moon books that feature Oz's photos are *Yucatán Peninsula Handbook, Cancún Handbook, Mexico Handbook*, and *Belize Handbook*. His work also appears in Pine Press's *Guide to Catalina Island*.

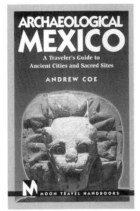

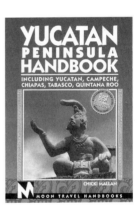

MOON TRAVEL HANDBOOKS

LOSE YOURSELF IN THE EXPERIENCE, NOT THE CROWD

For 25 years, Moon Travel Handbooks have been the guidebooks of choice for adventurous travelers. Our award-winning Handbook series provides focused, comprehensive coverage of distinct destinations all over the world. Each Handbook is like an entire bookcase of cultural insight and introductory information in one portable volume. Our goal at Moon is to give travelers all the background and practical information they'll need for an extraordinary travel experience.

The following pages include a complete list of Handbooks, covering North America and Hawaii, Mexico, Latin America and the Caribbean, and Asia and the Pacific.To purchase Moon Travel Handbooks, check your local bookstore or order by phone: (800) 345-5473 M-F 8 am.-5 p.m. PST or outside the U.S. phone: (530) 345-5473.

> "An in-depth dunk into the land, the people and their history, arts, and politics."
> —*Student Travels*

> "I consider these books to be superior to Lonely Planet. When Moon produces a book it is more humorous, incisive, and off-beat."
> —*Toronto Sun*

> "Outdoor enthusiasts gravitate to the well-written Moon Travel Handbooks. In addition to politically correct historic and cultural features, the series focuses on flora, fauna and outdoor recreation. Maps and meticulous directions also are a trademark of Moon guides."
> —*Houston Chronicle*

> "Moon [Travel Handbooks] . . . bring a healthy respect to the places they investigate. Best of all, they provide a host of odd nuggets that give a place texture and prod the wary traveler from the beaten path. The finest are written with such care and insight they deserve listing as literature."
> —*American Geographical Society*

> "Moon Travel Handbooks offer in-depth historical essays and useful maps, enhanced by a sense of humor and a neat, compact format."
> —*Swing*

> "Perfect for the more adventurous, these are long on history, sightseeing and nitty-gritty information and very price-specific."
> —*Columbus Dispatch*

> "Moon guides manage to be comprehensive and countercultural at the same time . . . Handbooks are packed with maps, photographs, drawings, and sidebars that constitute a college-level introduction to each country's history, culture, people, and crafts."
> —*National Geographic Traveler*

> "Few travel guides do a better job helping travelers create their own itineraries than the Moon Travel Handbook series. The authors have a knack for homing in on the essentials."
> —**Colorado Springs** *Gazette Telegraph*

MEXICO

"These books will delight the armchair traveler, aid the undecided person in selecting a destination, and guide the seasoned road warrior looking for lesser-known hideaways."

—*Mexican Meanderings* Newsletter

"From tourist traps to off-the-beaten track hideaways, these guides offer consistent, accurate details without pretension."

—*Foreign Service Journal*

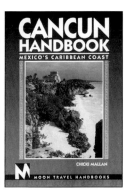

Archaeological Mexico	**$19.95**
Andrew Coe	410 pages, 34 maps
Baja Handbook	**$16.95**
Joe Cummings	544 pages, 46 maps
Cabo Handbook	**$14.95**
Joe Cummings	272 pages, 17 maps
Cancún Handbook	**$14.95**
Chicki Mallan	270 pages, 25 maps
Colonial Mexico	**$18.95**
Chicki Mallan	360 pages, 38 maps
Mexico Handbook	**$21.95**
Joe Cummings and Chicki Mallan	1,200 pages, 201 maps
Northern Mexico Handbook	**$17.95**
Joe Cummings	590 pages, 69 maps
Pacific Mexico Handbook	**$17.95**
Bruce Whipperman	580 pages, 68 maps
Puerto Vallarta Handbook	**$14.95**
Bruce Whipperman	330 pages, 36 maps
Yucatán Handbook	**$16.95**
Chicki Mallan	470 pages, 52 maps

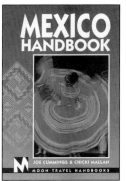

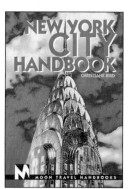

LATIN AMERICA
AND THE CARIBBEAN

"Solidly packed with practical information and full of significant cultural asides that will enlighten you on the whys and wherefores of things you might easily see but not easily grasp."

—*Boston Globe*

Belize Handbook	**$15.95**
Chicki Mallan and Patti Lange	390 pages, 45 maps
Caribbean Handbook	**$16.95**
Karl Luntta	400 pages, 56 maps
Costa Rica Handbook	**$19.95**
Christopher P. Baker	780 pages, 73 maps
Cuba Handbook	**$19.95**
Christopher P. Baker	740 pages, 70 maps
Dominican Republic Handbook	**$15.95**
Gaylord Dold	420 pages, 24 maps
Ecuador Handbook	**$16.95**
Julian Smith	450 pages, 43 maps
Honduras Handbook	**$15.95**
Chris Humphrey	330 pages, 40 maps
Jamaica Handbook	**$15.95**
Karl Luntta	330 pages, 17 maps
Virgin Islands Handbook	**$13.95**
Karl Luntta	220 pages, 19 maps

NORTH AMERICA AND HAWAII

"These domestic guides convey the same sense of exoticism that their foreign counterparts do, making home-country travel seem like far-flung adventure."

—*Sierra Magazine*

Alaska-Yukon Handbook	**$17.95**
Deke Castleman and Don Pitcher	530 pages, 92 maps
Alberta and the Northwest Territories Handbook	**$17.95**
Andrew Hempstead and Nadina Purdon	530 pages, 72 maps,
Arizona Traveler's Handbook	**$17.95**
Bill Weir and Robert Blake	512 pages,54 maps
Atlantic Canada Handbook	**$17.95**
Nan Drosdick and Mark Morris	460 pages, 61 maps
Big Island of Hawaii Handbook	**$15.95**
J.D. Bisignani	390 pages, 23 maps
British Columbia Handbook	**$16.95**
Jane King and Andrew Hempstead	430 pages, 69 maps

Colorado Handbook	**$18.95**
Stephen Metzger	480 pages, 59 maps
Georgia Handbook	**$17.95**
Kap Stann	370 pages, 50 maps
Hawaii Handbook	**$19.95**
J.D. Bisignani	1,030 pages, 90 maps
Honolulu-Waikiki Handbook	**$14.95**
J.D. Bisignani	380 pages, 20 maps
Idaho Handbook	**$18.95**
Don Root	610 pages, 42 maps
Kauai Handbook	**$15.95**
J.D. Bisignani	320 pages, 23 maps
Maine Handbook	**$18.95**
Kathleen M. Brandes	660 pages, 27 maps
Massachusetts Handbook	**$18.95**
Jeff Perk	600 pages, 23 maps
Maui Handbook	**$14.95**
J.D. Bisignani	410 pages, 35 maps
Montana Handbook	**$17.95**
Judy Jewell and W.C. McRae	480 pages, 52 maps
Nevada Handbook	**$18.95**
Deke Castleman	530 pages, 40 maps
New Hampshire Handbook	**$18.95**
Steve Lantos	500 pages, 18 maps
New Mexico Handbook	**$15.95**
Stephen Metzger	360 pages, 47 maps
New York City Handbook	**$13.95**
Christiane Bird	300 pages, 20 maps
New York Handbook	**$19.95**
Christiane Bird	780 pages, 95 maps
Northern California Handbook	**$19.95**
Kim Weir	800 pages, 50 maps
Oregon Handbook	**$17.95**
Stuart Warren and Ted Long Ishikawa	588 pages, 34 maps
Pennsylvania Handbook	**$18.95**
Joanne Miller	448 pages, 40 maps
Road Trip USA	**$22.50**
Jamie Jensen	800 pages, 165 maps
Southern California Handbook	**$19.95**
Kim Weir	720 pages, 26 maps
Tennessee Handbook	**$17.95**
Jeff Bradley	530 pages, 44 maps
Texas Handbook	**$18.95**
Joe Cummings	690 pages, 70 maps
Utah Handbook	**$17.95**
Bill Weir and W.C. McRae	490 pages, 40 maps

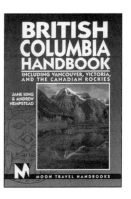

Washington Handbook	$19.95
Don Pitcher	870 pages, 113 maps
Wisconsin Handbook	$18.95
Thomas Huhti	590 pages, 69 maps
Wyoming Handbook	$17.95
Don Pitcher	610 pages, 80 maps

ASIA AND THE PACIFIC

"Scores of maps, detailed practical info down to business hours of small-town libraries. You can't beat the Asian titles for sheer heft. (The) series is sort of an American Lonely Planet, with better writing but fewer titles. (The) individual voice of researchers comes through."

—Travel & Leisure

Australia Handbook	$21.95
Marael Johnson, Andrew Hempstead, and Nadina Purdon	940 pages, 141 maps
Bali Handbook	$19.95
Bill Dalton	750 pages, 54 maps
Bangkok Handbook	$13.95
Michael Buckley	244 pages, 30 maps
Fiji Islands Handbook	$13.95
David Stanley	280 pages, 38 maps
Hong Kong Handbook	$16.95
Kerry Moran	378 pages, 49 maps
Indonesia Handbook	$25.00
Bill Dalton	1,380 pages, 249 maps
Japan Handbook	$22.50
J.D. Bisignani	970 pages, 213 maps
Micronesia Handbook	$14.95
Neil M. Levy	340 pages, 70 maps
Nepal Handbook	$18.95
Kerry Moran	490 pages, 51 maps
New Zealand Handbook	$19.95
Jane King	620 pages, 81 maps
Outback Australia Handbook	$18.95
Marael Johnson	450 pages, 57 maps
Philippines Handbook	$17.95
Peter Harper and Laurie Fullerton	670 pages, 116 maps
Singapore Handbook	$15.95
Carl Parkes	350 pages, 29 maps
Southeast Asia Handbook	$21.95
Carl Parkes	1,000 pages, 203 maps

South Korea Handbook	$19.95
Robert Nilsen	820 pages, 141 maps
South Pacific Handbook	$22.95
David Stanley	920 pages, 147 maps
Tahiti-Polynesia Handbook	$13.95
David Stanley	270 pages, 35 maps
Thailand Handbook	$19.95
Carl Parkes	860 pages, 142 maps
Vietnam, Cambodia & Laos Handbook	$18.95
Michael Buckley	730 pages, 116 maps

OTHER GREAT TITLES FROM MOON

"For hardy wanderers, few guides come more highly recommended than the Handbooks. They include good maps, steer clear of fluff and flackery, and offer plenty of money-saving tips. They also give you the kind of information that visitors to strange lands—on any budget—need to survive."

—*US News & World Report*

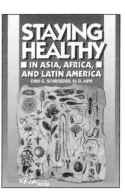

Moon Handbook	$10.00
Carl Koppeschaar	141 pages, 8 maps
Moscow-St. Petersburg Handbook	$13.95
Masha Nordbye	259 pages, 16 maps
The Practical Nomad: How to Travel Around the World	$17.95
Edward Hasbrouck	575 pages
Staying Healthy in Asia, Africa, and Latin America	$11.95
Dirk Schroeder	197 pages, 4 maps

MOONBELT

A new concept in moneybelts. Made of heavy-duty Cordura nylon, the Moonbelt offers maximum protection for your money and important papers. This pouch, designed for all-weather comfort, slips under your shirt or waistband, rendering it virtually undetectable and inaccessible to pickpockets. It features a one-inch high-test quick-release buckle so there's no more fumbling around for the strap or repeated adjustments. This handy plastic buckle opens and closes with a touch but won't come undone until you want it to. Moonbelts accommodate traveler's checks, passports, cash, photos, etc. Size 5 x 9 inches. Available in black only. **$8.95**

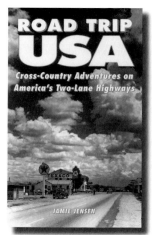

THE PRACTICAL NOMAD

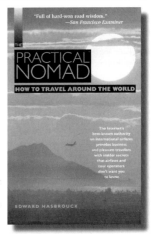

> "Full of hard-won road wisdom."
> —*San Francisco Examiner*

✈ TAKE THE PLUNGE

"The greatest barriers to long-term travel by Americans are the disempowered feelings that leave them afraid to ask for the time off. Just do it."

✈ TAKE NOTHING FOR GRANTED

"Even 'What time is it?' is a highly politicized question in some areas, and the answer may depend on your informant's ethnicity and political allegiance as well as the proximity of the secret police."

✈ TAKE THIS BOOK

$17.95   576 pages

With experience helping thousands of his globetrotting clients plan their trips around the world, travel industry insider Edward Hasbrouck provides the secrets that can save readers money and valuable travel time.
An indispensable complement to destination-specific travel guides,
The Practical Nomad includes:

airfare strategies

ticket discounts

long-term travel considerations

travel documents

border crossings

entry requirements

government offices

travel publications

Internet information resources

WHERE TO BUY MOON TRAVEL HANDBOOKS

BOOKSTORES AND LIBRARIES: Moon Travel Handbooks are distributed worldwide. Please contact our sales manager for a list of wholesalers and distributors in your area.

TRAVELERS: We would like to have Moon Travel Handbooks available throughout the world. Please ask your bookstore to write or call us for ordering information. If your bookstore will not order our guides for you, please contact us for a free catalog.

Moon Travel Handbooks
P.O. Box 3040
Chico, CA 95927-3040 U.S.A.
tel.: (800) 345-5473, outside the U.S. (530) 345-5473
fax: (530) 345-6751
e-mail: travel@moon.com

IMPORTANT ORDERING INFORMATION

PRICES: All prices are subject to change. We always ship the most current edition. We will let you know if there is a price increase on the book you order.

SHIPPING AND HANDLING OPTIONS: Domestic UPS or USPS first class (allow 10 working days for delivery): $4.50 for the first item, $1.00 for each additional item.

Moonbelt shipping is $1.50 for one, 50 cents for each additional belt.

UPS 2nd Day Air or Printed Airmail requires a special quote.

International Surface Bookrate 8-12 weeks delivery: $4.00 for the first item, $1.00 for each additional item. Note: We cannot guarantee international surface bookrate shipping. We recommends sending international orders via air mail, which requires a special quote.

FOREIGN ORDERS: Orders that originate outside the U.S.A. must be paid for with an international money order, a check in U.S. currency drawn on a major U.S. bank based in the U.S.A., or Visa, MasterCard, or Discover.

TELEPHONE ORDERS: We accept Visa, MasterCard, or Discover payments. Call in your order: (800) 345-5473, 8 a.m.-5 p.m. Pacific standard time. Outside the U.S. the number is (530) 345-5473.

INTERNET ORDERS: Visit our site at: www.moon.com

ORDER FORM

Prices are subject to change without notice. Be sure to call (800) 345-5473,
or (530) 345-5473 from outside the U.S. 8 a.m.–5 p.m. PST for current prices and editions.
(See important ordering information on preceding page.)

Name: _____ Date: _____

Street: _____

City: _____ Daytime Phone: _____

State or Country: _____ Zip Code: _____

QUANTITY	TITLE	PRICE

Taxable Total_____

Sales Tax (7.25%) for California Residents_____

Shipping & Handling_____

TOTAL_____

Ship: ☐ UPS (no P.O. Boxes) ☐ 1st class ☐ International surface mail
Ship to: ☐ address above ☐ other _____

Make checks payable to: **MOON TRAVEL HANDBOOKS**, P.O. Box 3040, Chico, CA 95927-3040
U.S.A. We accept Visa, MasterCard, or Discover. **To Order**: Call in your Visa, MasterCard, or Discover number,
or send a written order with your Visa, MasterCard, or Discover number and expiration date clearly written.

Card Number: ☐ **Visa** ☐ **MasterCard** ☐ **Discover**

☐ ☐ ☐ ☐ ☐ ☐ ☐ ☐ ☐ ☐ ☐ ☐ ☐ ☐ ☐ ☐

Exact Name on Card: _____

Expiration date:_____

Signature: _____

NOTES

NOTES

U.S.~METRIC CONVERSION

1 inch = 2.54 centimeters (cm)
1 foot = .304 meters (m)
1 yard = 0.914 meters (m)
1 mile = 1.6093 kilometers (km)
1 km = .6214 miles
1 fathom = 1.8288 m
1 chain = 20.1168 m
1 furlong = 201.168 m
1 acre = .4047 hectares
1 sq km = 100 hectares
1 sq mile = 2.59 square km
1 ounce = 28.35 grams
1 pound = .4536 kilograms
1 short ton = .90718 metric ton
1 short ton = 2000 pounds
1 long ton = 1.016 metric tons
1 long ton = 2240 pounds
1 metric ton = 1000 kilograms
1 quart = .94635 liters
1 US gallon = 3.7854 liters
1 Imperial gallon = 4.5459 liters
1 nautical mile = 1.852 km

To compute celsius temperatures, subtract 32 from Fahrenheit and divide by 1.8. To go the other way, multiply celsius by 1.8 and add 32.

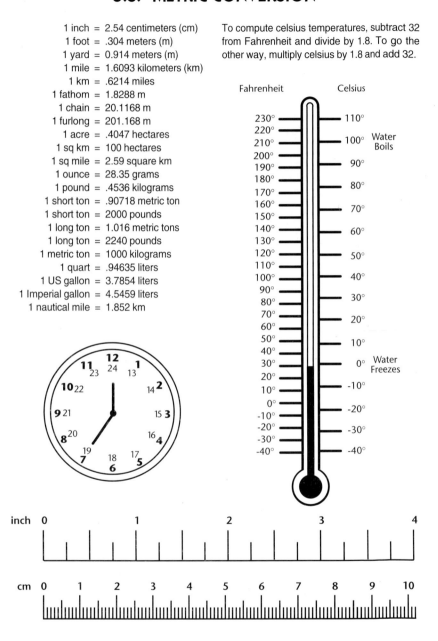